The beach is only about ten minutes away from my workplace, so you can usually find me there the day after I'm done with work. Driving is nice, but I run there! The weather was great this summer, so I was happy. For someone who loves summer as much as I do, writing manga indoors all day seems like a waste of a great day. I almost wish I could work at the beach.

- Takeshi Konomi, 2004

About Takeshi Konomi

Takeshi Konomi exploded onto the manga scene with the incredible **THE PRINCE OF TENNIS**. His refined art style and sleek character designs proved popular with **Weekly Shonen Jump** readers, and **THE PRINCE OF TENNIS** became the number one sports manga in Japan almost overnight. Its cast of fascinating male tennis players attracted legions of female readers even though it was originally intended to be a boys' comic. The manga continues to be a success in Japan and has inspired a hit anime series, as well as several video games and mountains of merchandise.

THE PRINCE OF TENNIS
VOL. 25
The SHONEN JUMP Manga Edition

STORY AND ART BY
TAKESHI KONOMI

Translation/Joe Yamazaki
Consultant/Michelle Pangilinan
Touch-up Art & Lettering/Vanessa Satone
Design/Sam Elzway
Editor/Leyla Aker

Editor in Chief, Books/Alvin Lu
Editor in Chief, Magazines/Marc Weidenbaum
VP of Publishing Licensing/Rika Inouye
VP of Sales/Gonzalo Ferreyra
Sr. VP of Marketing/Liza Coppola
Publisher/Hyoe Narita

Printed in the U.S.A.

Published by VIZ Media, LLC
P.O. Box 77010
San Francisco, CA 94107

SHONEN JUMP Manga Edition
10 9 8 7 6 5 4 3 2 1
First printing, May 2008

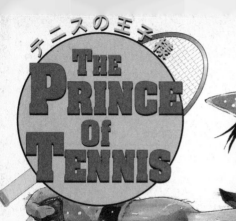

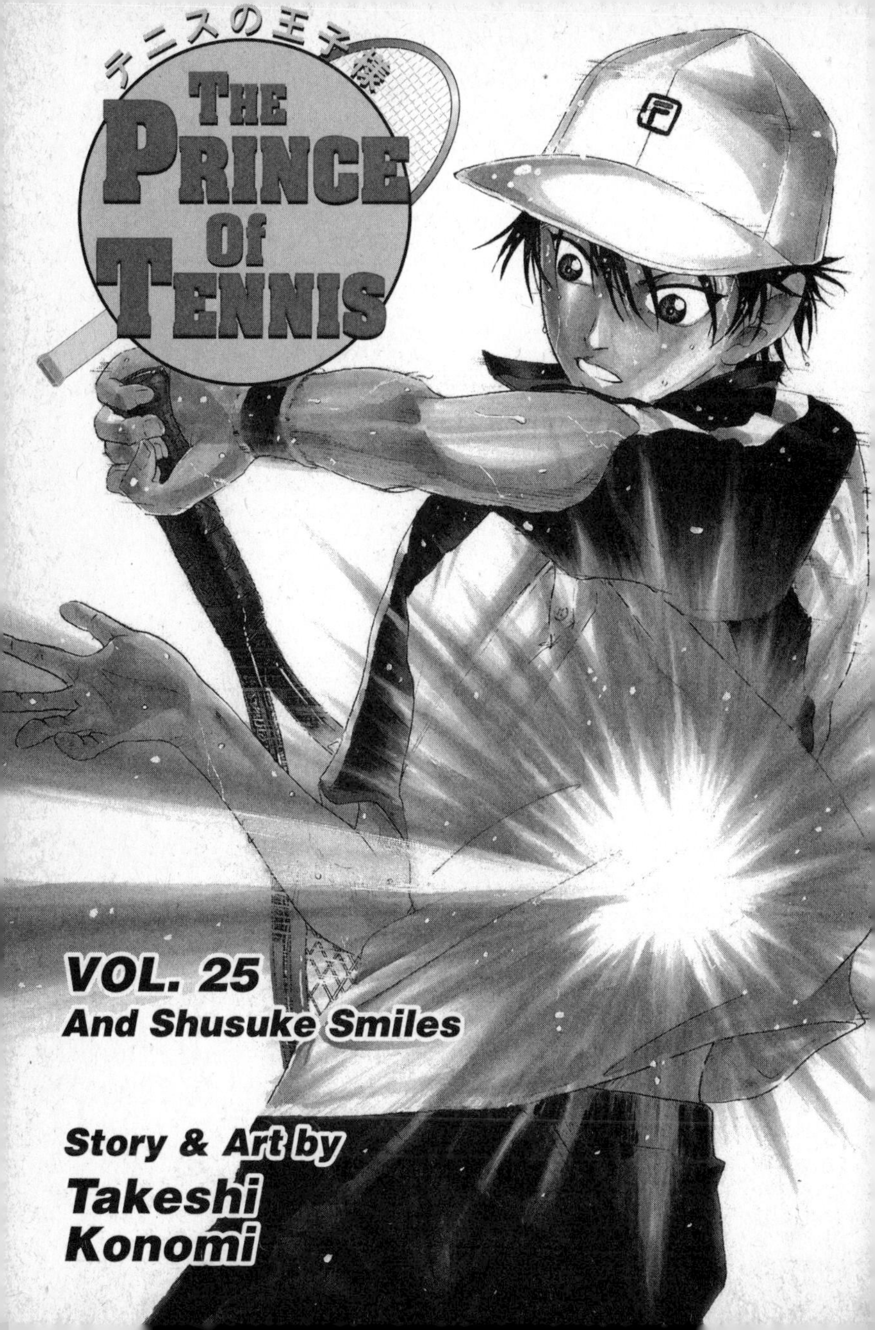

THE PRINCE OF TENNIS

テニスの王子

VOL. 25
And Shusuke Smiles

Story & Art by
Takeshi Konomi

ENNIS CLUB

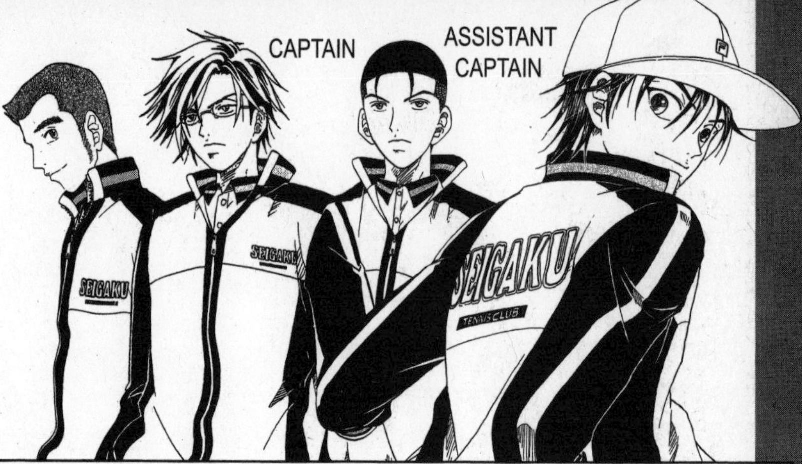
CAPTAIN
ASSISTANT CAPTAIN

●TAKASHI KAWAMURA ●KUNIMITSU TEZUKA ● SHUICHIRO OISHI ● RYOMA ECHIZEN ●

Seishun Academy student Ryoma Echizen is a tennis prodigy, with wins in four consecutive U.S. Junior tournaments under his belt. He became a starter as a 7th grader and led his team to the District Preliminaries! Despite a few mishaps, Seishun won the District Prelims and the City Tournament, and even earned a ticket to the Kanto Tournament.

The team comes away victorious from its first-round matches against Hyotei, but Kunimitsu injures his shoulder and goes to Kyushu for treatment. Despite losing captain Kunimitsu and assistant captain Shuichiro to injury, Seishun defeats Midoriyama and Rokkaku, not only reaching the finals of the tournament but also earning a slot at the Nationals! Now their opponent is the number-one ranked Rikkai, a team full of national-level players. After losing consecutive doubles matches, Seishun's hopes rest on the shoulders of Sadaharu, playing in No. 3 Singles against his childhood friend Renji.

STORY & CHARACTERS

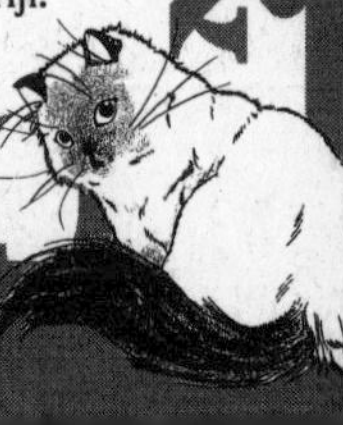

SEIGAKU T

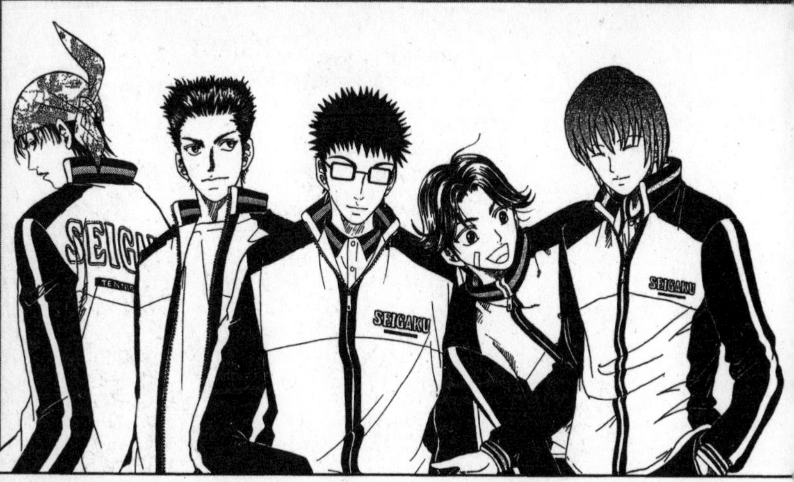

• KAORU KAIDO • TAKESHI MOMOSHIRO • SADAHARU INUI • EIJI KIKUMARU • SHUSUKE FUJI •

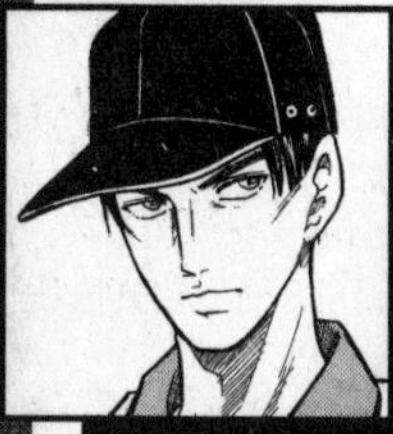

RIKKAI

GENICHIRO SANADA

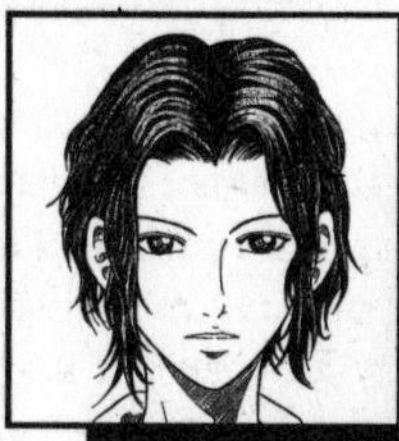

RIKKAI

SEIICHI YUKIMURA

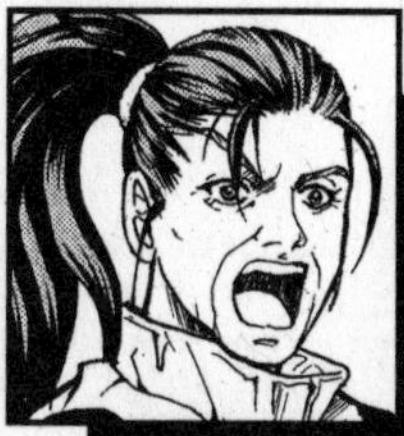

SEISHUN ACADEMY TENNIS COACH

SUMIRE RYUZAKI

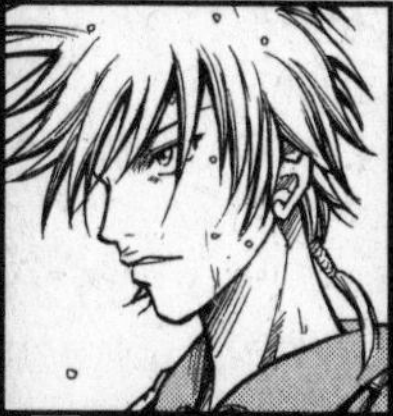

RIKKAI

MASAHARU NIO

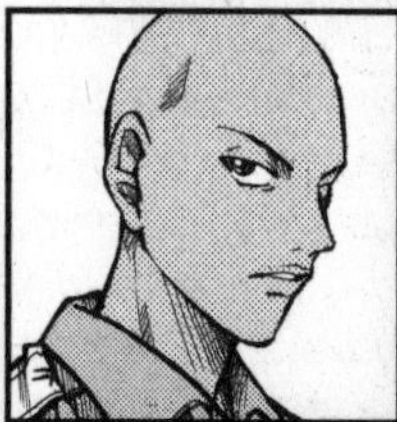

RIKKAI

JACKAL KUWAHARA

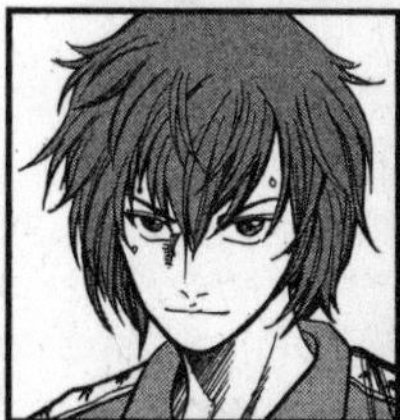

RIKKAI

BUNTA MARUI

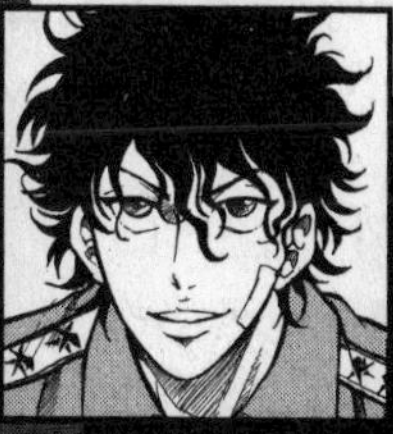

RIKKAI

AKAYA KIRIHARA

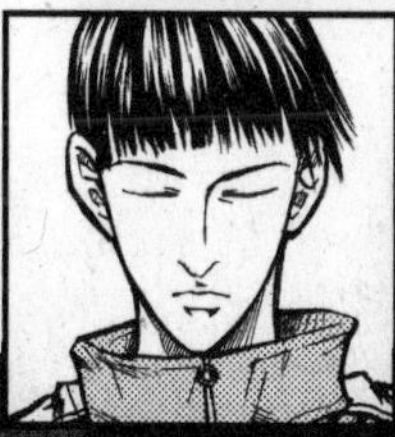

RIKKAI

RENJI YANAGI

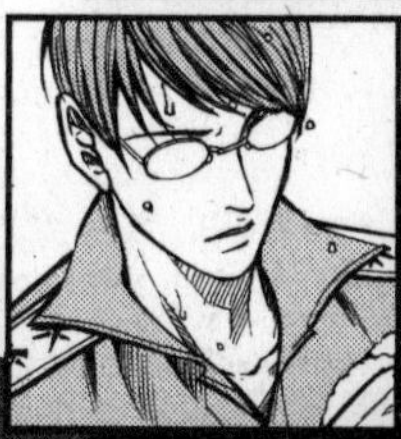

RIKKAI

HIROSHI YAGYU

CONTENTS

Vol. 25
And Shusuke Smiles

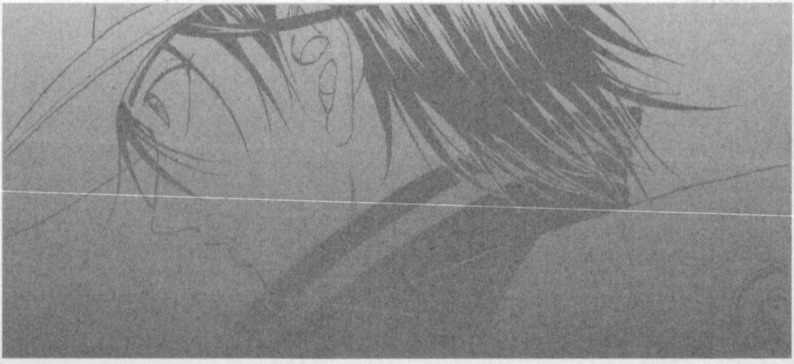

5th Match — No. 1 Singles	4th Match — No. 2 Singles	3rd Match — No. 3 Singles	2nd Match — No. 1 Doubles		1st Match — No. 2 Doubles	
RYOMA ECHIZEN (7th Grade) Blood Type: O	SHUSUKE FUJI (8th Grade) Blood Type: B	SADAHARU INUI (9th Grade) Blood Type: AB	SHUICHIRO OISHI (9th Grade) Blood Type: O	EIJI KIKUMARU (9th Grade) Blood Type: A	KAORU KAIDO (8th Grade) Blood Type: B	TAKESHI MOMOSHIRO (8th Grade) Blood Type: O

SEIGAKU
SEIGAKU
SEIGAKU
SEIGAKU
SEIGAKU

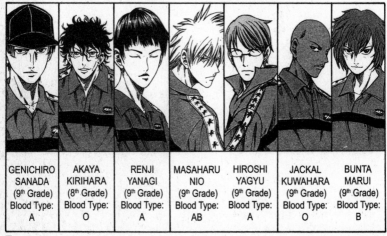

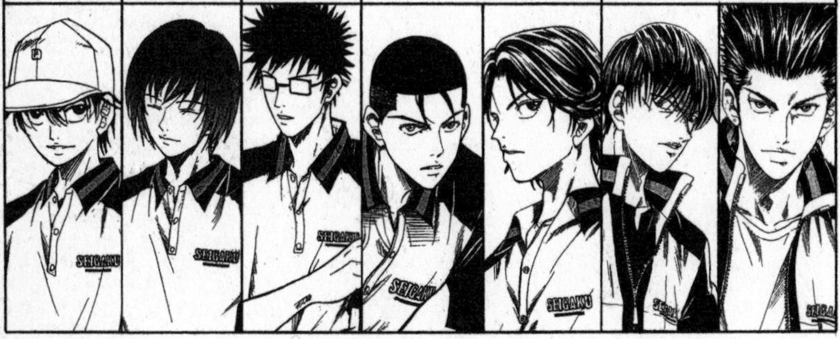

GENIUS 211: THE COLLAPSE OF DATA TENNIS

GENICHIRO SANADA (9th Grade) Blood Type: A	AKAYA KIRIHARA (8th Grade) Blood Type: O	RENJI YANAGI (9th Grade) Blood Type: A	MASAHARU NIO (9th Grade) Blood Type: AB	HIROSHI YAGYU (9th Grade) Blood Type: A	JACKAL KUWAHARA (9th Grade) Blood Type: O	BUNTA MARUI (9th Grade) Blood Type: B

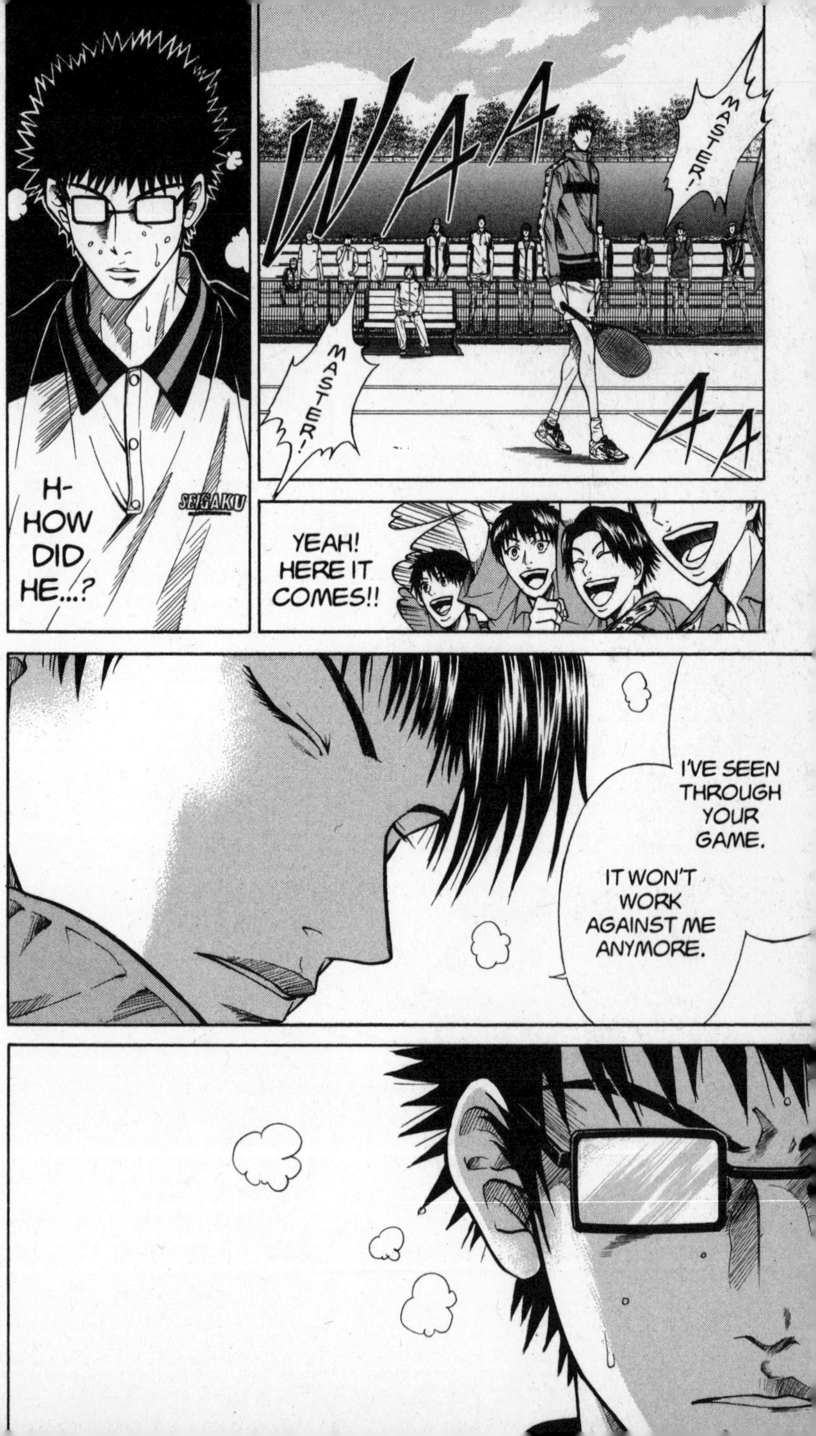
MASTER!
MASTER!
WAA
AA
YEAH! HERE IT COMES!!
H- HOW DID HE...?
SEIGAKU
I'VE SEEN THROUGH YOUR GAME.
IT WON'T WORK AGAINST ME ANYMORE.

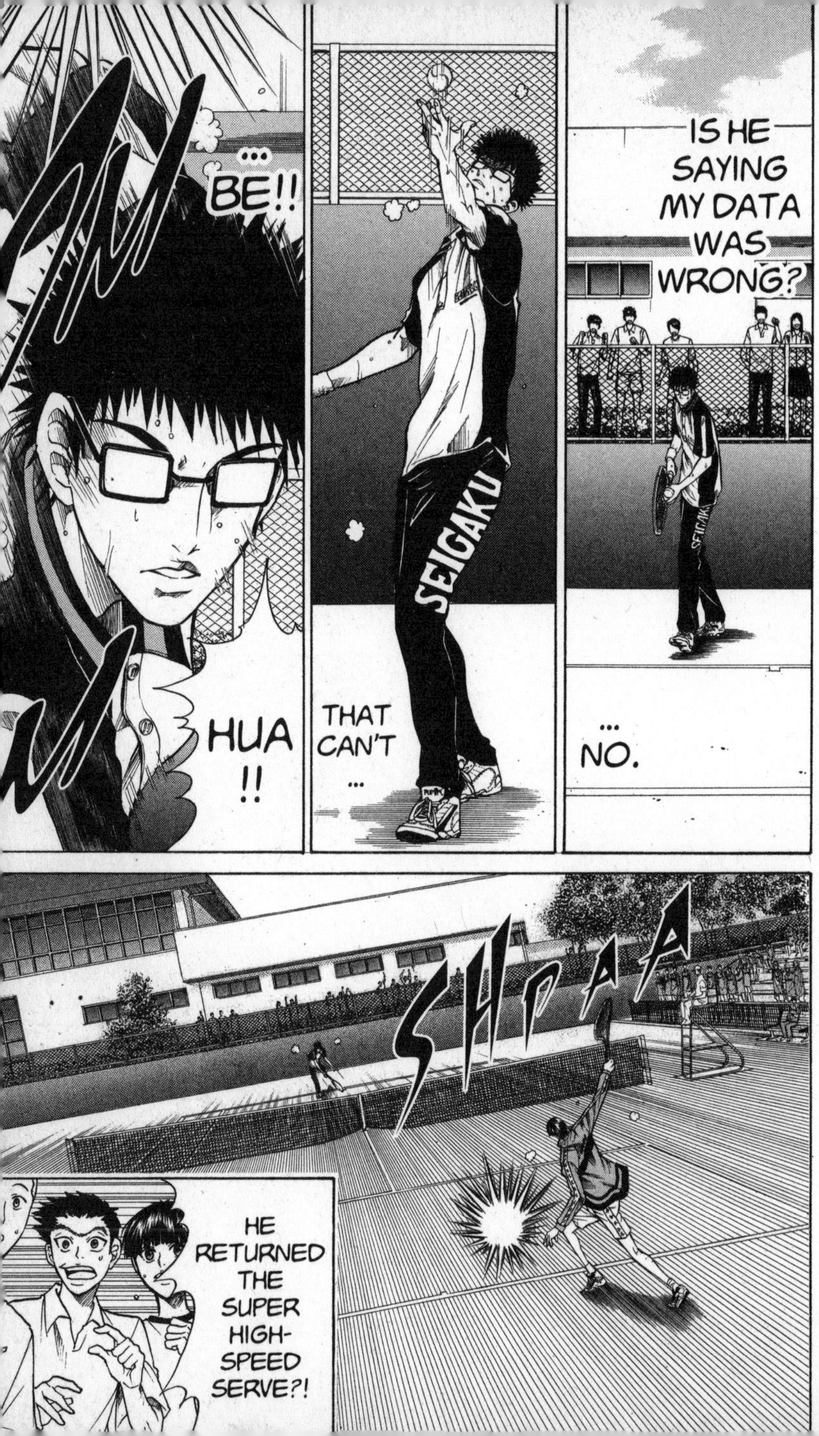
IS HE SAYING MY DATA WAS WRONG?
... NO.
THAT CAN'T ...
... BE!!
HUA !!
SHPAA
HE RETURNED THE SUPER HIGH-SPEED SERVE?!

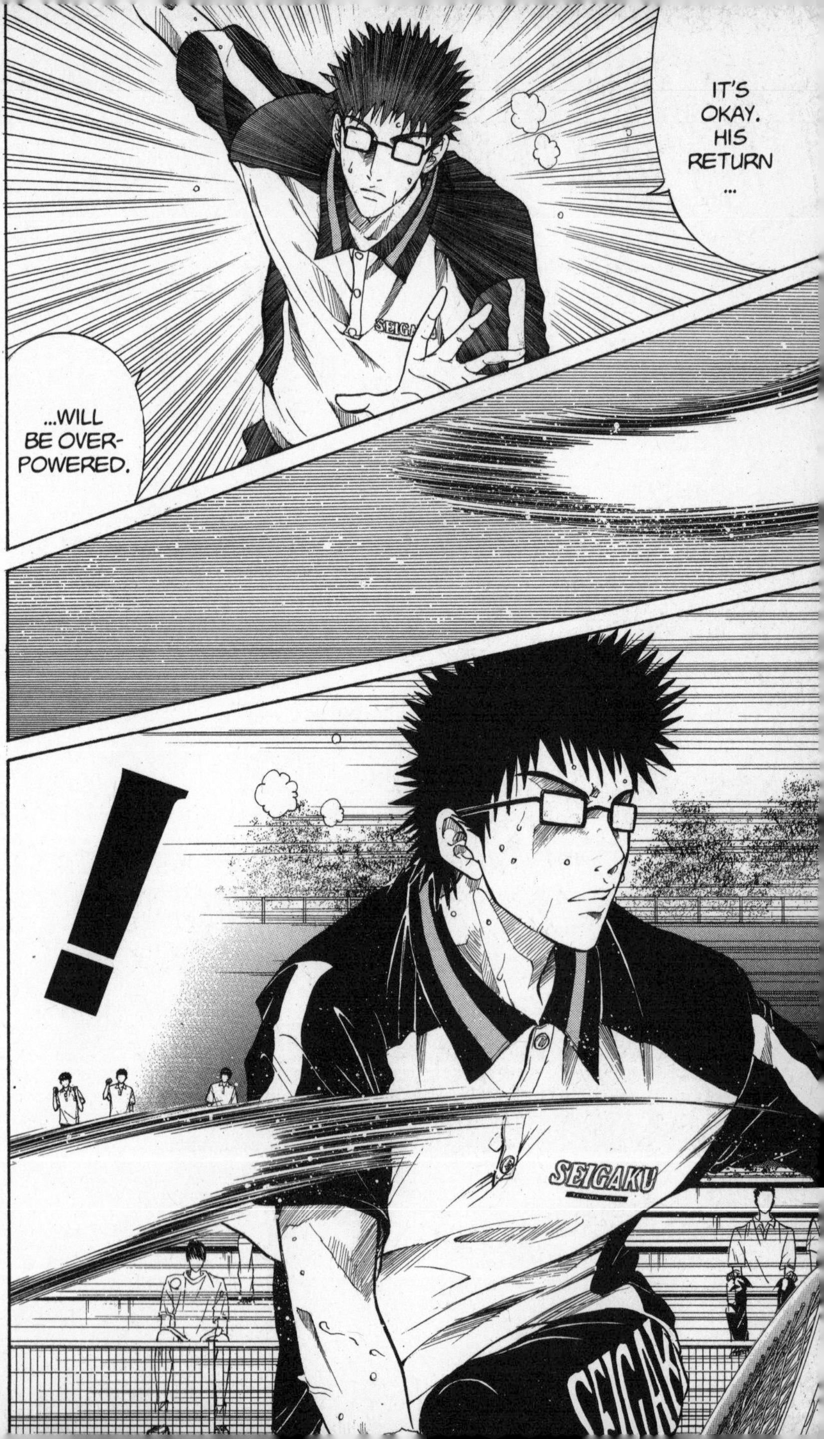
IT'S OKAY. HIS RETURN ...
...WILL BE OVER-POWERED.
!
SEIGAKU

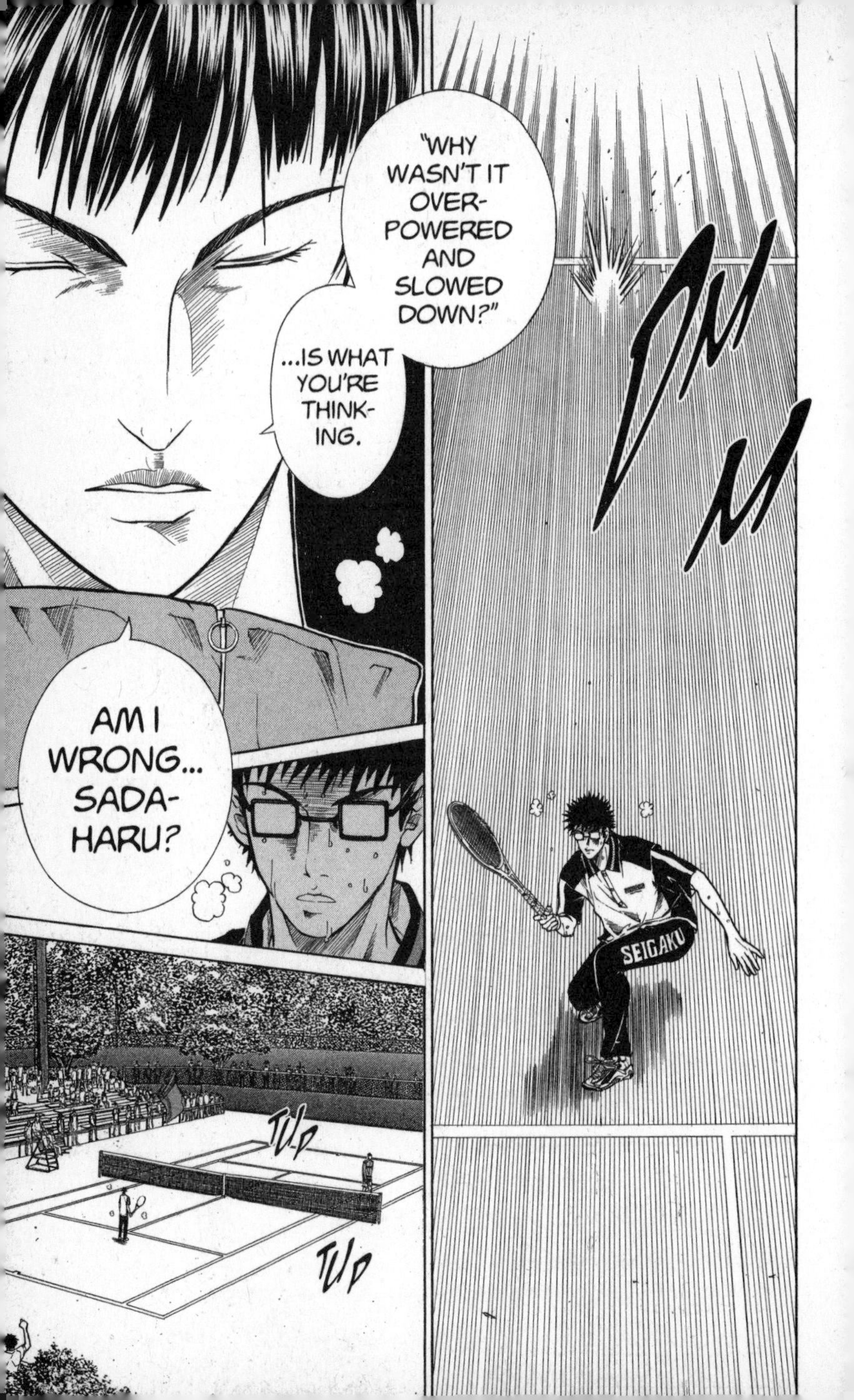
"WHY WASN'T IT OVER-POWERED AND SLOWED DOWN?"
...IS WHAT YOU'RE THINK-ING.
AM I WRONG... SADA-HARU?
SEIGAKU
TUP
TUP

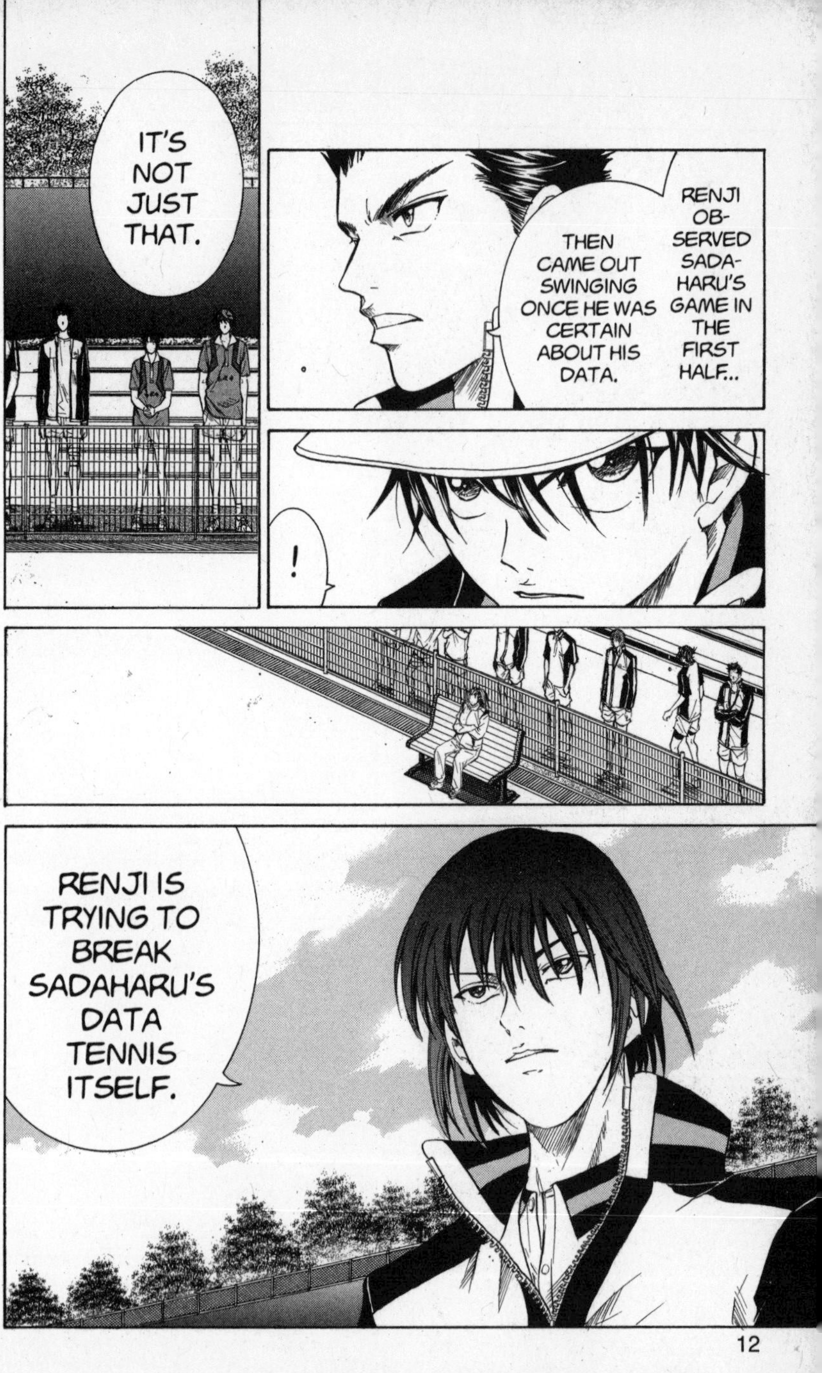
RENJI OBSERVED SADAHARU'S GAME IN THE FIRST HALF...
THEN CAME OUT SWINGING ONCE HE WAS CERTAIN ABOUT HIS DATA.
!
IT'S NOT JUST THAT.
RENJI IS TRYING TO BREAK SADAHARU'S DATA TENNIS ITSELF.

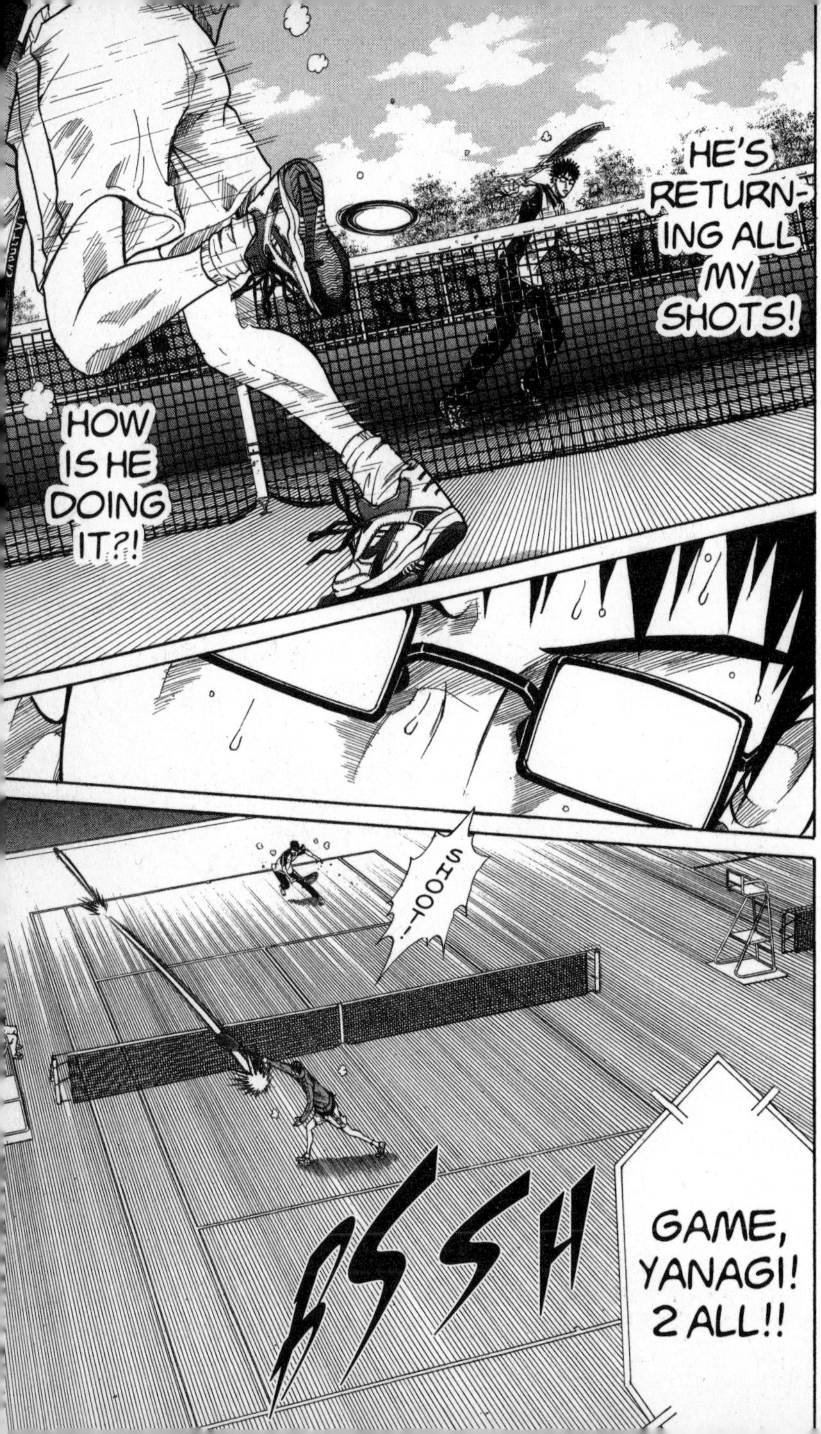
HE'S RETURNING ALL MY SHOTS!
HOW IS HE DOING IT?!
SHOOT--!
GAME, YANAGI! 2 ALL!!
BSSH

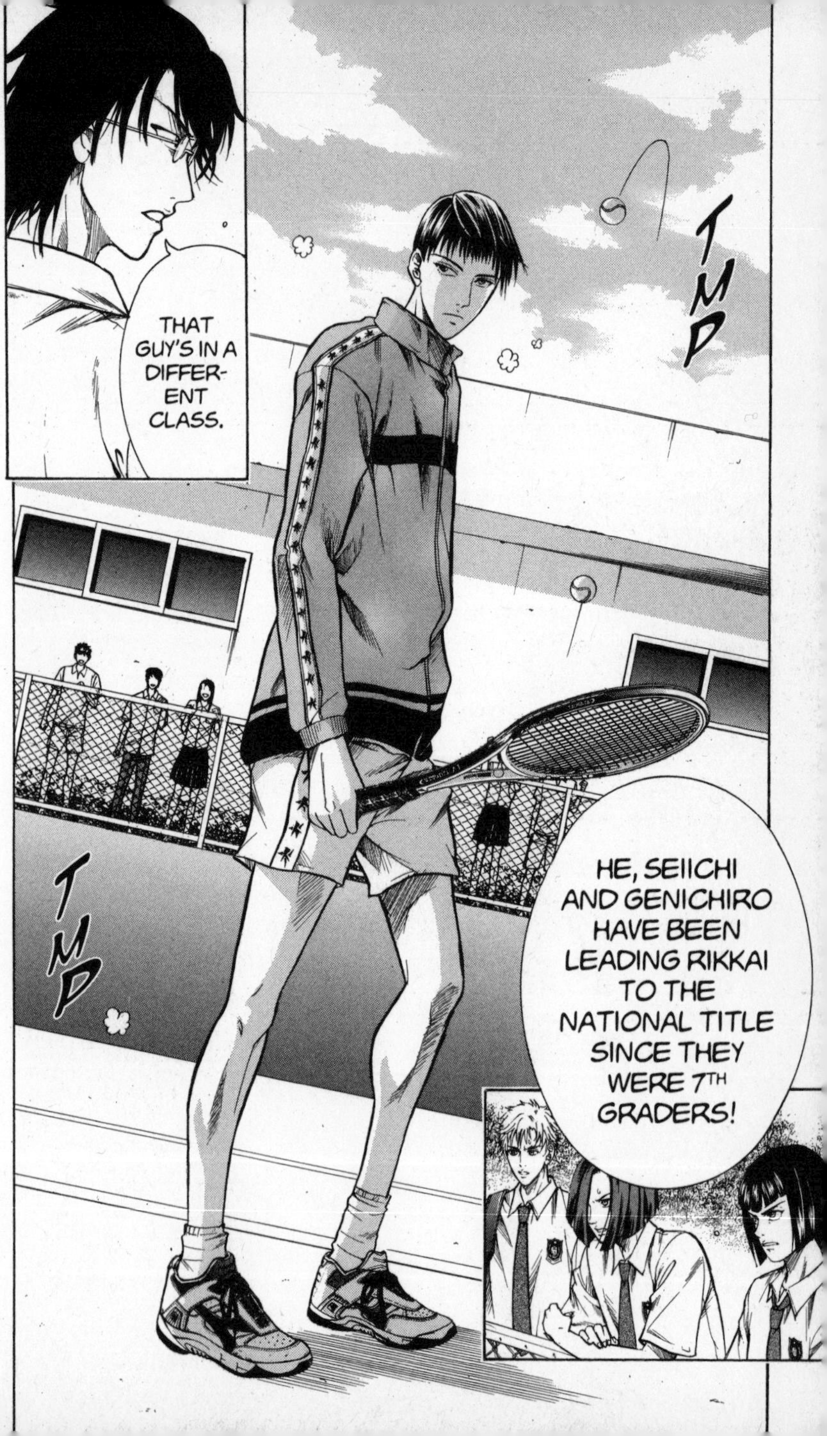
TMD
THAT GUY'S IN A DIFFERENT CLASS.
TMD
HE, SEIICHI AND GENICHIRO HAVE BEEN LEADING RIKKAI TO THE NATIONAL TITLE SINCE THEY WERE 7TH GRADERS!

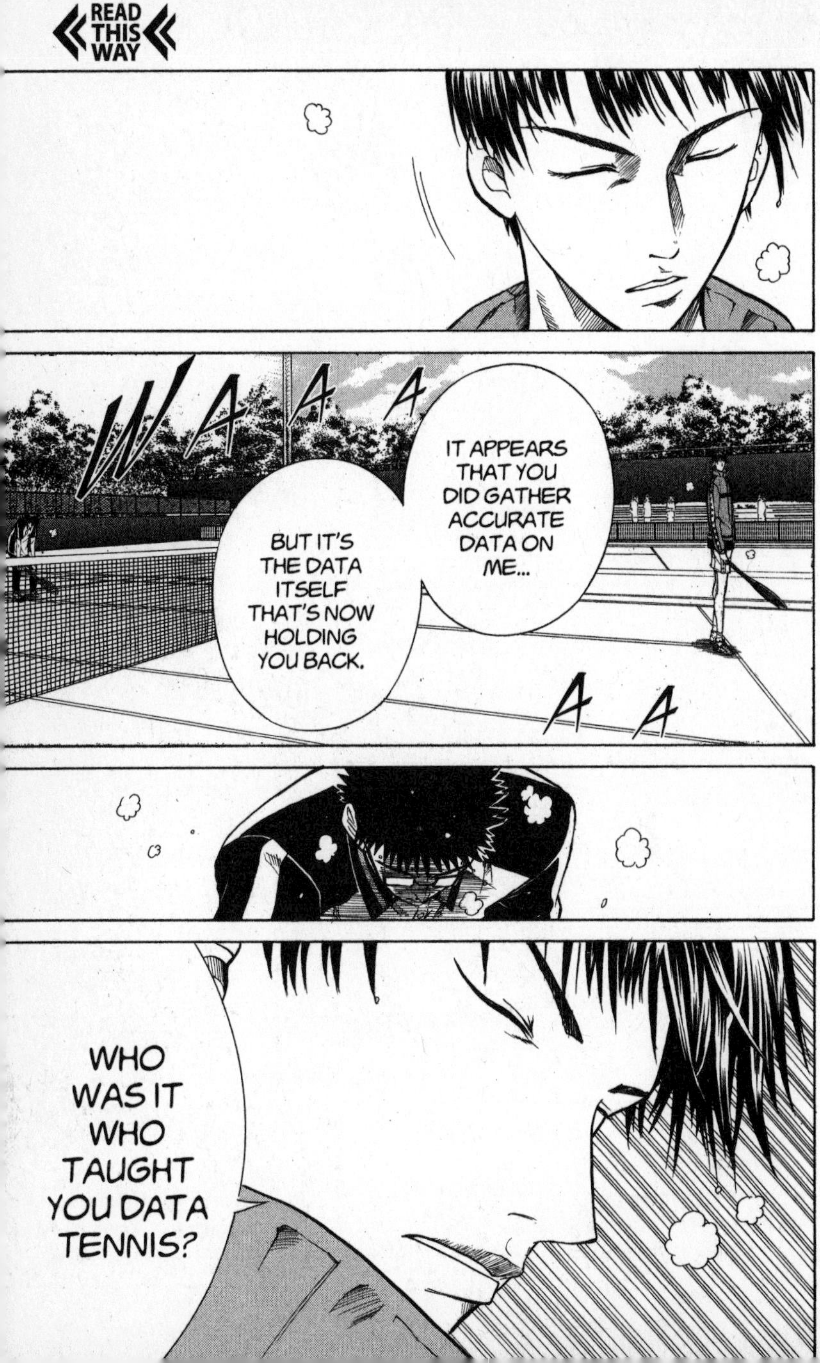
READ THIS WAY
IT APPEARS THAT YOU DID GATHER ACCURATE DATA ON ME...
BUT IT'S THE DATA ITSELF THAT'S NOW HOLDING YOU BACK.
WAAA
AA
WHO WAS IT WHO TAUGHT YOU DATA TENNIS?

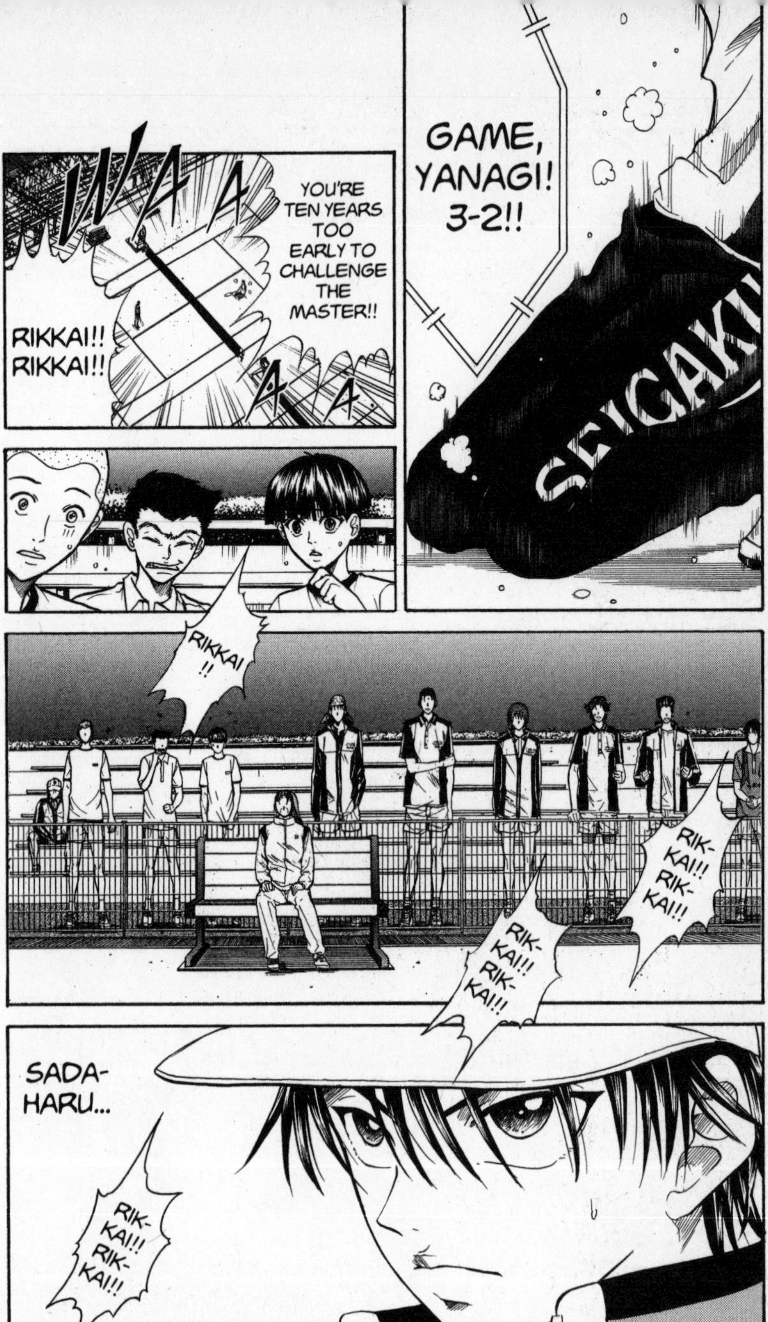
GAME, YANAGI! 3-2!!
YOU'RE TEN YEARS TOO EARLY TO CHALLENGE THE MASTER!!
WAAA
RIKKAI!! RIKKAI!!
RIKKAI!!
RIK-KAI!! RIK-KAI!!
RIK-KAI!! RIK-KAI!!
SADA-HARU...
RIK-KAI!! RIK-KAI!!

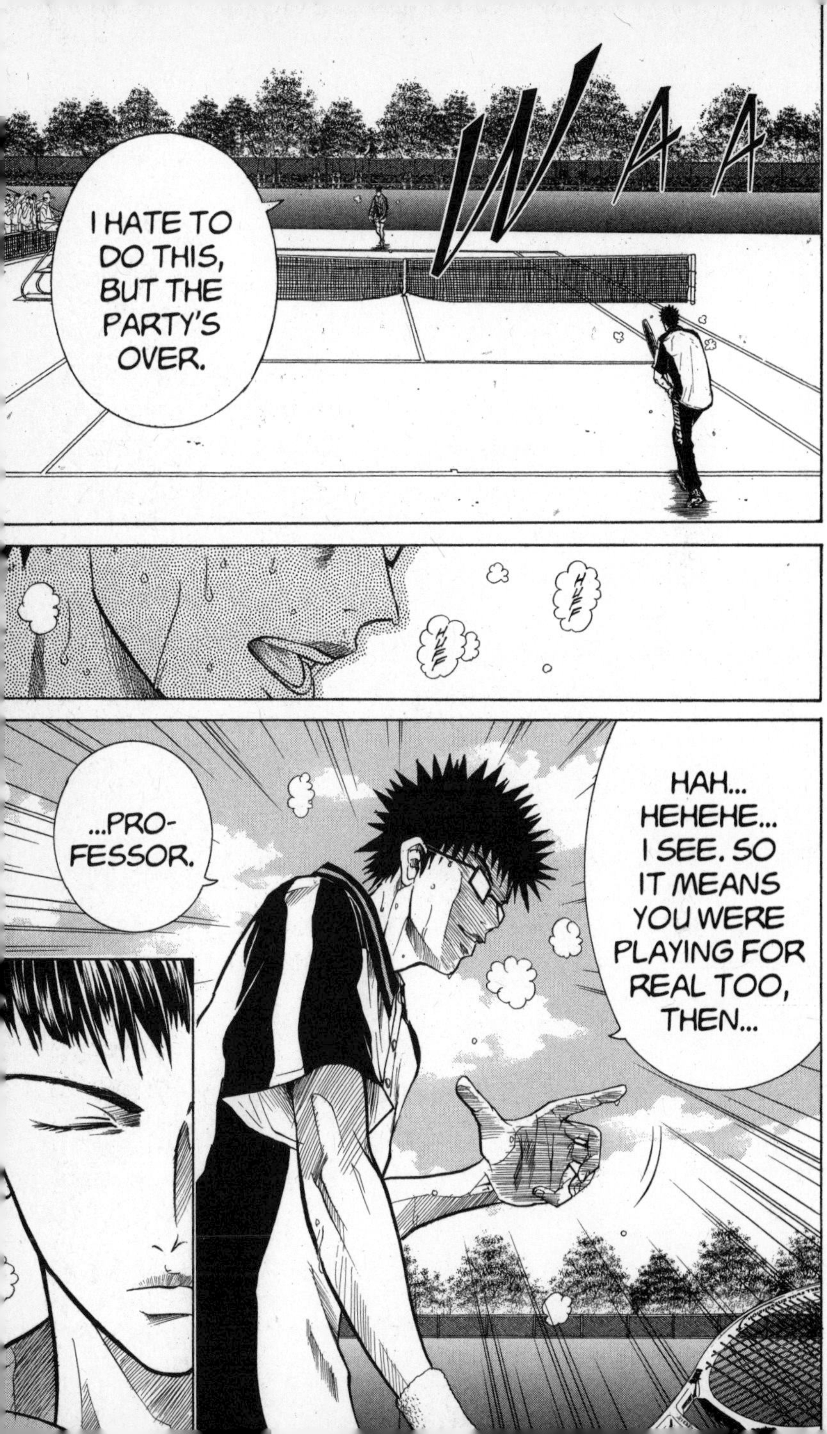
WAAA
I HATE TO DO THIS, BUT THE PARTY'S OVER.
HUFF
HUFF
HAH... HEHEHE... I SEE. SO IT MEANS YOU WERE PLAYING FOR REAL TOO, THEN...
...PRO-FESSOR.

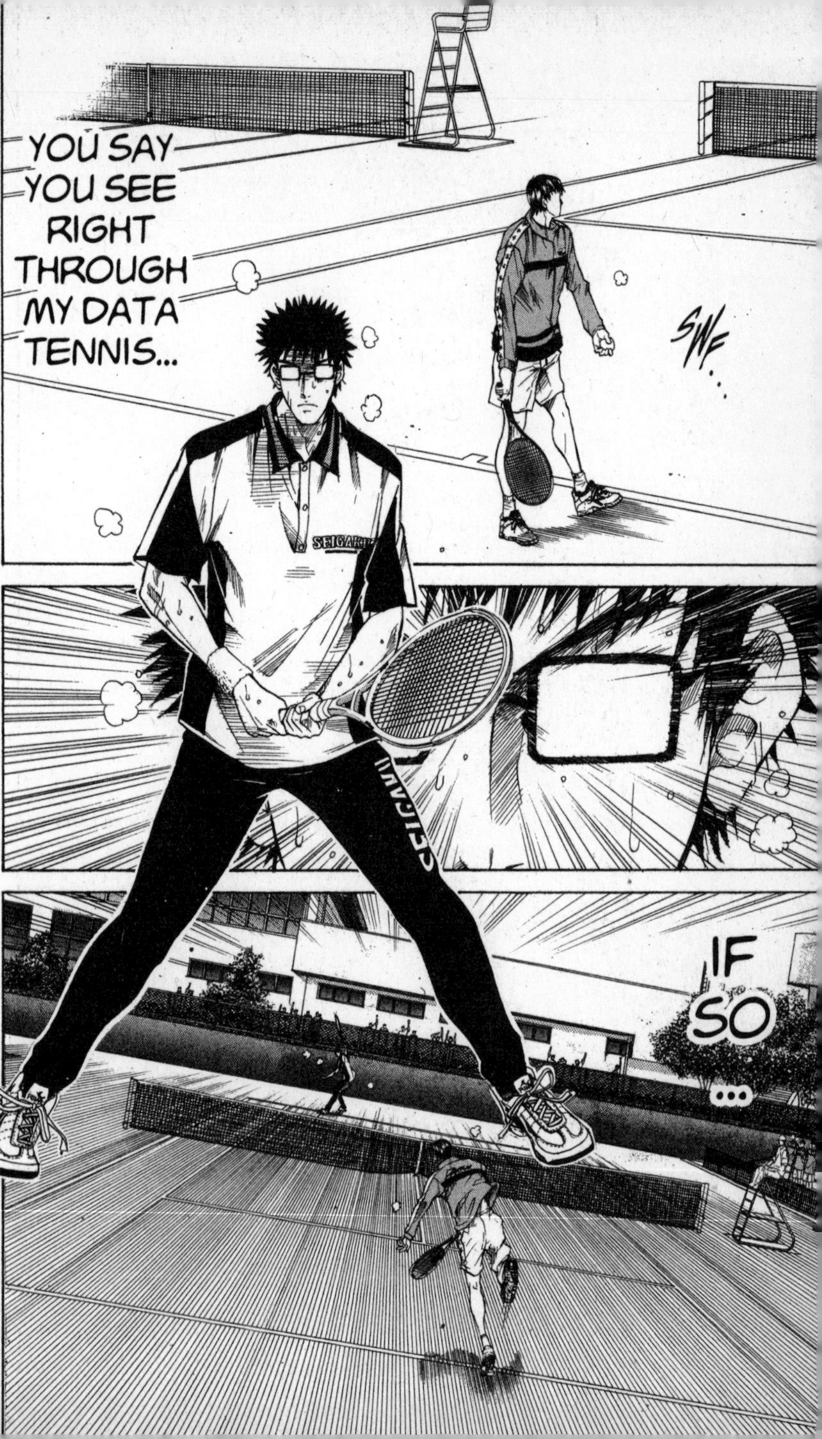
SWF...
YOU SAY YOU SEE RIGHT THROUGH MY DATA TENNIS...
IF SO...

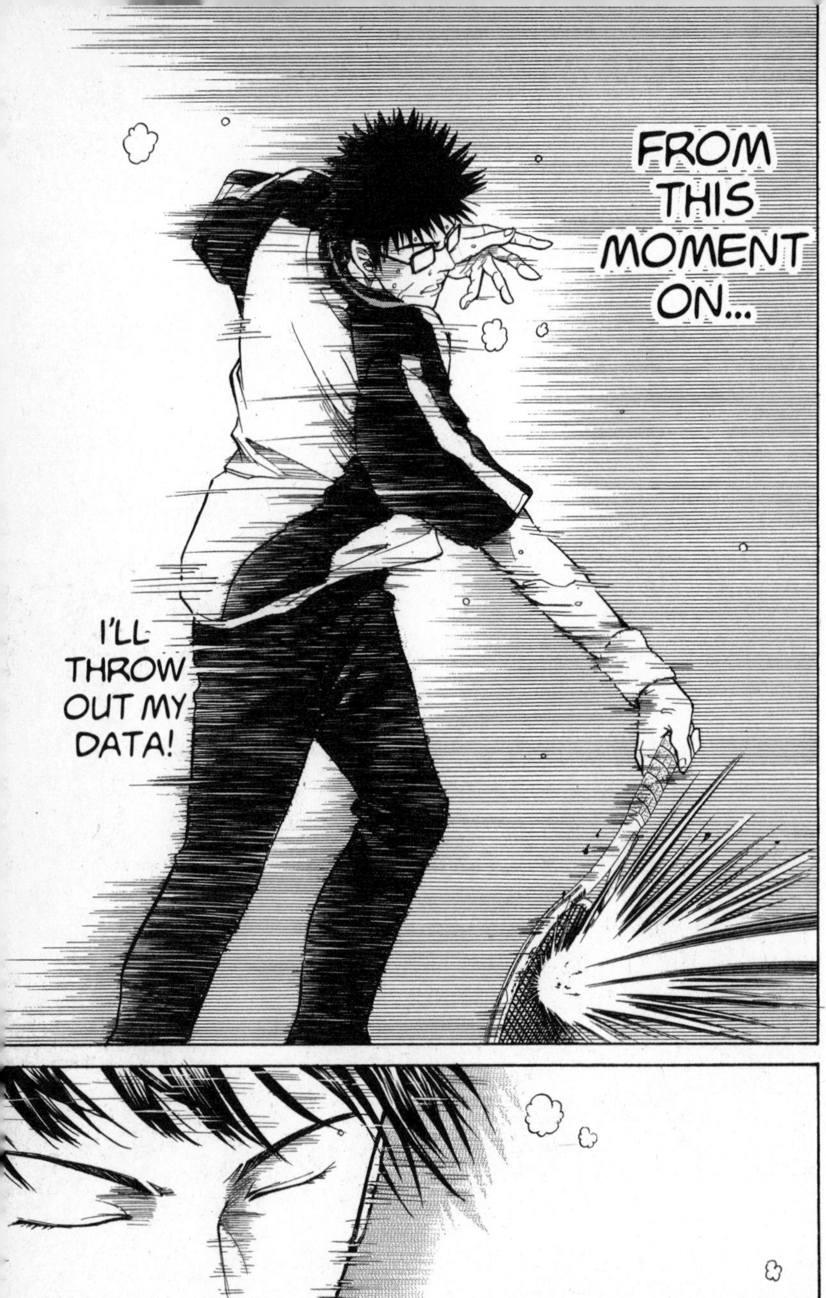
FROM THIS MOMENT ON...
I'LL THROW OUT MY DATA!

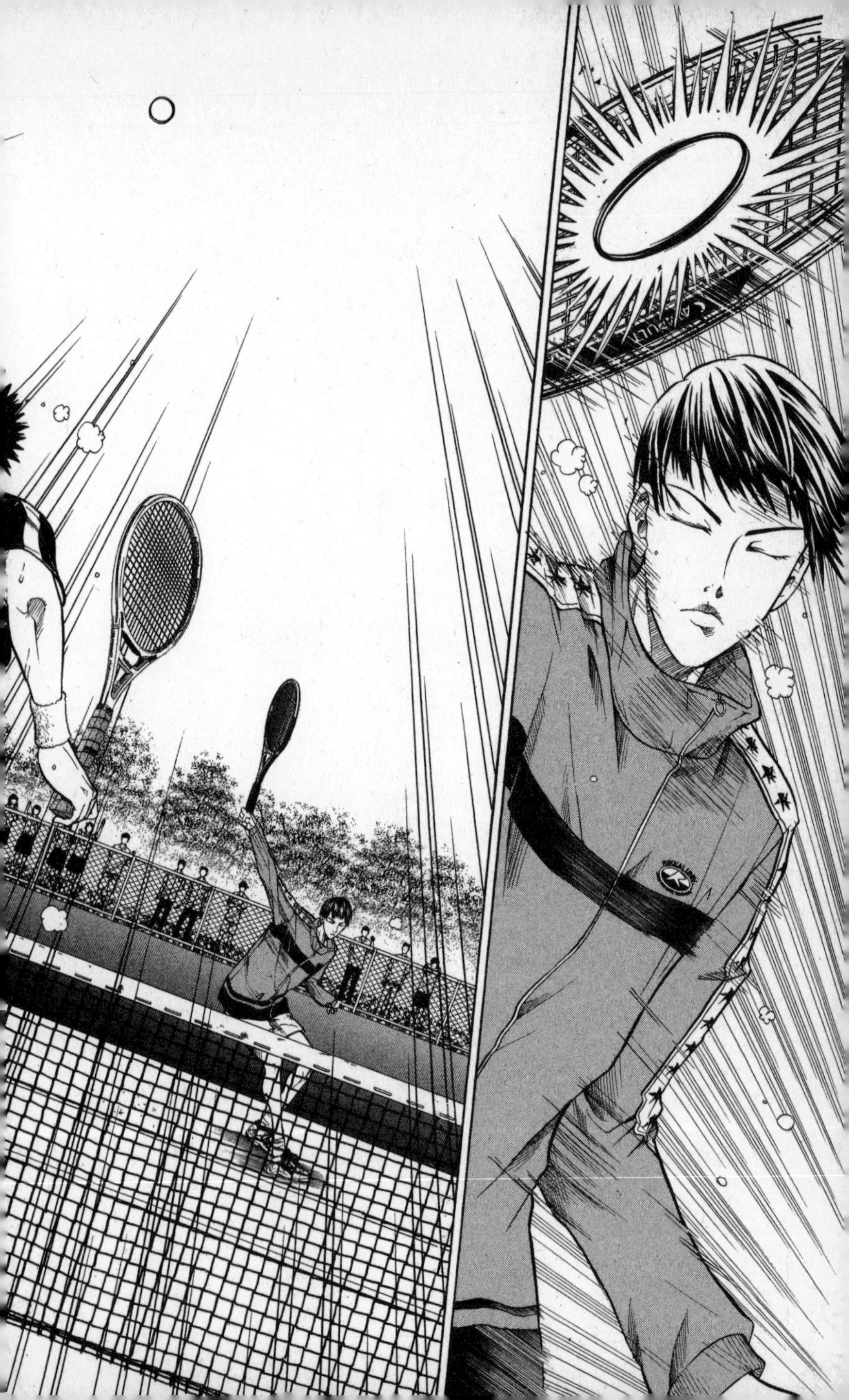

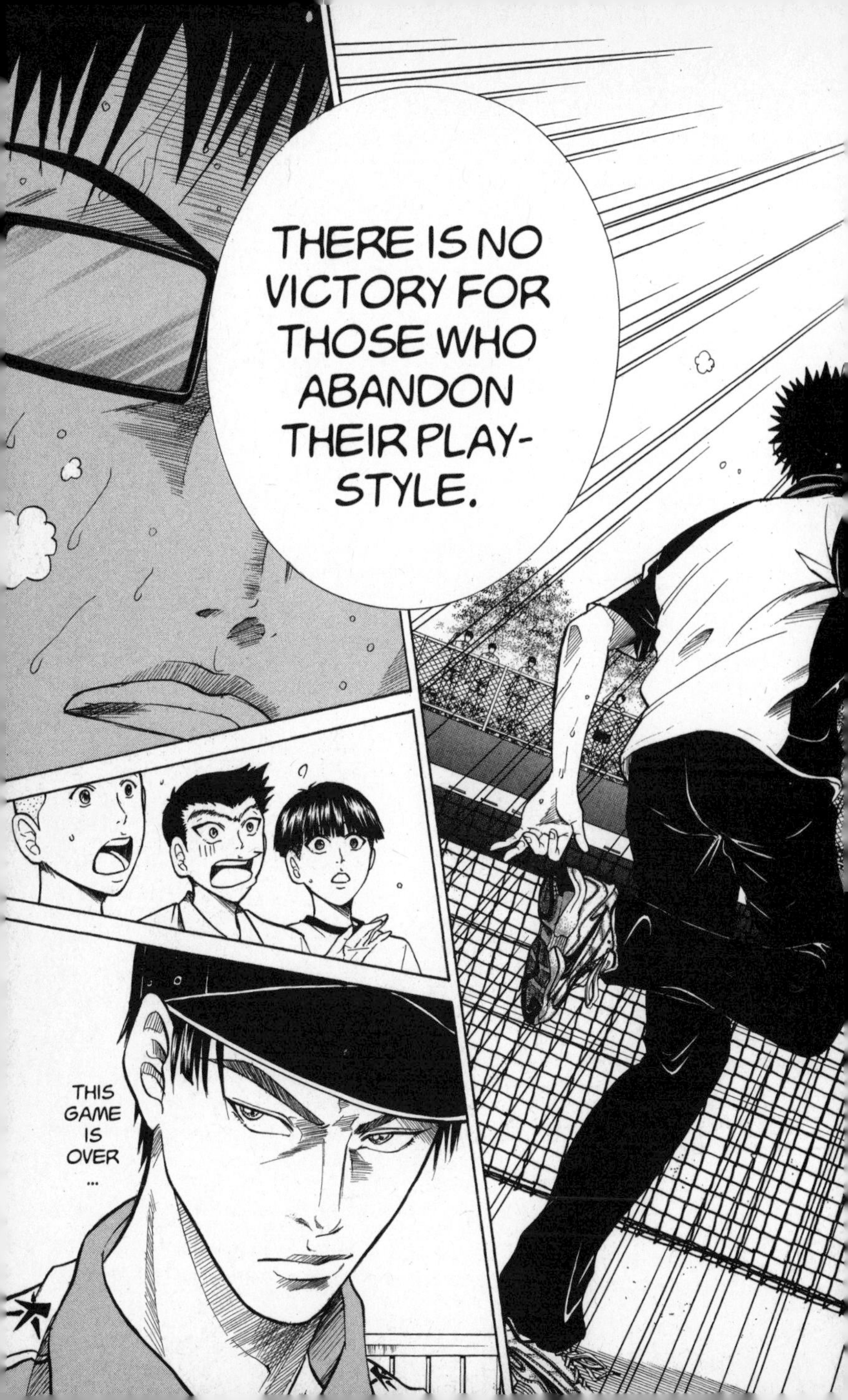
THERE IS NO VICTORY FOR THOSE WHO ABANDON THEIR PLAY-STYLE.
THIS GAME IS OVER ...

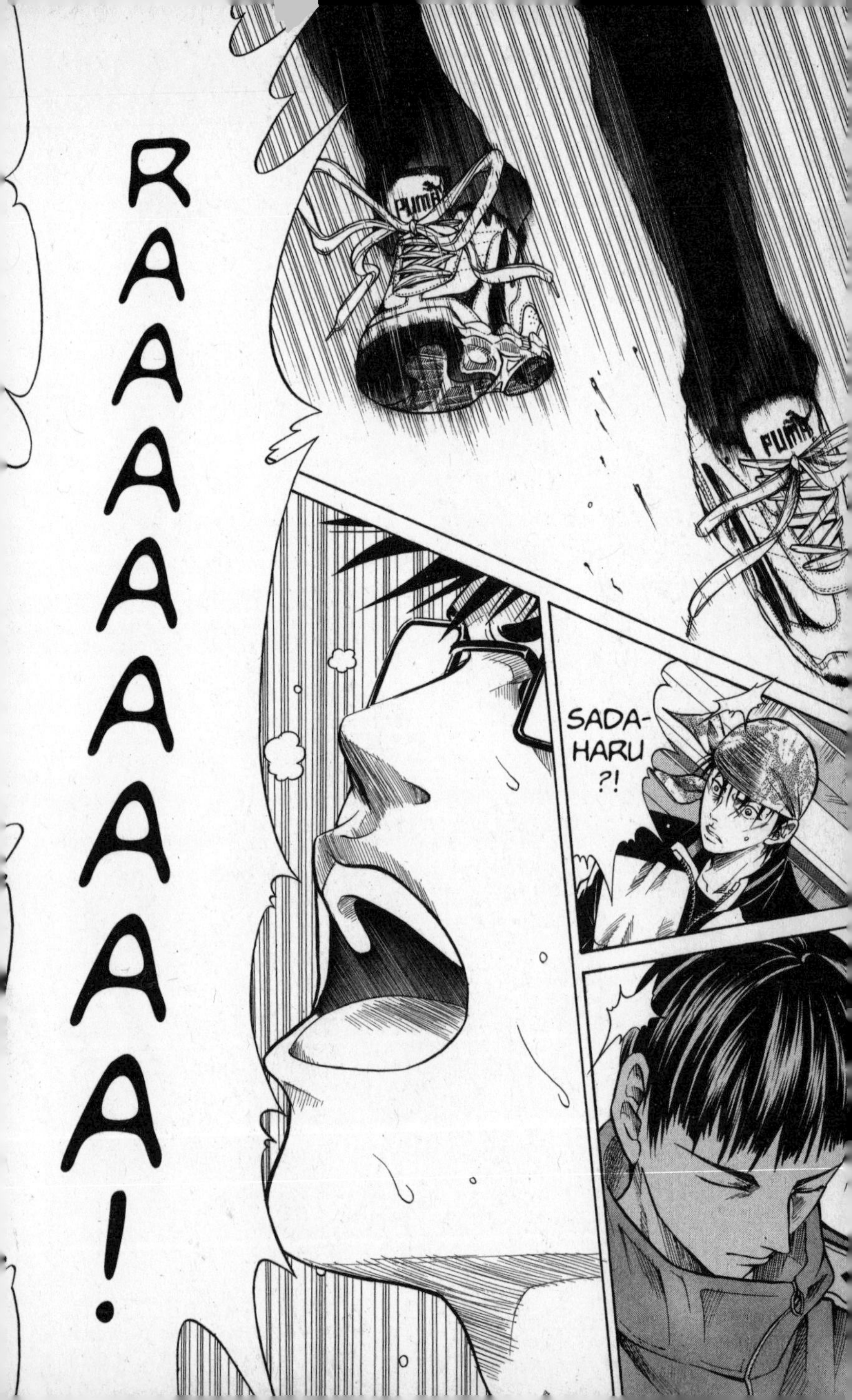
PUMA
PUMA
SADA-
HARU
?!
RAAAAAAAAA!

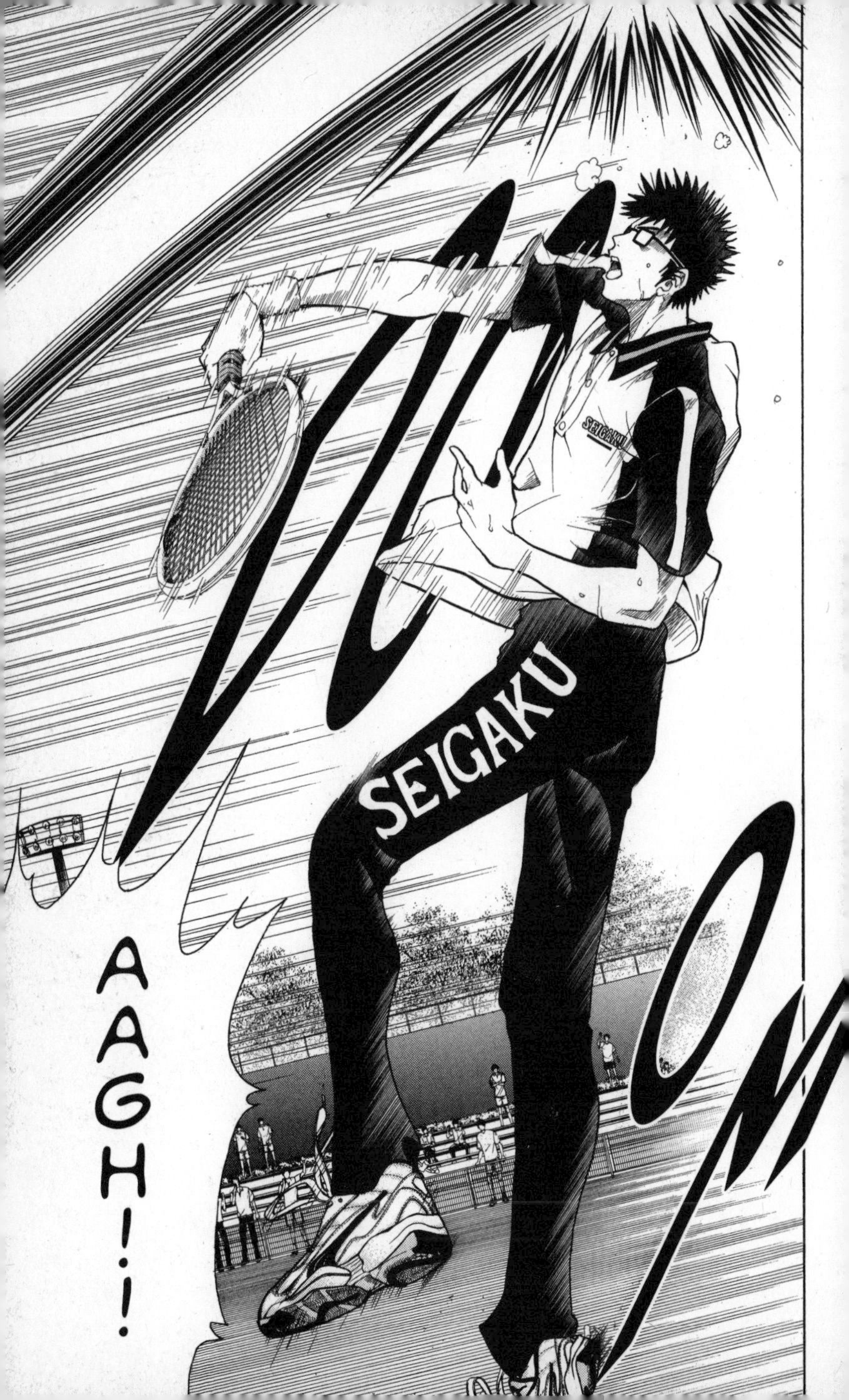
SEIGAKU
SEIGAKU
AAGH!!

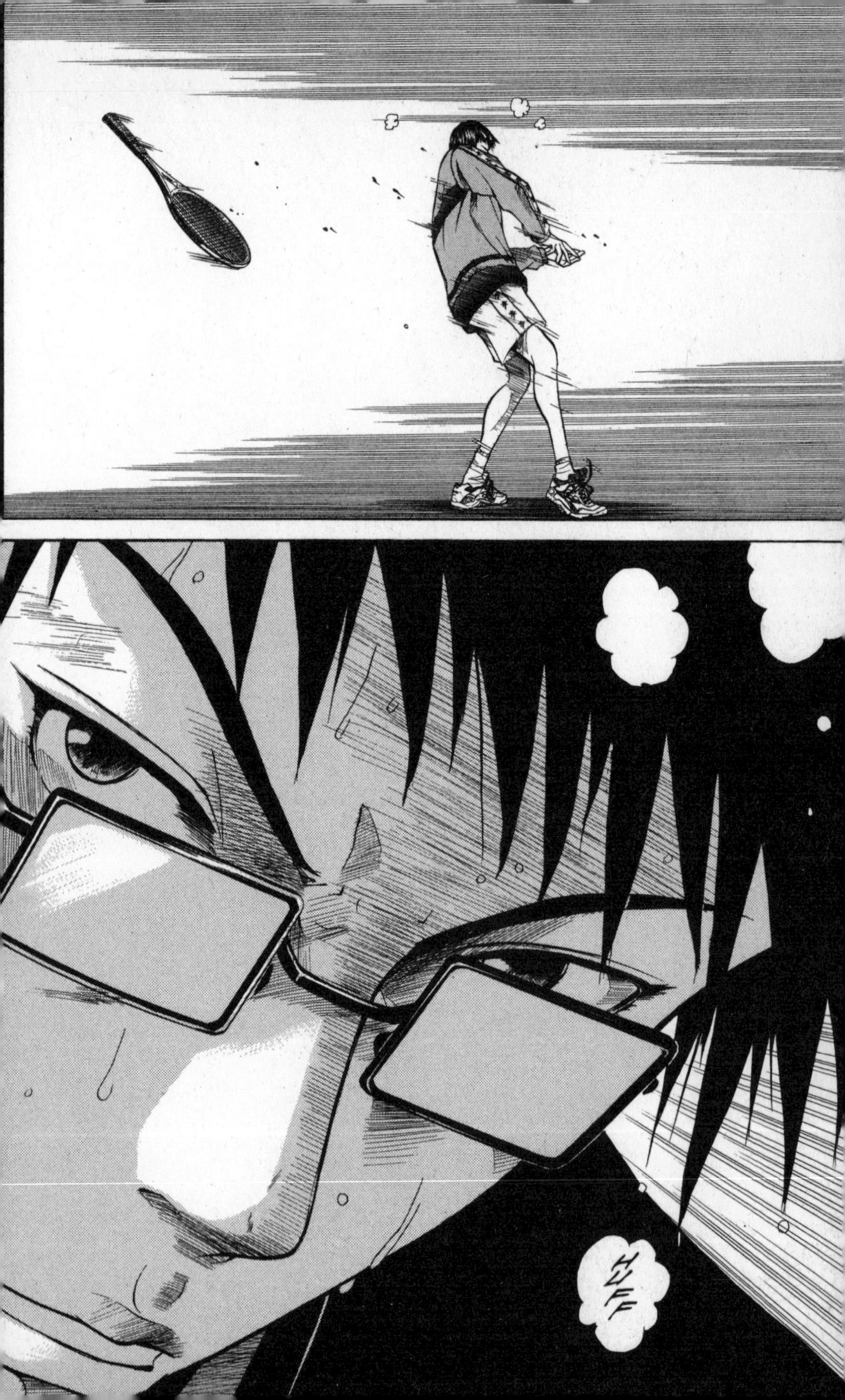
HUFF

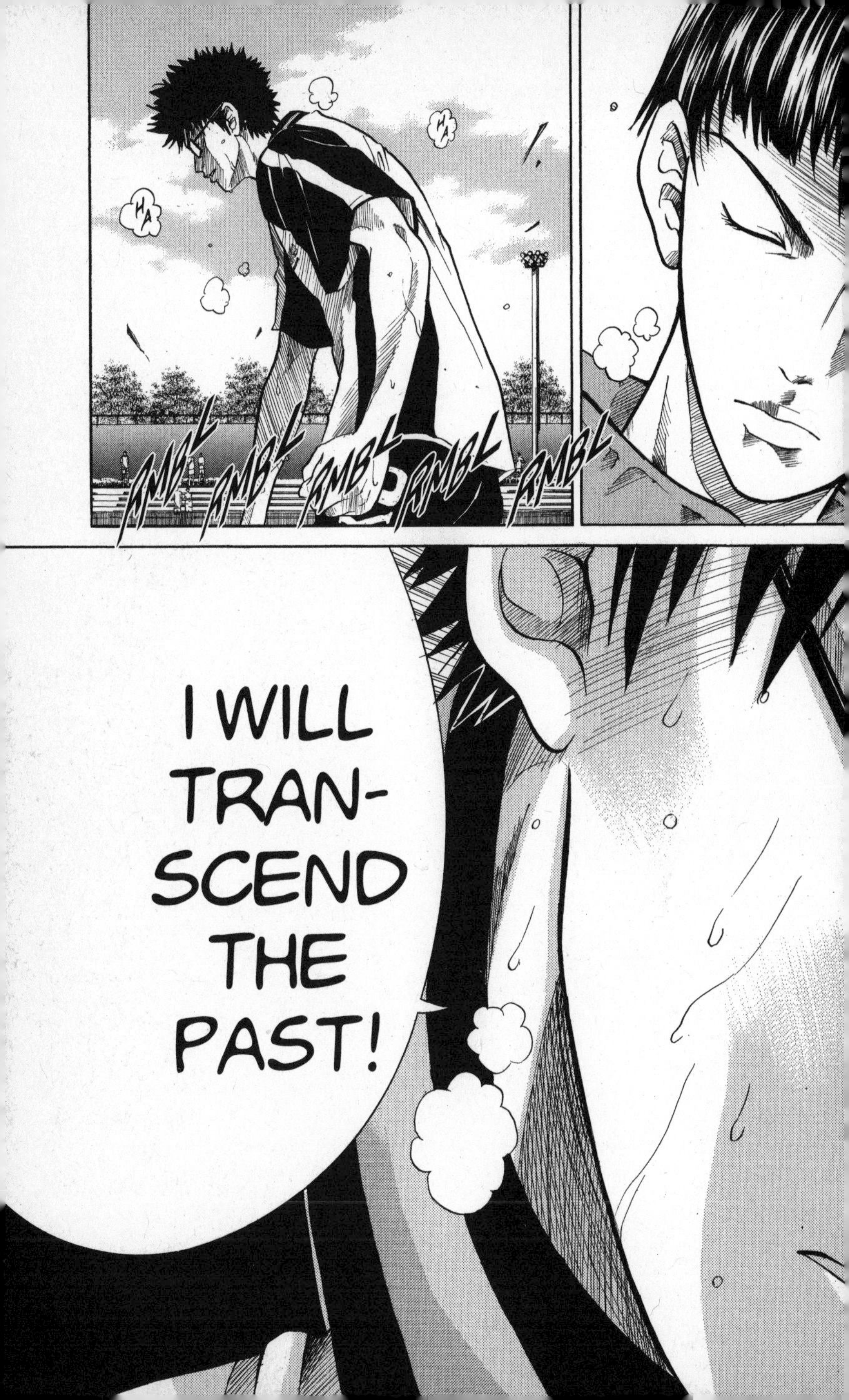
HA
HA
RMBL RMBL RMBL RMBL RMBL
I WILL TRAN-SCEND THE PAST!

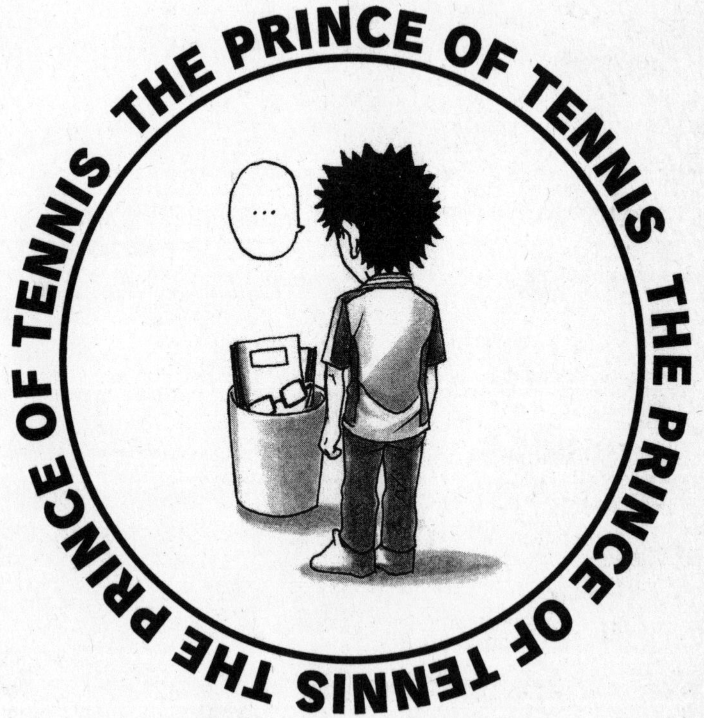
THE PRINCE OF TENNIS THE PRINCE OF TENNIS THE PRINCE OF TENNIS
...

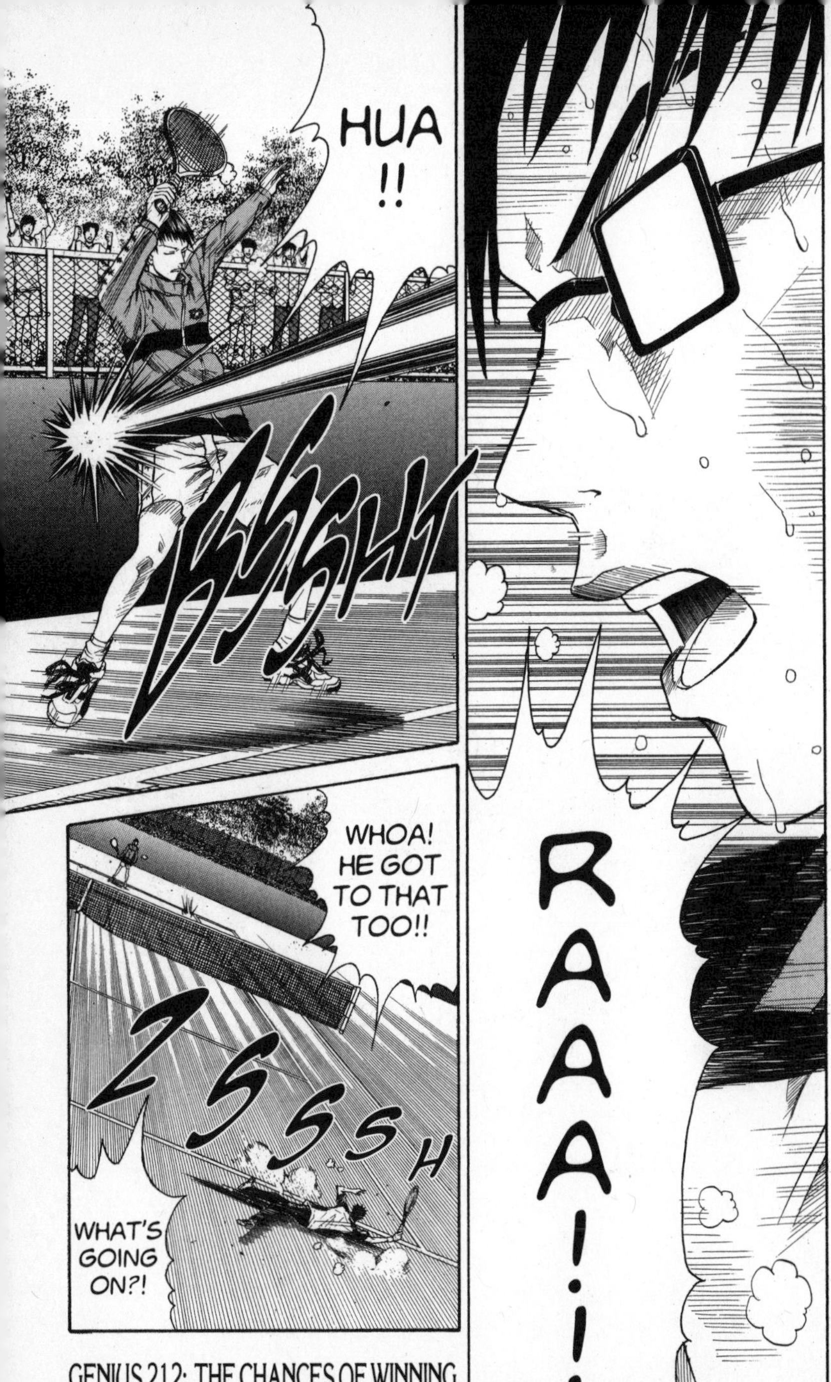
RAAAI!!
HUA!!
WHOA! HE GOT TO THAT TOO!!
ZSSSH
WHAT'S GOING ON?!

GENIUS 212: THE CHANCES OF WINNING

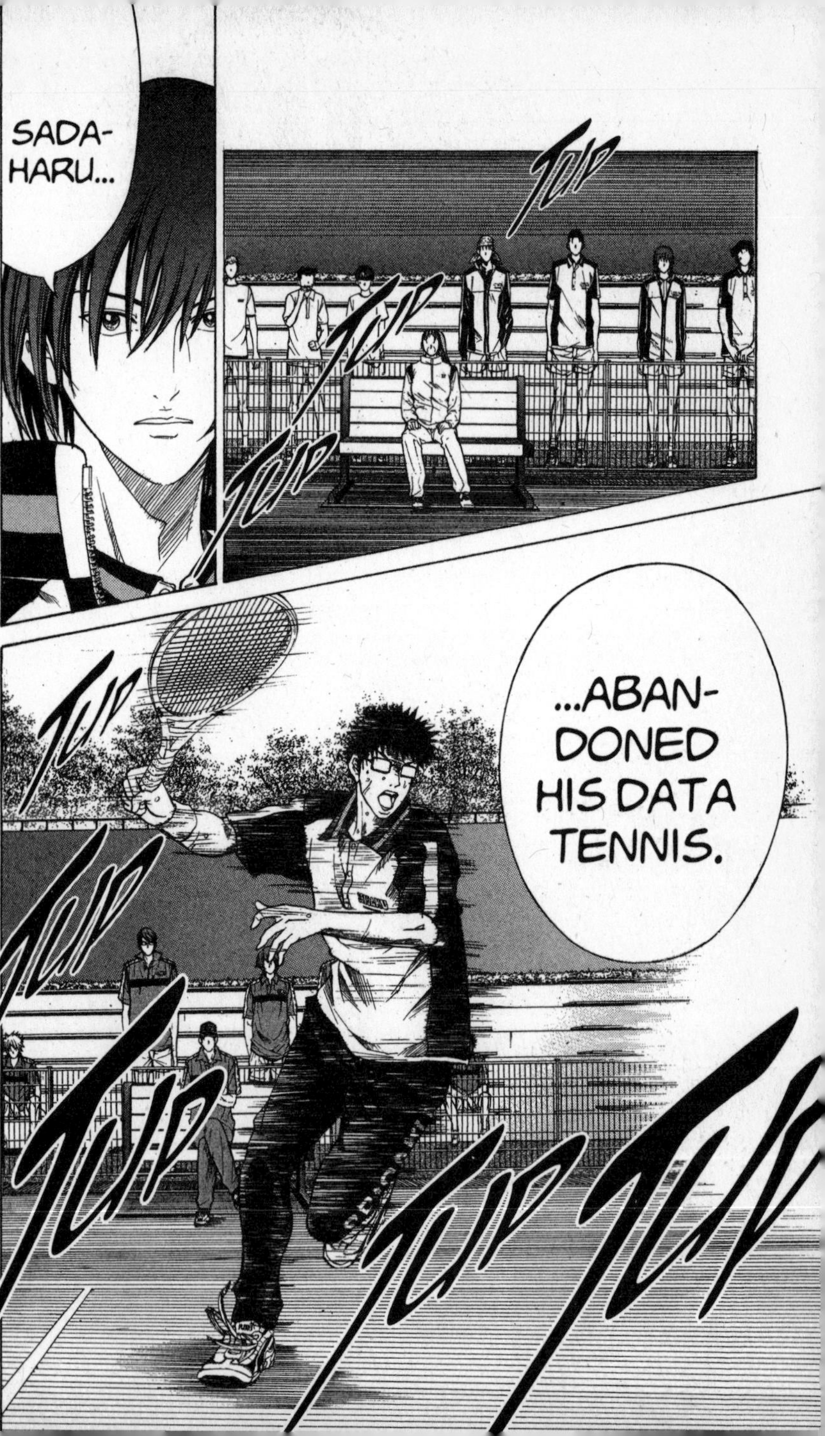
SADA-HARU...
...ABAN-DONED HIS DATA TENNIS.

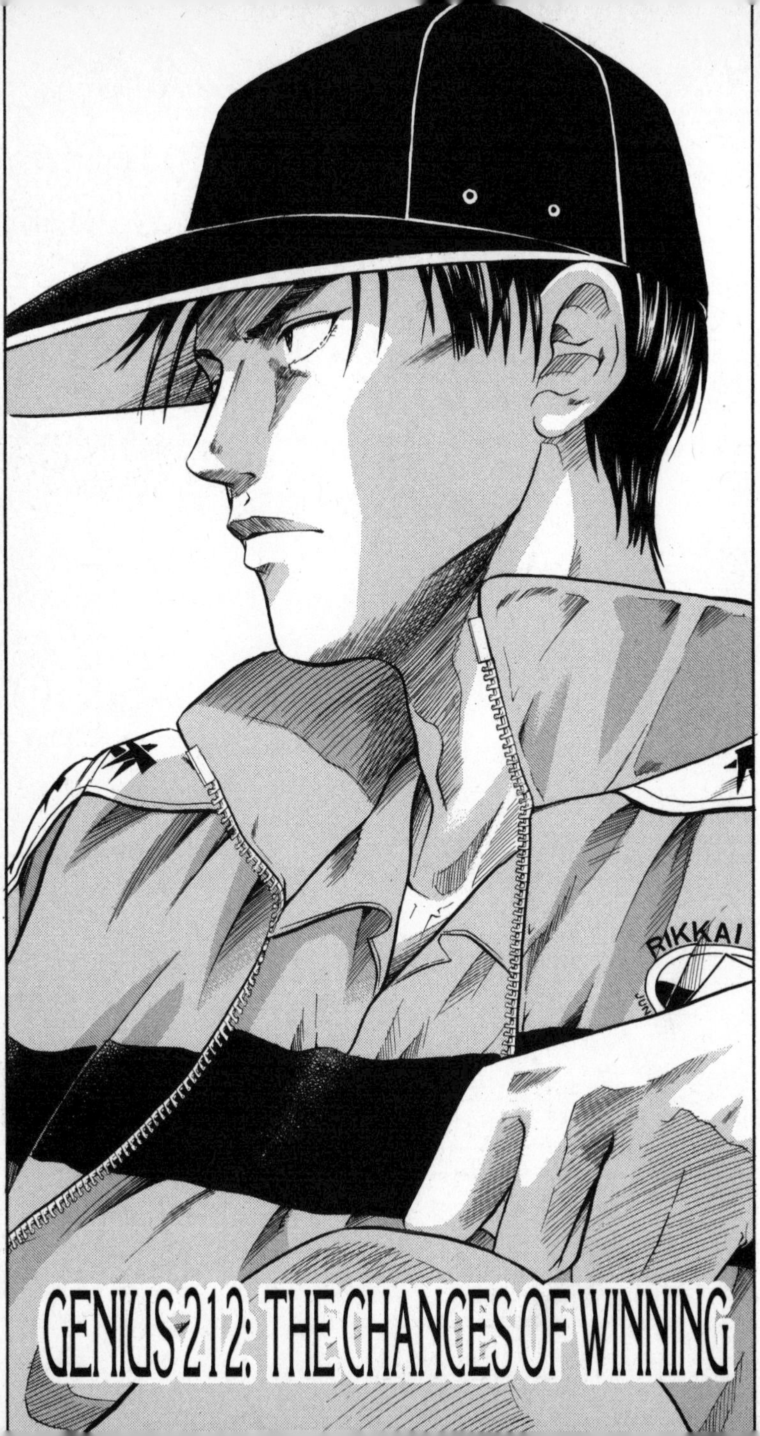
RIKKAI
GENIUS 212: THE CHANCES OF WINNING

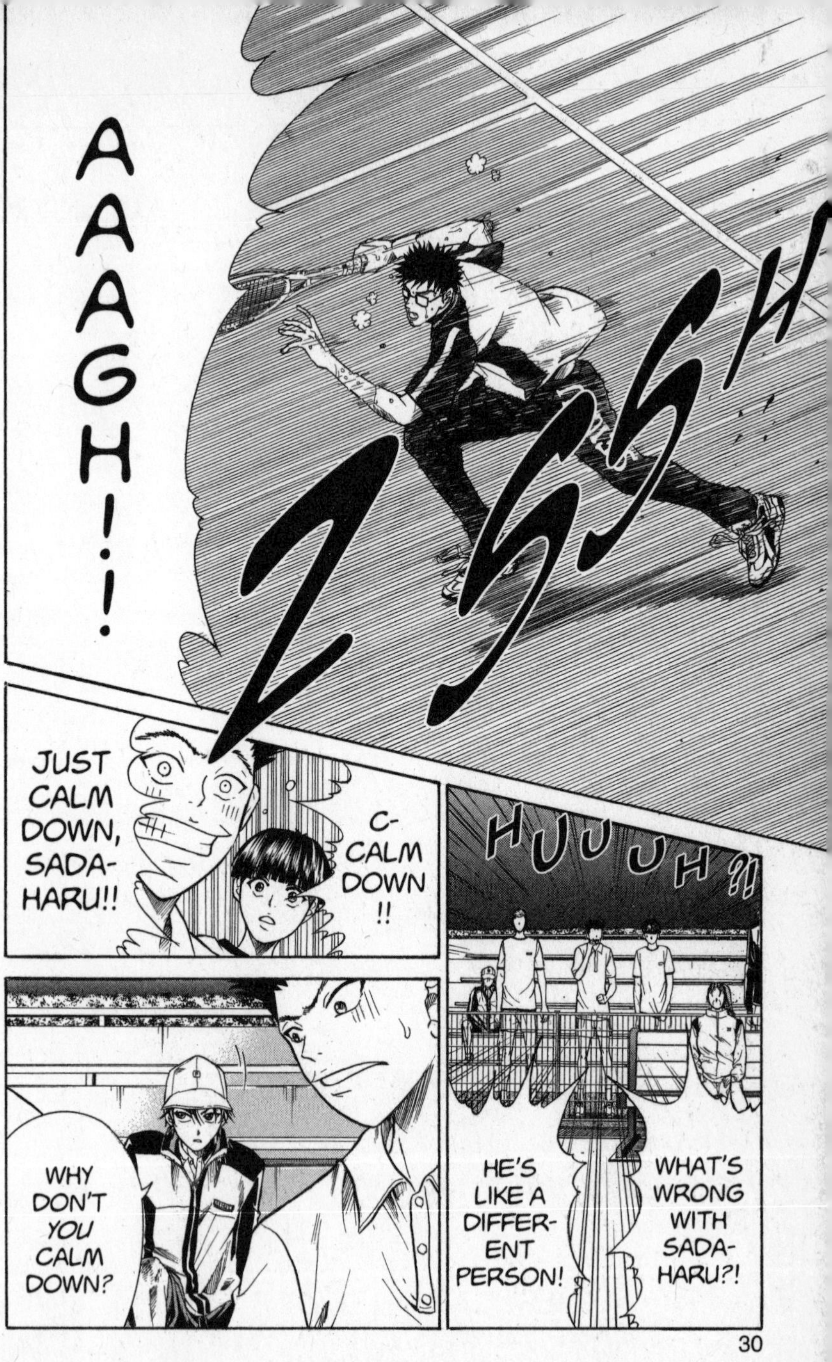
ZSSSH
AAAGH!!
HUUUJH?!
WHAT'S WRONG WITH SADA-HARU?!
HE'S LIKE A DIFFER-ENT PERSON!
C-CALM DOWN!!
JUST CALM DOWN, SADA-HARU!!
WHY DON'T YOU CALM DOWN?

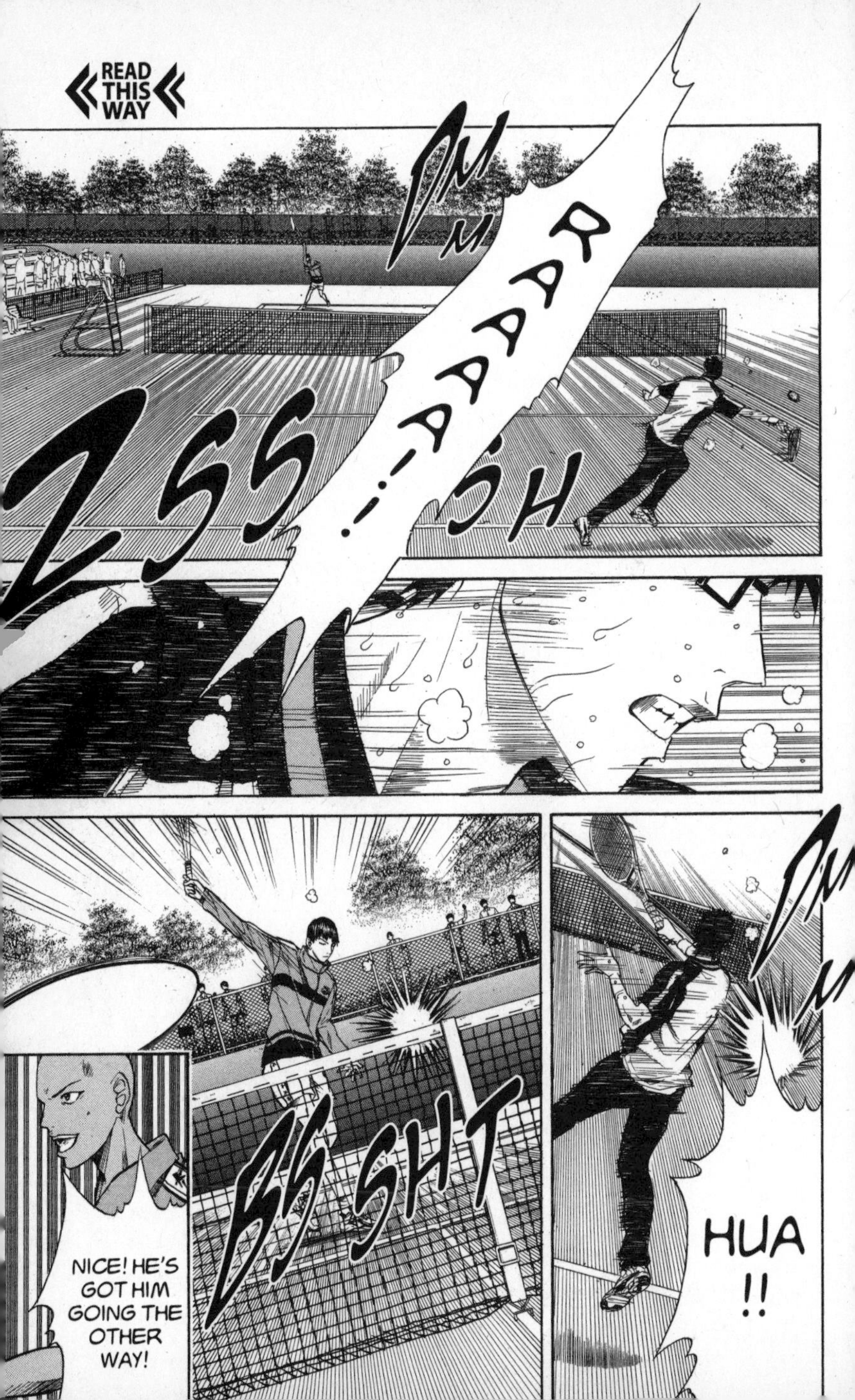
READ THIS WAY
RAAAA--!!
ZSS
SH
HUA!!
BS SHT
NICE! HE'S GOT HIM GOING THE OTHER WAY!

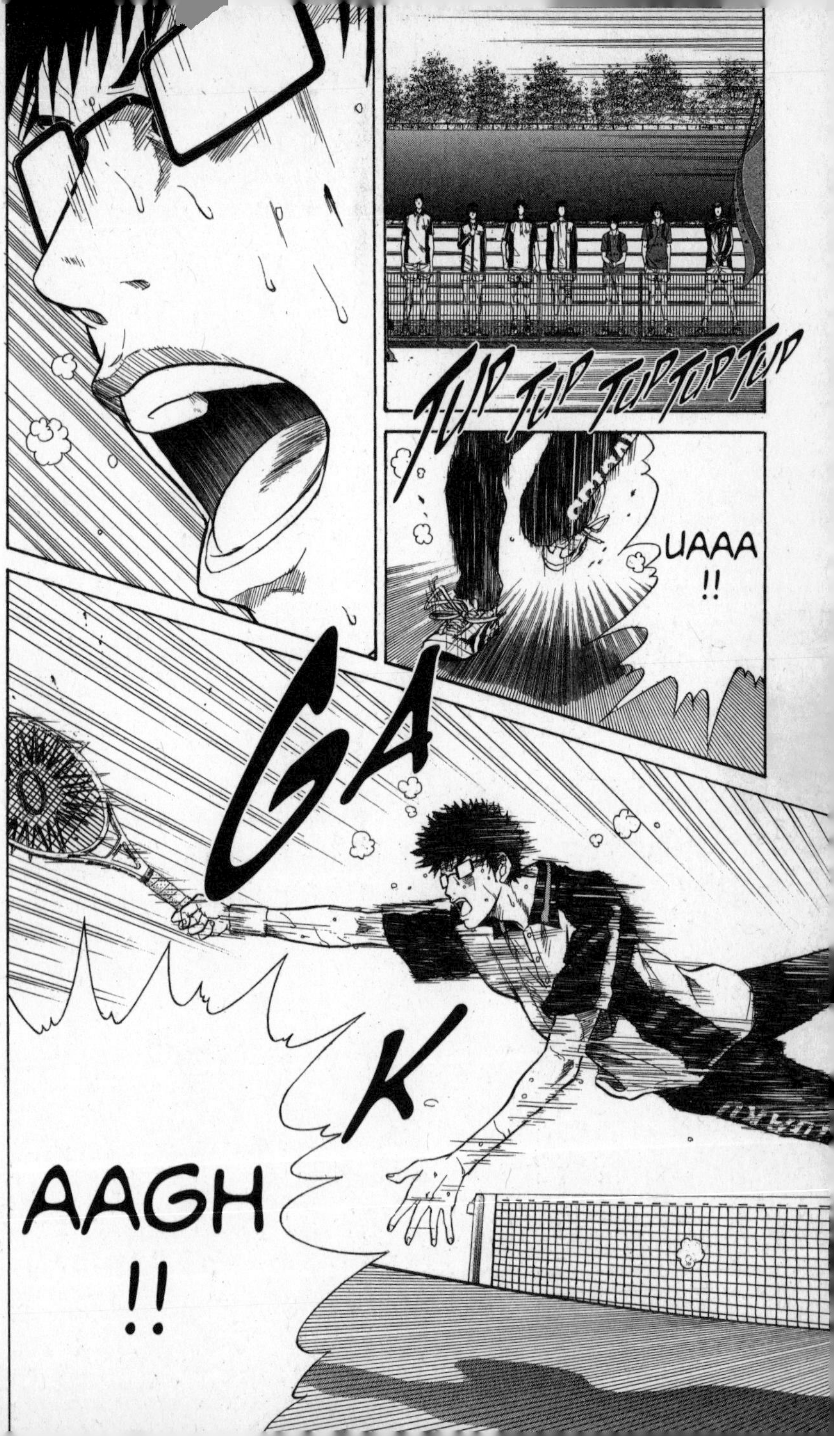
TUP TUP TUP TUP TUP
UAAA !!
GAK
AAGH !!

READ THIS WAY

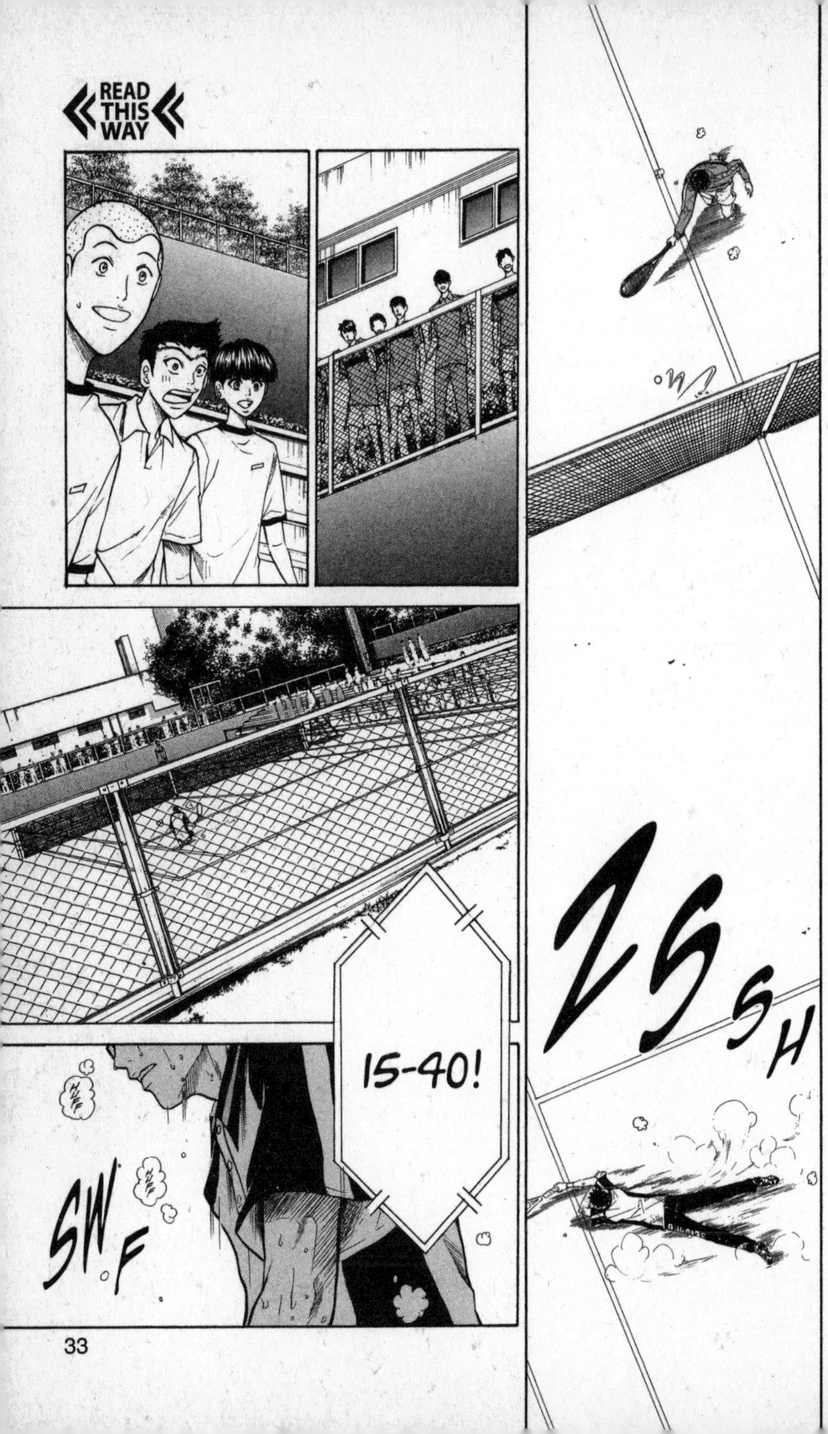
ZSSH
15-40!
SWF

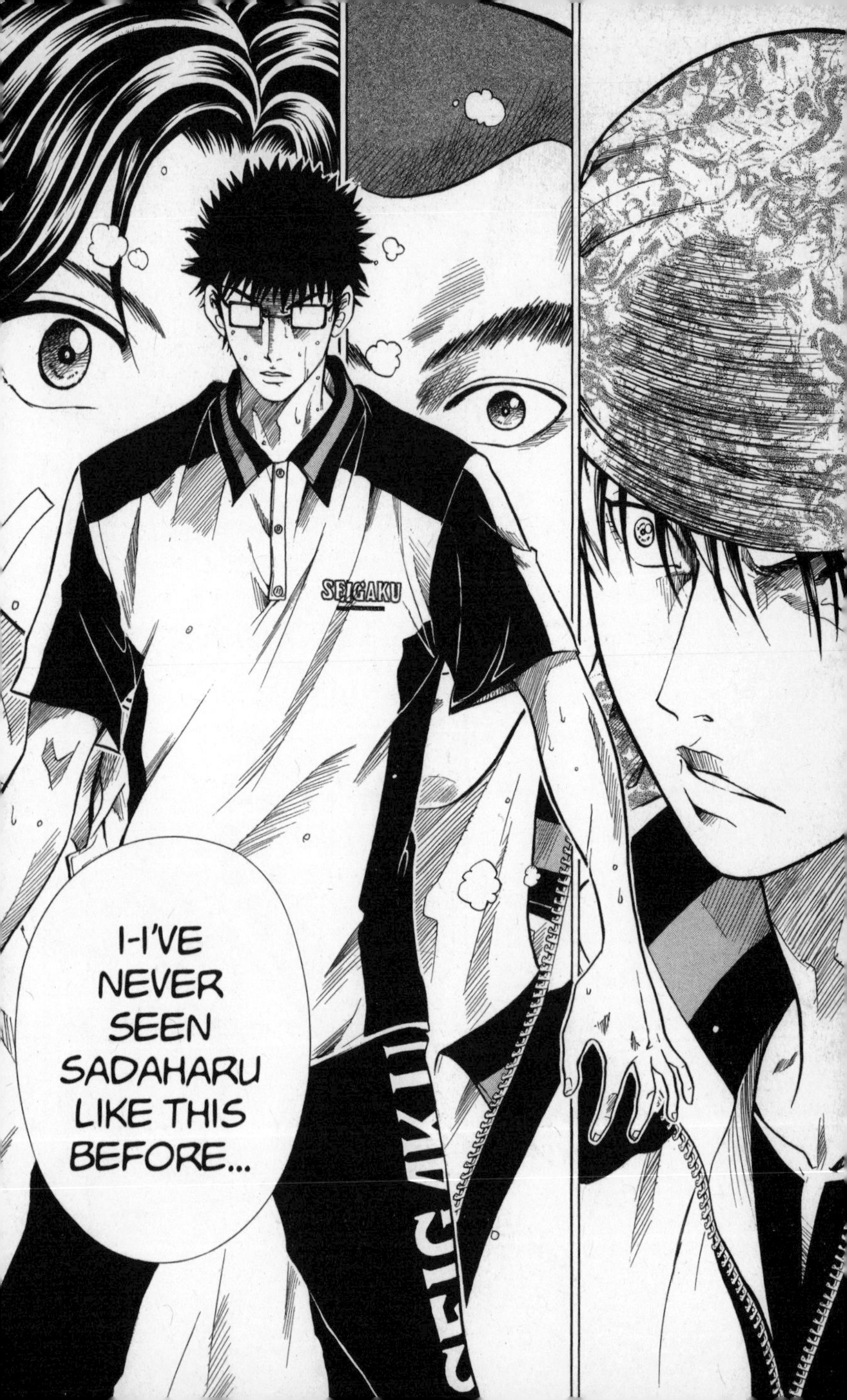
SEIGAKU
I-I'VE NEVER SEEN SADAHARU LIKE THIS BEFORE...

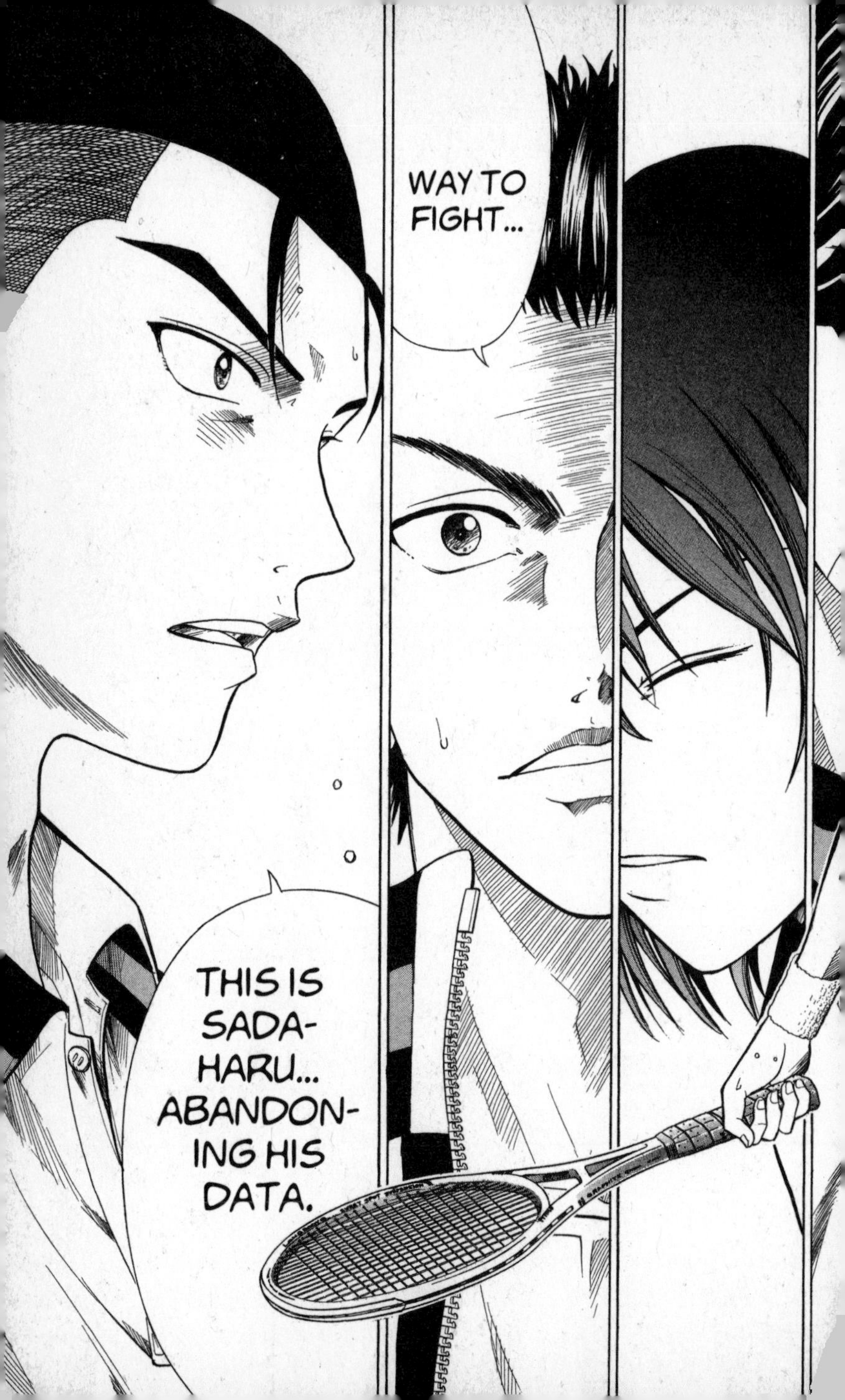
WAY TO FIGHT...
THIS IS SADAHARU... ABANDONING HIS DATA.

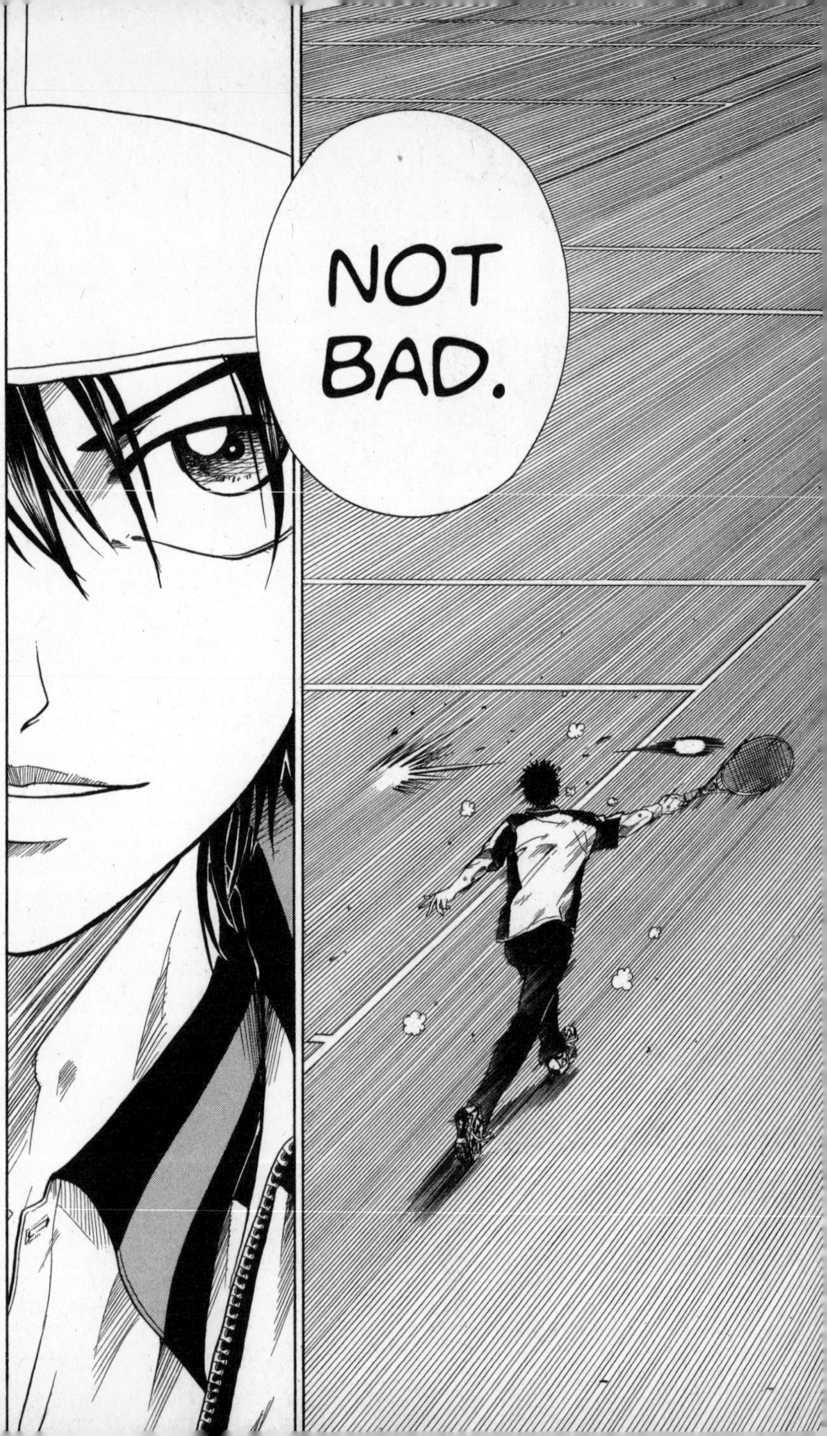
NOT BAD.

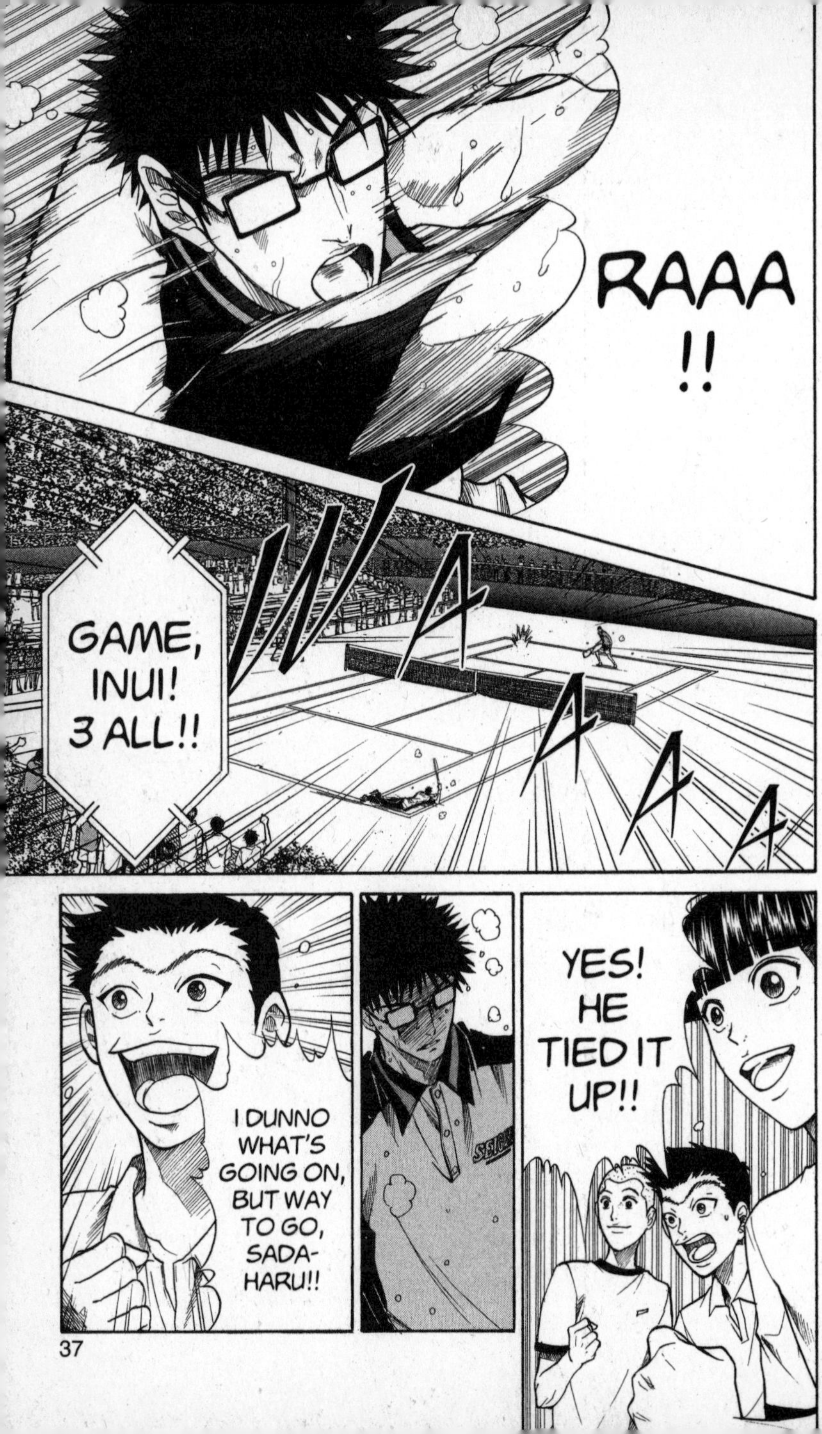
RAAA!!
WAAAAA
GAME, INUI! 3 ALL!!
YES! HE TIED IT UP!!
I DUNNO WHAT'S GOING ON, BUT WAY TO GO, SADA-HARU!!

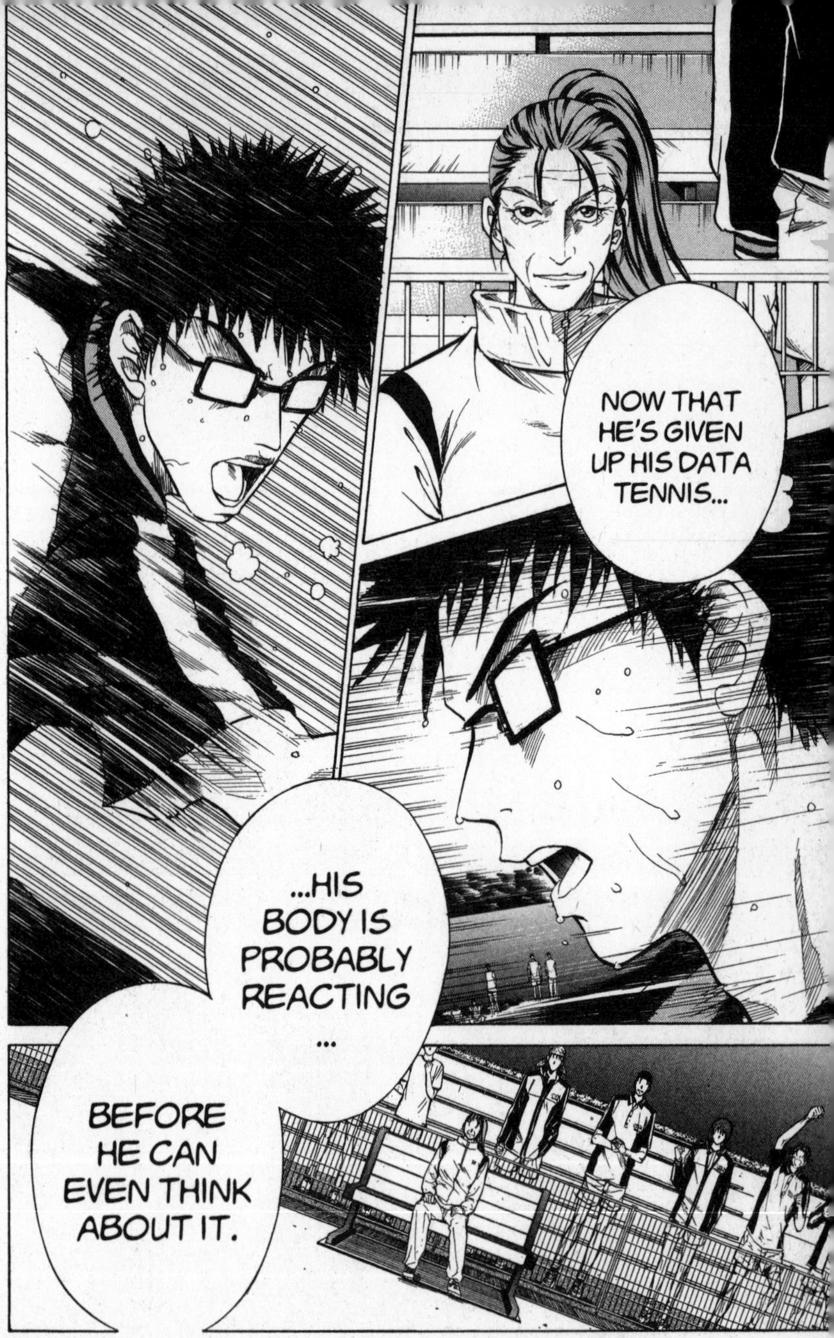
NOW THAT HE'S GIVEN UP HIS DATA TENNIS...
...HIS BODY IS PROBABLY REACTING ...
BEFORE HE CAN EVEN THINK ABOUT IT.

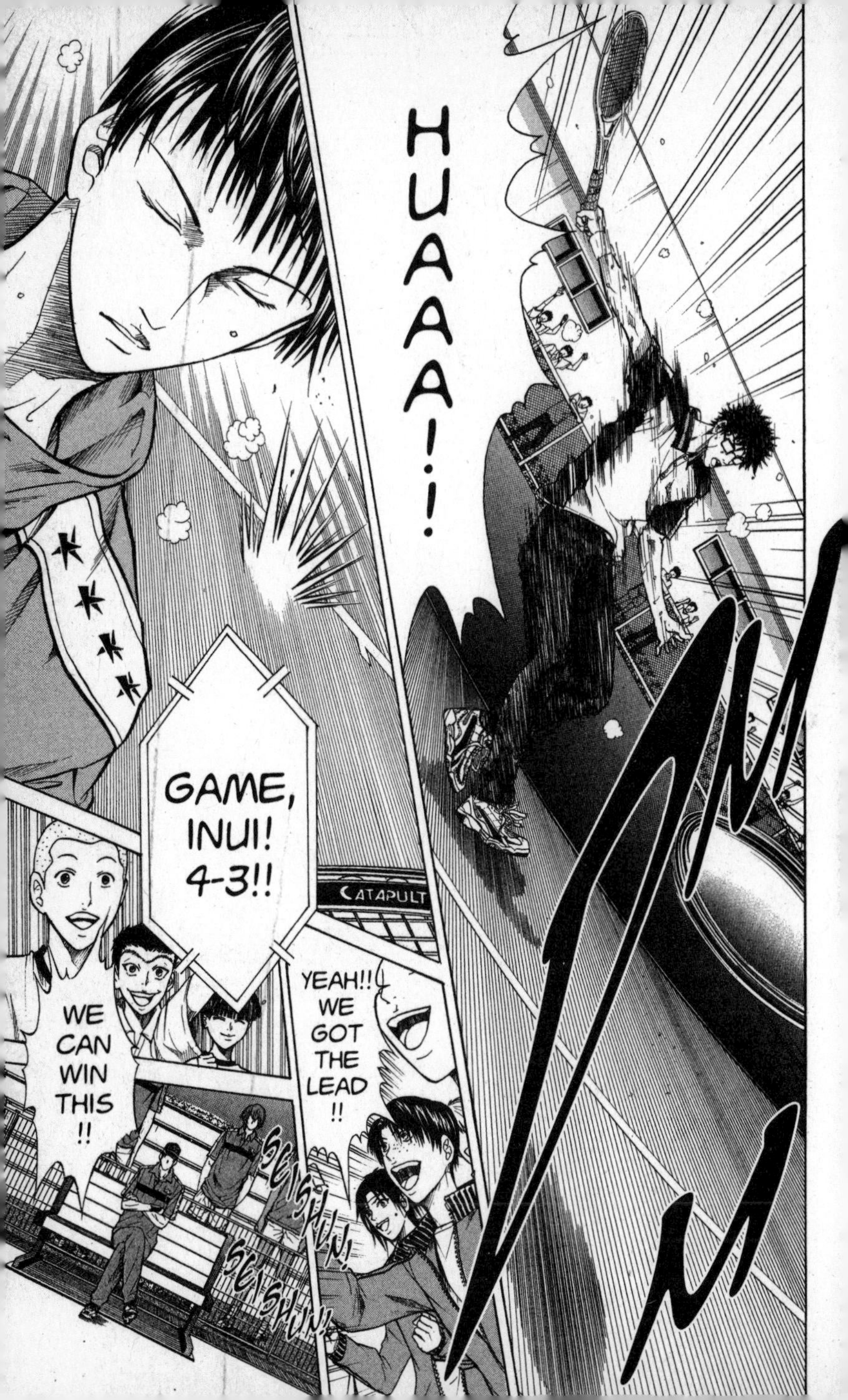
HUAAAI!!
GAME, INUI! 4-3!!
CATAPULT
YEAH!! WE GOT THE LEAD!!
SEISHUN! SEISHUN!
WE CAN WIN THIS!!

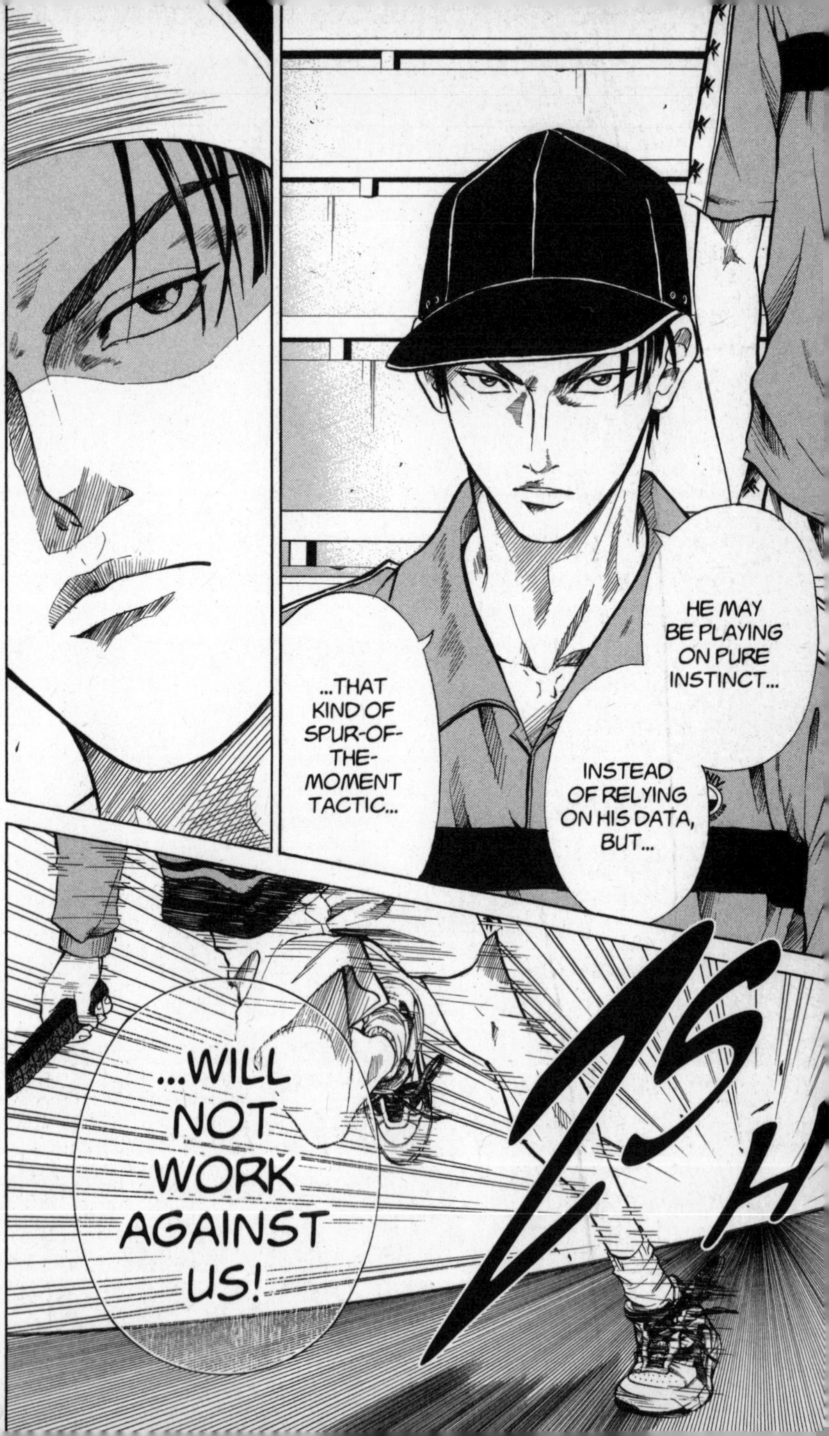
HE MAY BE PLAYING ON PURE INSTINCT...
INSTEAD OF RELYING ON HIS DATA, BUT...
...THAT KIND OF SPUR-OF-THE-MOMENT TACTIC...
...WILL NOT WORK AGAINST US!

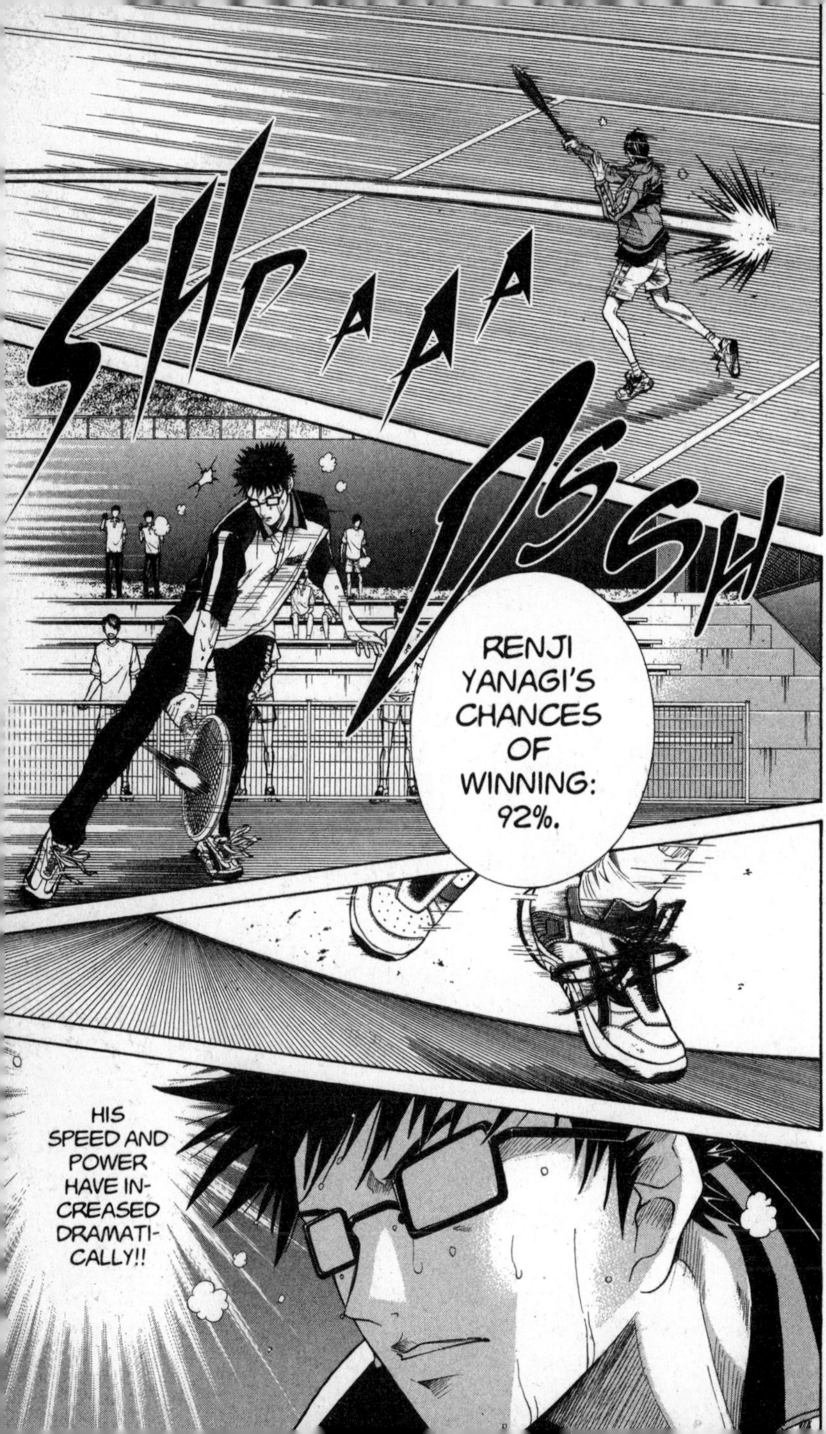
SHPAAAASSH
RENJI YANAGI'S CHANCES OF WINNING: 92%.
HIS SPEED AND POWER HAVE IN-CREASED DRAMATI-CALLY!!

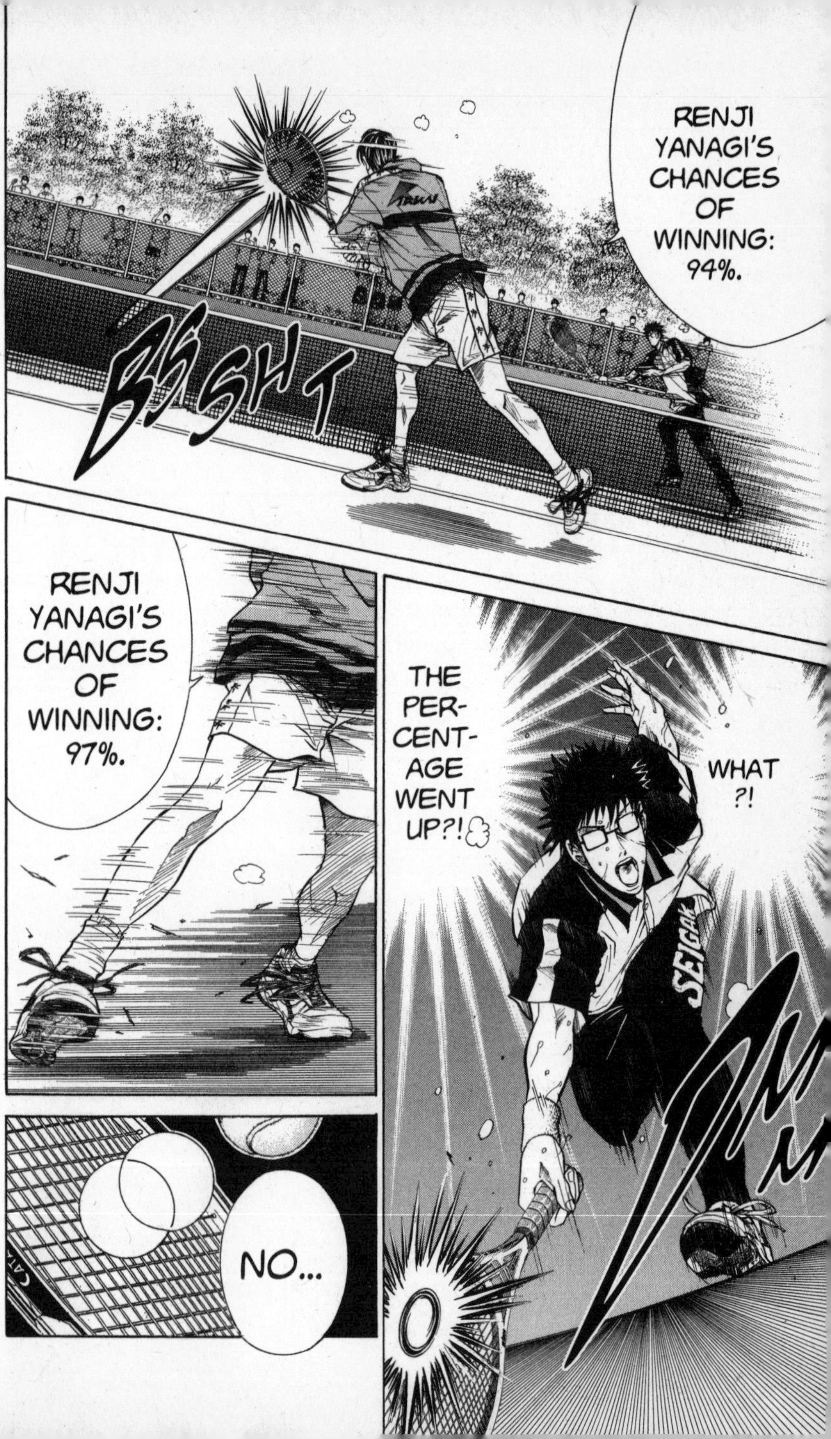
RENJI YANAGI'S CHANCES OF WINNING: 94%.
BSSHT
RENJI YANAGI'S CHANCES OF WINNING: 97%.
WHAT ?!
THE PER-CENT-AGE WENT UP?!
NO...

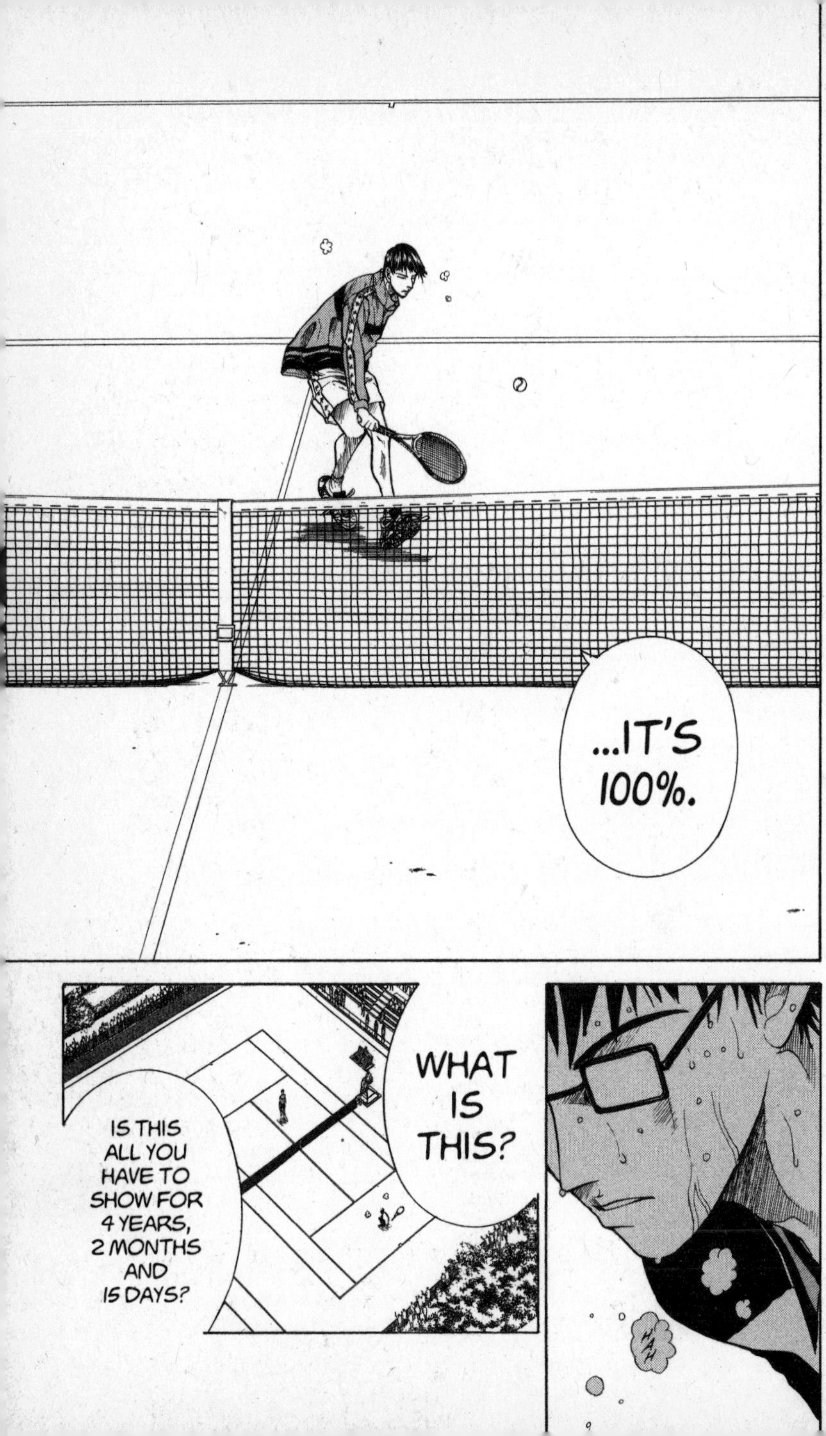

...IT'S 100%.
WHAT IS THIS?
IS THIS ALL YOU HAVE TO SHOW FOR 4 YEARS, 2 MONTHS AND 15 DAYS?

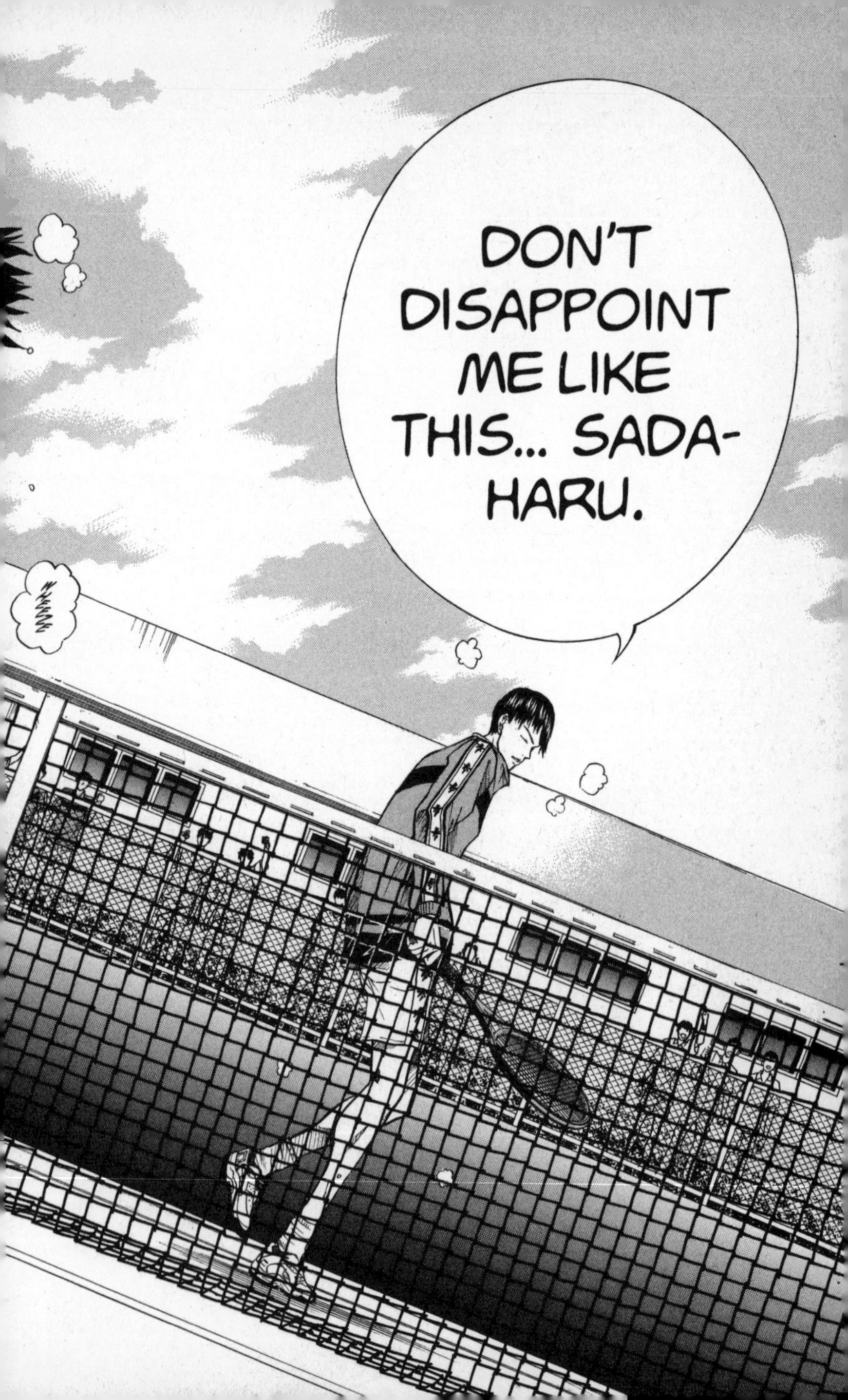
DON'T DISAPPOINT ME LIKE THIS... SADA-HARU.

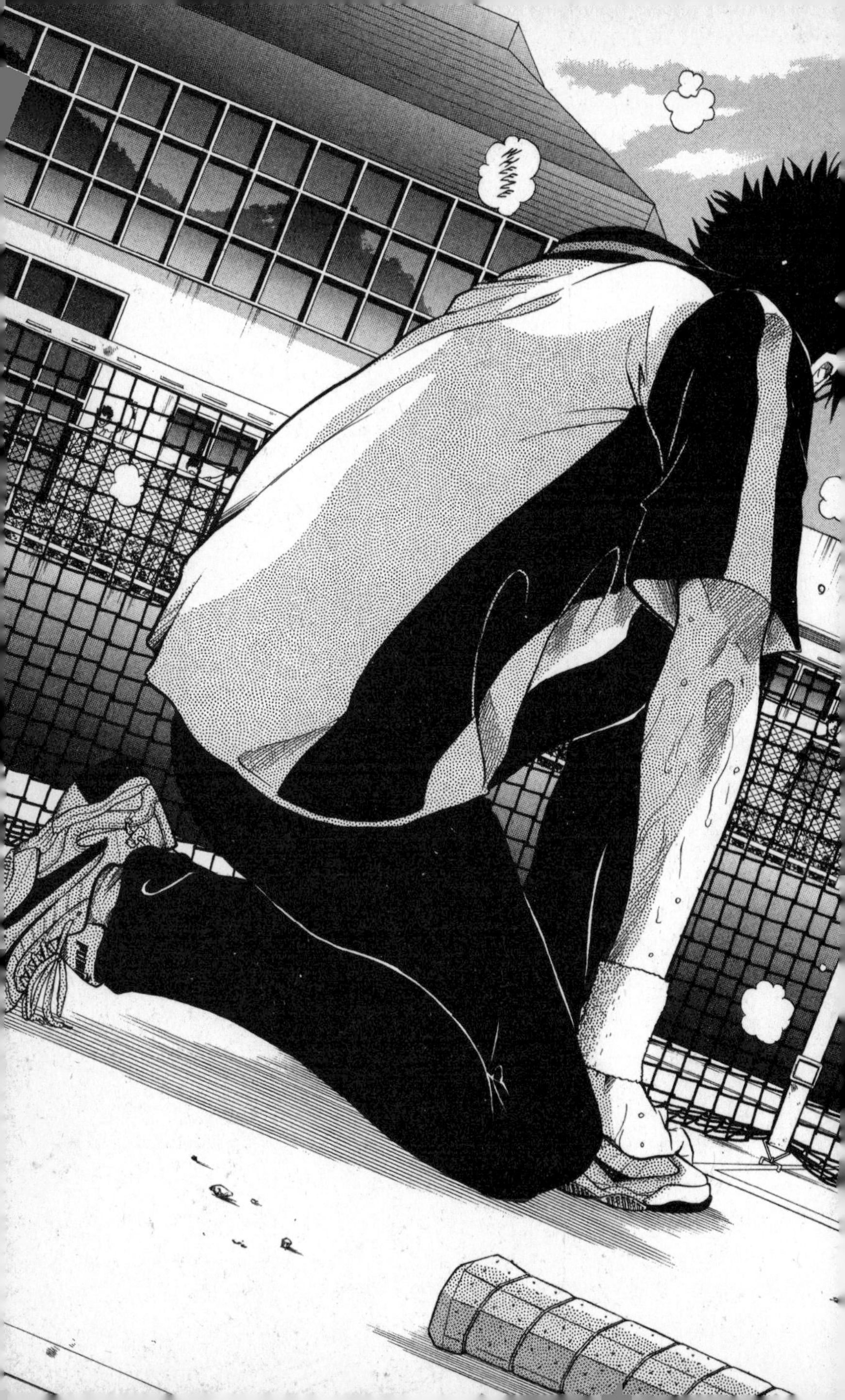

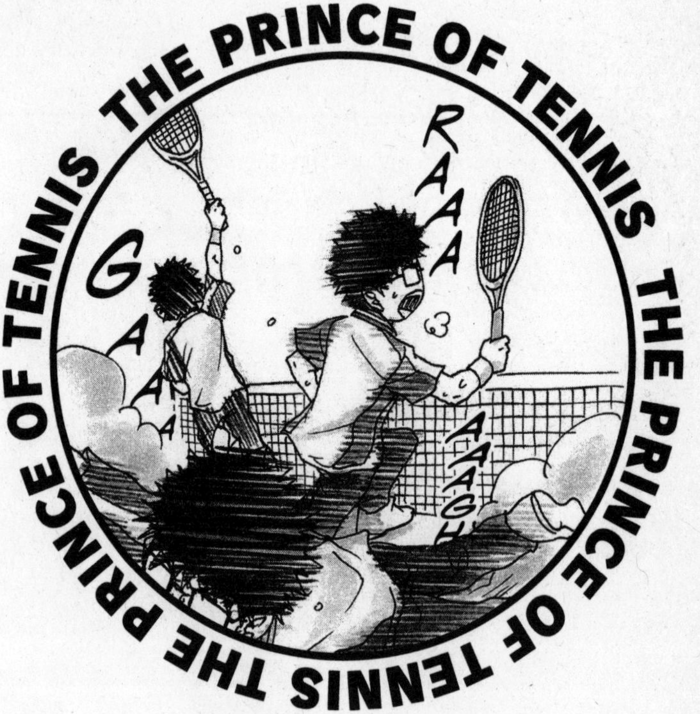
THE PRINCE OF TENNIS THE PRINCE OF TENNIS THE PRINCE OF TENNIS THE PRINCE OF TENNIS
GAAAA
RAAA
AAAGH

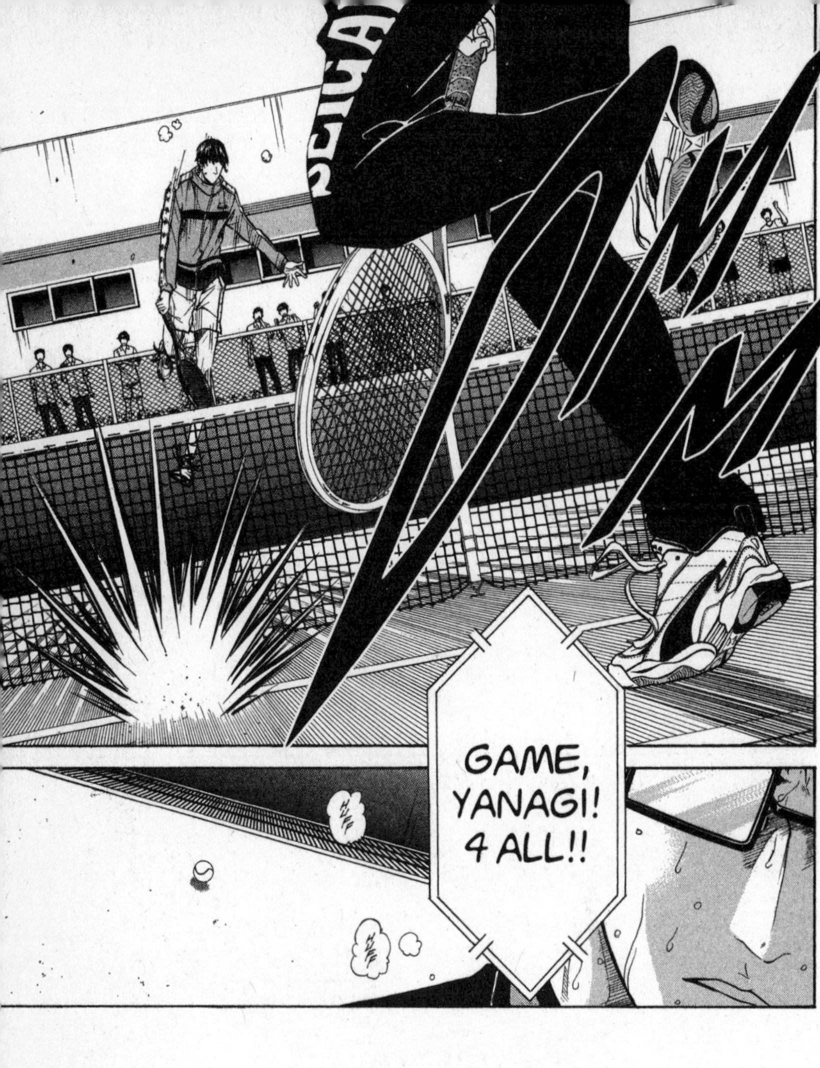
GAME, YANAGI! 4 ALL!!

GENIUS 213: THOUGHTS

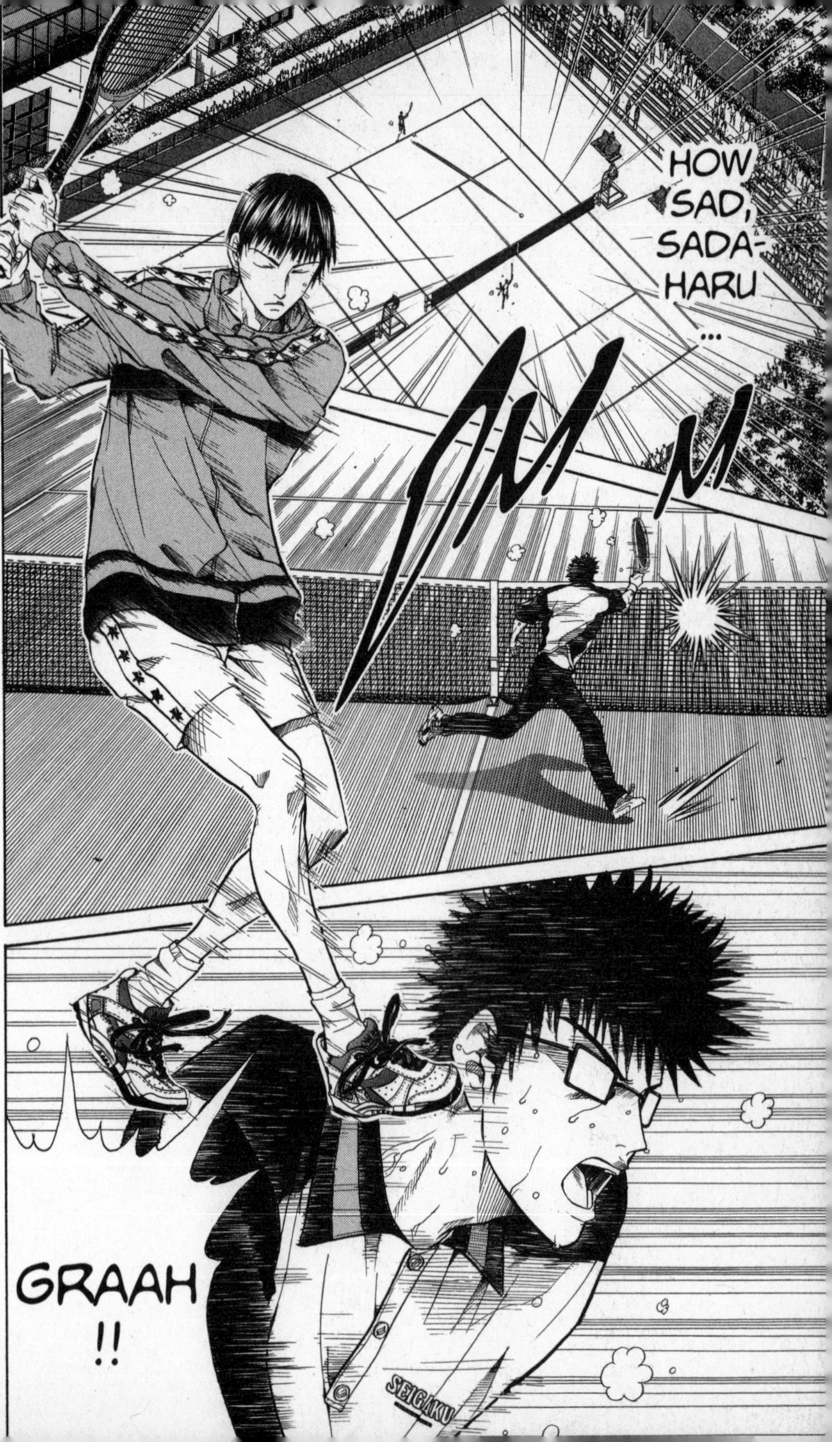
HOW SAD, SADA-HARU...
GRAAH!!
SEIGAKU

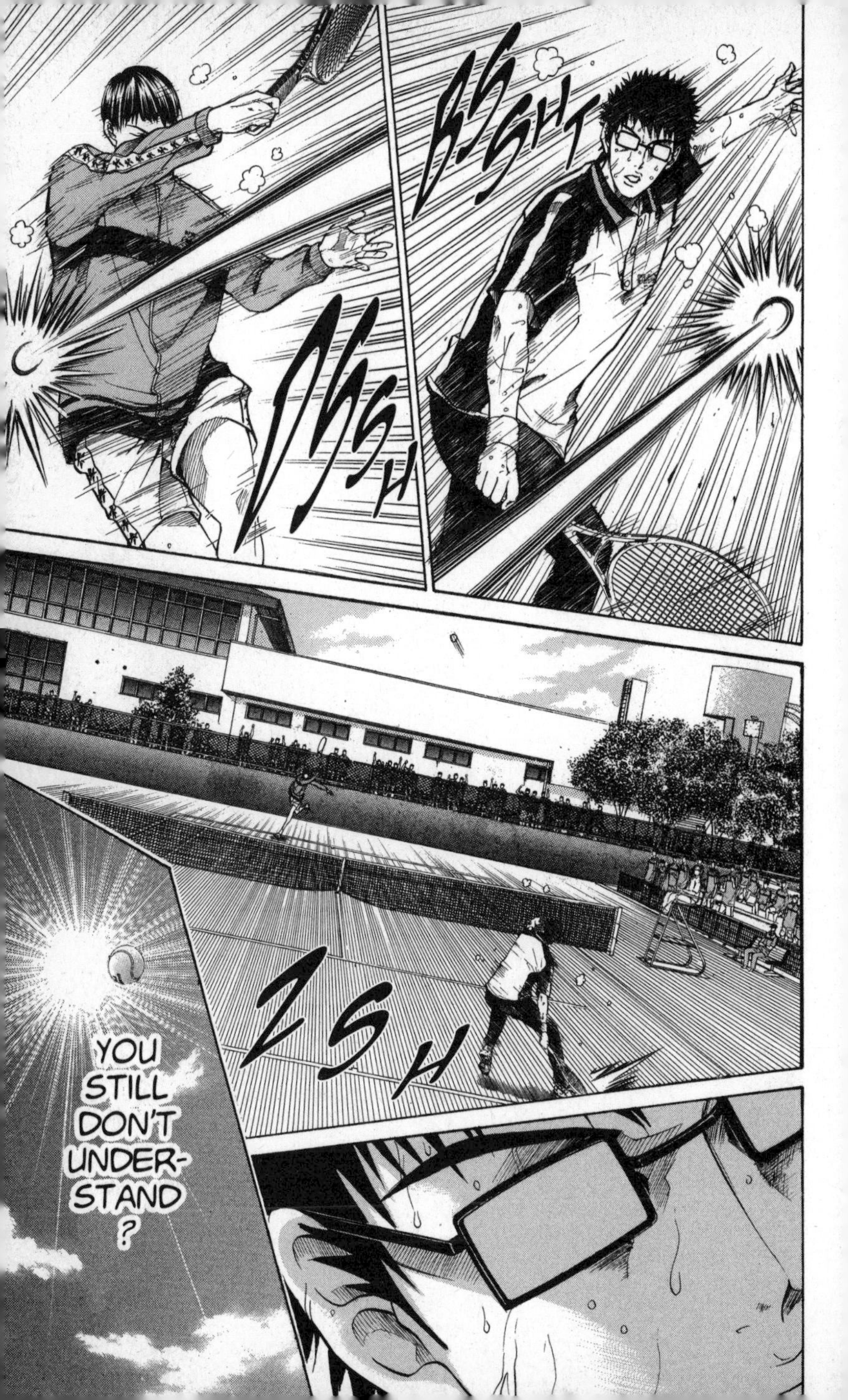
ZSH
YOU STILL DON'T UNDER-STAND?

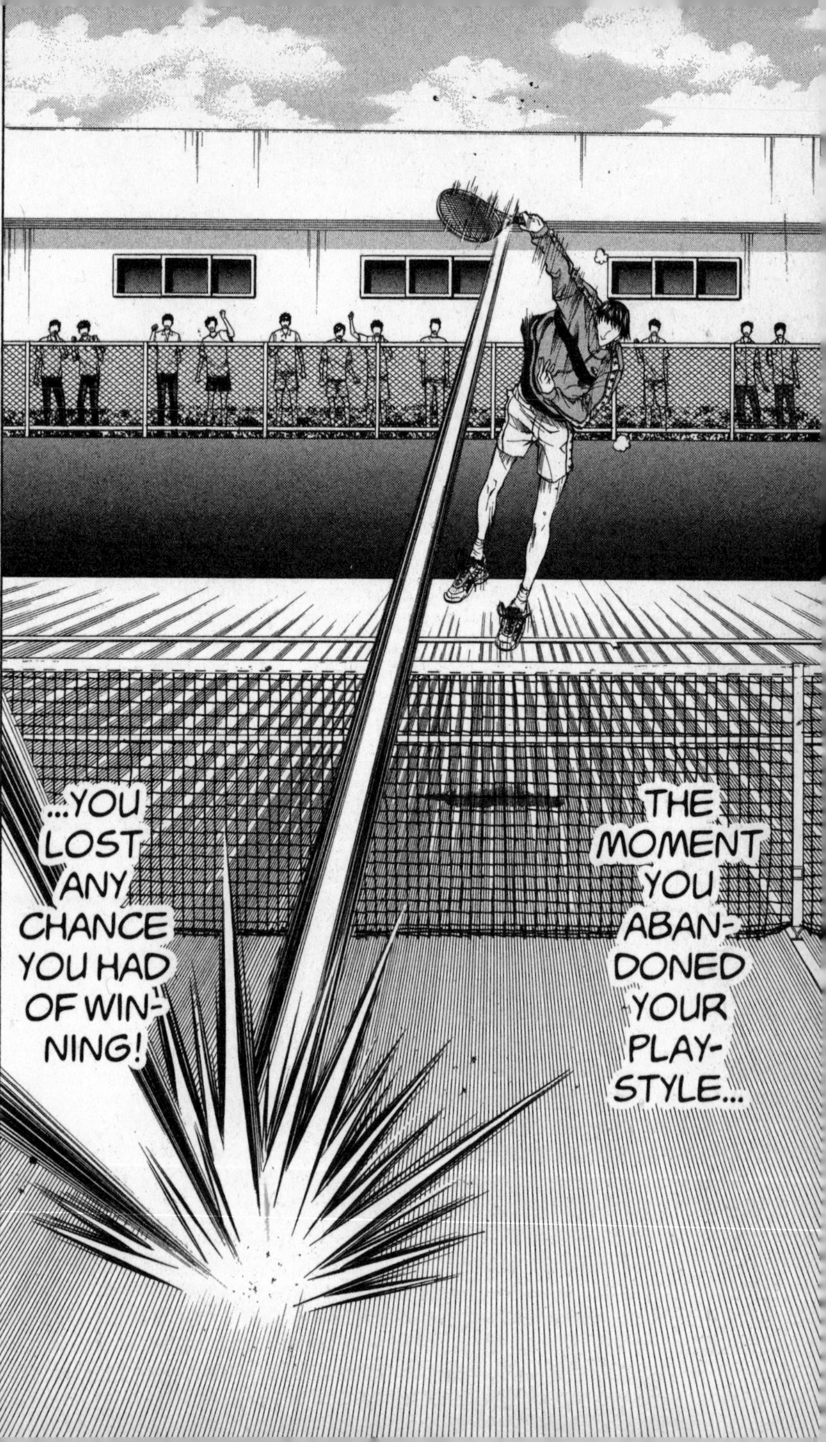
THE MOMENT YOU ABAN-DONED YOUR PLAY-STYLE...
...YOU LOST ANY CHANCE YOU HAD OF WIN-NING!

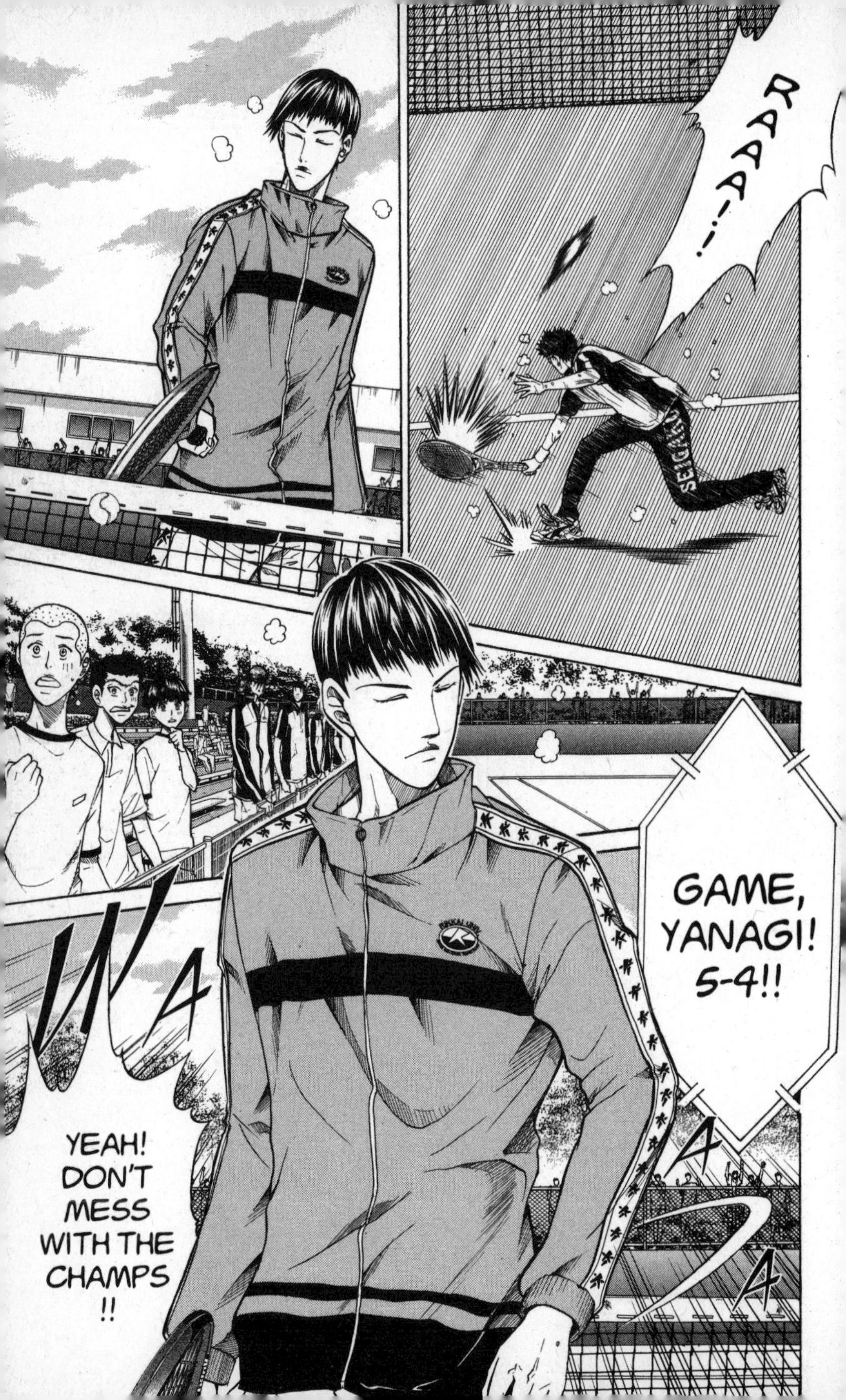
RAAAA!!
GAME, YANAGI! 5-4!!
WAAAA
YEAH! DON'T MESS WITH THE CHAMPS !!

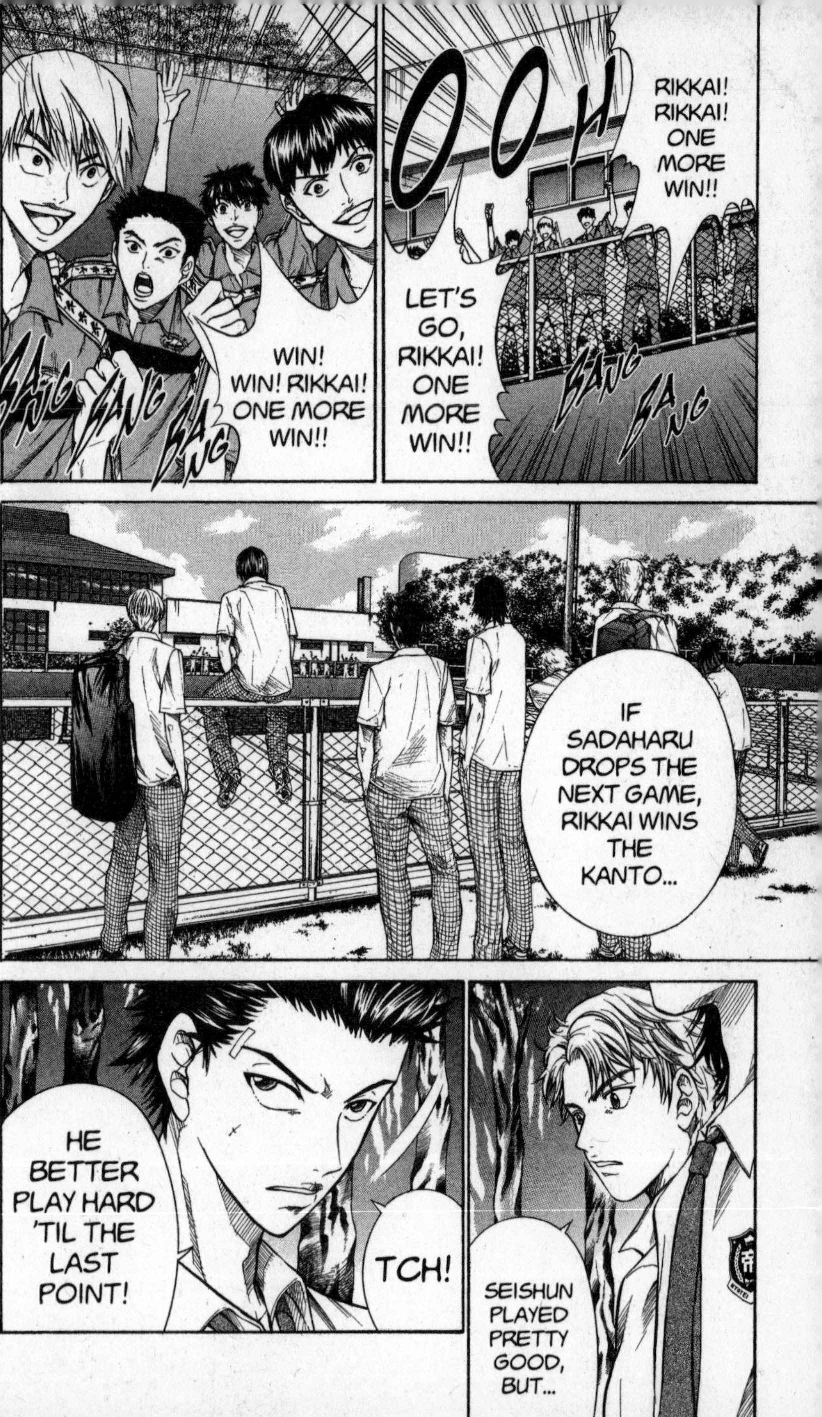
RIKKAI! RIKKAI! ONE MORE WIN!!
OOH
LET'S GO, RIKKAI! ONE MORE WIN!!
BANG
BANG
WIN! WIN! RIKKAI! ONE MORE WIN!!
BANG
BANG
BANG
IF SADAHARU DROPS THE NEXT GAME, RIKKAI WINS THE KANTO...
SEISHUN PLAYED PRETTY GOOD, BUT...
TCH!
HE BETTER PLAY HARD 'TIL THE LAST POINT!

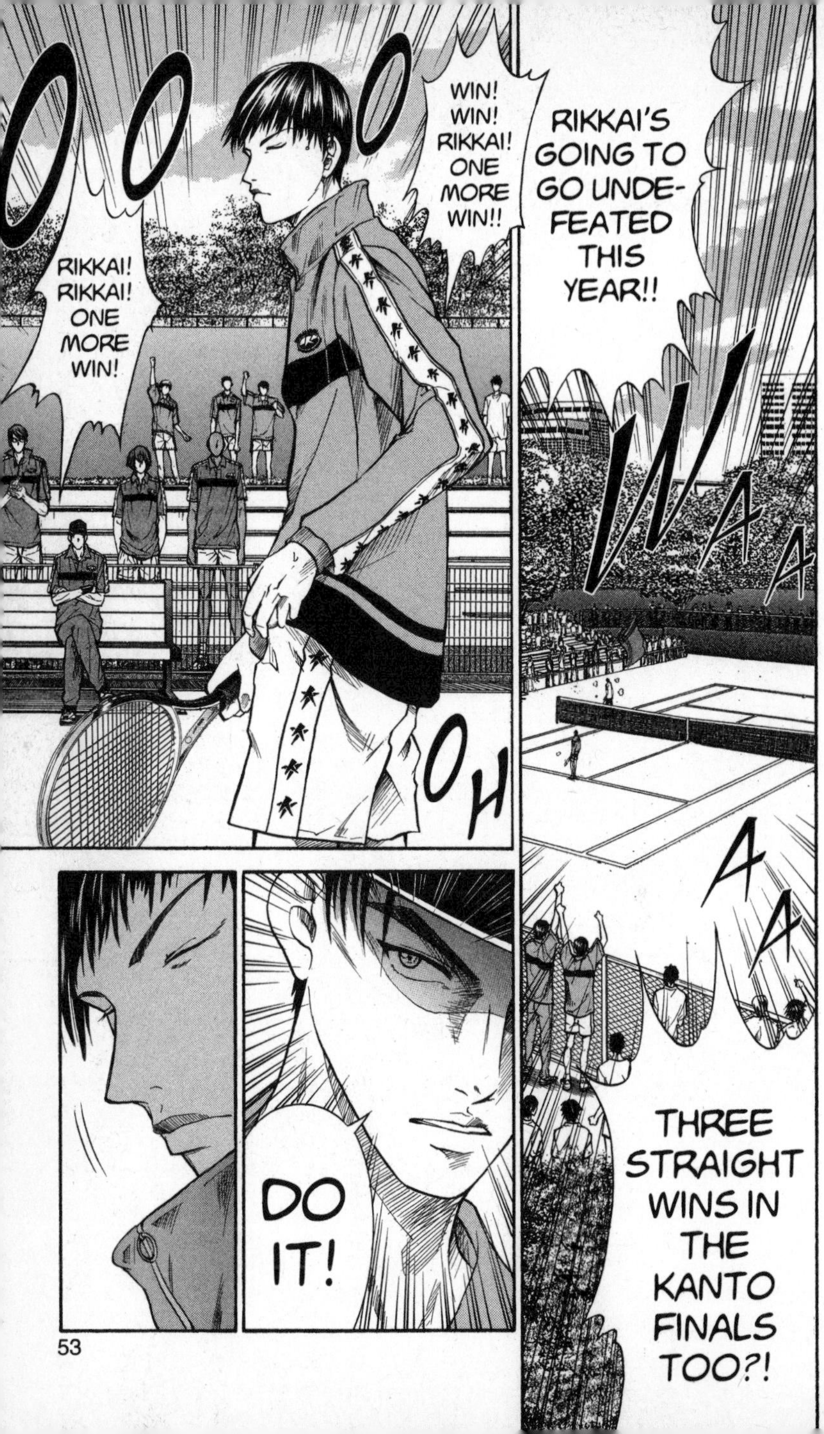
RIKKAI'S GOING TO GO UNDE-FEATED THIS YEAR!!
WAAAA
THREE STRAIGHT WINS IN THE KANTO FINALS TOO?!
OOOO
WIN! WIN! RIKKAI! ONE MORE WIN!!
RIKKAI! RIKKAI! ONE MORE WIN!
OH
DO IT!

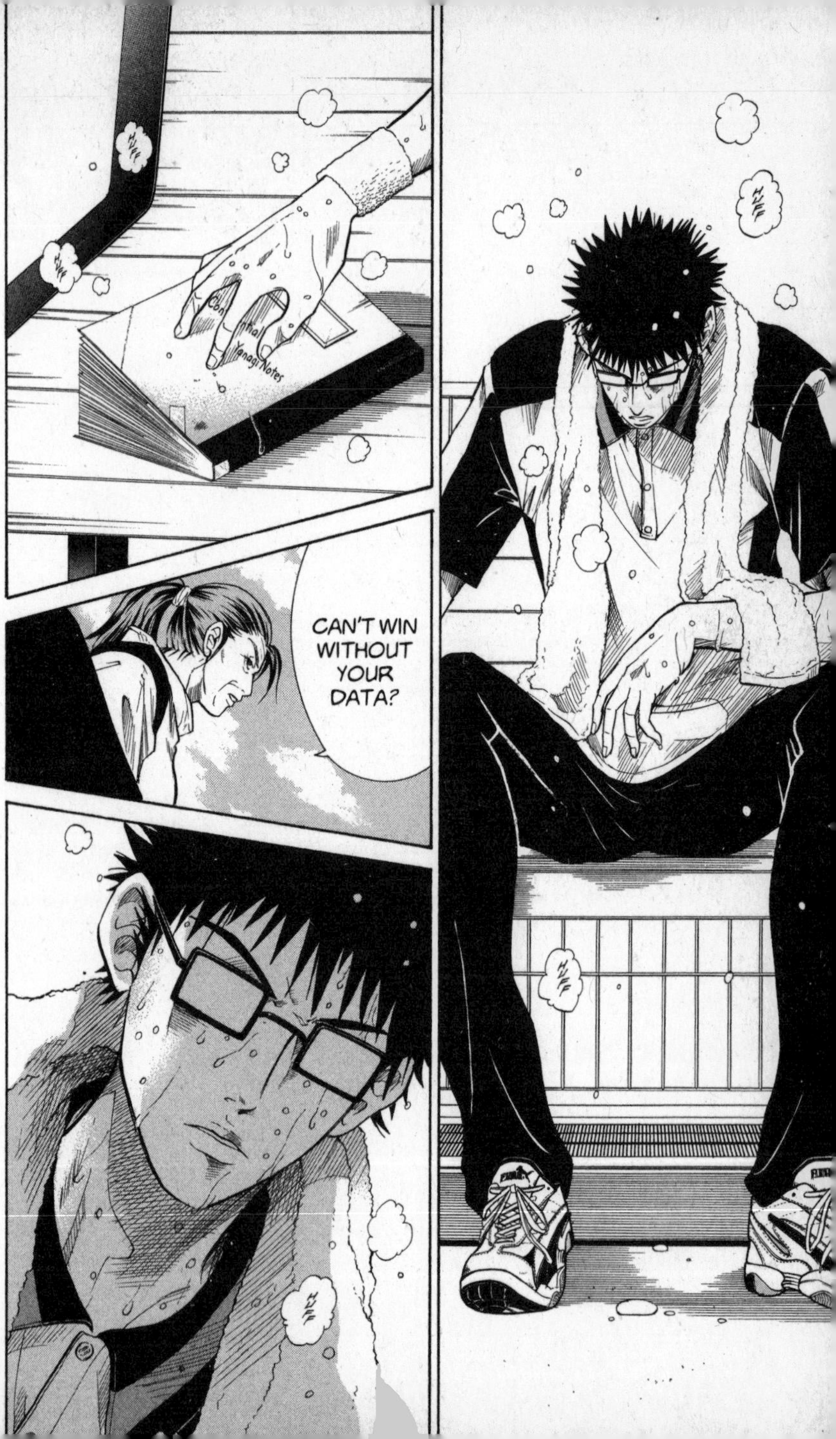
HUFF
HUFF
HUFF
HUFF
Yanagi Notes
CAN'T WIN WITHOUT YOUR DATA?
HUFF

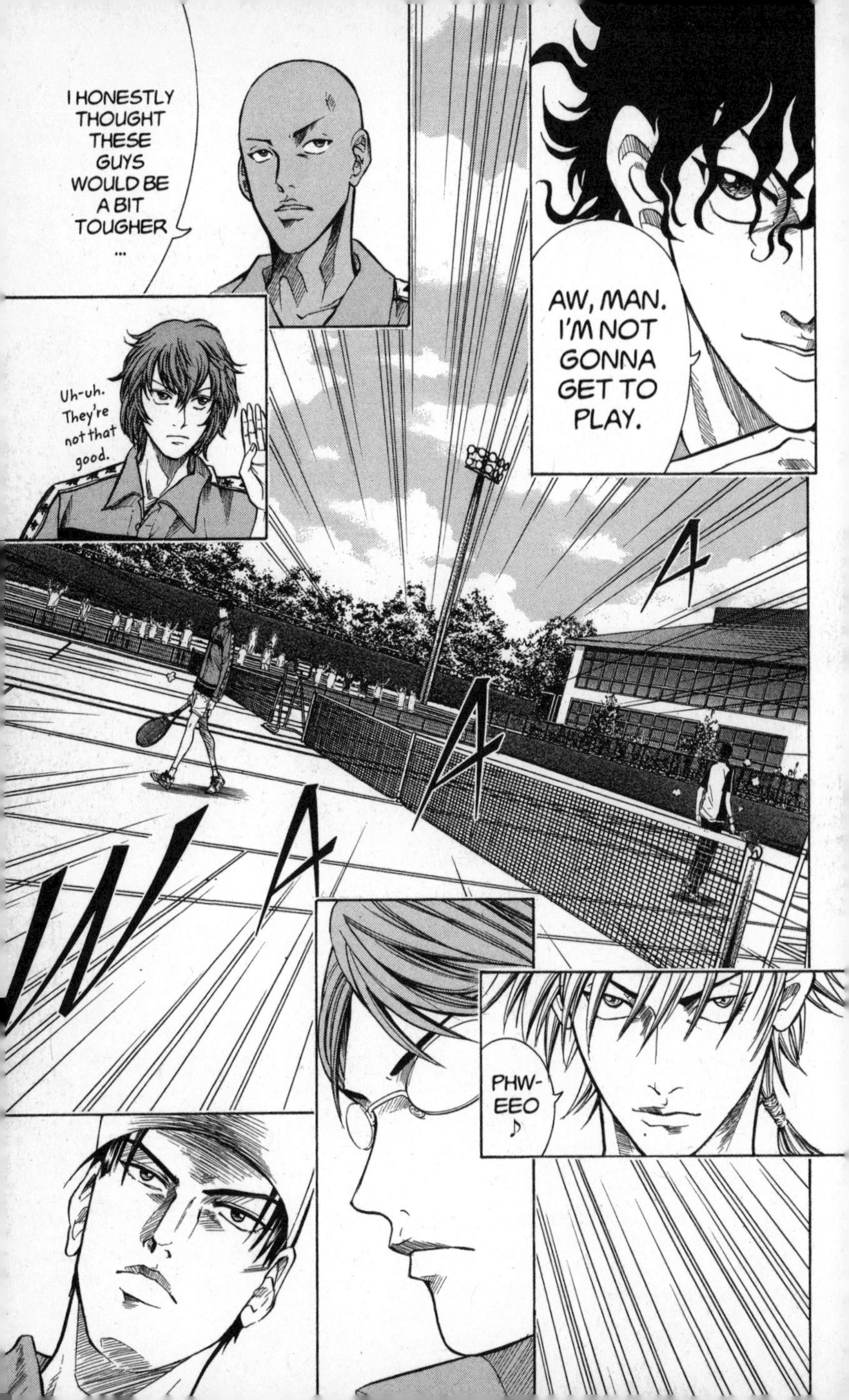
AW, MAN. I'M NOT GONNA GET TO PLAY.
I HONESTLY THOUGHT THESE GUYS WOULD BE A BIT TOUGHER ...
Uh-uh. They're not that good.
WAAA
PHWEEO ♪

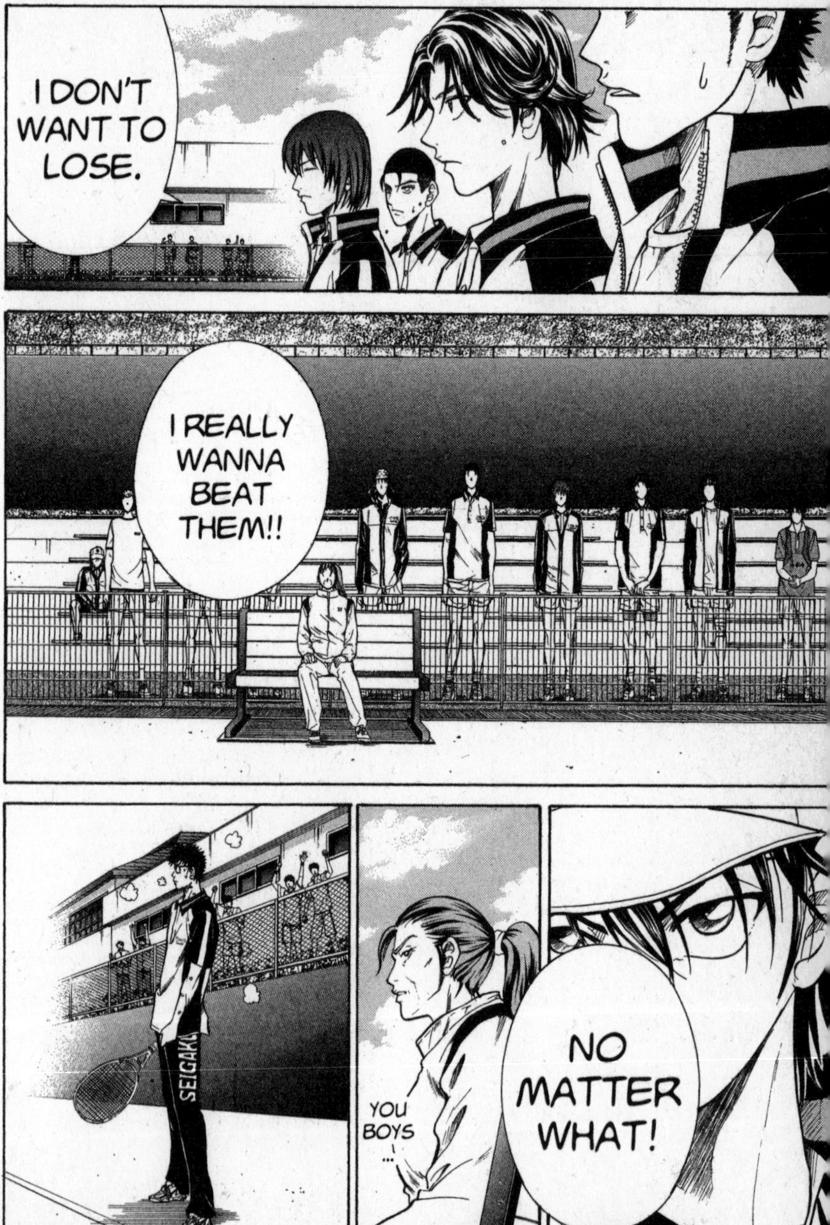
I DON'T WANT TO LOSE.
I REALLY WANNA BEAT THEM!!
NO MATTER WHAT!
YOU BOYS...

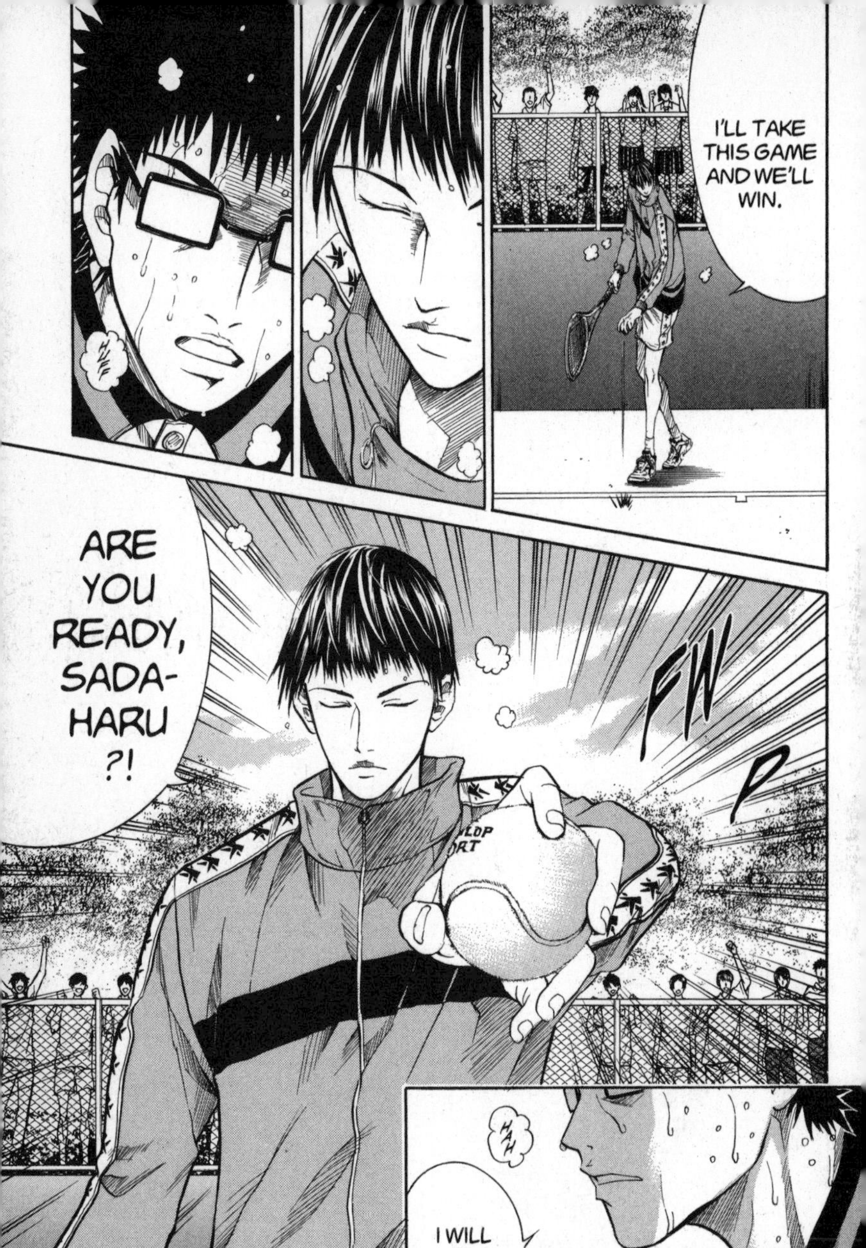
I'LL TAKE THIS GAME AND WE'LL WIN.
ARE YOU READY, SADA-HARU?!
FWP
I WILL NOT LOSE...

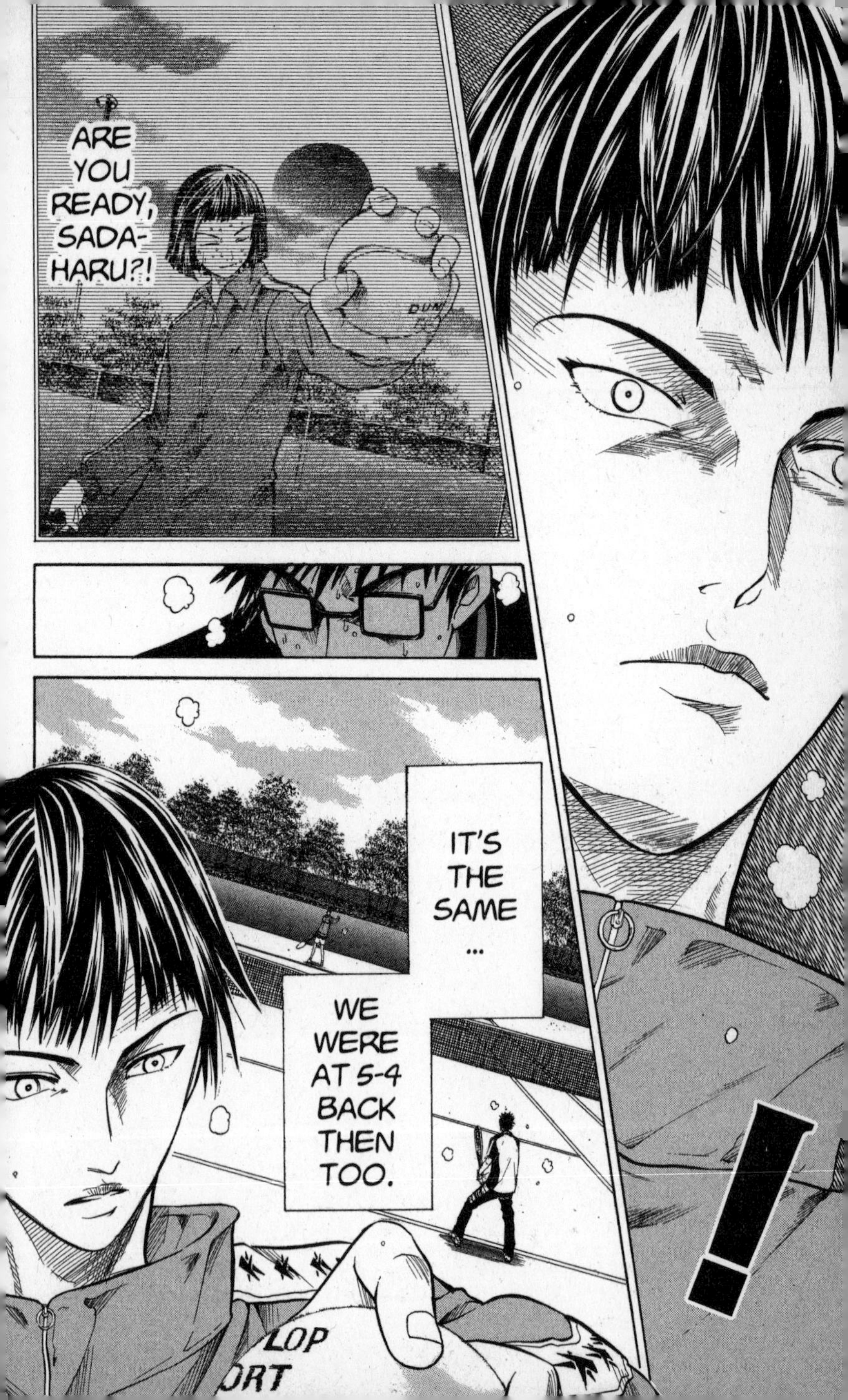
!
ARE YOU READY, SADA-HARU?!
IT'S THE SAME ...
WE WERE AT 5-4 BACK THEN TOO.

READ THIS WAY

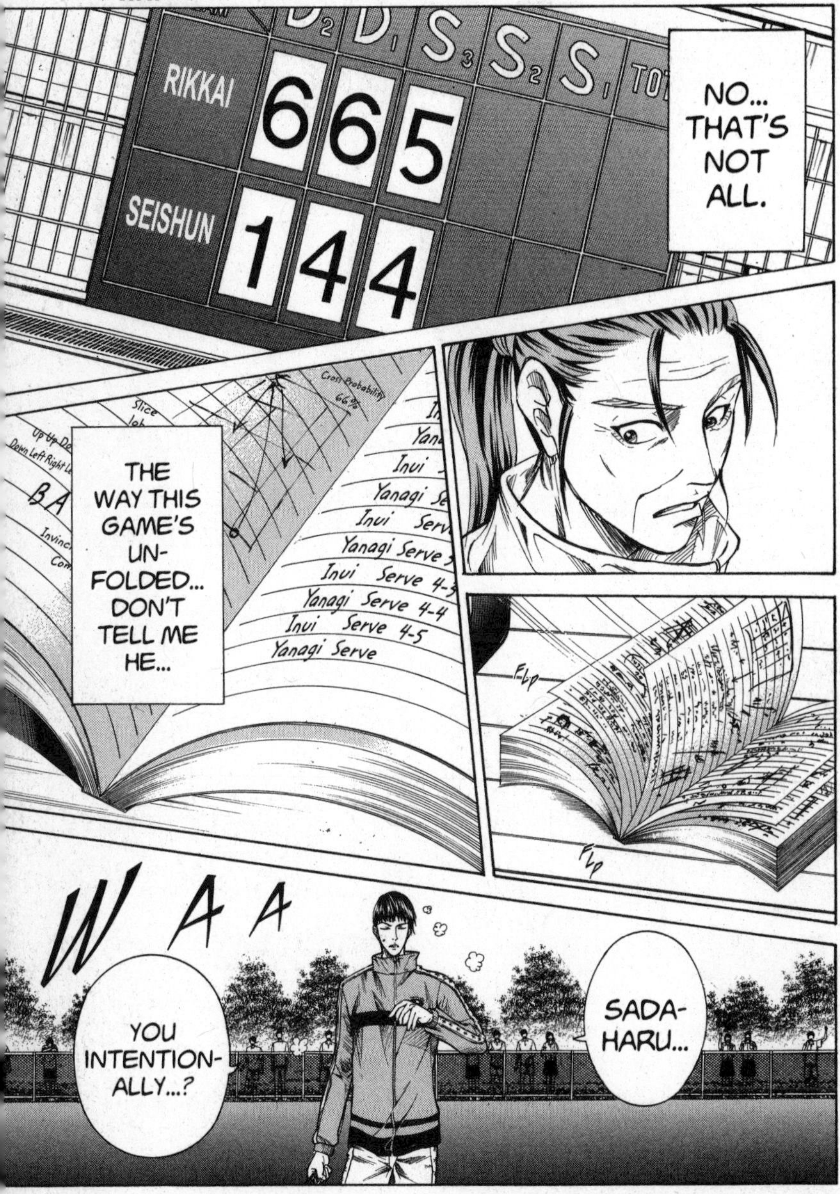
RIKKAI 6 6 5
SEISHUN 1 4 4
NO... THAT'S NOT ALL.
Cross Probability 66%
Inui Serve 4-3
Yanagi Serve 4-4
Inui Serve 4-5
Yanagi Serve
THE WAY THIS GAME'S UN-FOLDED... DON'T TELL ME HE...
WAA
SADA-HARU...
YOU INTENTION-ALLY...?

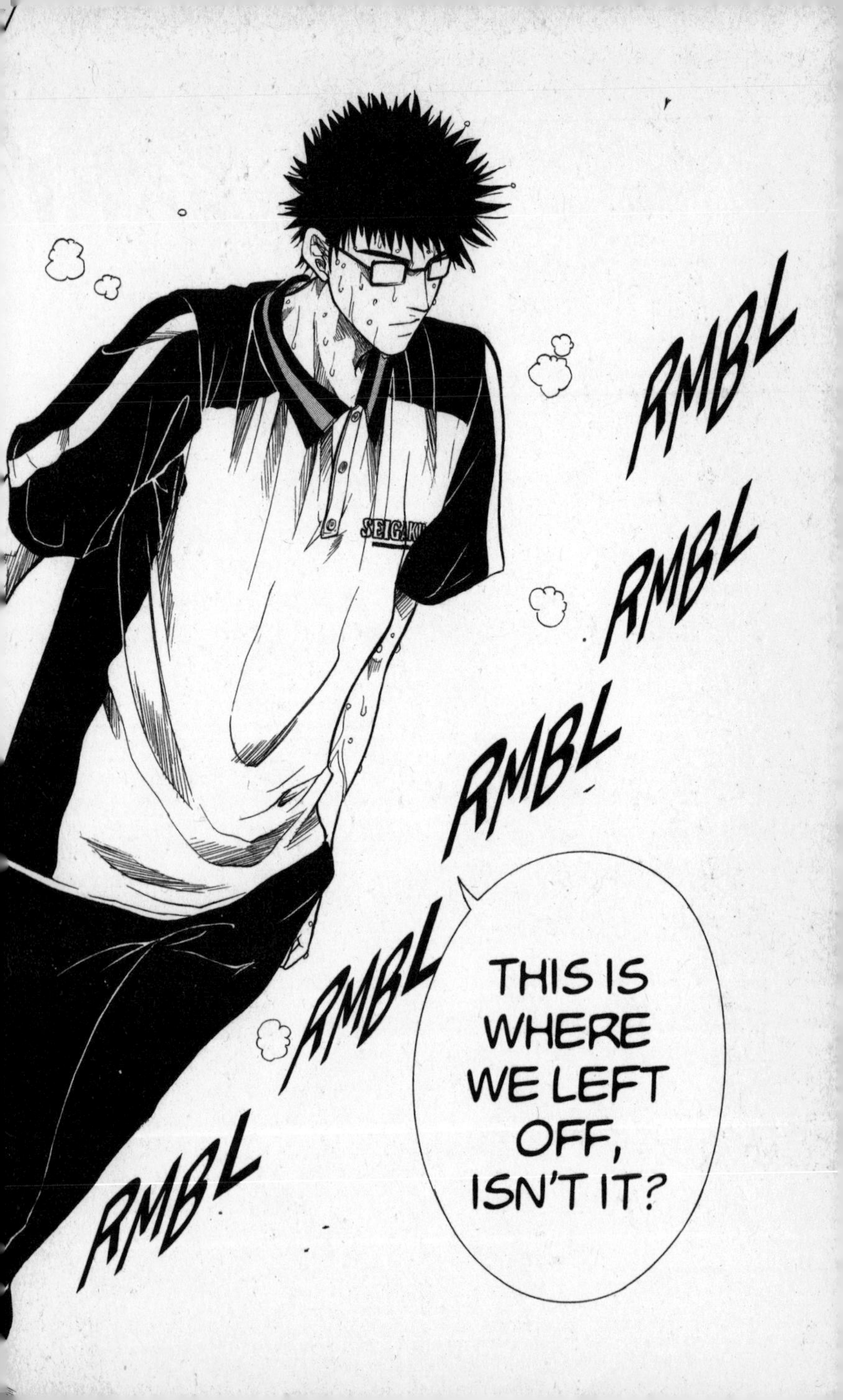

RMBL
RMBL
RMBL
THIS IS WHERE WE LEFT OFF, ISN'T IT?
RMBL
RMBL

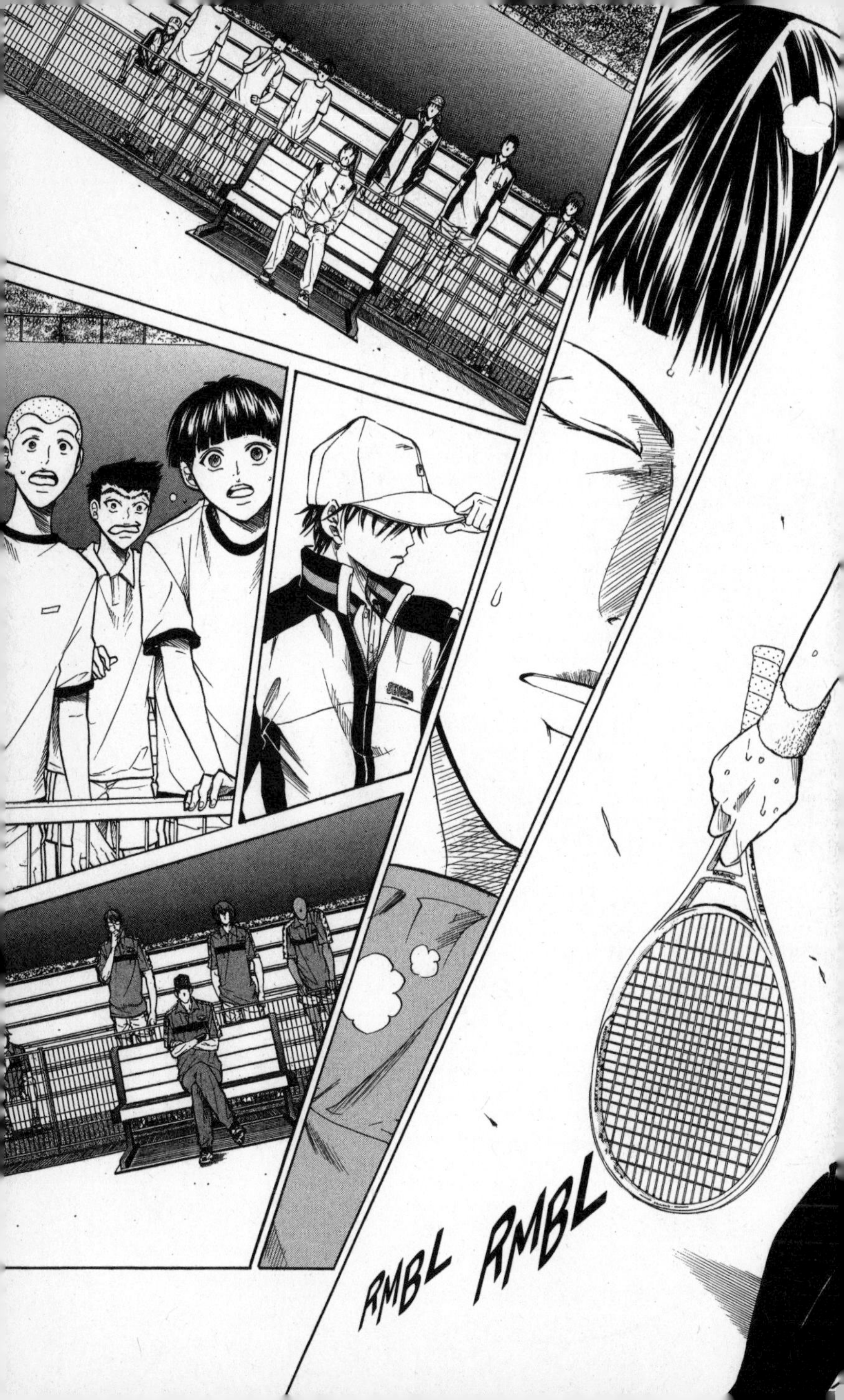
RMBL RMBL

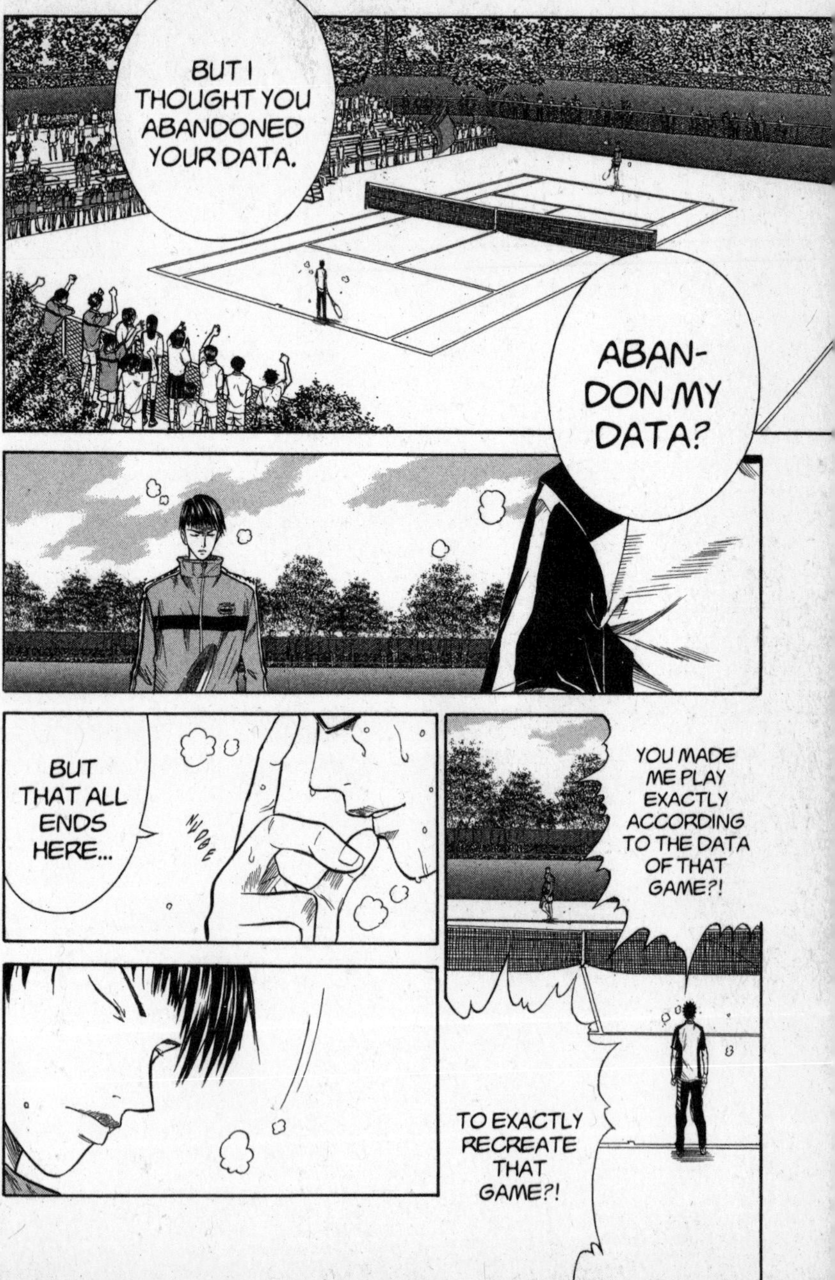
BUT I THOUGHT YOU ABANDONED YOUR DATA.
ABAN-DON MY DATA?
YOU MADE ME PLAY EXACTLY ACCORDING TO THE DATA OF THAT GAME?!
TO EXACTLY RECREATE THAT GAME?!
BUT THAT ALL ENDS HERE...
NUDGE

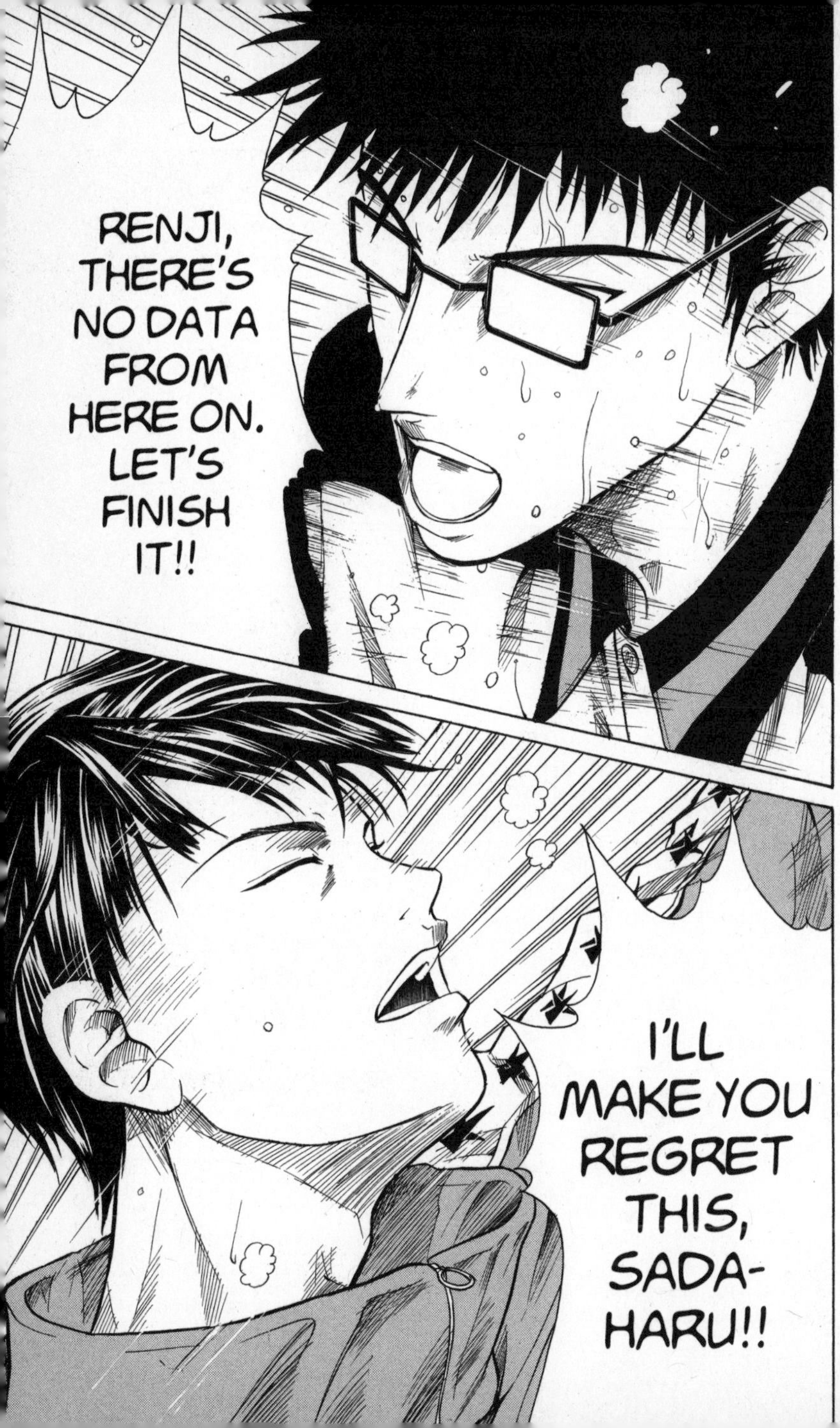
RENJI, THERE'S NO DATA FROM HERE ON. LET'S FINISH IT!!
I'LL MAKE YOU REGRET THIS, SADA-HARU!!

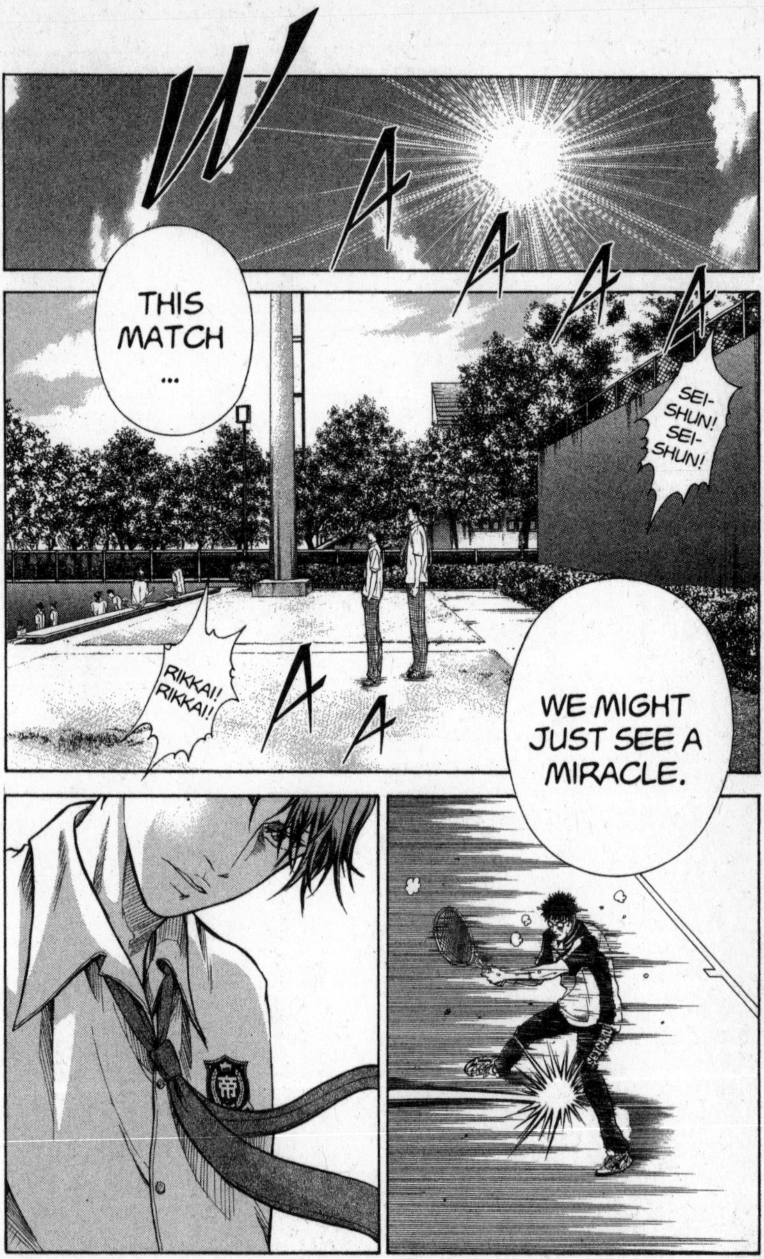
WAAAAAA
SEI-SHUN! SEI-SHUN!
THIS MATCH ...
RIKKAI! RIKKAI!
WE MIGHT JUST SEE A MIRACLE.

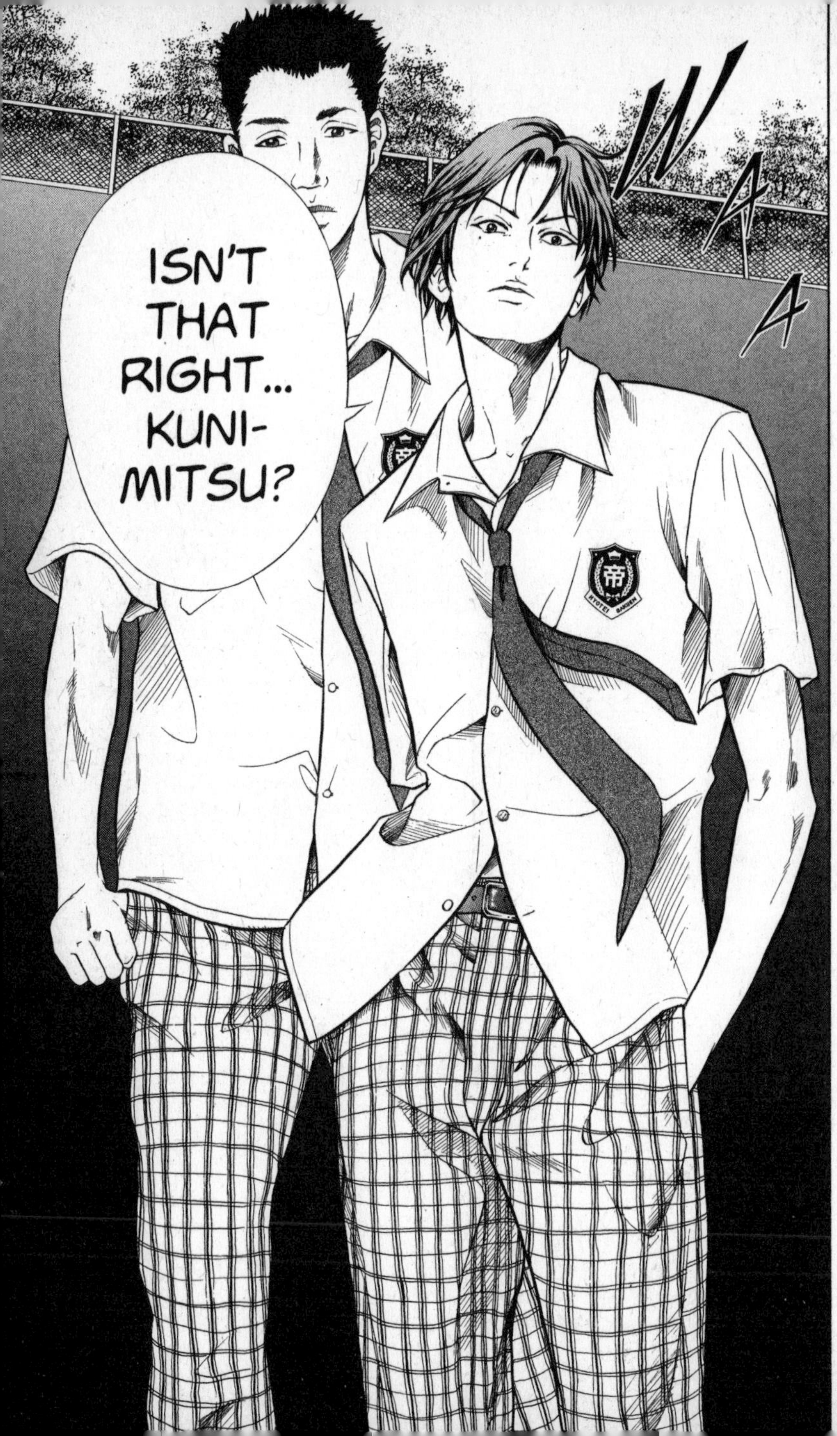
WAA
ISN'T THAT RIGHT... KUNI-MITSU?

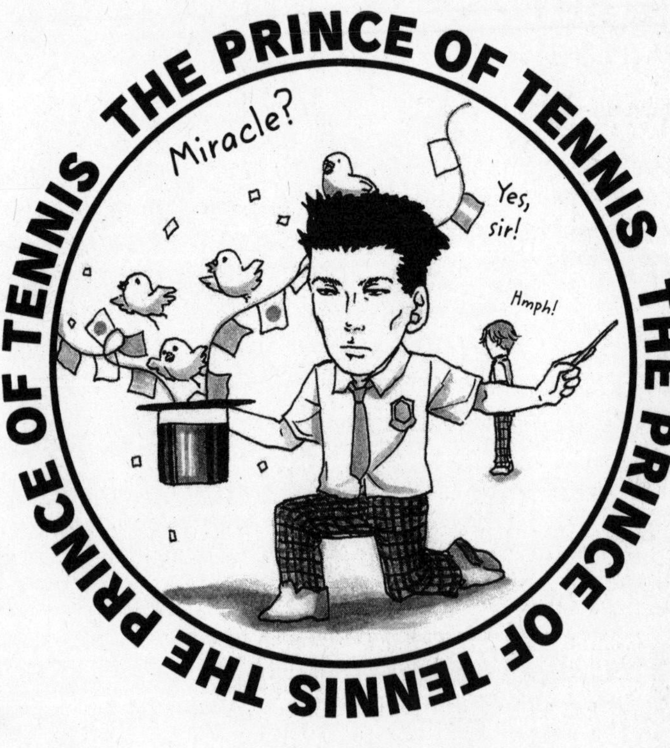
THE PRINCE OF TENNIS THE PRINCE OF TENNIS THE PRINCE OF TENNIS
Miracle?
Yes, sir!
Hmph!

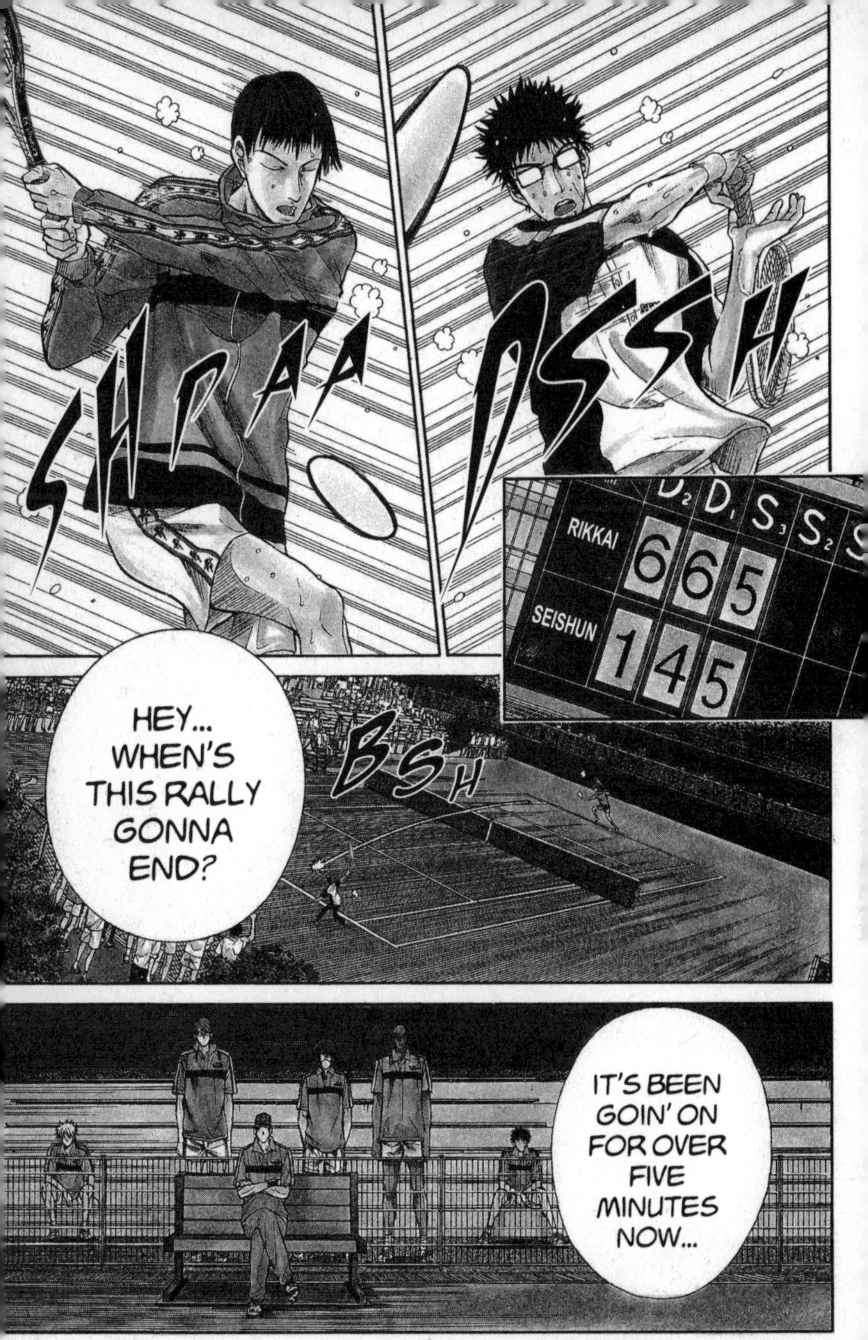
DSSSH
SHAAA
D2 D1 S3 S2
RIKKAI 6 6 5
SEISHUN 1 4 5
HEY... WHEN'S THIS RALLY GONNA END?
BSH
IT'S BEEN GOIN' ON FOR OVER FIVE MINUTES NOW...

GENIUS 214: SEISHUN DROPS THREE?!

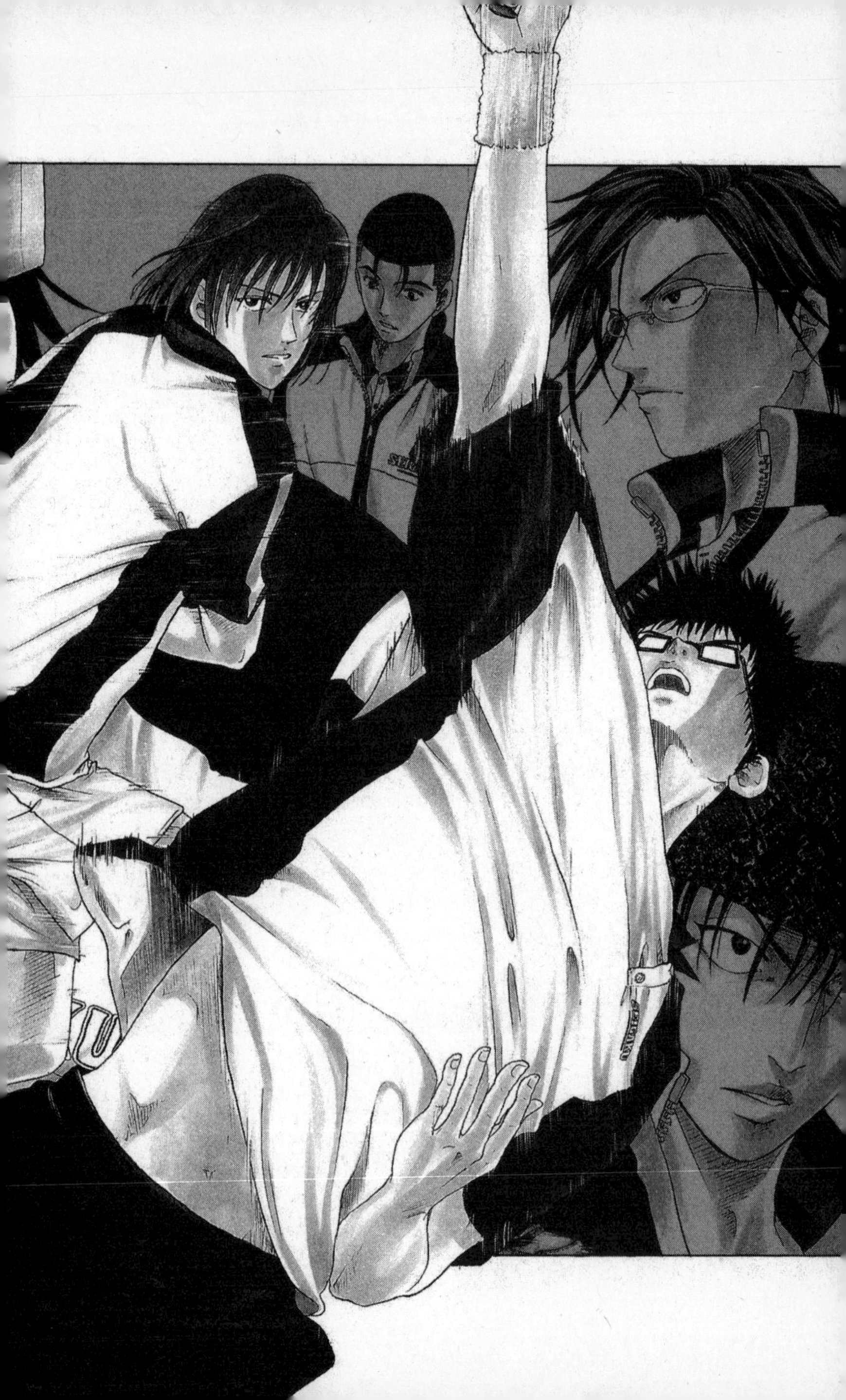

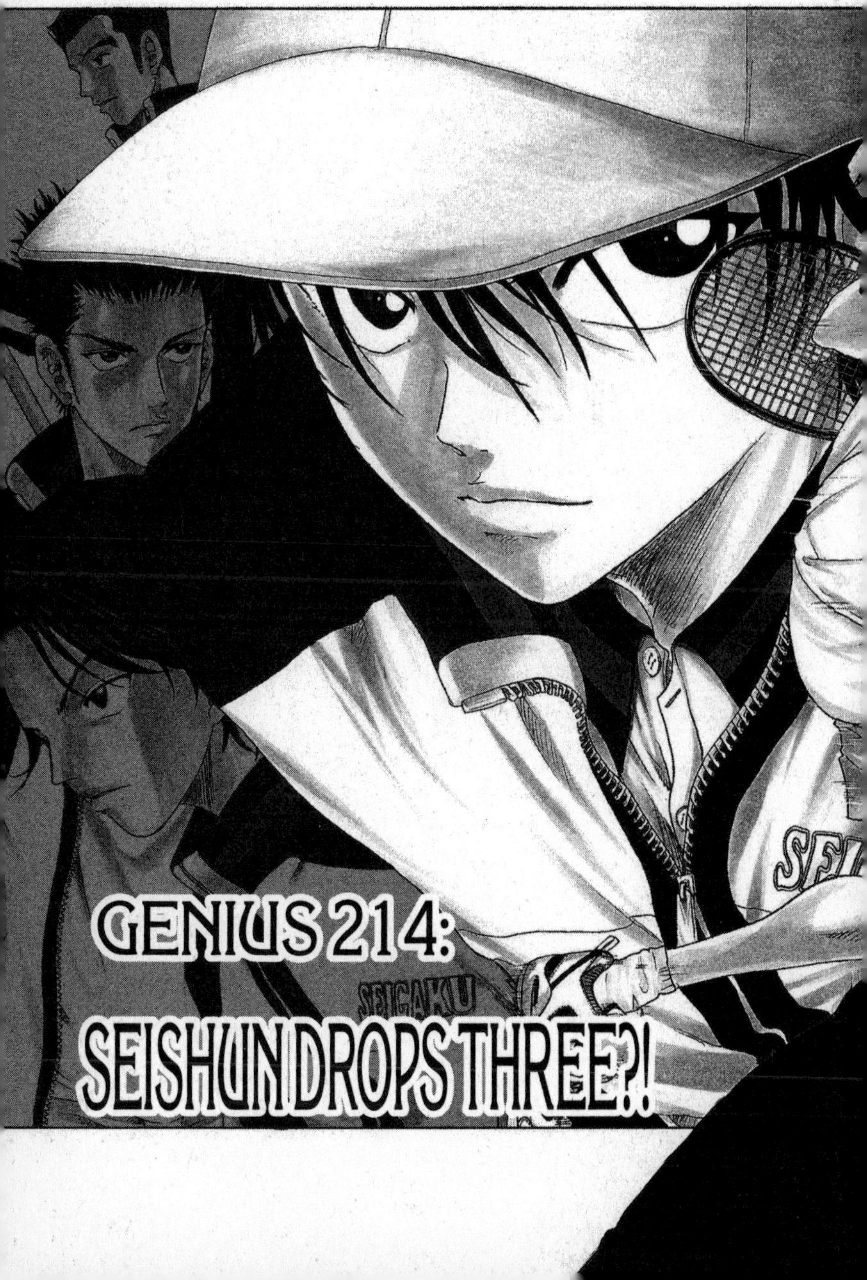
GENIUS 214:
SEISHUN DROPS THREE?!
SEIGAKU

テニスの王子様

THE PRINCE OF TENNIS

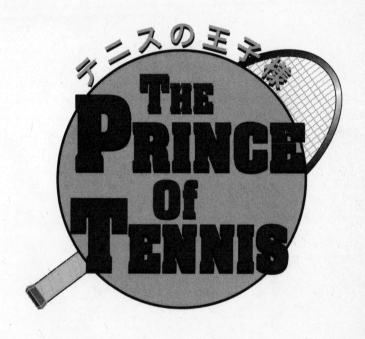

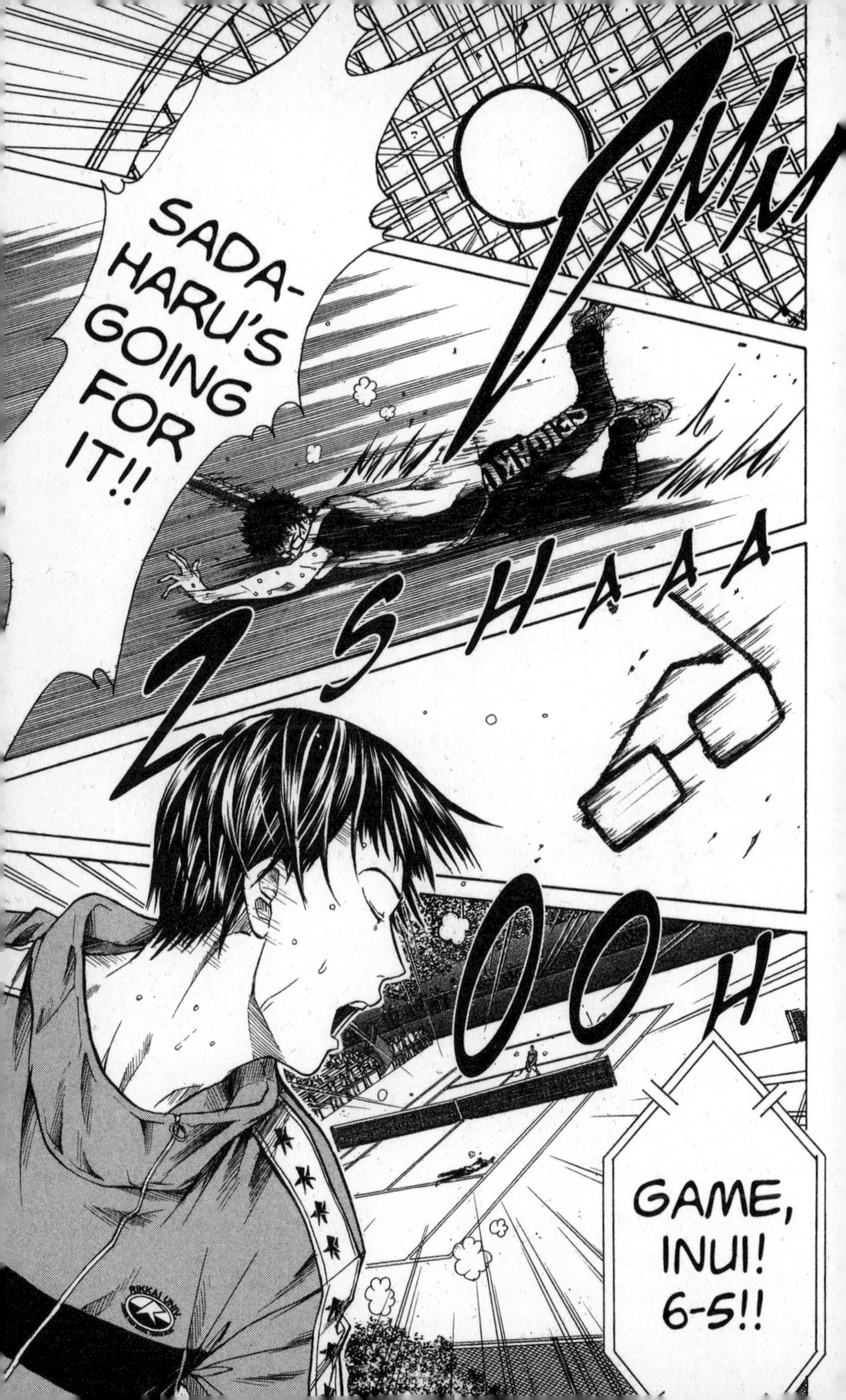
SADA-
HARU'S
GOING
FOR
IT!!
ZSHAAA
OOH
GAME,
INUI!
6-5!!

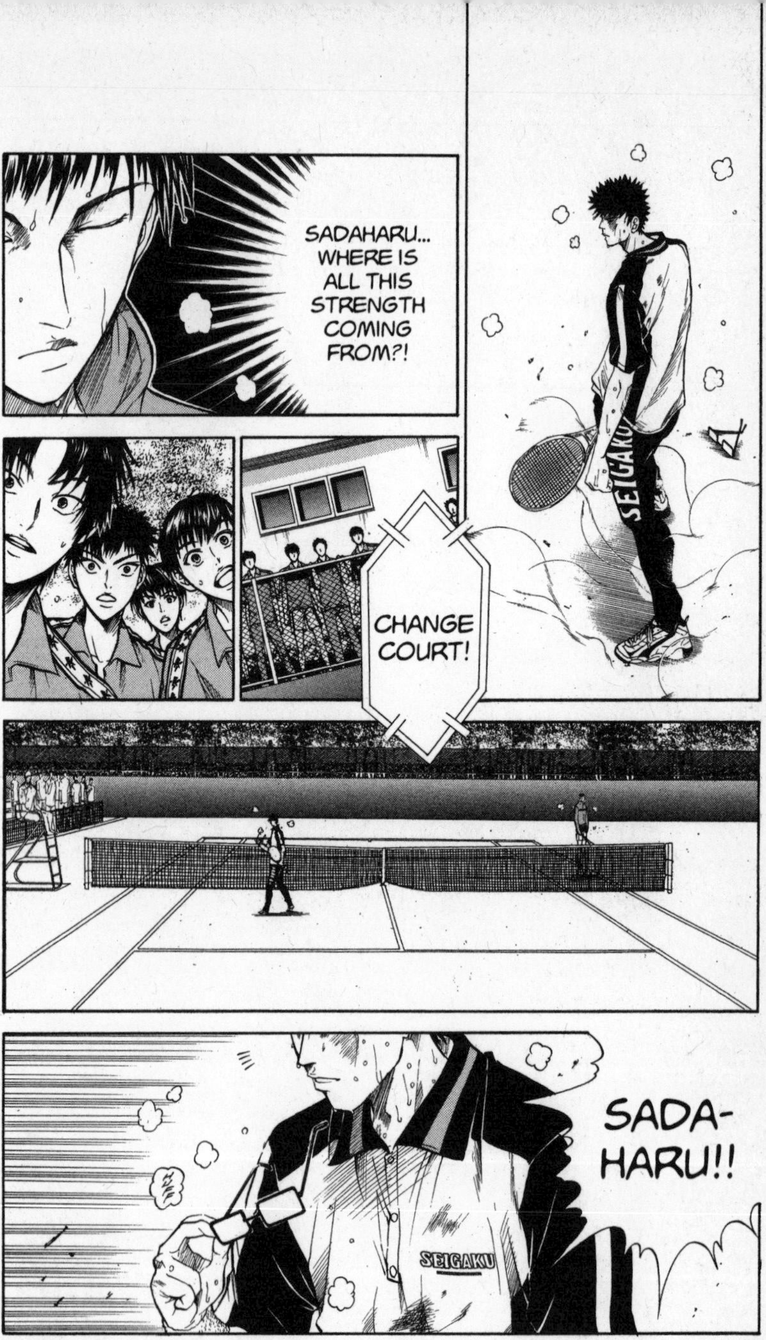
SADAHARU... WHERE IS ALL THIS STRENGTH COMING FROM?!
CHANGE COURT!
SADA-HARU!!

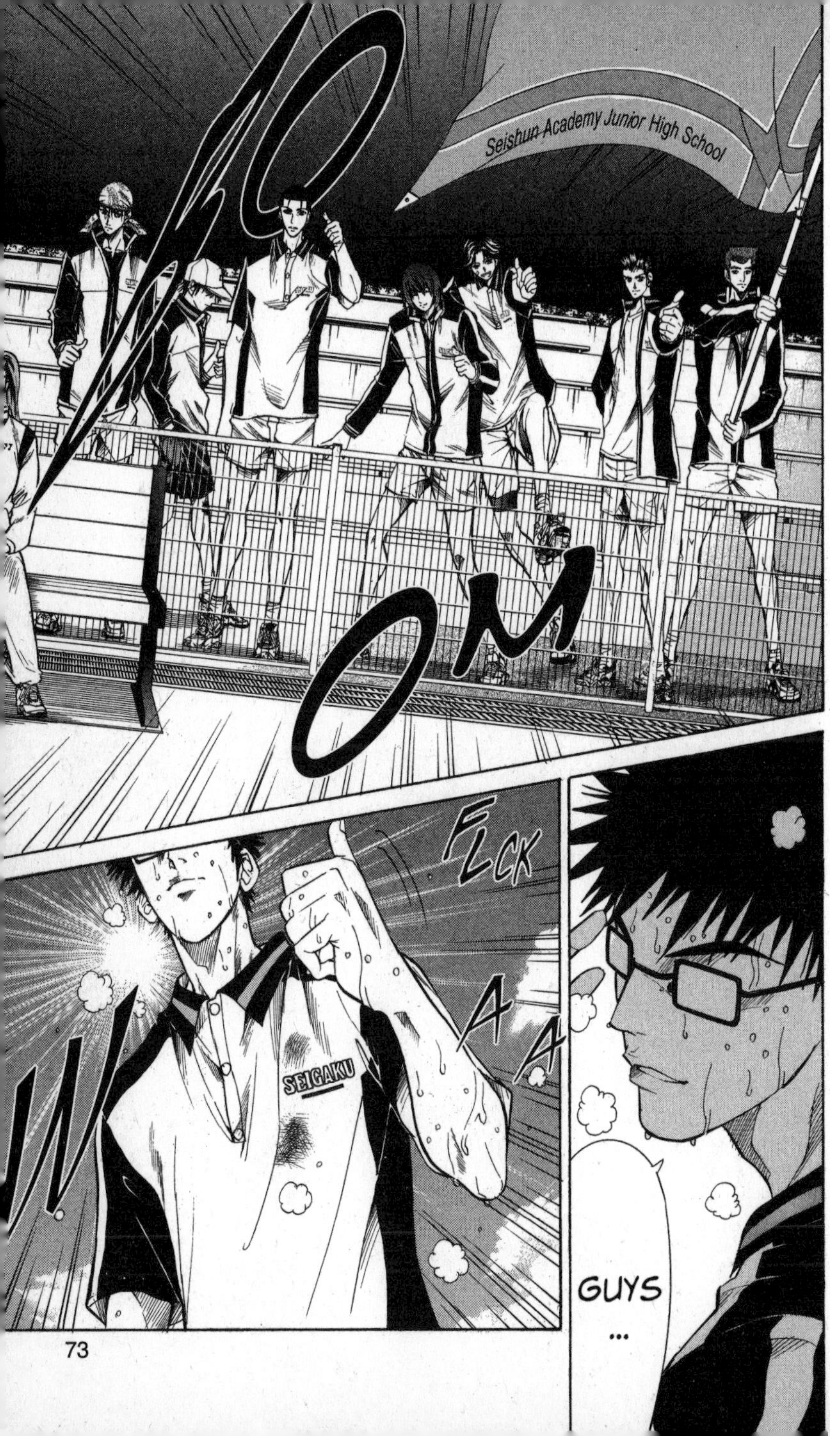
Seishun Academy Junior High School
OM
GUYS
...
FLCK
A
A
SEIGAKU

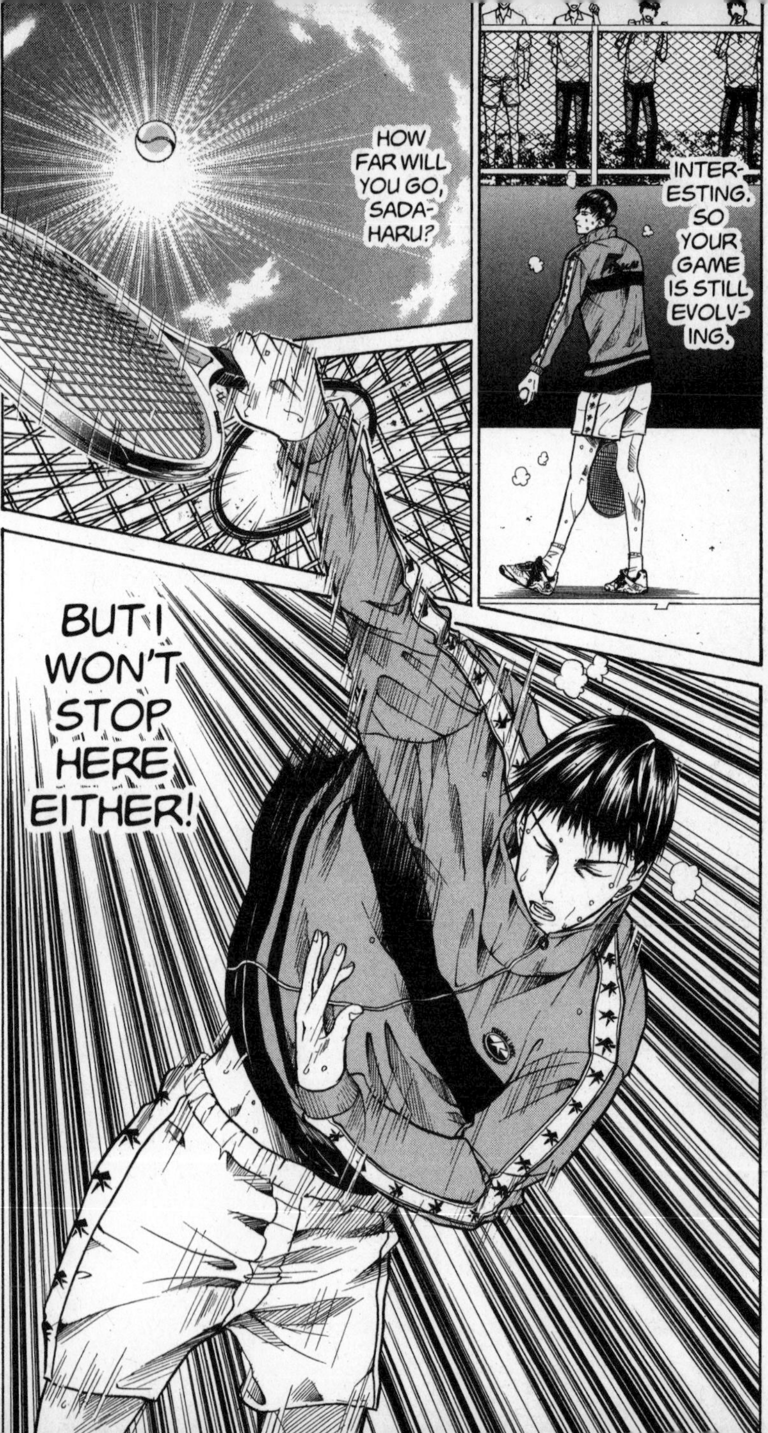
INTERESTING. SO YOUR GAME IS STILL EVOLVING.
HOW FAR WILL YOU GO, SADAHARU?
BUT I WON'T STOP HERE EITHER!

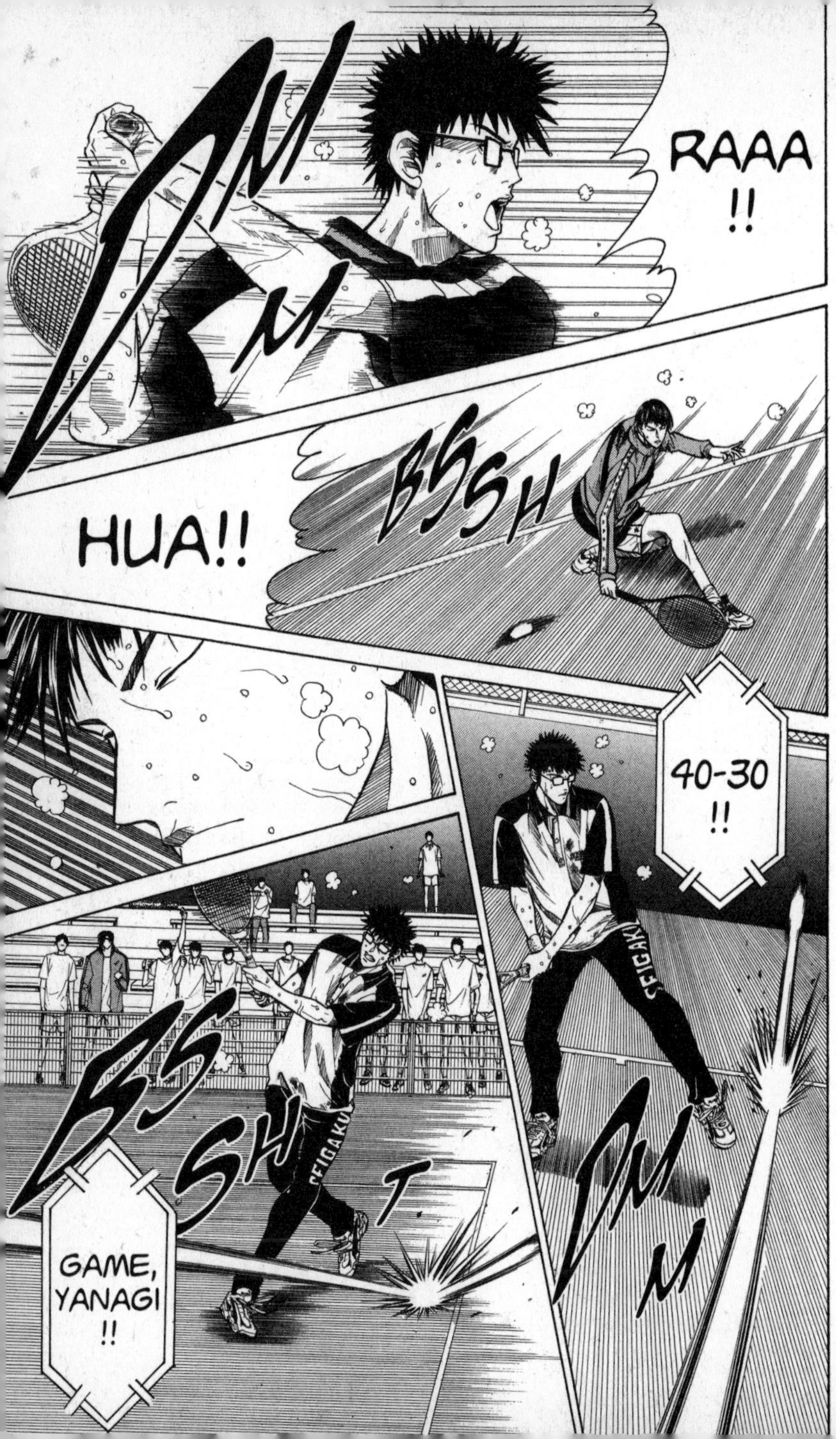

RAAA!!
DMM
BSSH
HUA!!
40-30!!
DMM
BSSHT
GAME, YANAGI!!

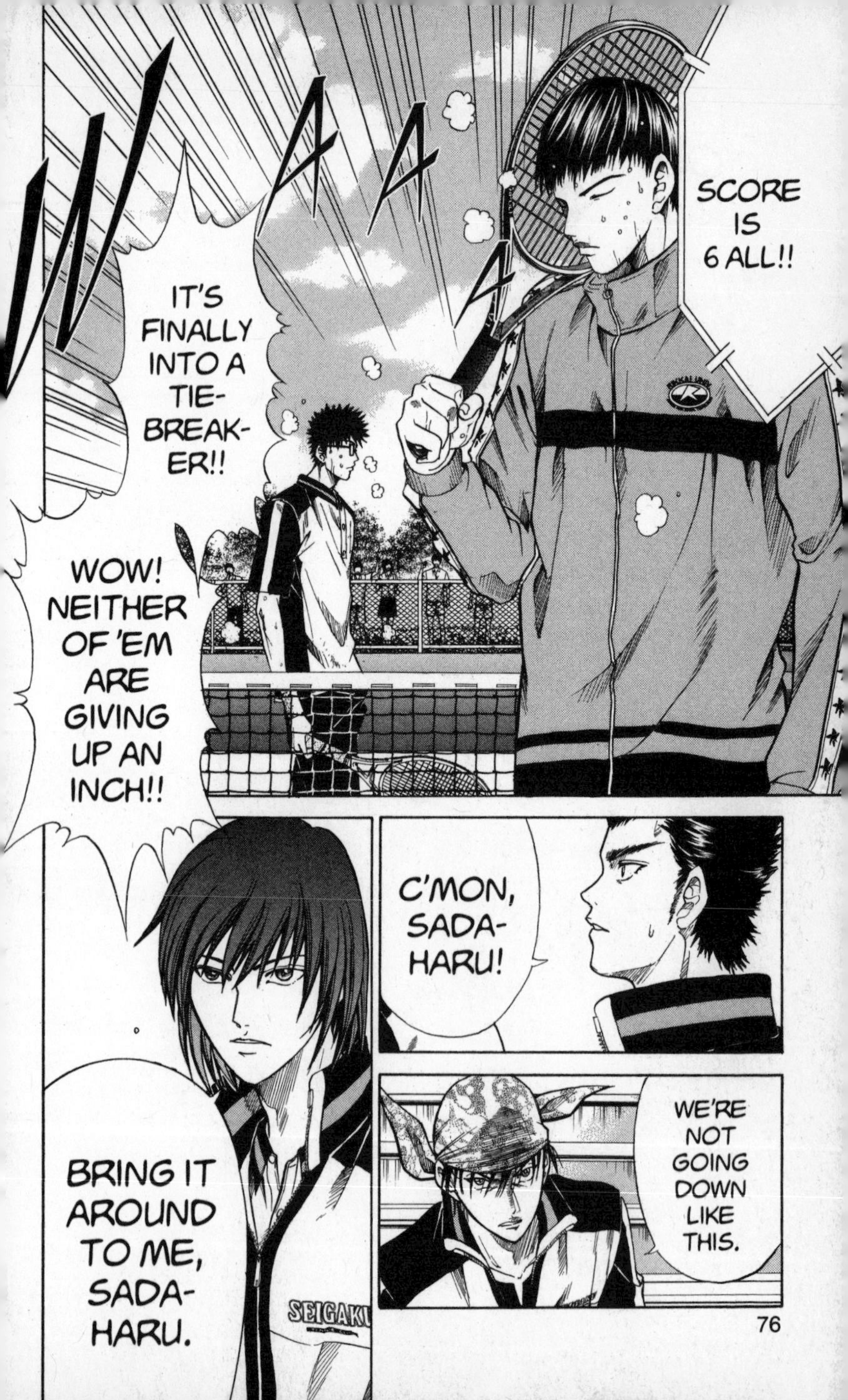
SCORE IS 6 ALL!!
WAAAA
IT'S FINALLY INTO A TIE-BREAKER!!
WOW! NEITHER OF 'EM ARE GIVING UP AN INCH!!
C'MON, SADA-HARU!
WE'RE NOT GOING DOWN LIKE THIS.
BRING IT AROUND TO ME, SADA-HARU.
SEIGAKU

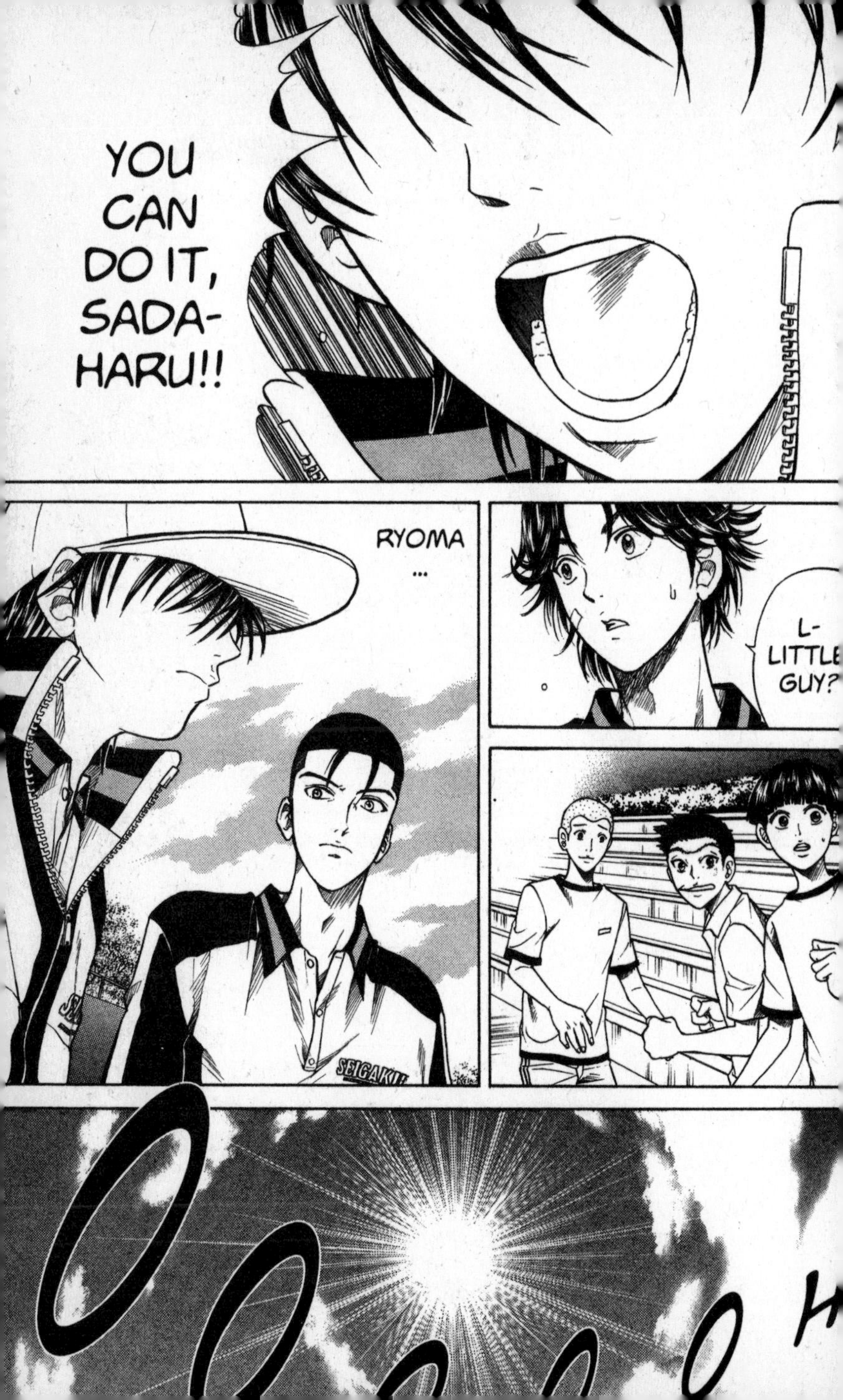
YOU CAN DO IT, SADAHARU!!
L-LITTLE GUY?
RYOMA ...
OOOOOOH

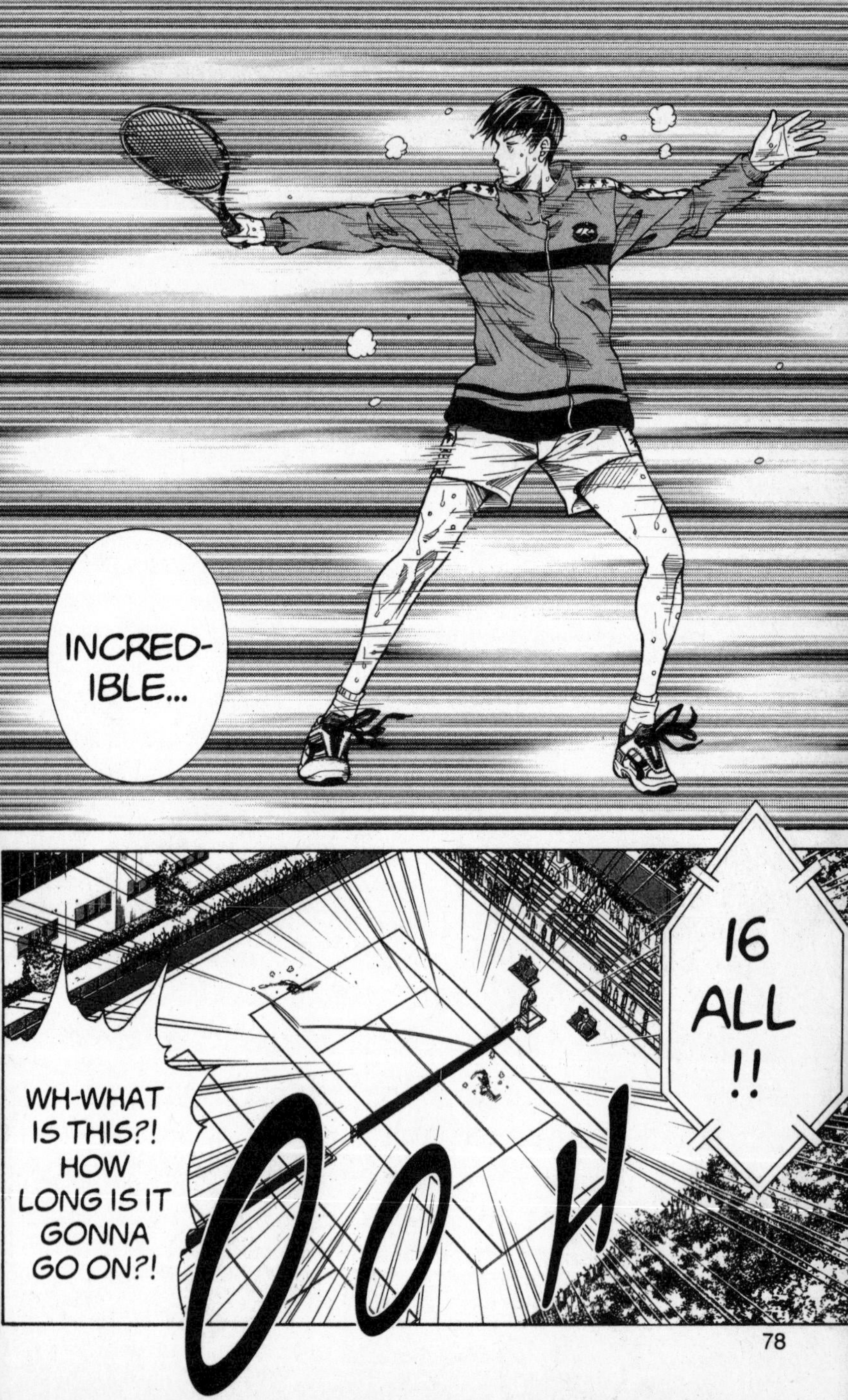
INCRED-IBLE...
16 ALL !!
WH-WHAT IS THIS?! HOW LONG IS IT GONNA GO ON?!
OOH

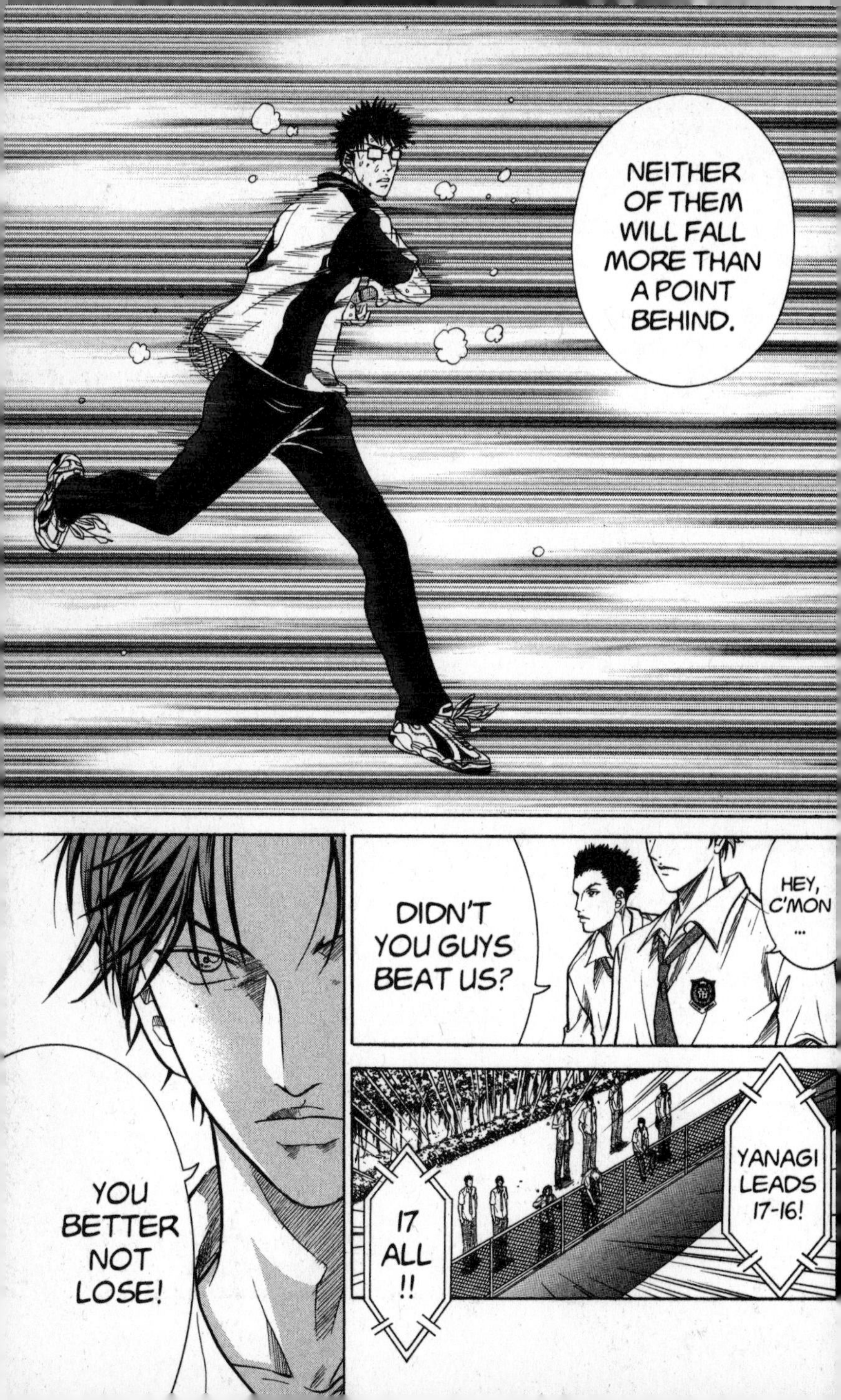
NEITHER OF THEM WILL FALL MORE THAN A POINT BEHIND.
HEY, C'MON ...
DIDN'T YOU GUYS BEAT US?
YANAGI LEADS 17-16!
17 ALL !!
YOU BETTER NOT LOSE!

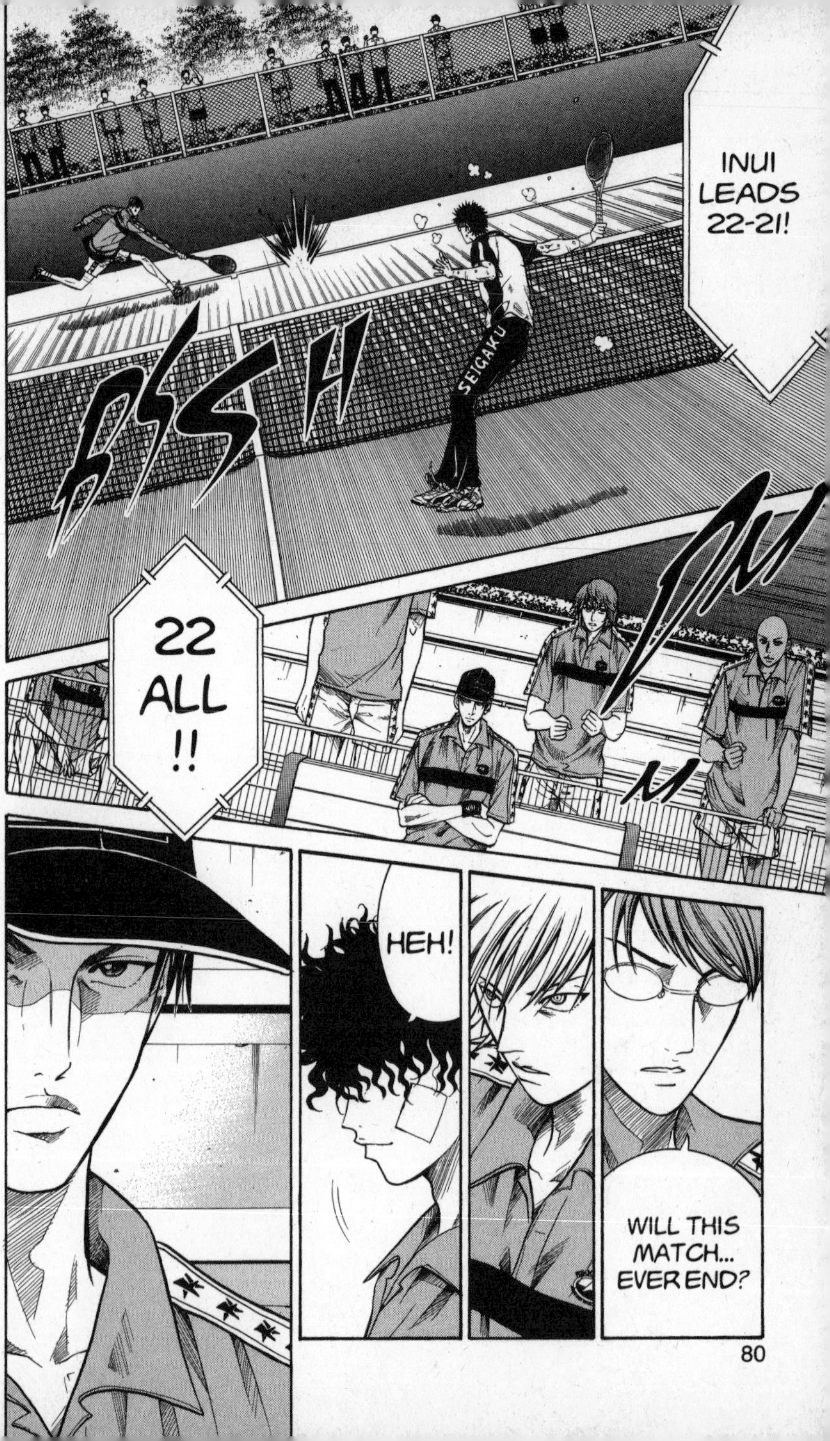
INUI LEADS 22-21!
BSSH
MM
22 ALL !!
WILL THIS MATCH... EVER END?
HEH!

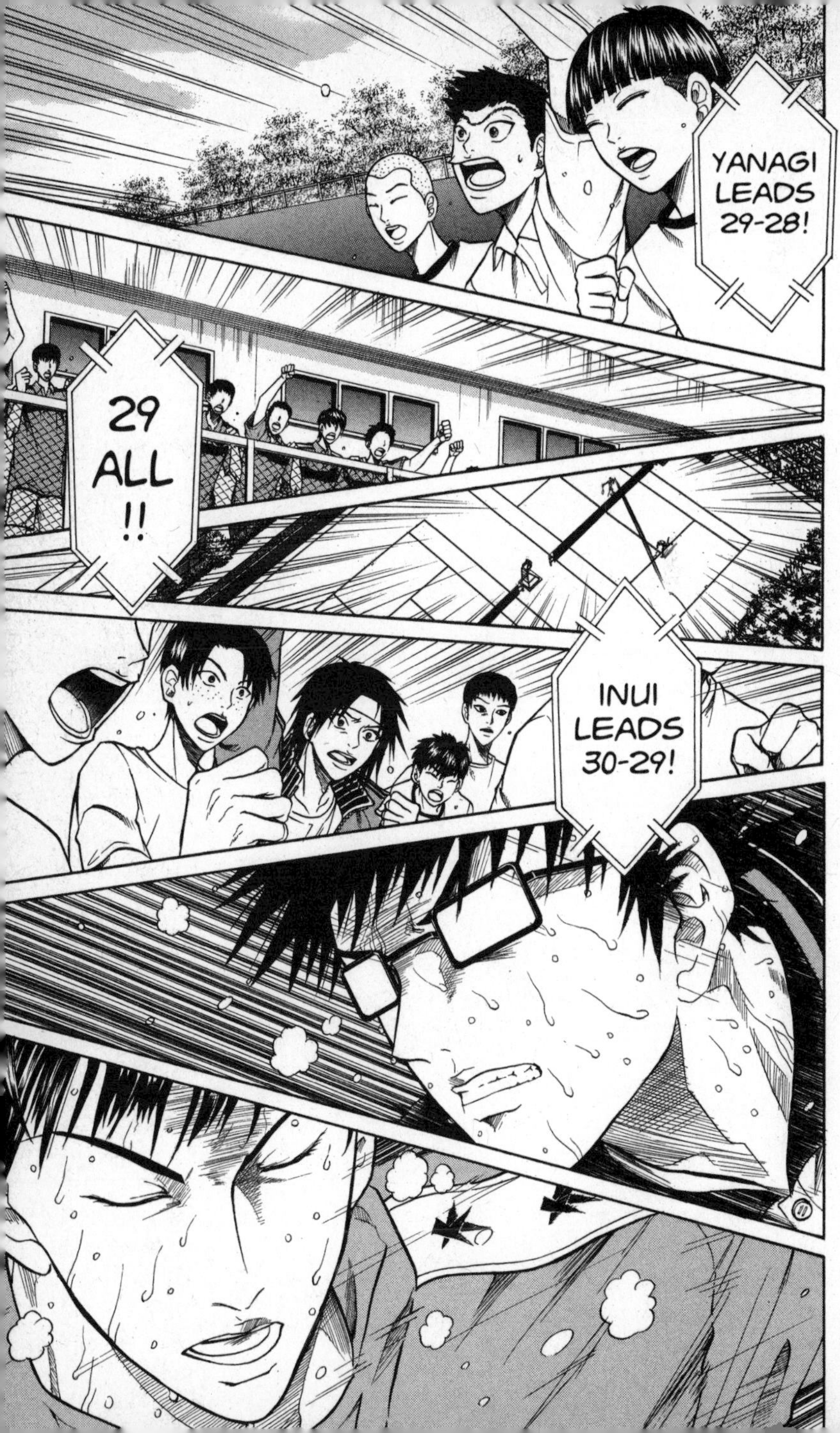
YANAGI LEADS 29-28!
29 ALL !!
INUI LEADS 30-29!

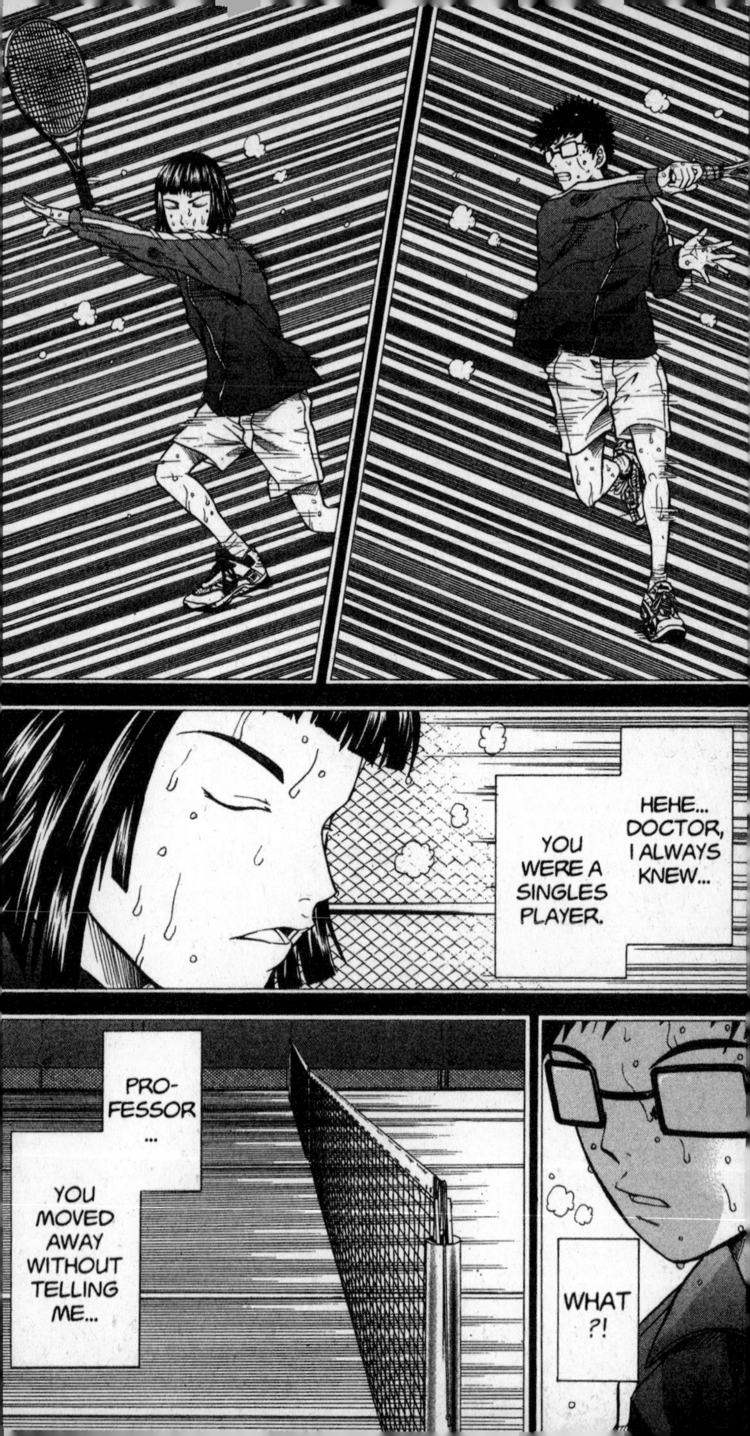
HEHE... DOCTOR, I ALWAYS KNEW...
YOU WERE A SINGLES PLAYER.
WHAT ?!
PRO-FESSOR ...
YOU MOVED AWAY WITHOUT TELLING ME...

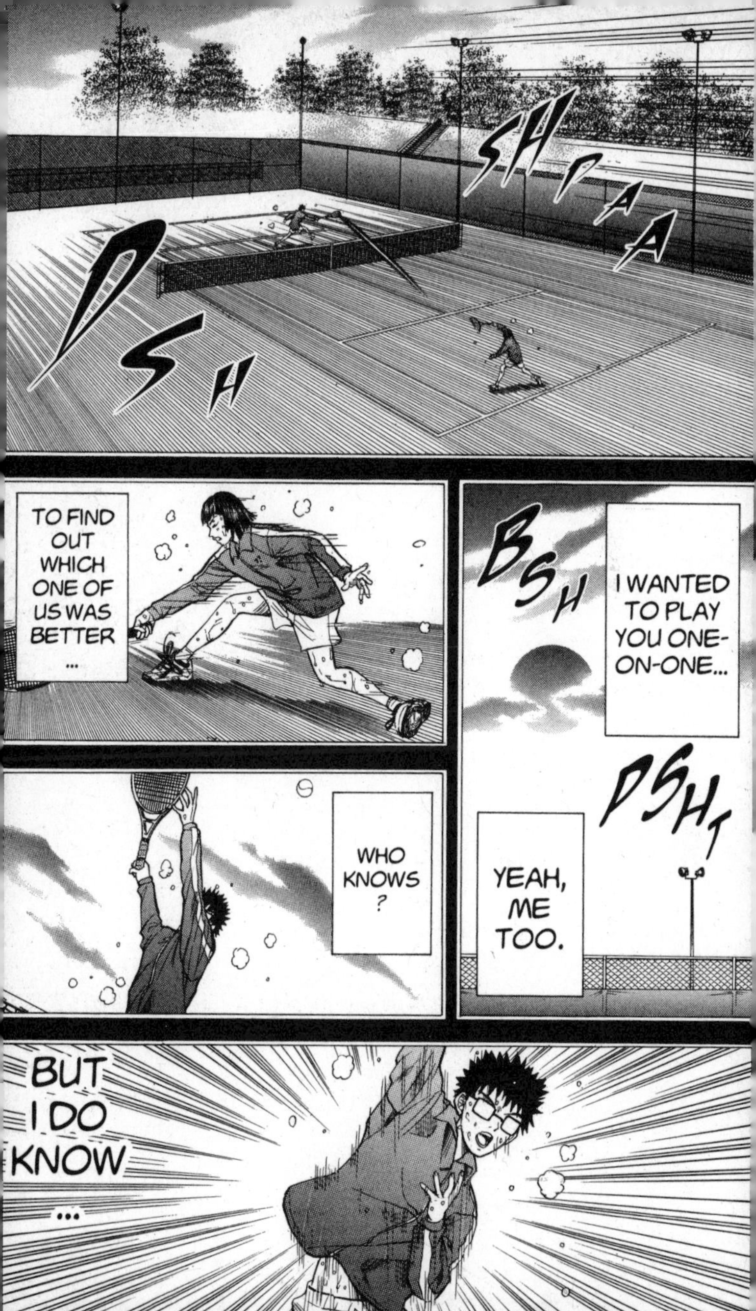
SHPAAA
DSH
BSH
I WANTED TO PLAY YOU ONE-ON-ONE...
DSHT
YEAH, ME TOO.
TO FIND OUT WHICH ONE OF US WAS BETTER...
WHO KNOWS?
BUT I DO KNOW...

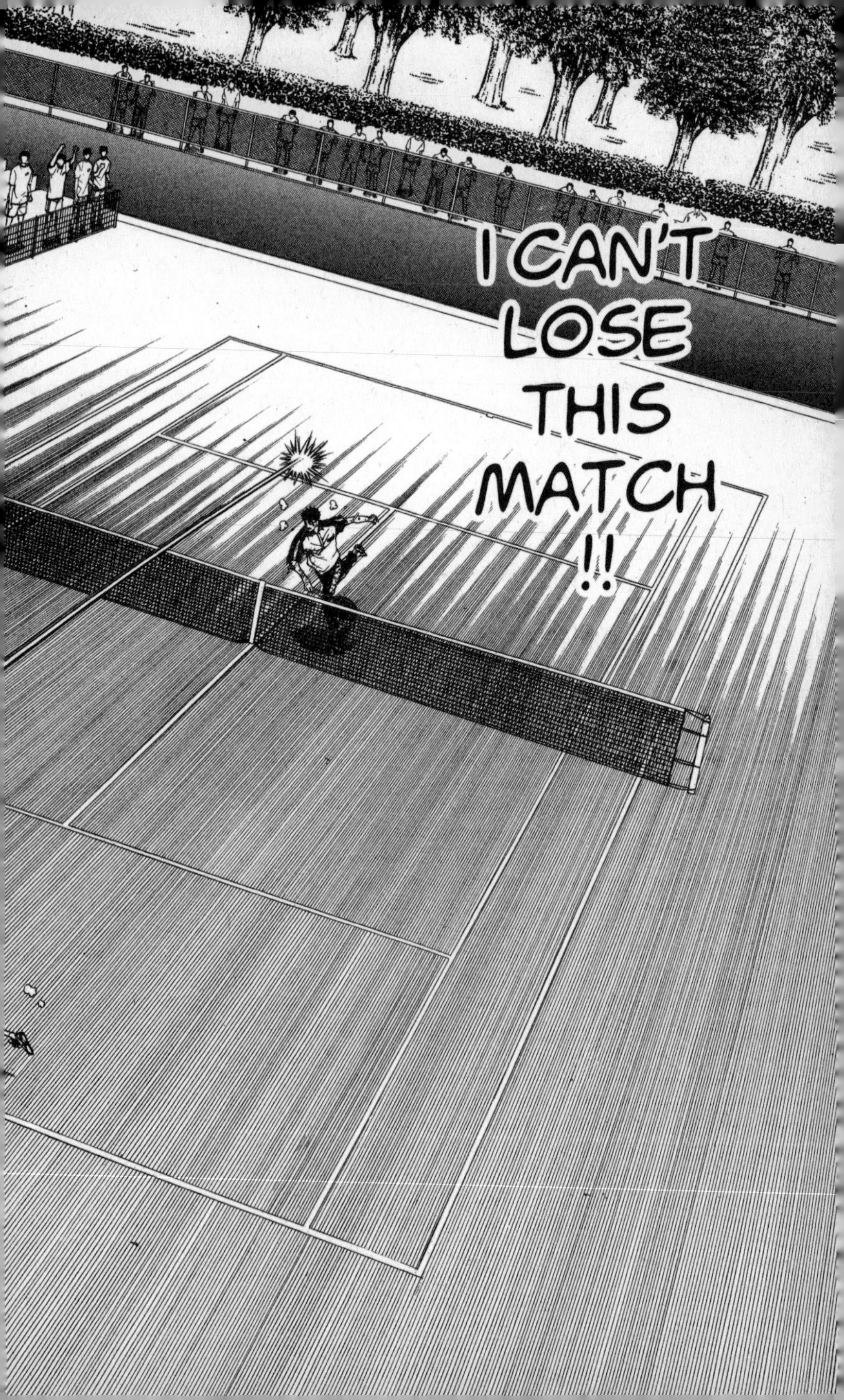
I CAN'T LOSE THIS MATCH !!

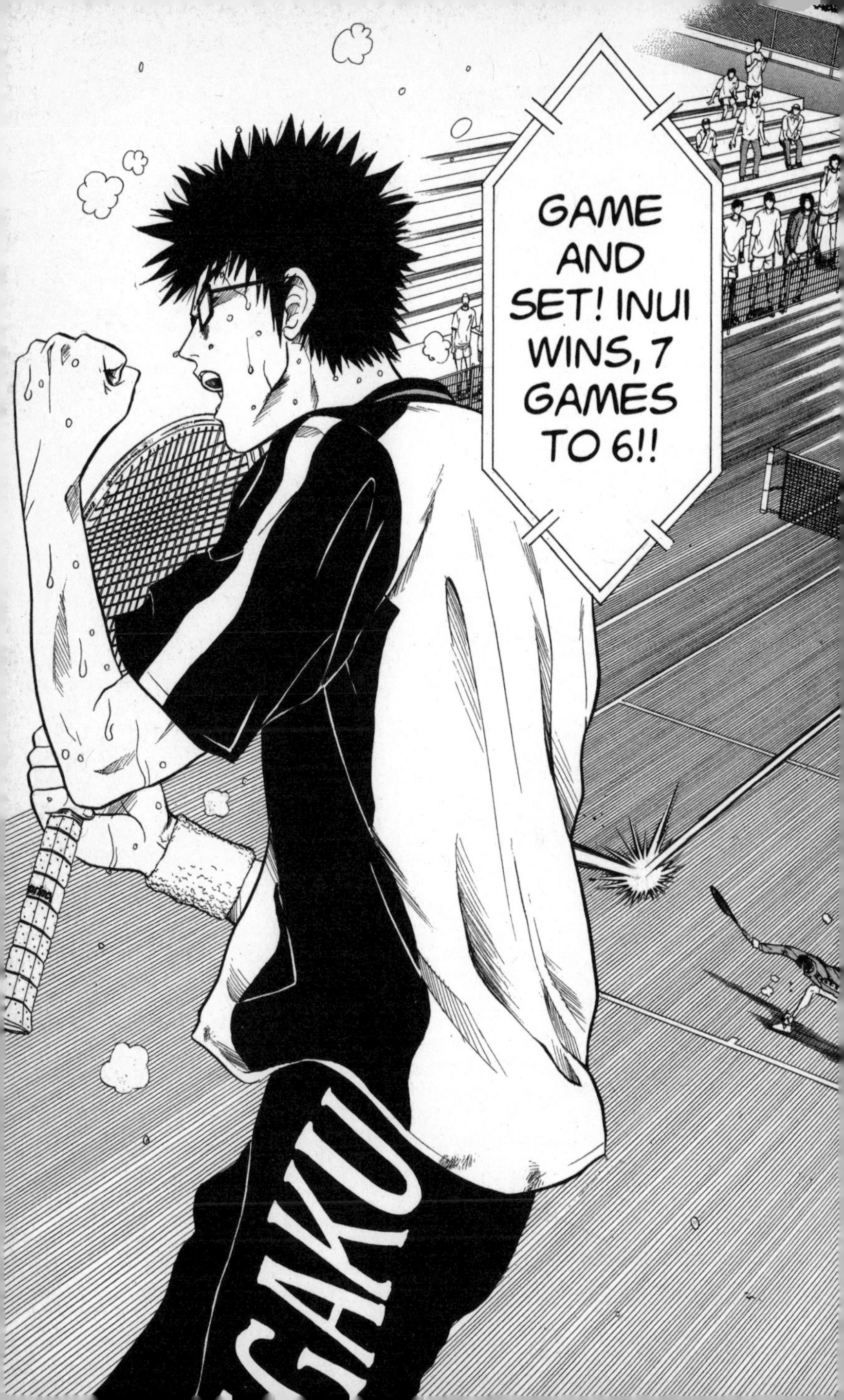
GAME AND SET! INUI WINS, 7 GAMES TO 6!!
SEIGAKU

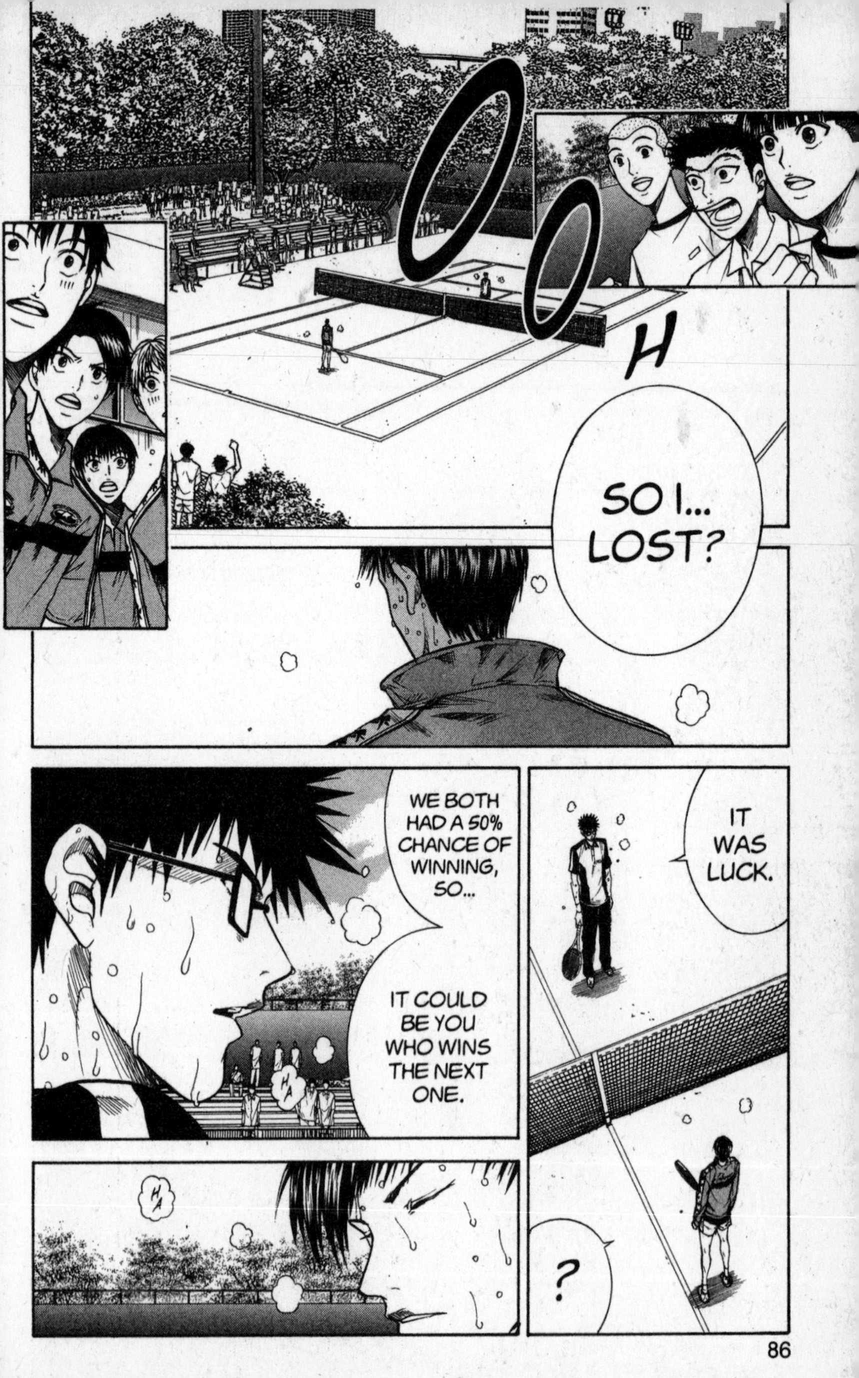
OOOH
SO I... LOST?
IT WAS LUCK.
?
WE BOTH HAD A 50% CHANCE OF WINNING, SO...
IT COULD BE YOU WHO WINS THE NEXT ONE.
HA
HA

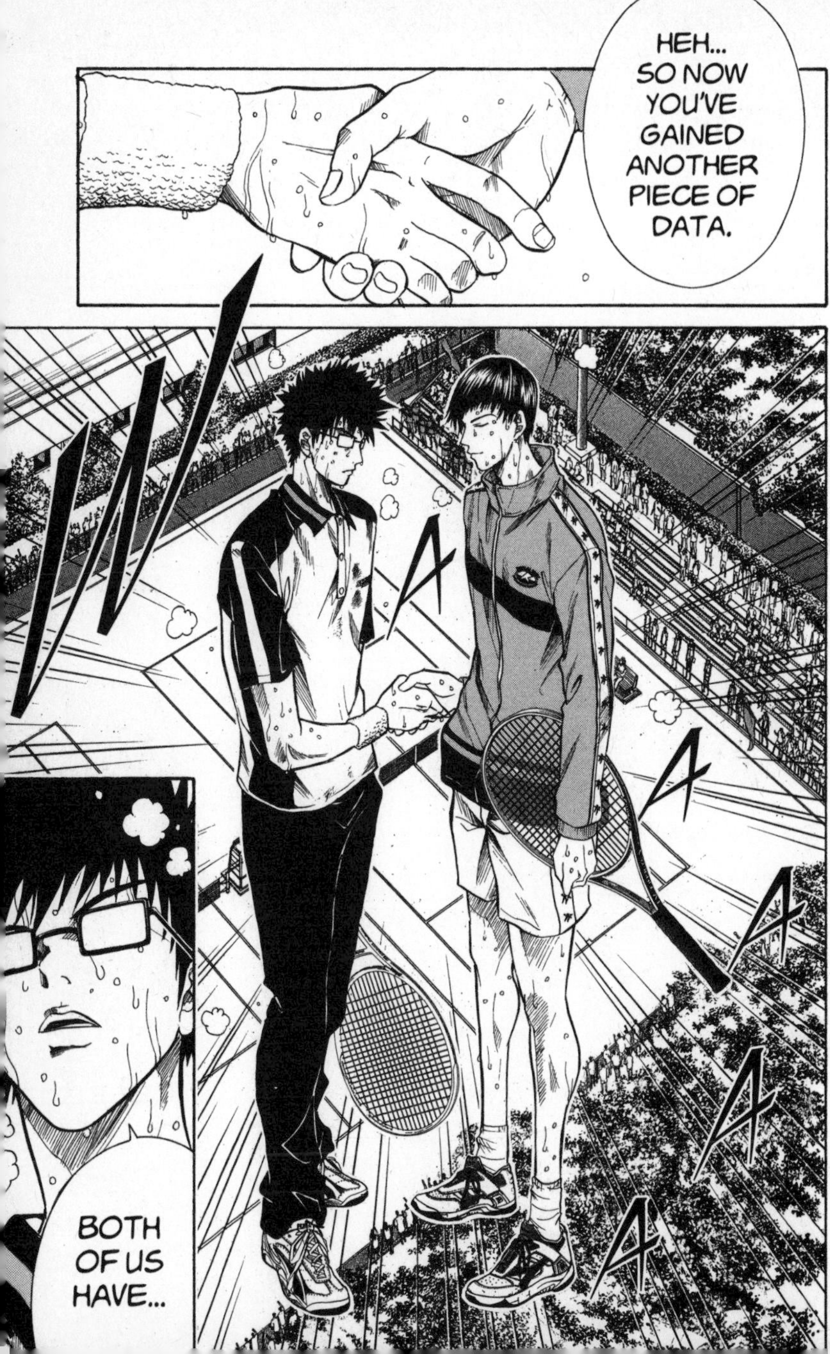
HEH... SO NOW YOU'VE GAINED ANOTHER PIECE OF DATA.
BOTH OF US HAVE...

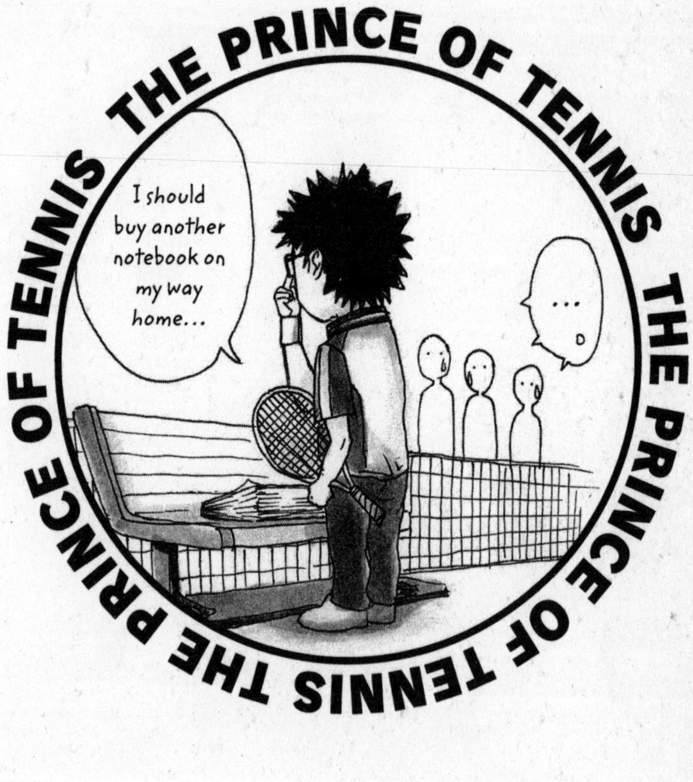
THE PRINCE OF TENNIS THE PRINCE OF TENNIS
I should buy another notebook on my way home...
...

GENIUS 215: NOT ALLOWED TO LOSE

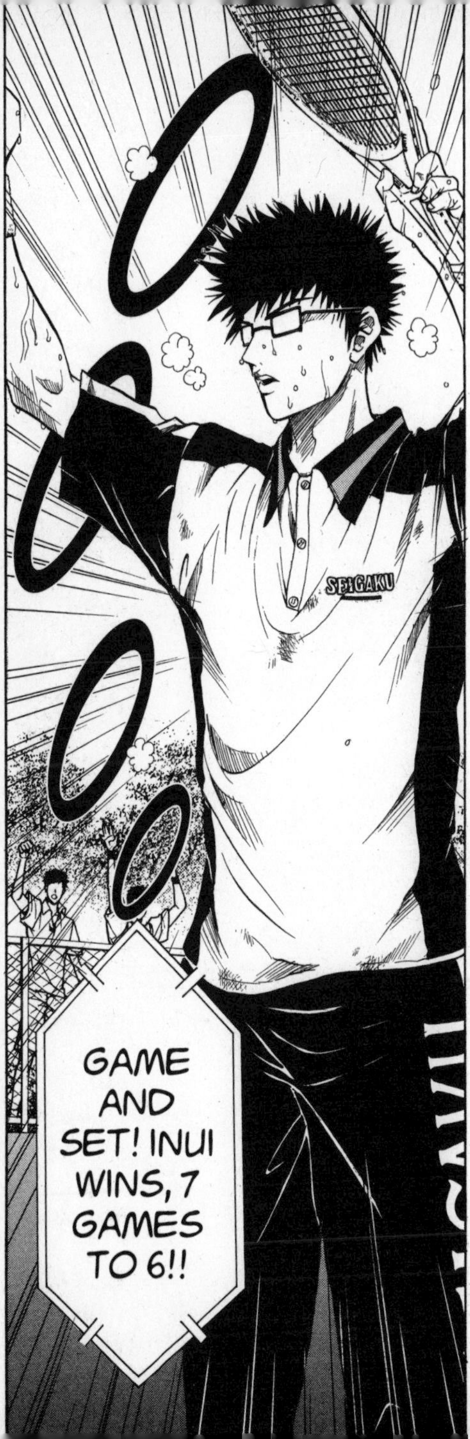
GAME AND SET! INUI WINS, 7 GAMES TO 6!!

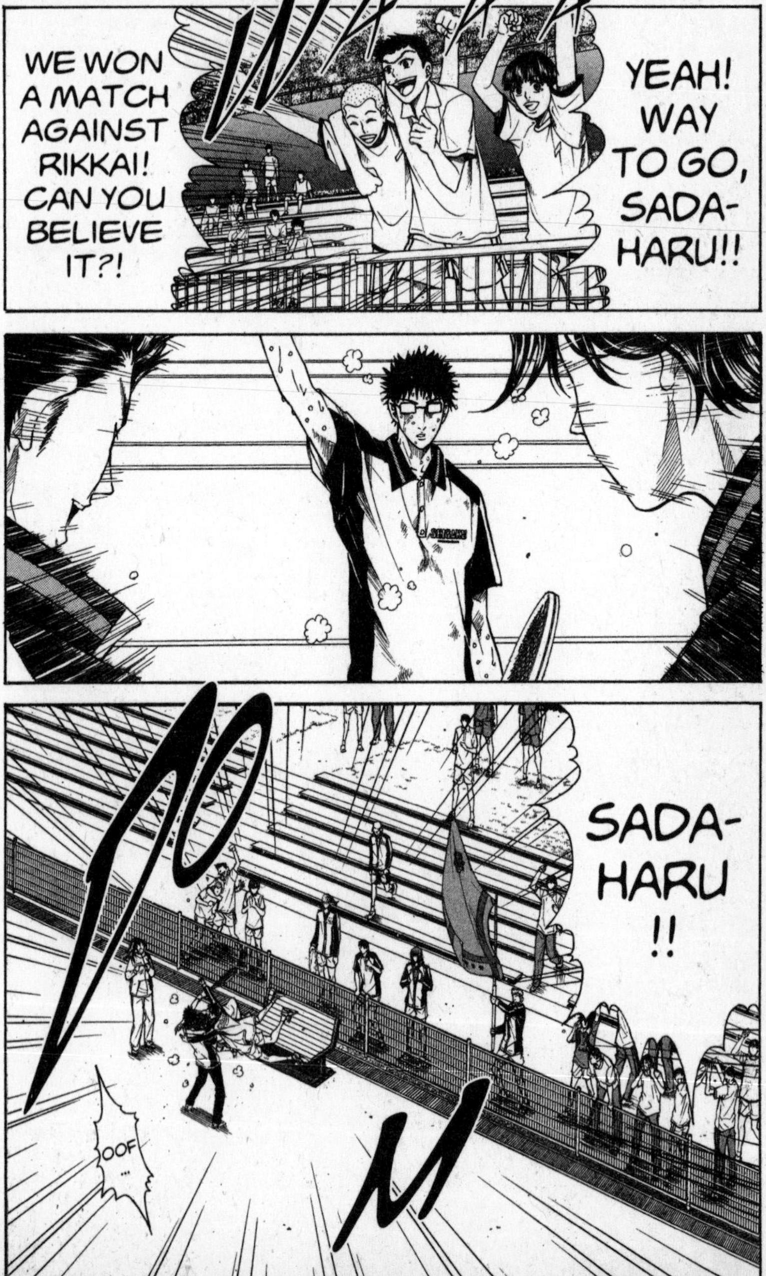
YEAH! WAY TO GO, SADAHARU!!
WAAA
WE WON A MATCH AGAINST RIKKAI! CAN YOU BELIEVE IT?!
SADAHARU!!
OOF...

READ THIS WAY

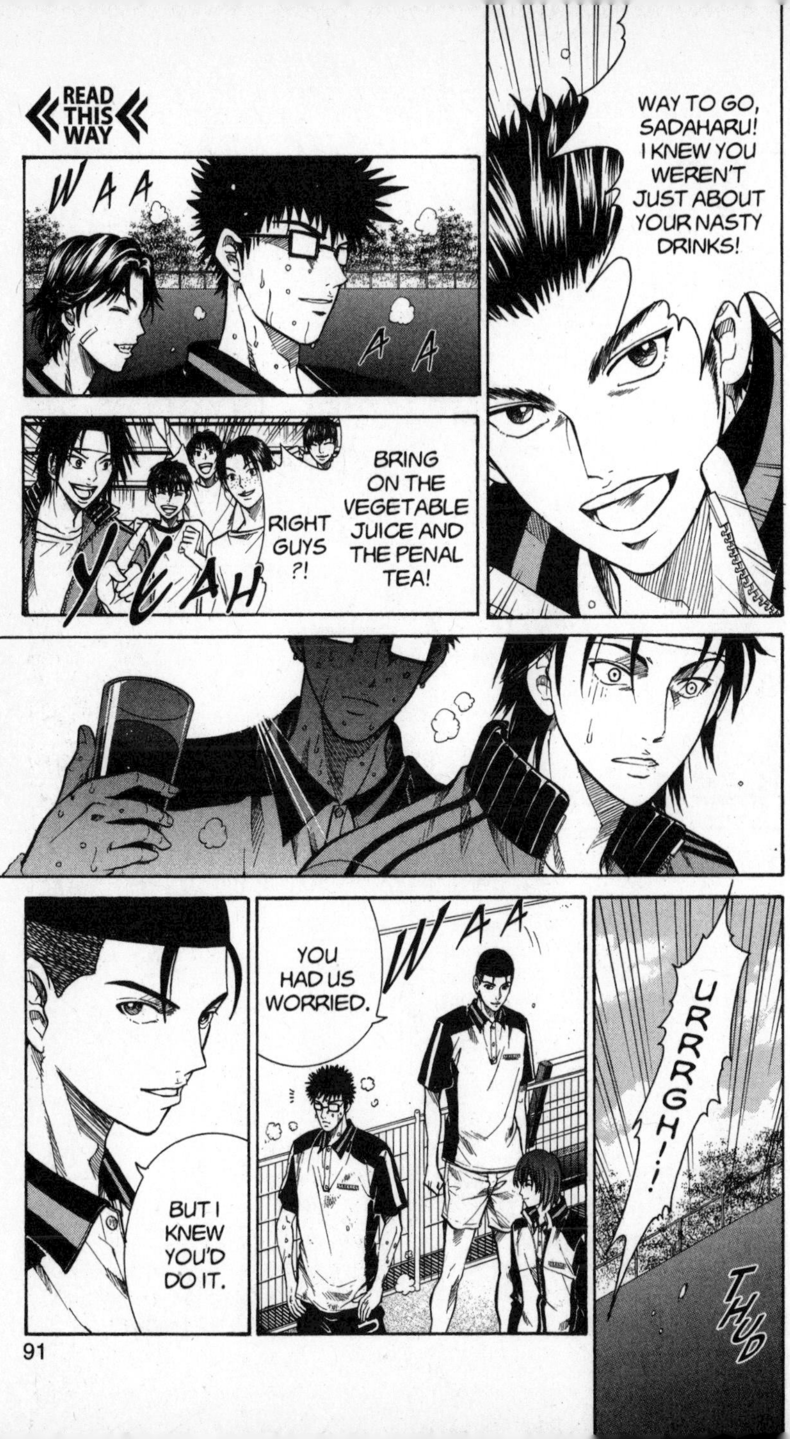

WAY TO GO, SADAHARU! I KNEW YOU WEREN'T JUST ABOUT YOUR NASTY DRINKS!
WAA
AA
BRING ON THE VEGETABLE JUICE AND THE PENAL TEA!
RIGHT GUYS ?!
YEAH
URRRGH!!
THUD
WAA
YOU HAD US WORRIED.
BUT I KNEW YOU'D DO IT.

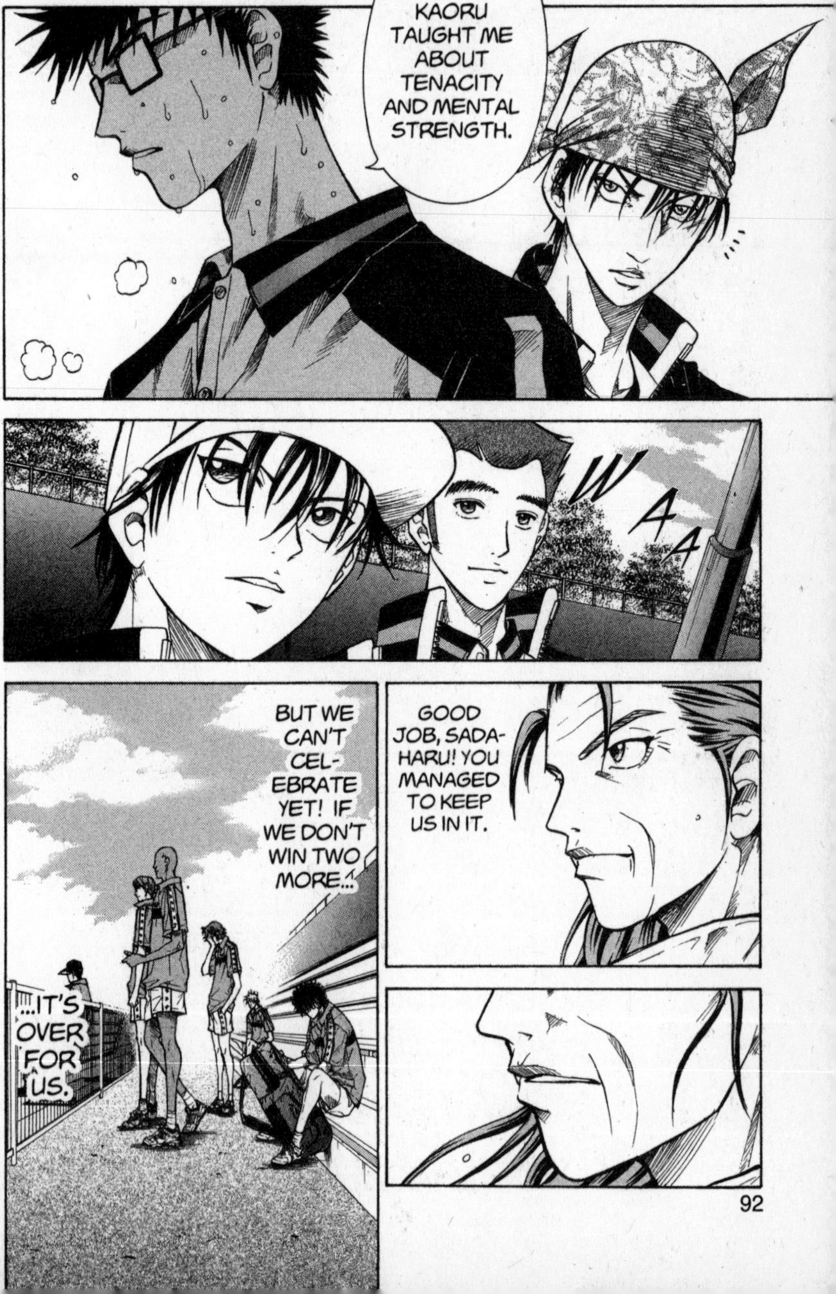
KAORU TAUGHT ME ABOUT TENACITY AND MENTAL STRENGTH.
WAA
GOOD JOB, SADA-HARU! YOU MANAGED TO KEEP US IN IT.
BUT WE CAN'T CEL-EBRATE YET! IF WE DON'T WIN TWO MORE...!
...IT'S OVER FOR US.

READ THIS WAY

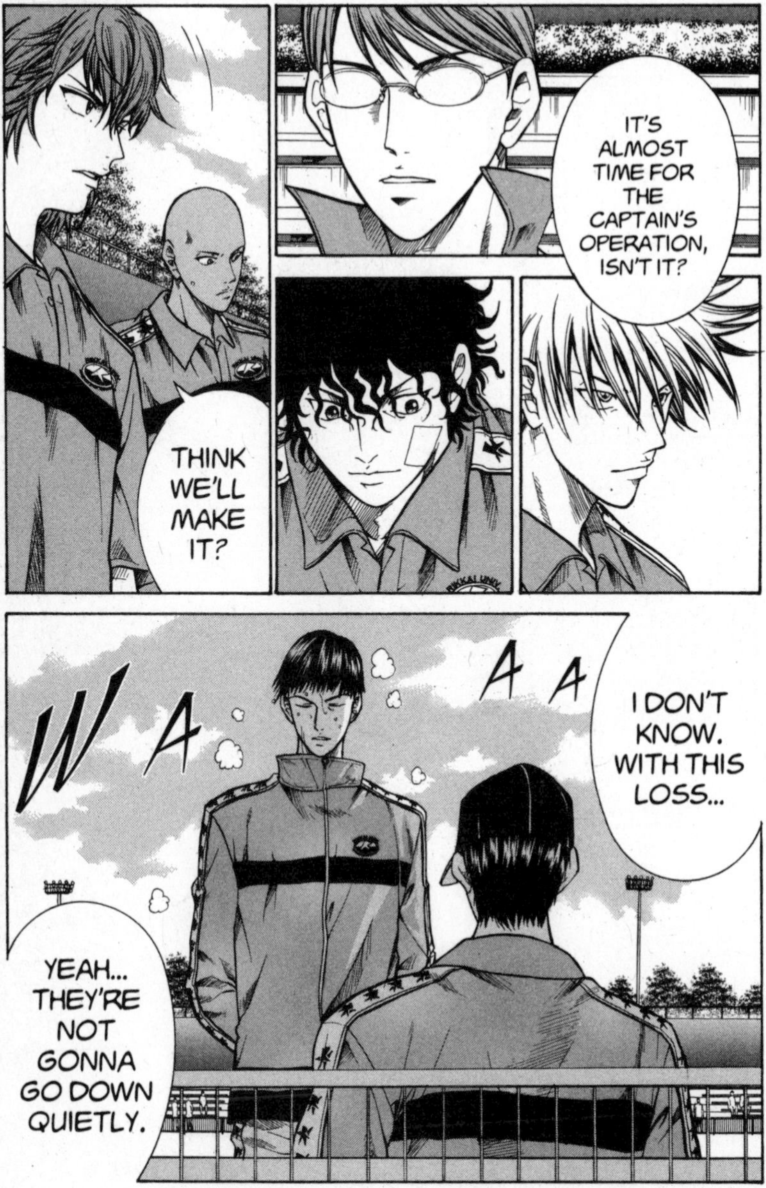
IT'S ALMOST TIME FOR THE CAPTAIN'S OPERATION, ISN'T IT?
THINK WE'LL MAKE IT?
I DON'T KNOW. WITH THIS LOSS...
WA A A A
YEAH... THEY'RE NOT GONNA GO DOWN QUIETLY.

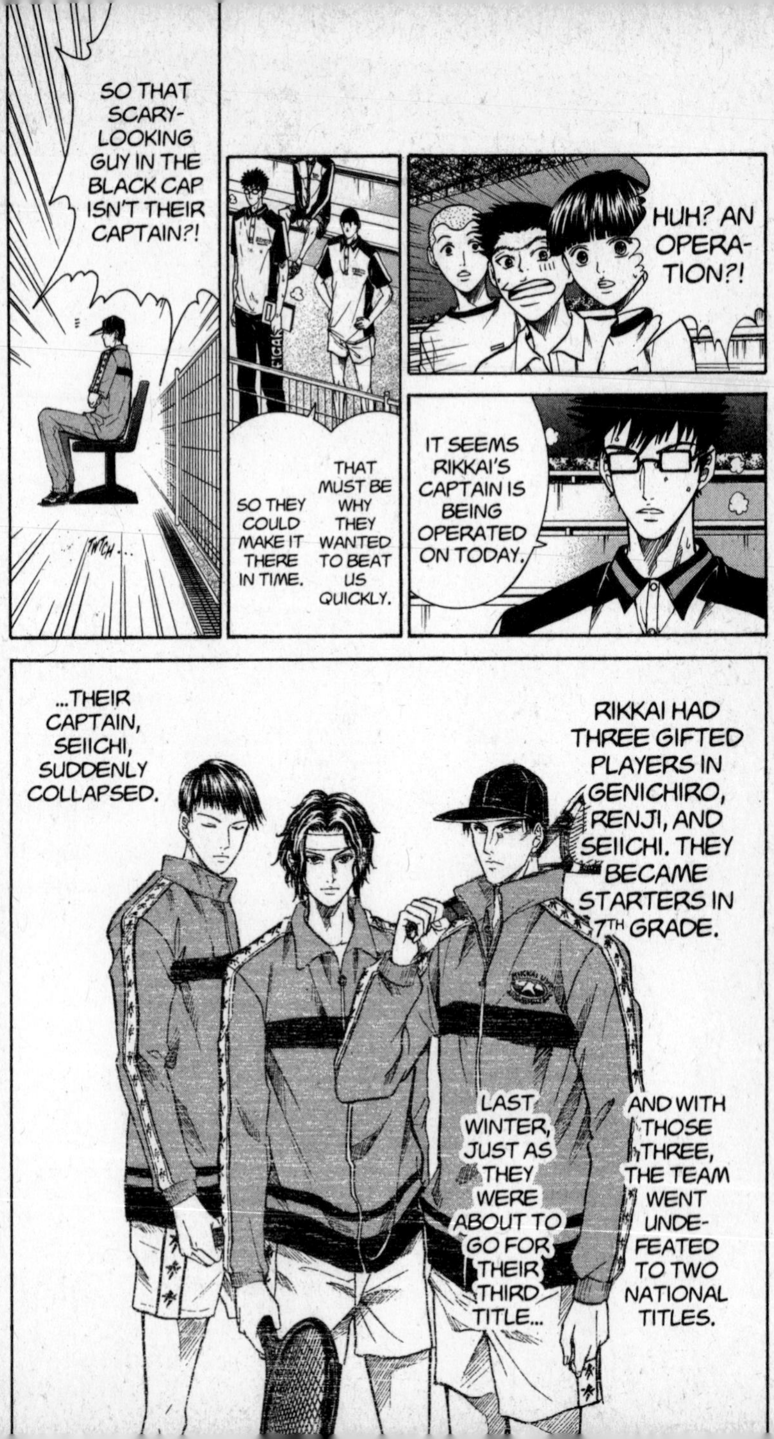
HUH? AN OPERATION?!
IT SEEMS RIKKAI'S CAPTAIN IS BEING OPERATED ON TODAY.
THAT MUST BE WHY THEY WANTED TO BEAT US QUICKLY.
SO THEY COULD MAKE IT THERE IN TIME.
SO THAT SCARY-LOOKING GUY IN THE BLACK CAP ISN'T THEIR CAPTAIN?!
TWITCH...
RIKKAI HAD THREE GIFTED PLAYERS IN GENICHIRO, RENJI, AND SEIICHI. THEY BECAME STARTERS IN 7TH GRADE.
AND WITH THOSE THREE, THE TEAM WENT UNDEFEATED TO TWO NATIONAL TITLES.
LAST WINTER, JUST AS THEY WERE ABOUT TO GO FOR THEIR THIRD TITLE...
...THEIR CAPTAIN, SEIICHI, SUDDENLY COLLAPSED.

READ THIS WAY

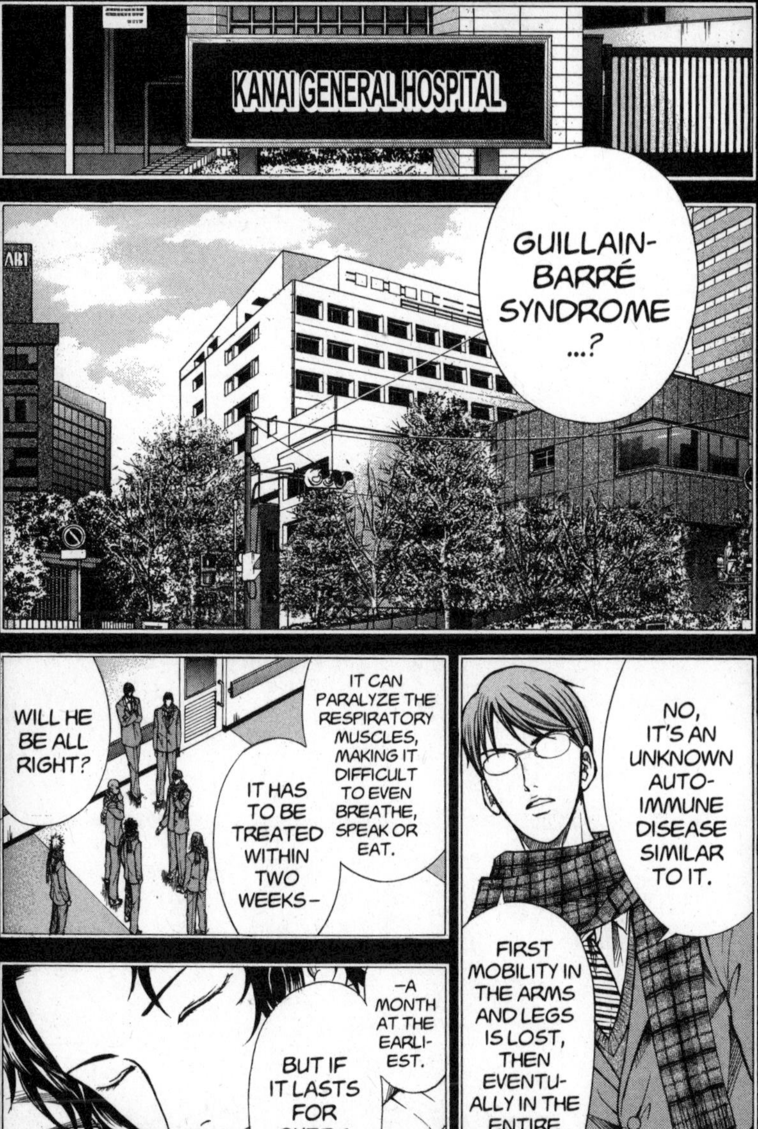
KANAI GENERAL HOSPITAL
GUILLAIN-BARRÉ SYNDROME ...?
NO, IT'S AN UNKNOWN AUTO-IMMUNE DISEASE SIMILAR TO IT.
FIRST MOBILITY IN THE ARMS AND LEGS IS LOST, THEN EVENTUALLY IN THE ENTIRE BODY.
IT CAN PARALYZE THE RESPIRATORY MUSCLES, MAKING IT DIFFICULT TO EVEN BREATHE, SPEAK OR EAT.
IT HAS TO BE TREATED WITHIN TWO WEEKS-
WILL HE BE ALL RIGHT?
-A MONTH AT THE EARLIEST.
BUT IF IT LASTS FOR OVER A YEAR...

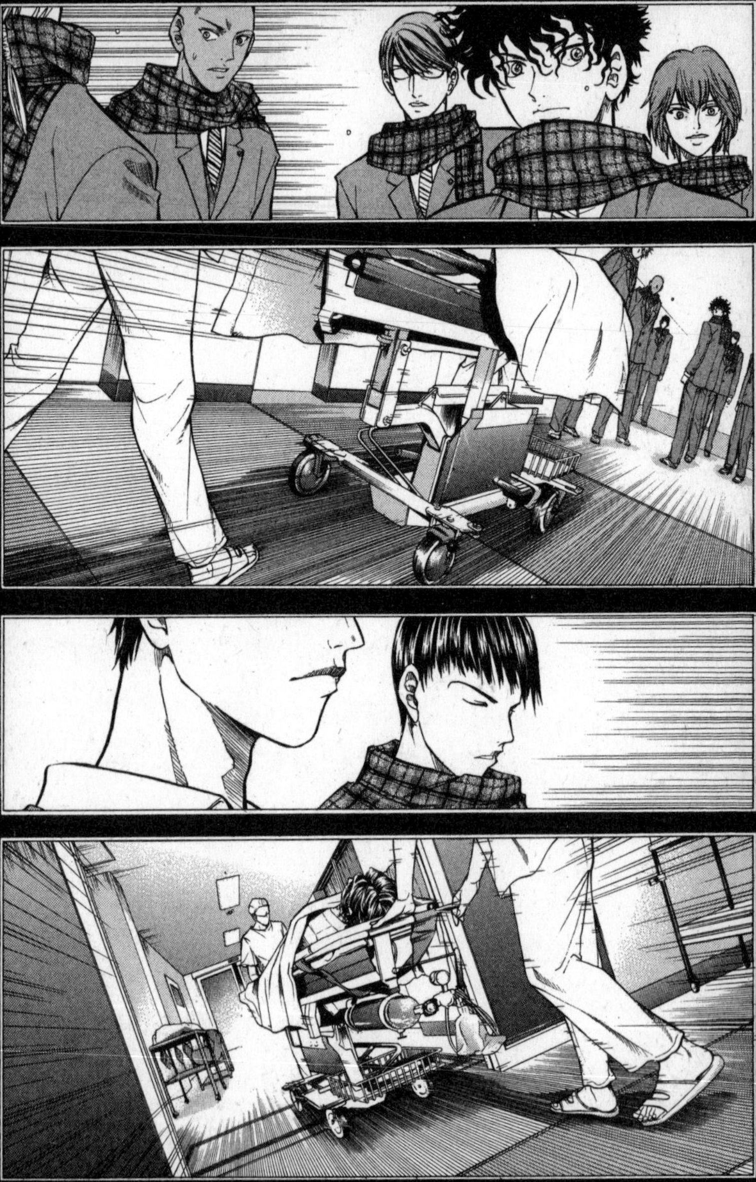

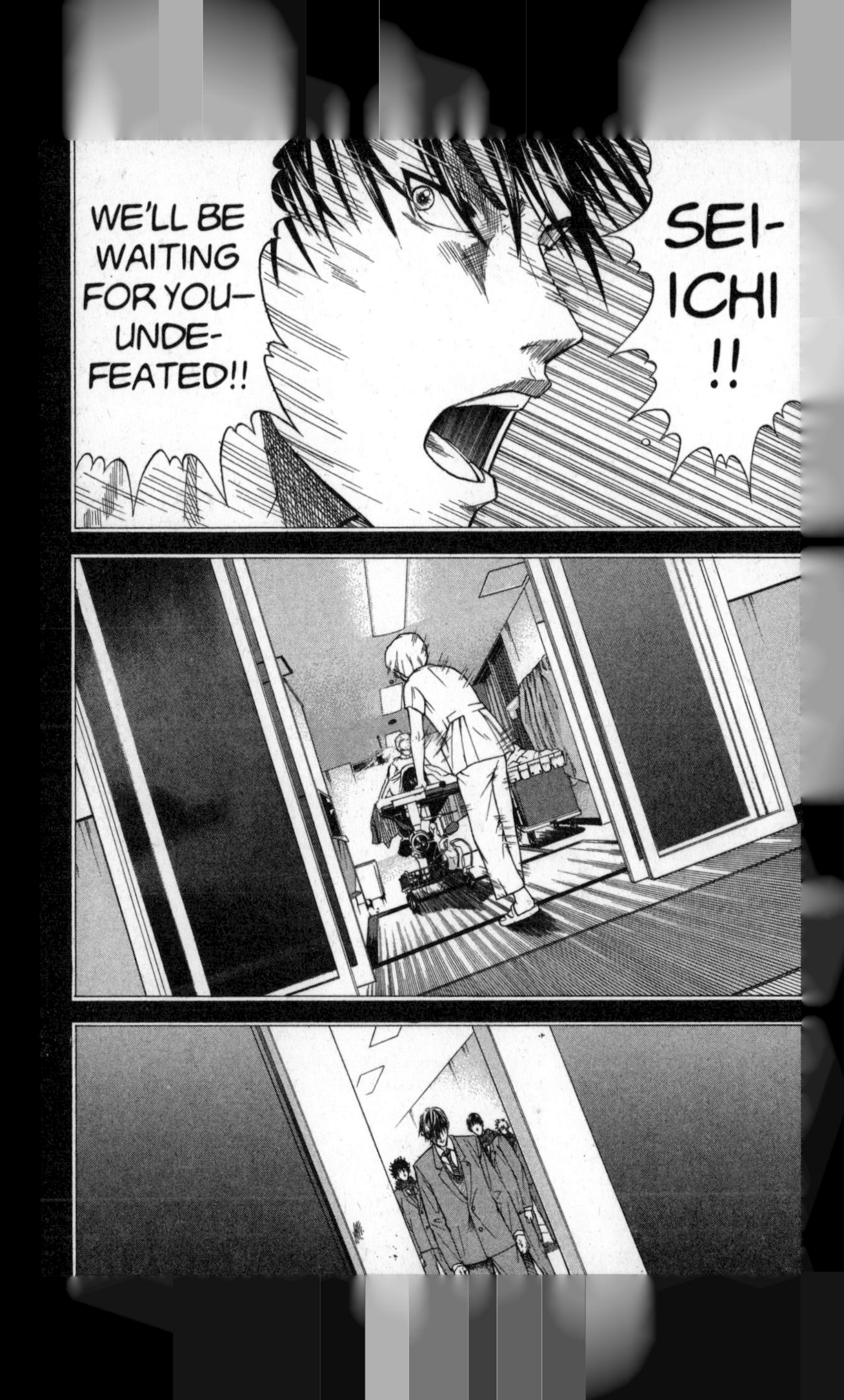
SEI-ICHI!!
WE'LL BE WAITING FOR YOU—UNDE-FEATED!!

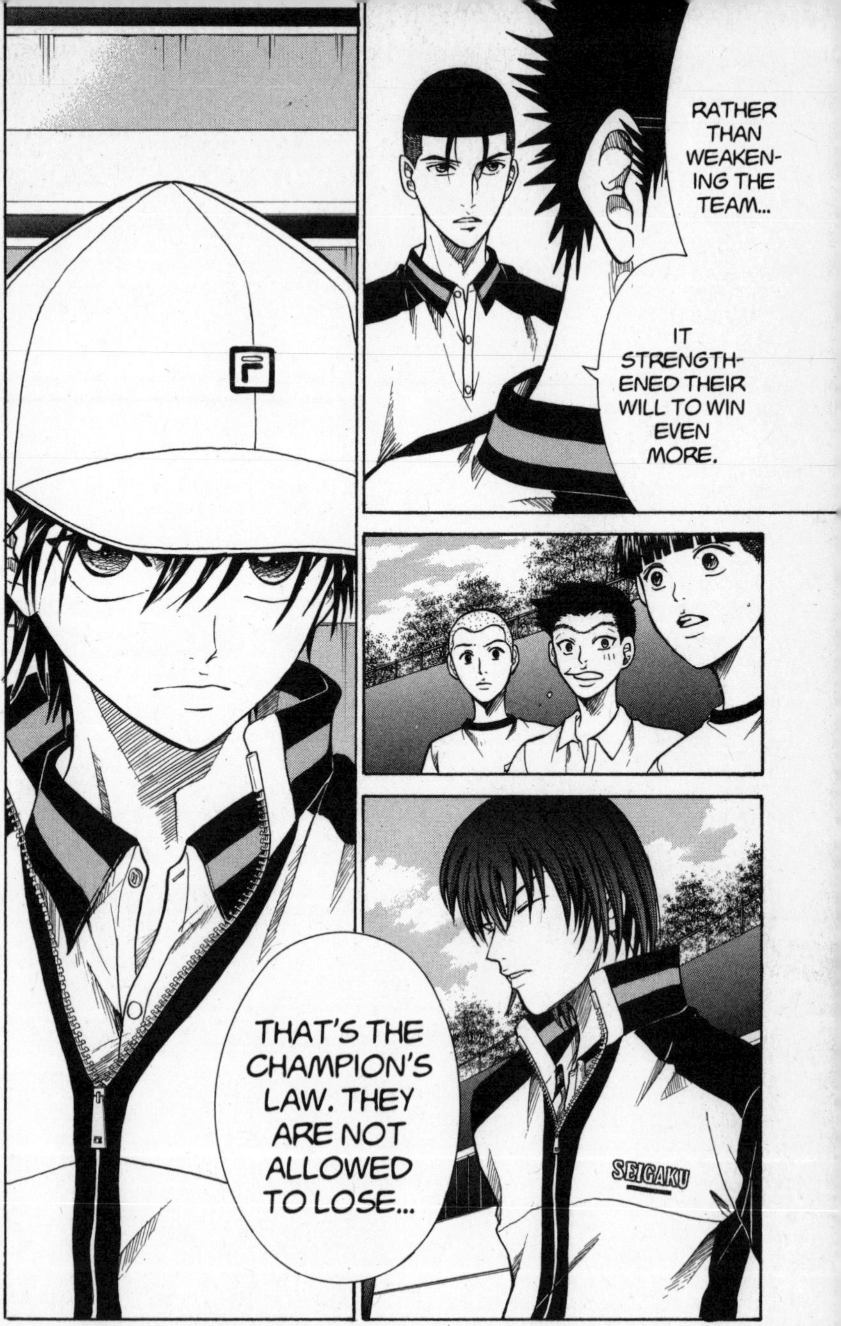
RATHER THAN WEAKENING THE TEAM...
IT STRENGTHENED THEIR WILL TO WIN EVEN MORE.
THAT'S THE CHAMPION'S LAW. THEY ARE NOT ALLOWED TO LOSE...
SEIGAKU

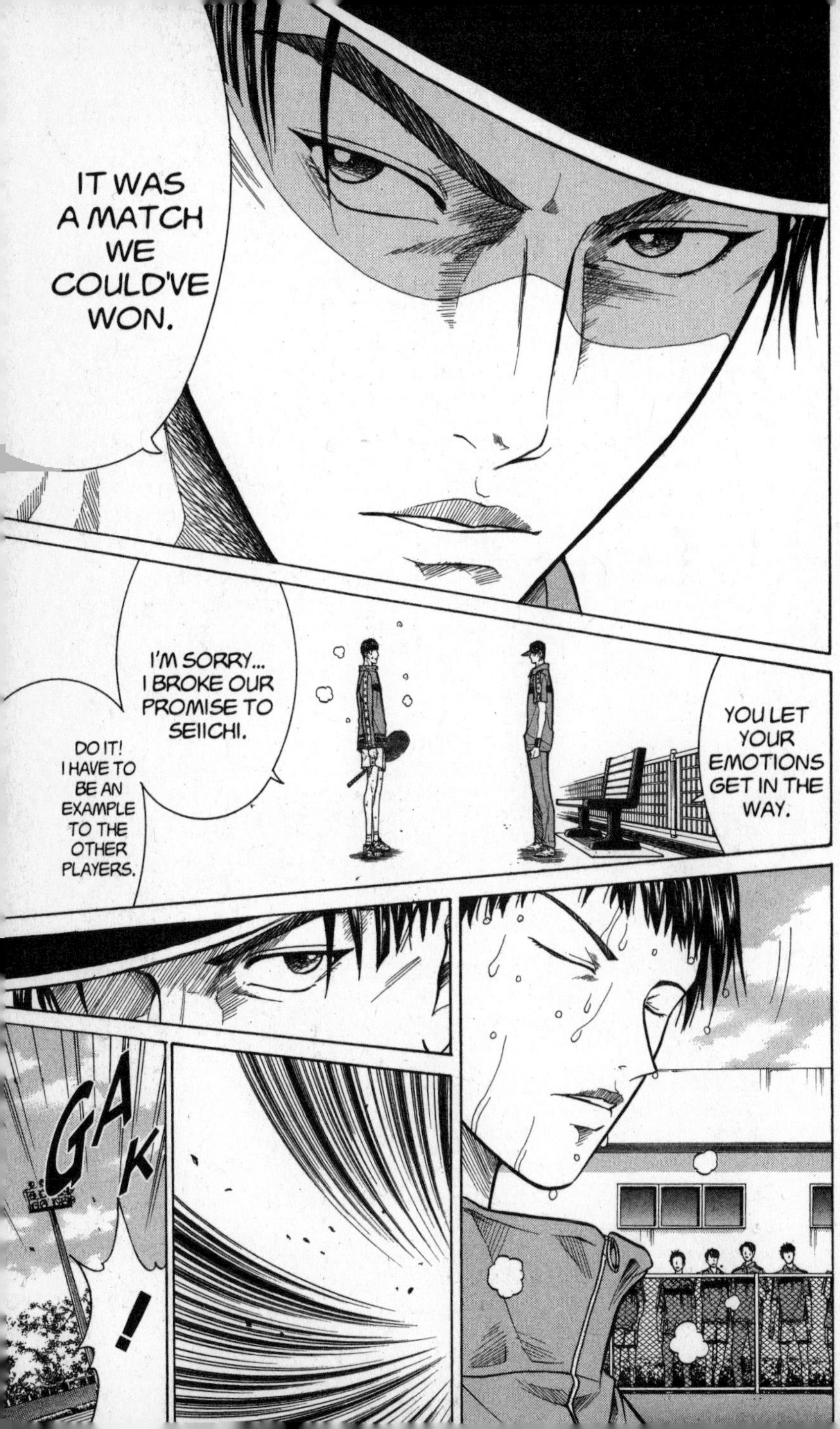
IT WAS A MATCH WE COULD'VE WON.
YOU LET YOUR EMOTIONS GET IN THE WAY.
I'M SORRY... I BROKE OUR PROMISE TO SEIICHI.
DO IT! I HAVE TO BE AN EXAMPLE TO THE OTHER PLAYERS.
GAK
!

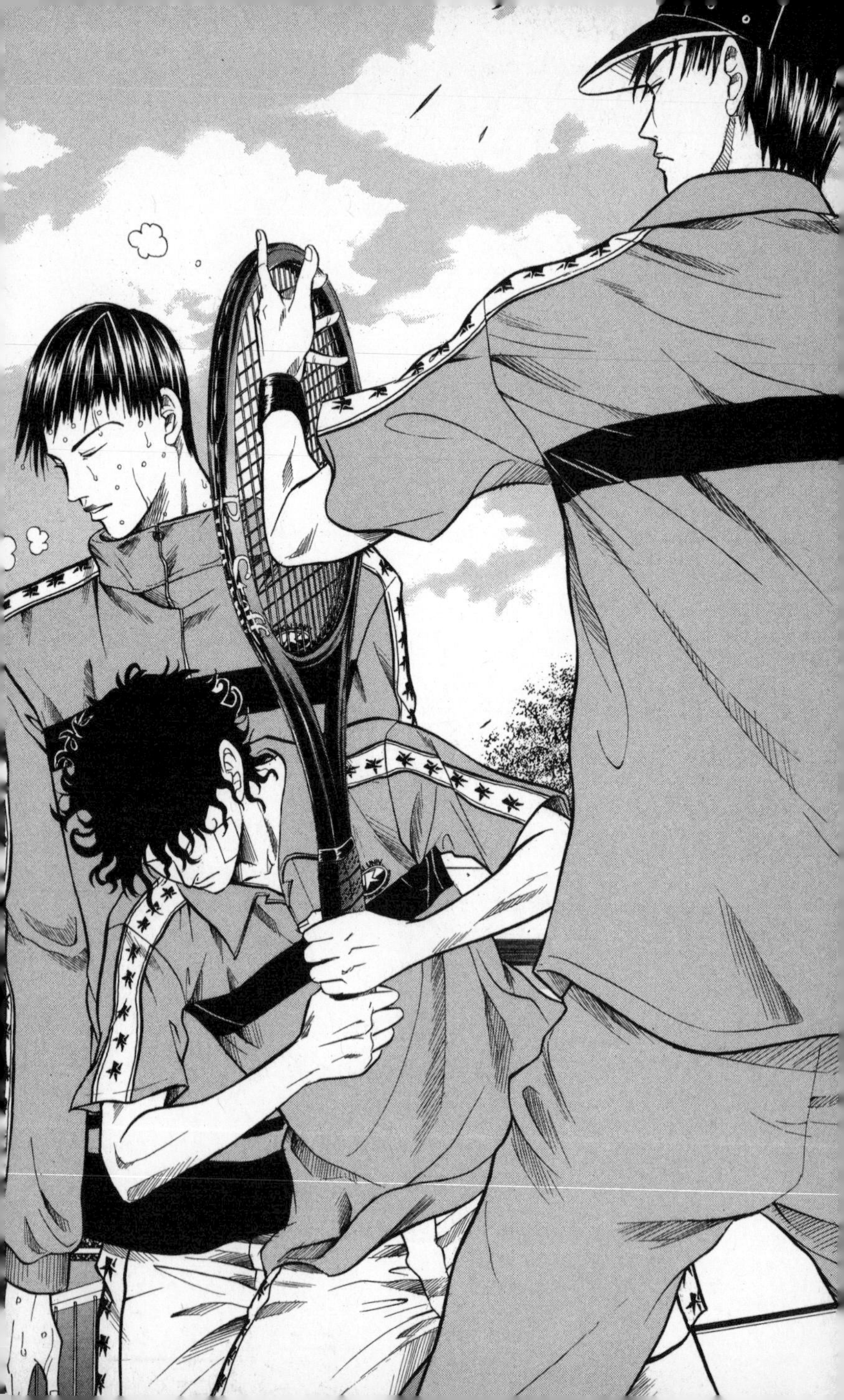

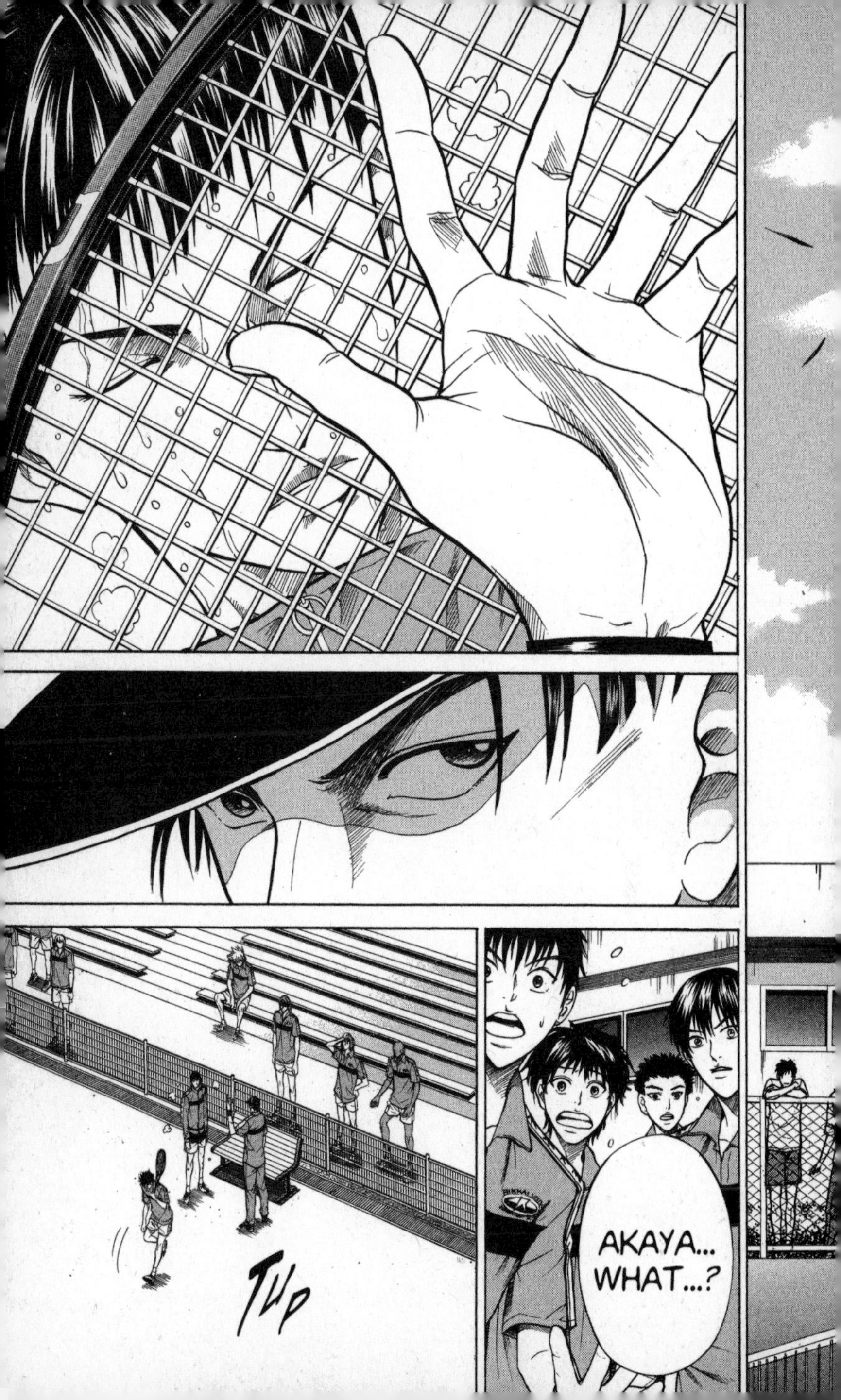
AKAYA... WHAT...?
TUP

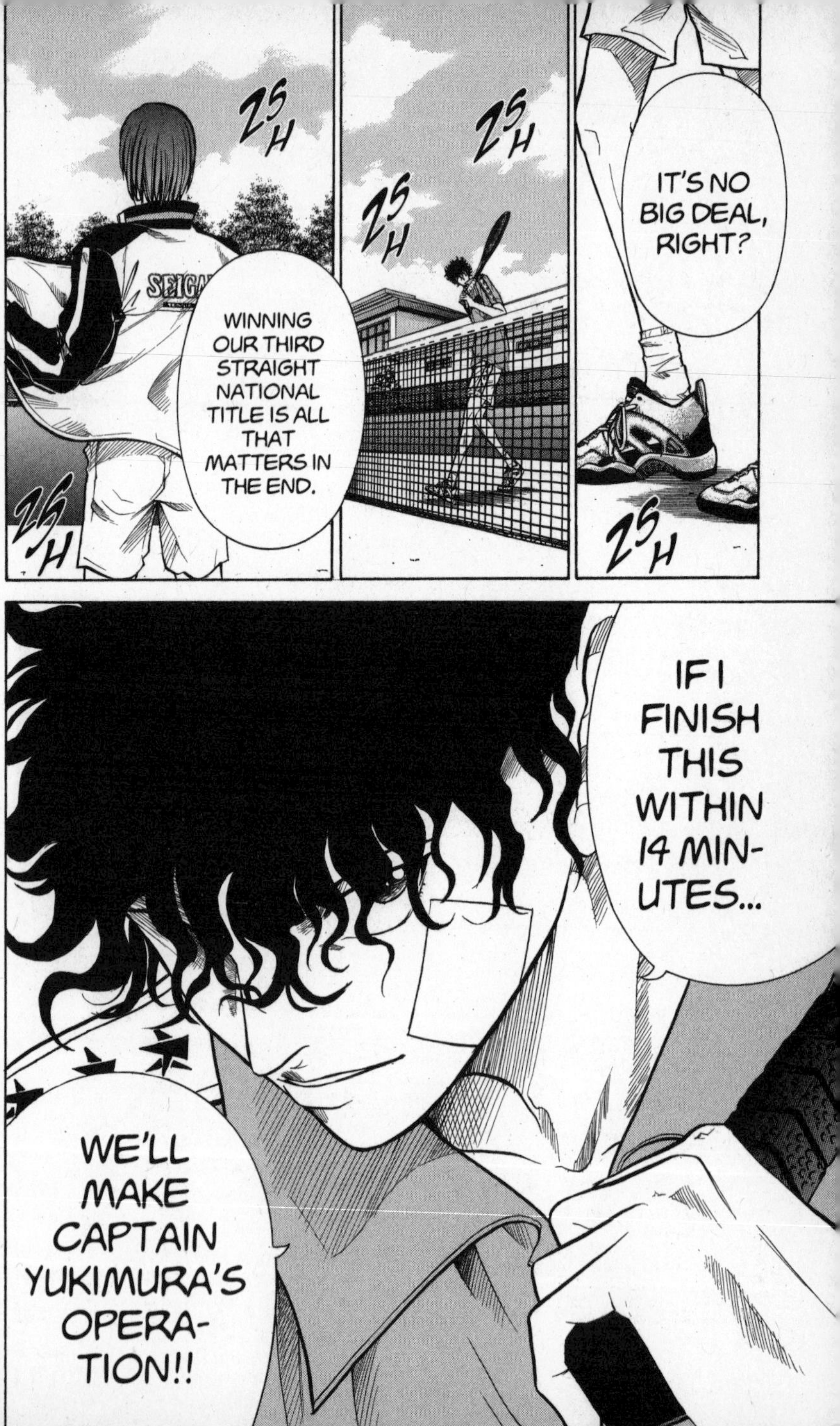
IT'S NO BIG DEAL, RIGHT?
ZSH
ZSH
ZSH
WINNING OUR THIRD STRAIGHT NATIONAL TITLE IS ALL THAT MATTERS IN THE END.
ZSH
IF I FINISH THIS WITHIN 14 MIN-UTES...
WE'LL MAKE CAPTAIN YUKIMURA'S OPERA-TION!!

READ THIS WAY

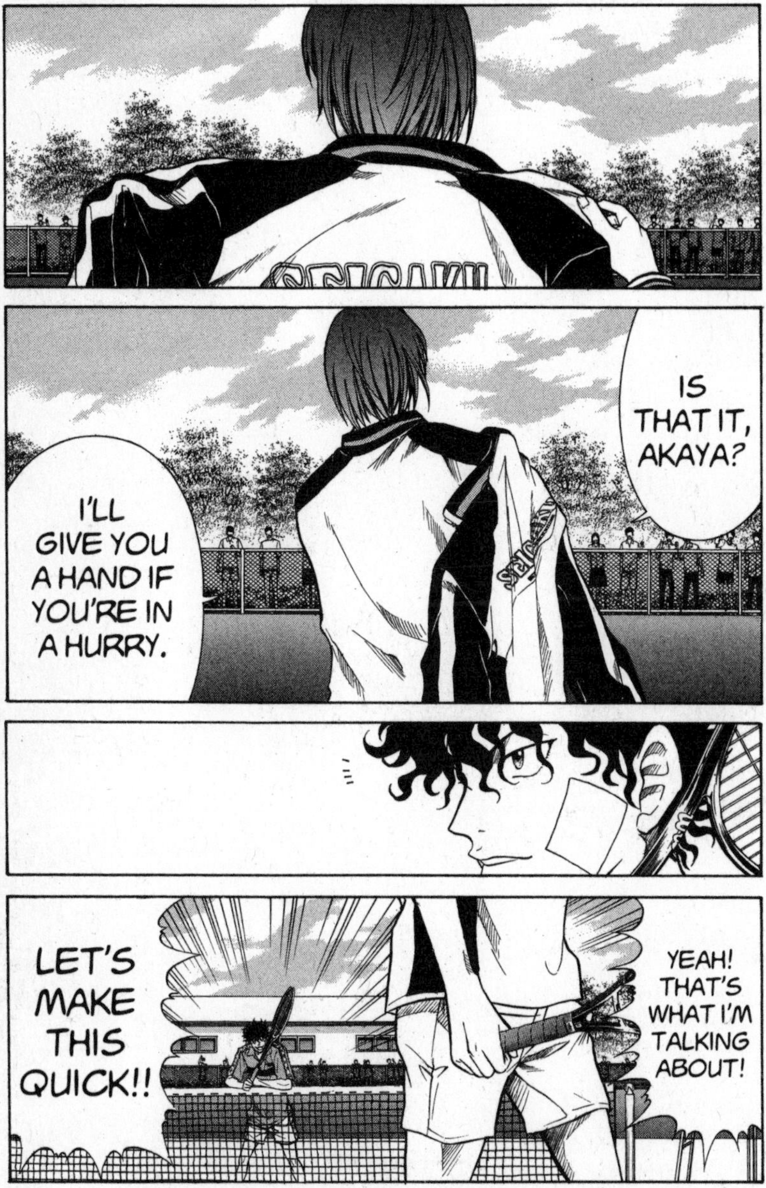

IS THAT IT, AKAYA?
I'LL GIVE YOU A HAND IF YOU'RE IN A HURRY.
YEAH! THAT'S WHAT I'M TALKING ABOUT!
LET'S MAKE THIS QUICK!!

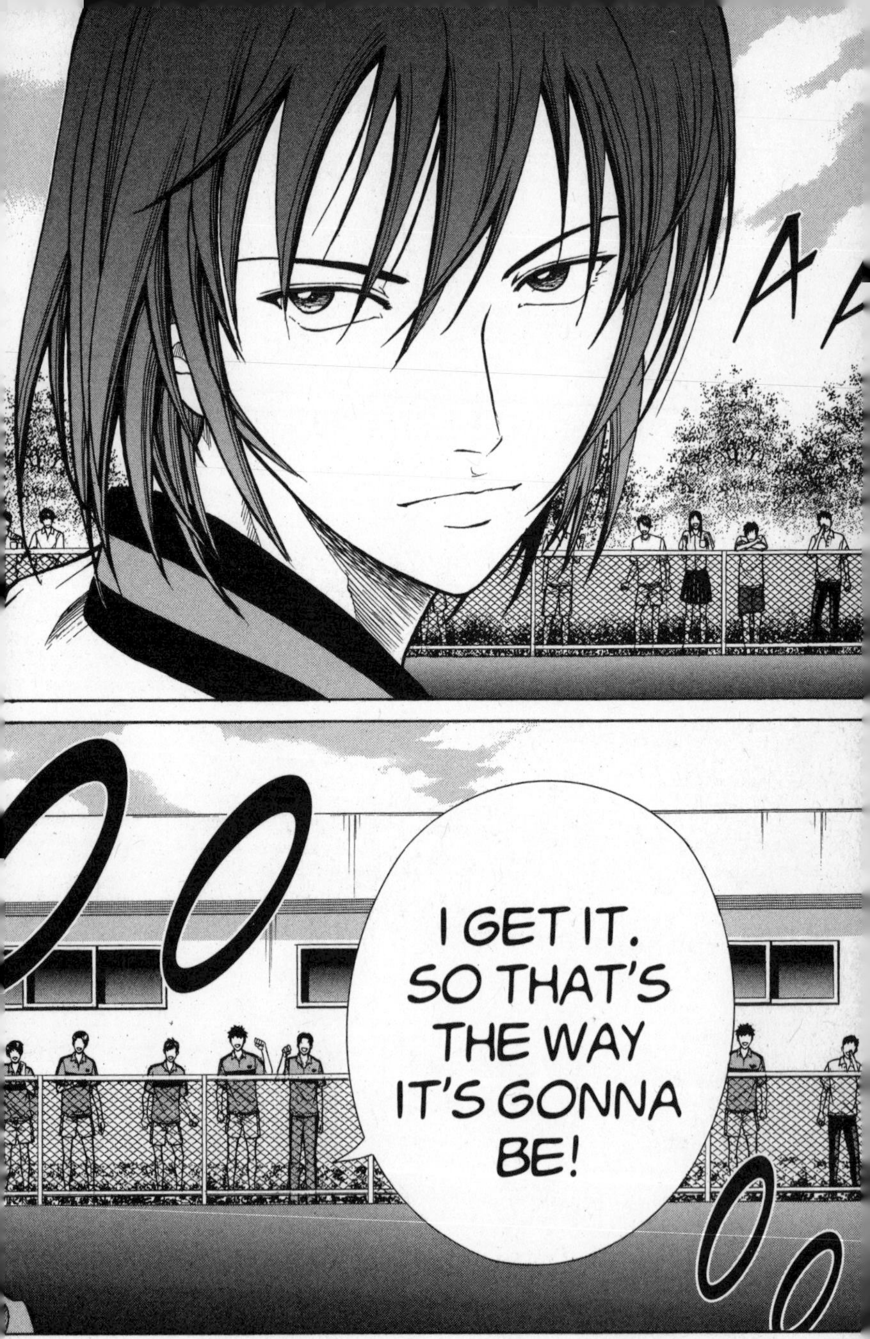
AA
I GET IT. SO THAT'S THE WAY IT'S GONNA BE!
OO
OO

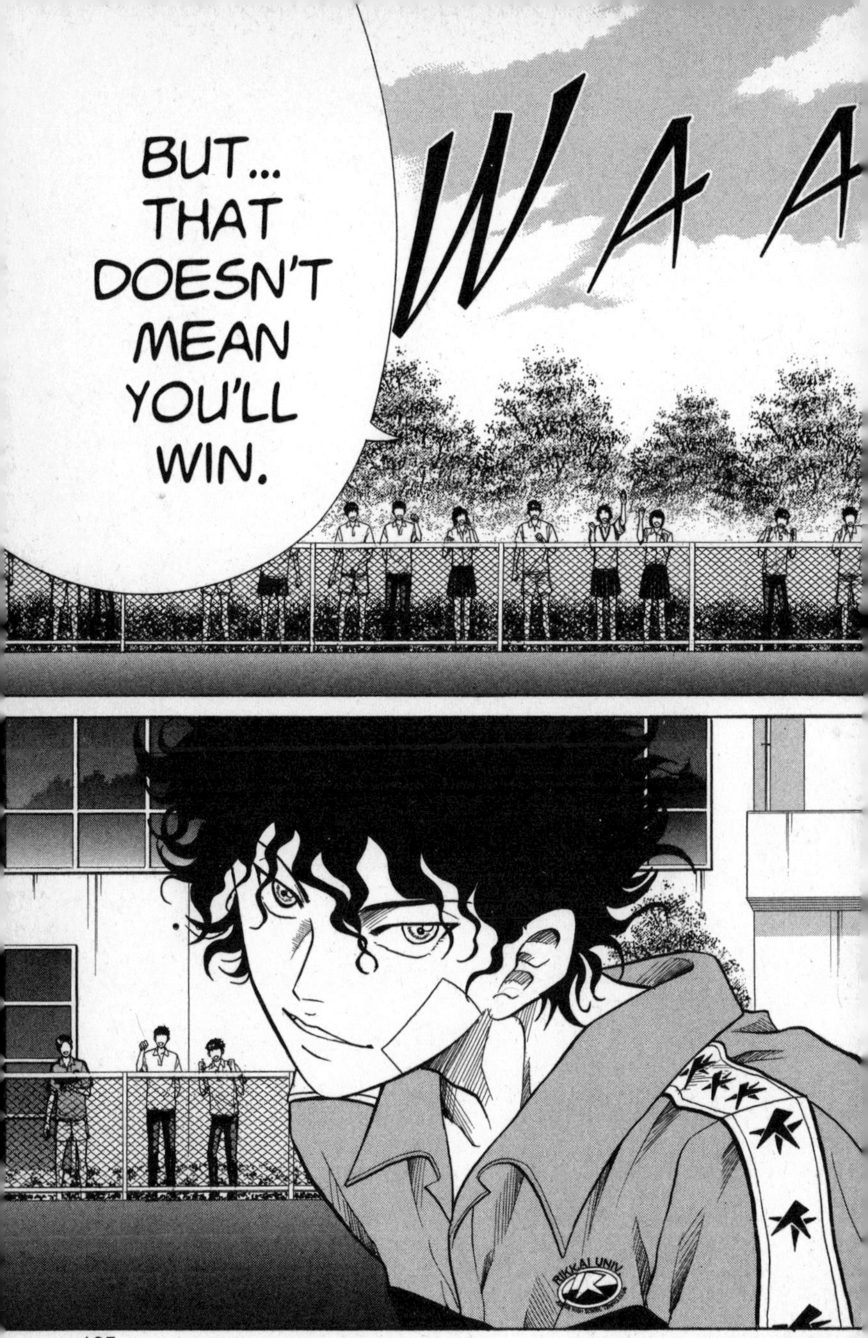
WAA
BUT... THAT DOESN'T MEAN YOU'LL WIN.
RIKKAI UNIV.

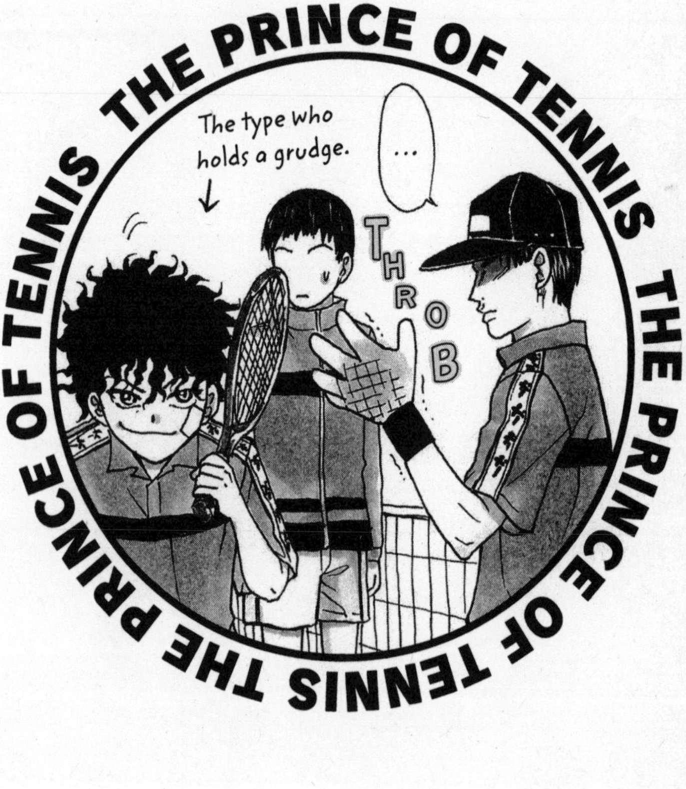

THE PRINCE OF TENNIS THE PRINCE OF TENNIS THE PRINCE OF TENNIS THE PRINCE OF TENNIS
...
THROB
The type who holds a grudge.

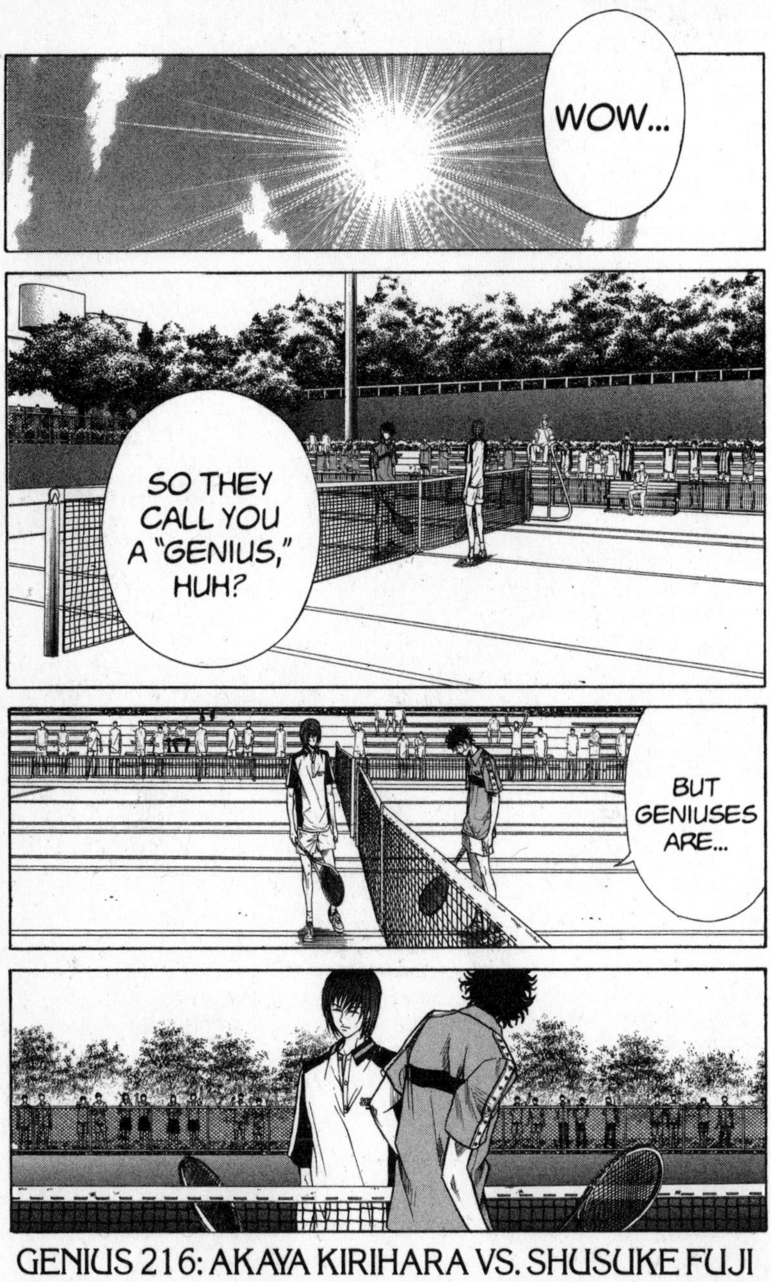
WOW...
SO THEY CALL YOU A "GENIUS," HUH?
BUT GENIUSES ARE...

GENIUS 216: AKAYA KIRIHARA VS. SHUSUKE FUJI

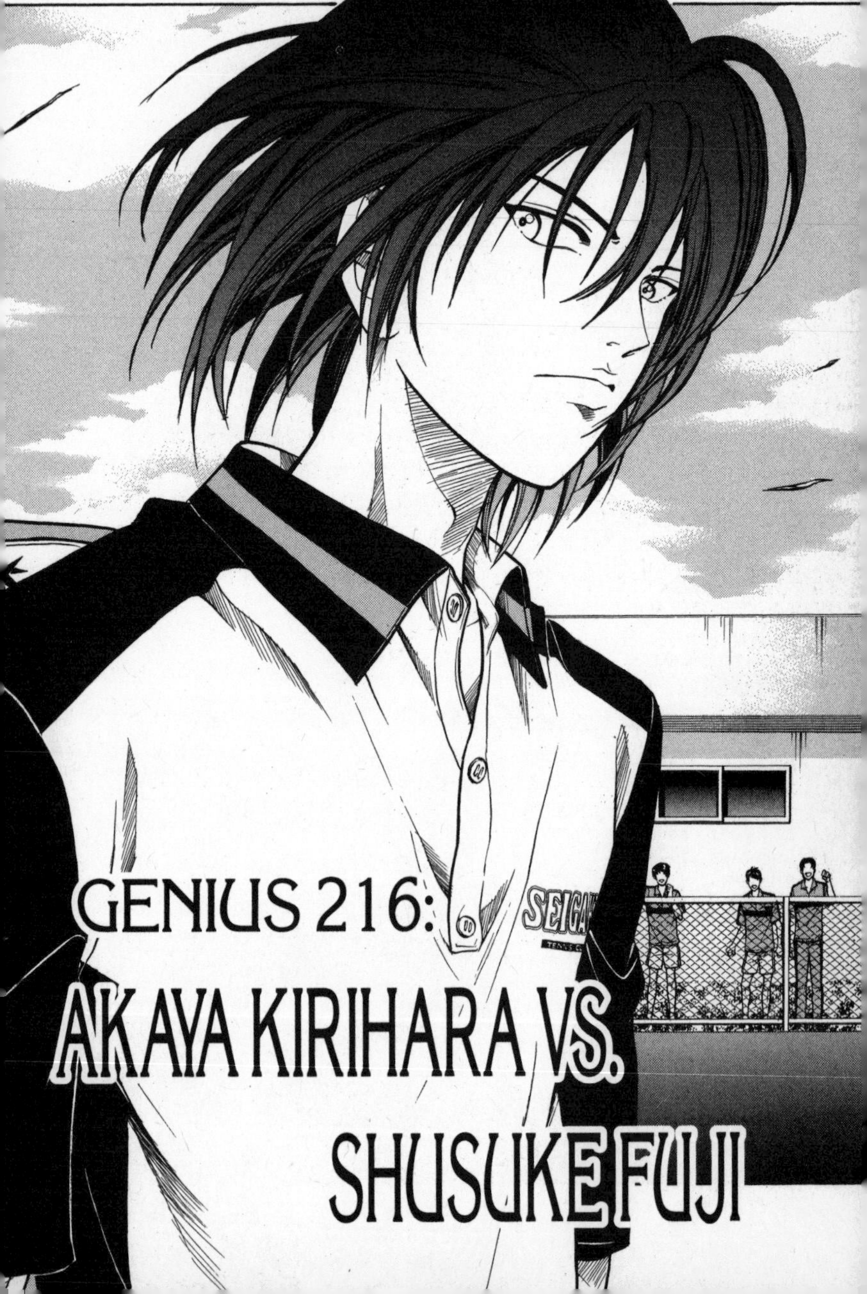

GENIUS 216:
AKAYA KIRIHARA VS. SHUSUKE FUJI

READ THIS WAY

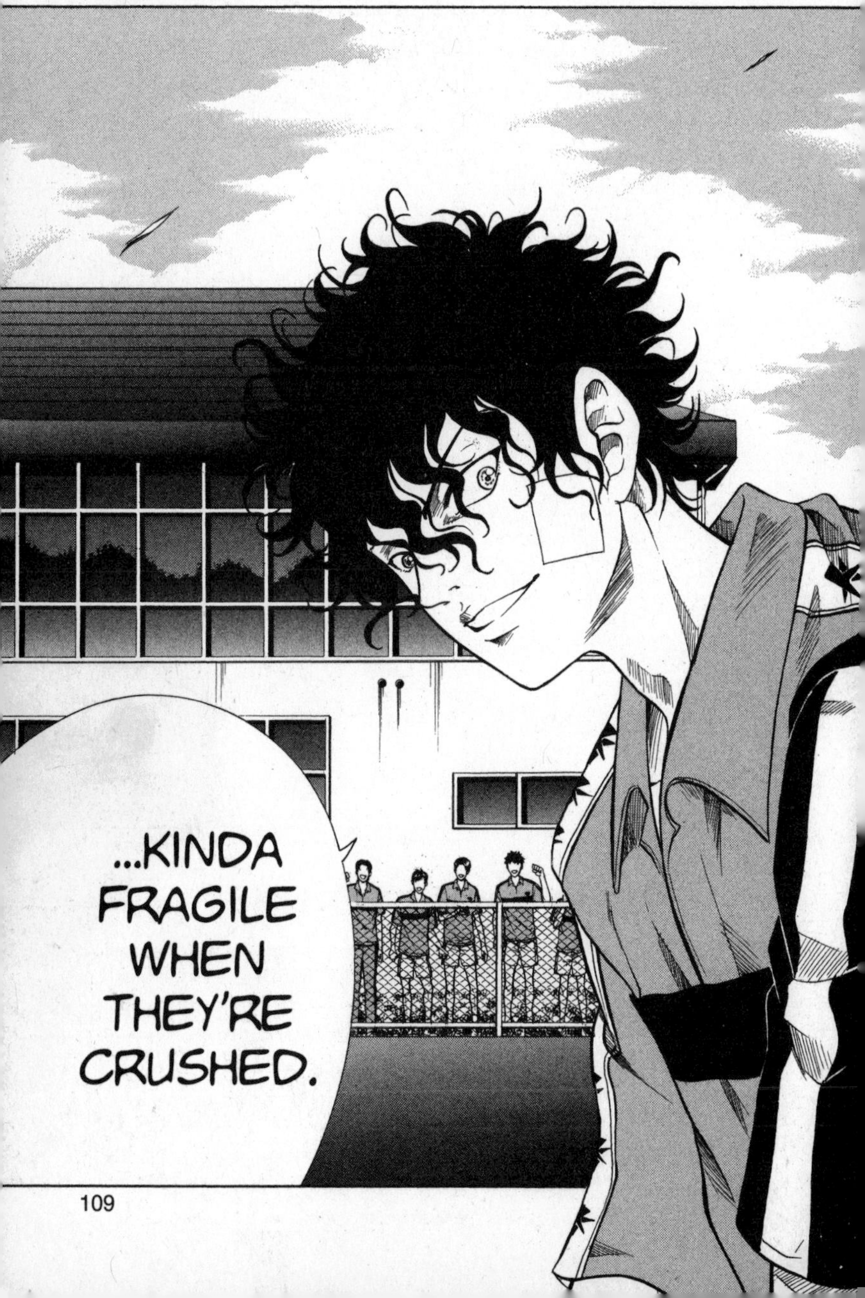
...KINDA FRAGILE WHEN THEY'RE CRUSHED.

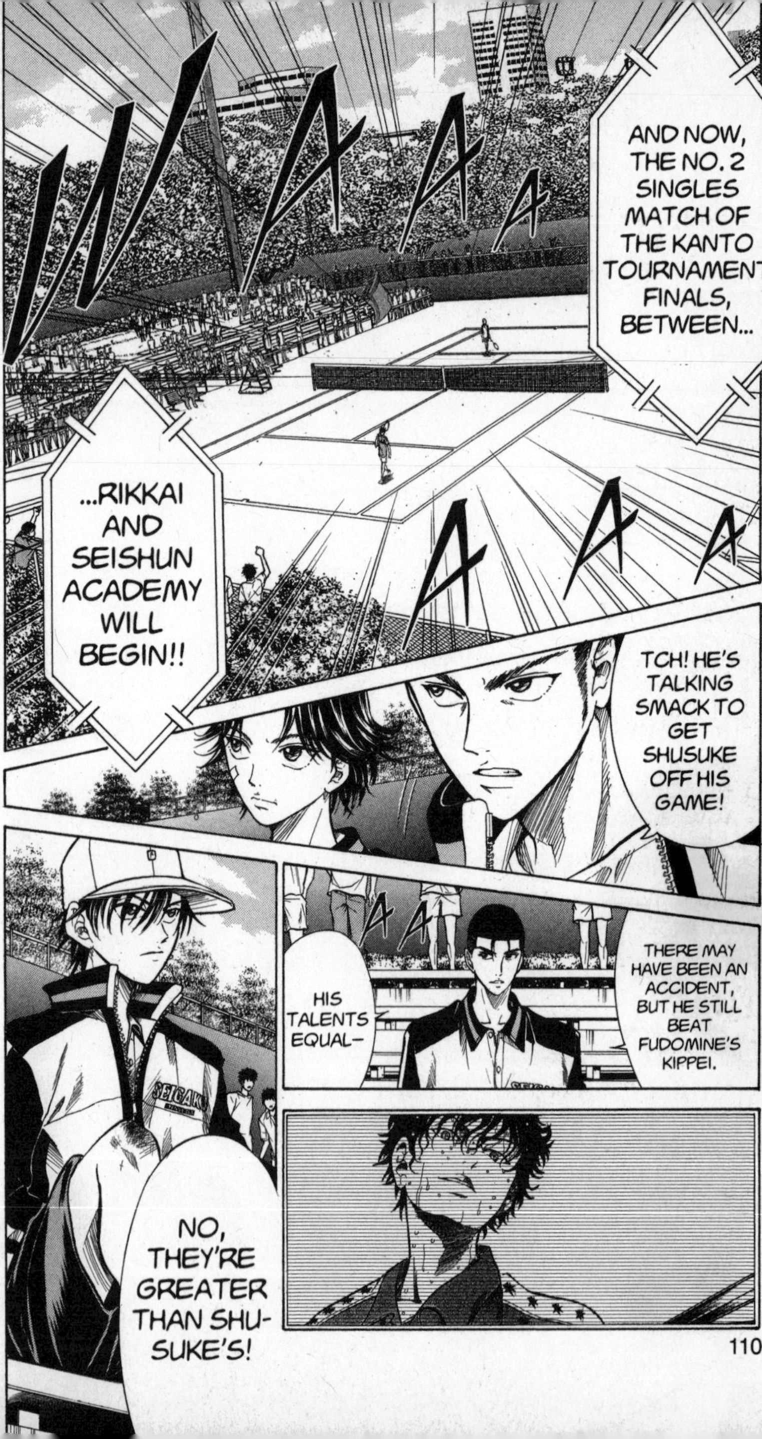
WAAAA
AND NOW, THE NO. 2 SINGLES MATCH OF THE KANTO TOURNAMENT FINALS, BETWEEN...
...RIKKAI AND SEISHUN ACADEMY WILL BEGIN!!
AAA
TCH! HE'S TALKING SMACK TO GET SHUSUKE OFF HIS GAME!
AA
THERE MAY HAVE BEEN AN ACCIDENT, BUT HE STILL BEAT FUDOMINE'S KIPPEI.
HIS TALENTS EQUAL—
NO, THEY'RE GREATER THAN SHU-SUKE'S!

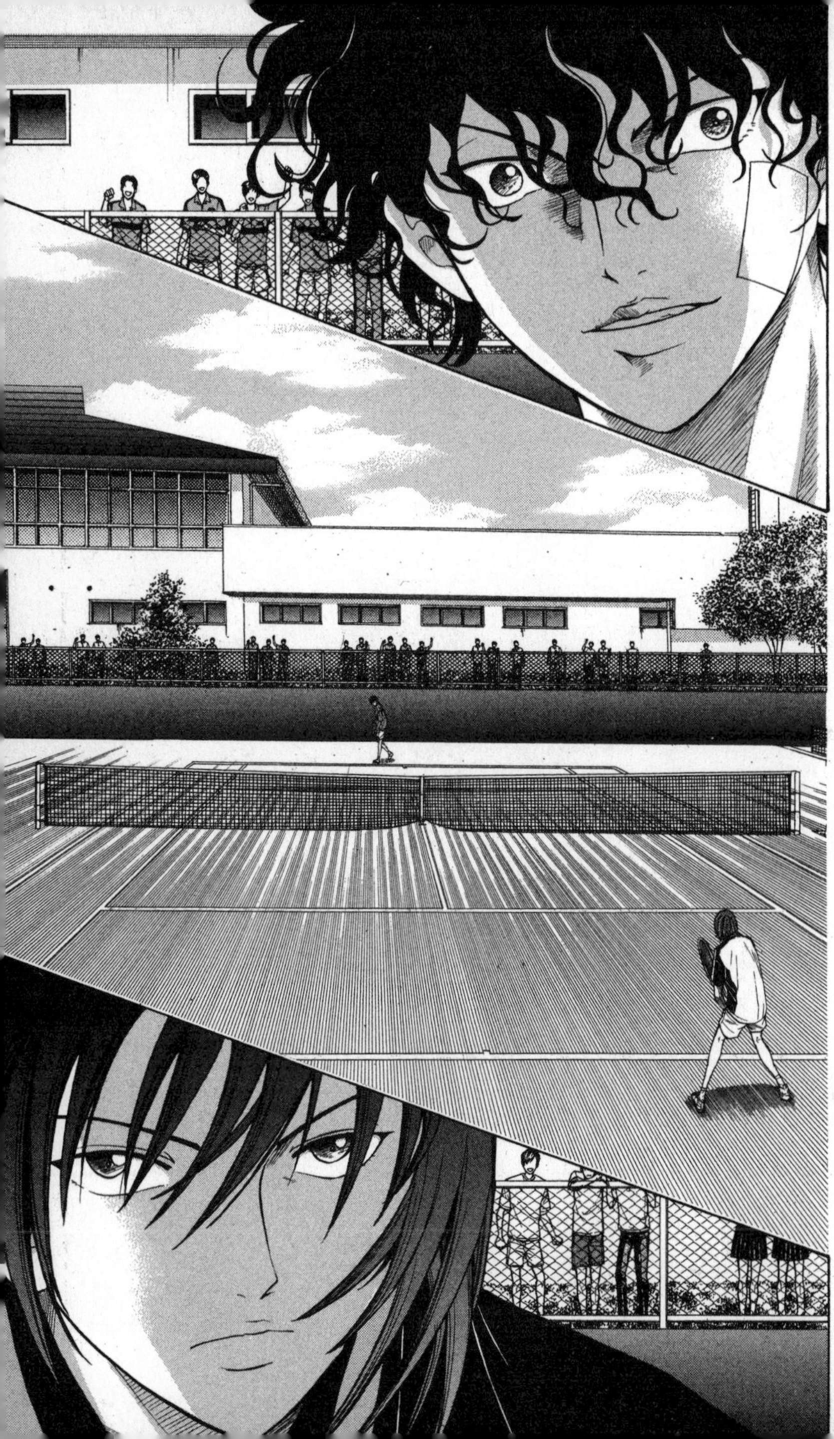

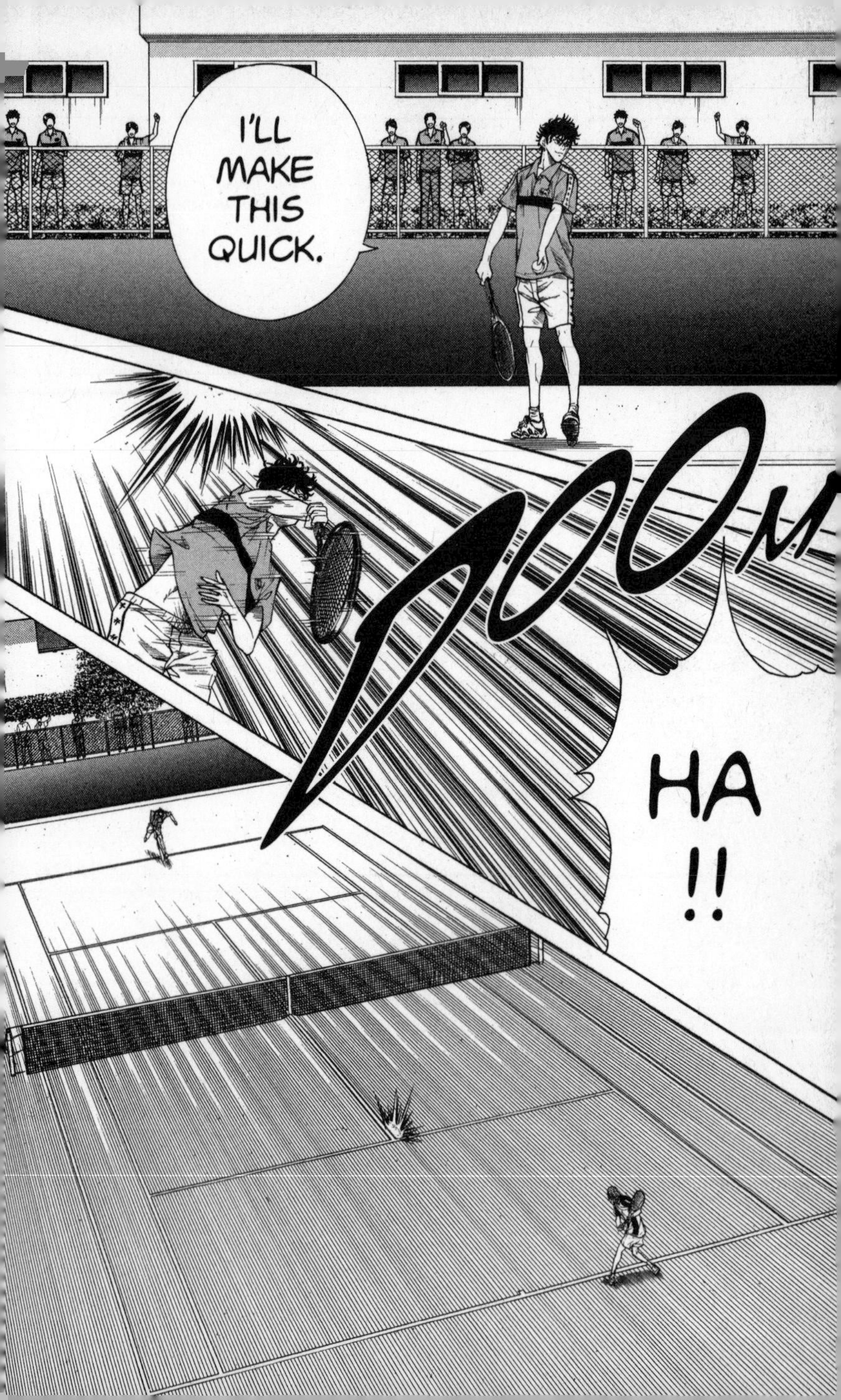
I'LL MAKE THIS QUICK.
ZOOM
HA !!

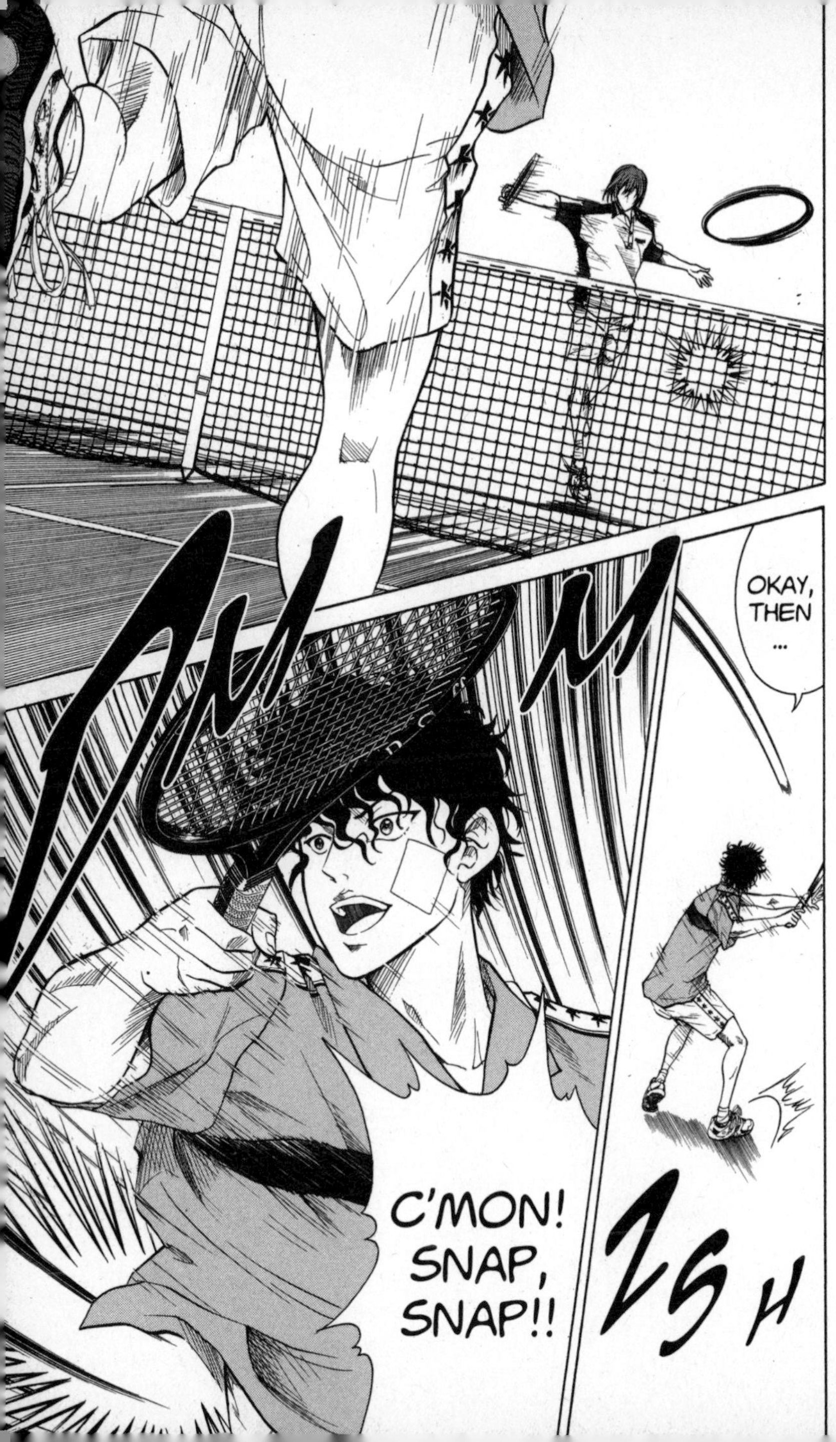
OKAY, THEN ...
C'MON! SNAP, SNAP!!

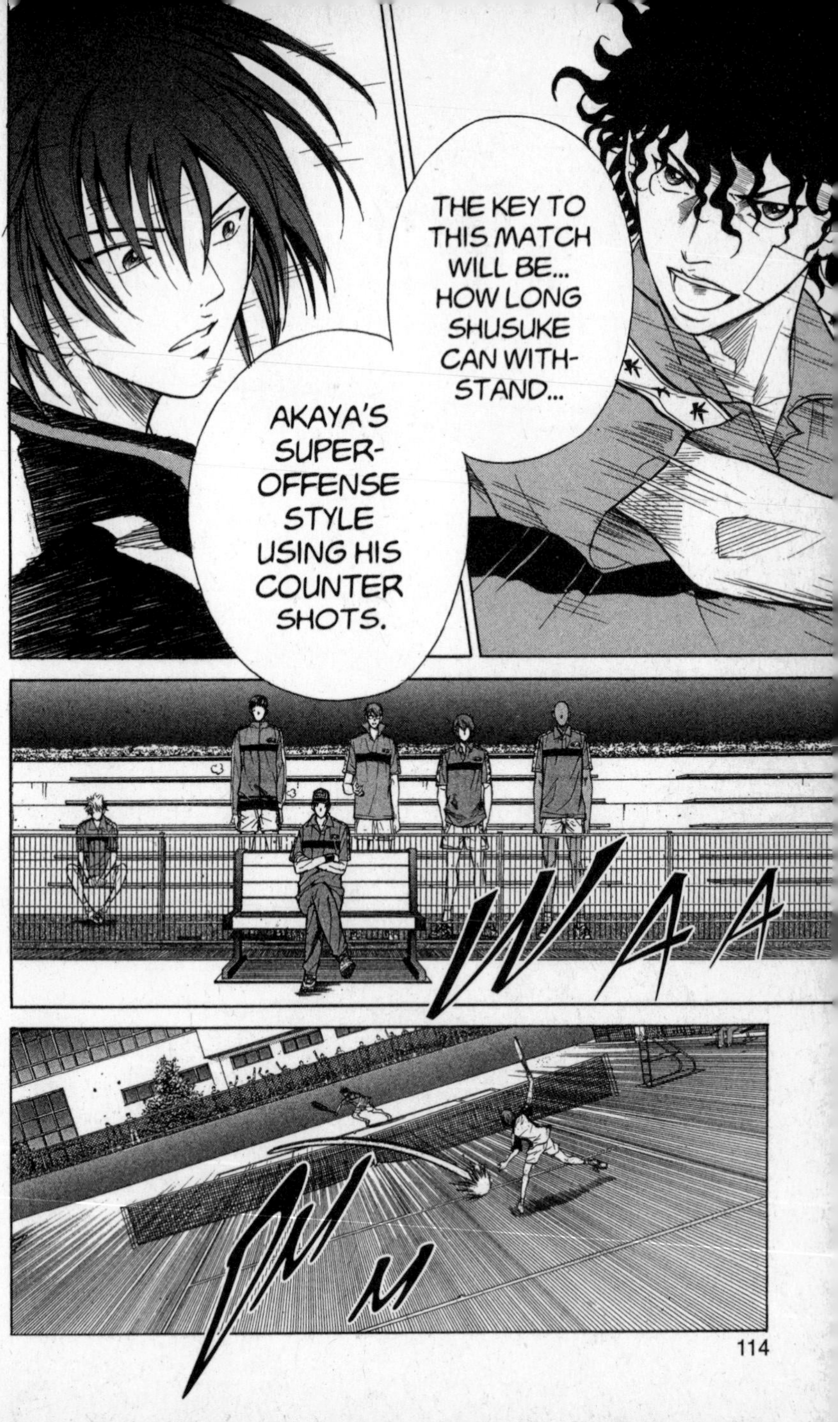
THE KEY TO THIS MATCH WILL BE... HOW LONG SHUSUKE CAN WITH-STAND...
AKAYA'S SUPER-OFFENSE STYLE USING HIS COUNTER SHOTS.
WAA
MM

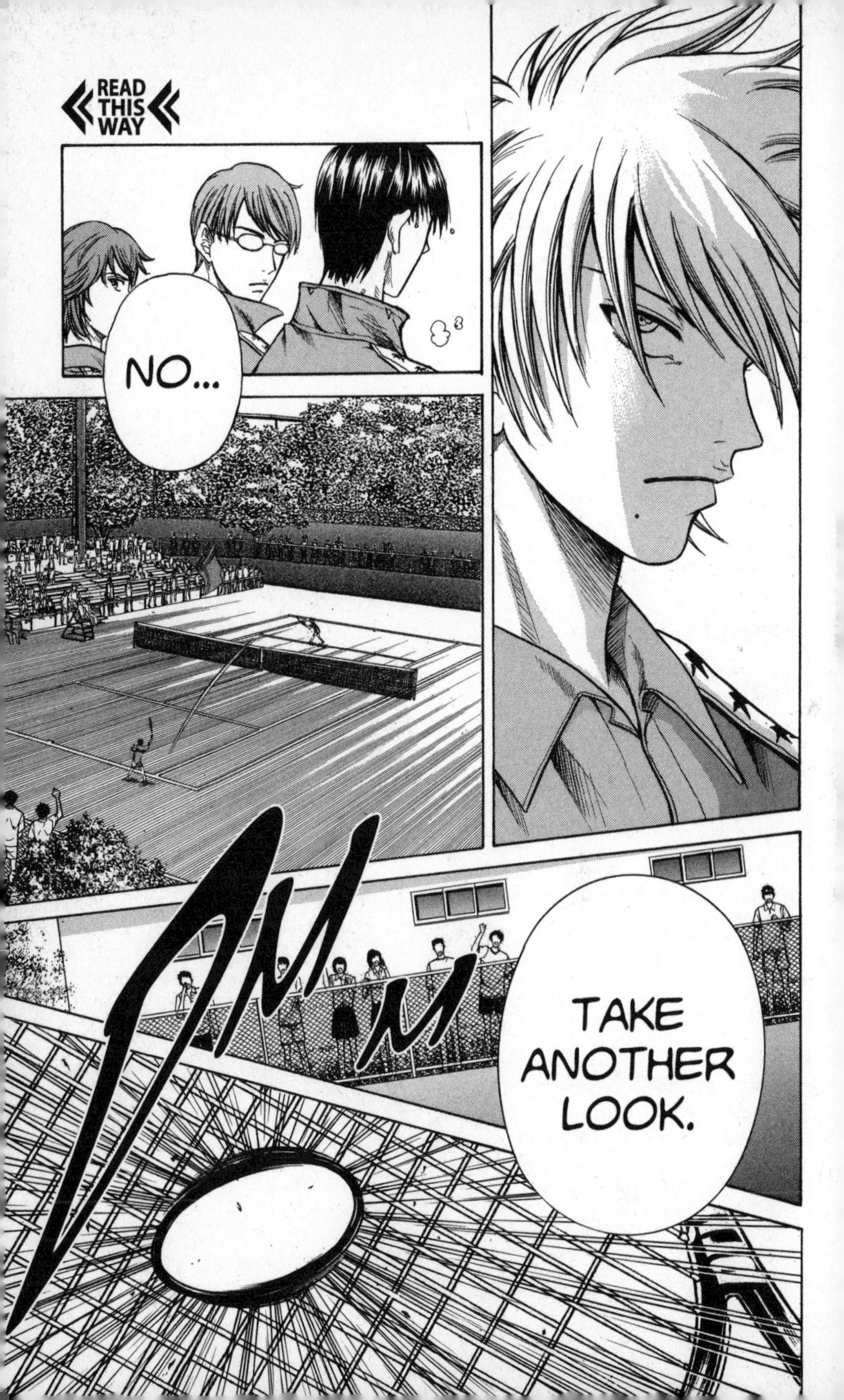
READ THIS WAY
NO...
TAKE ANOTHER LOOK.

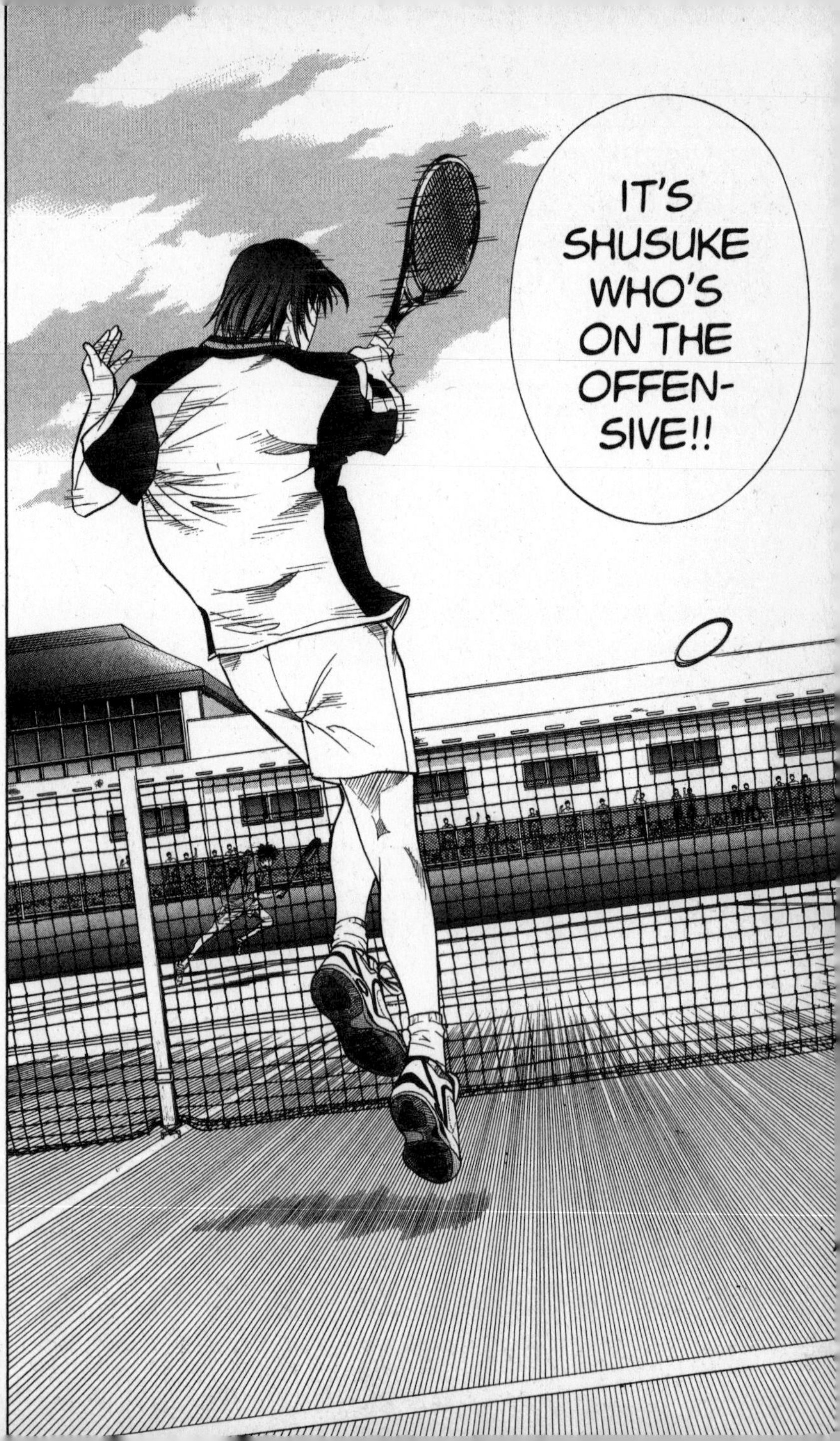
IT'S SHUSUKE WHO'S ON THE OFFEN-SIVE!!

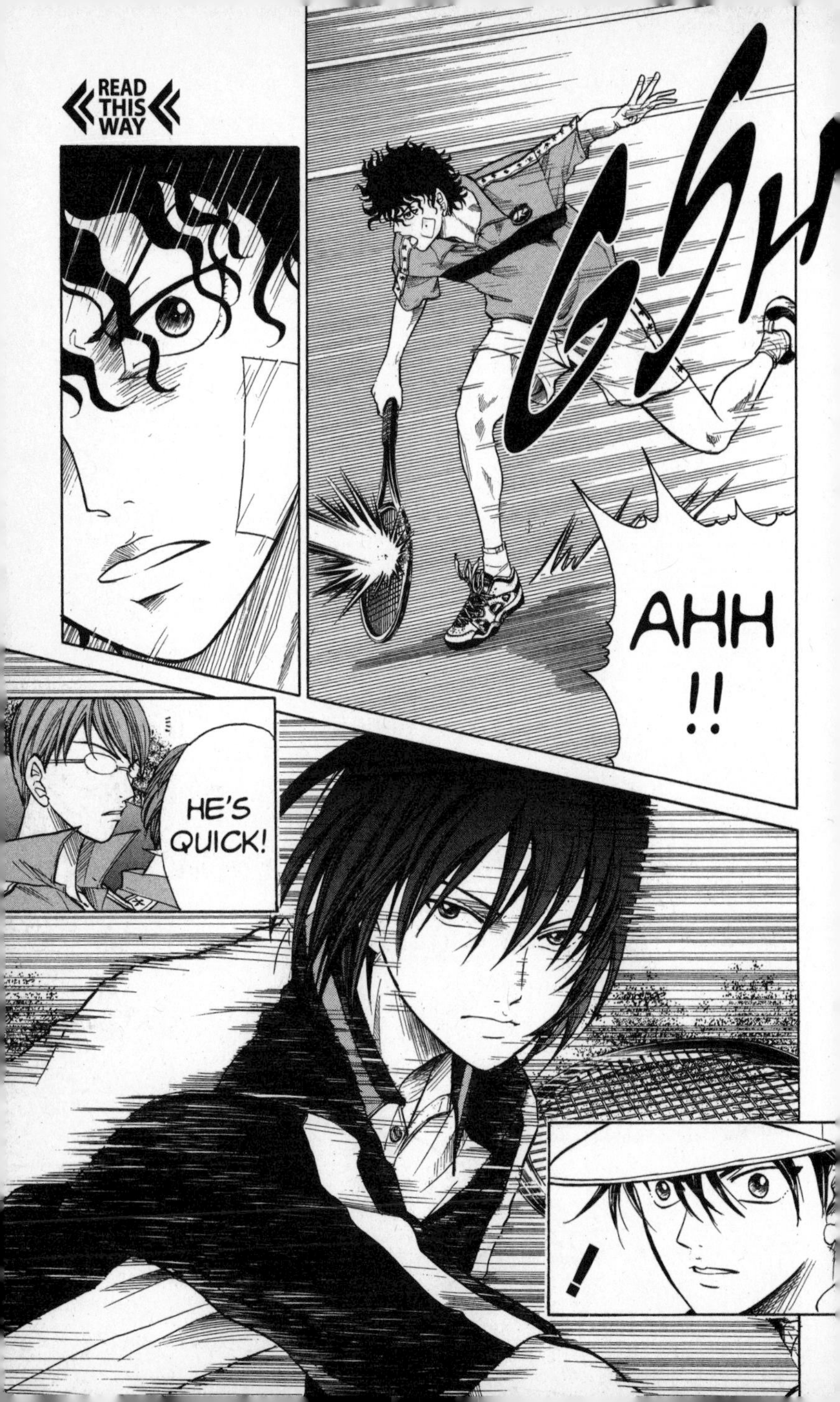
READ THIS WAY
GSSH
AHH !!
HE'S QUICK!
!

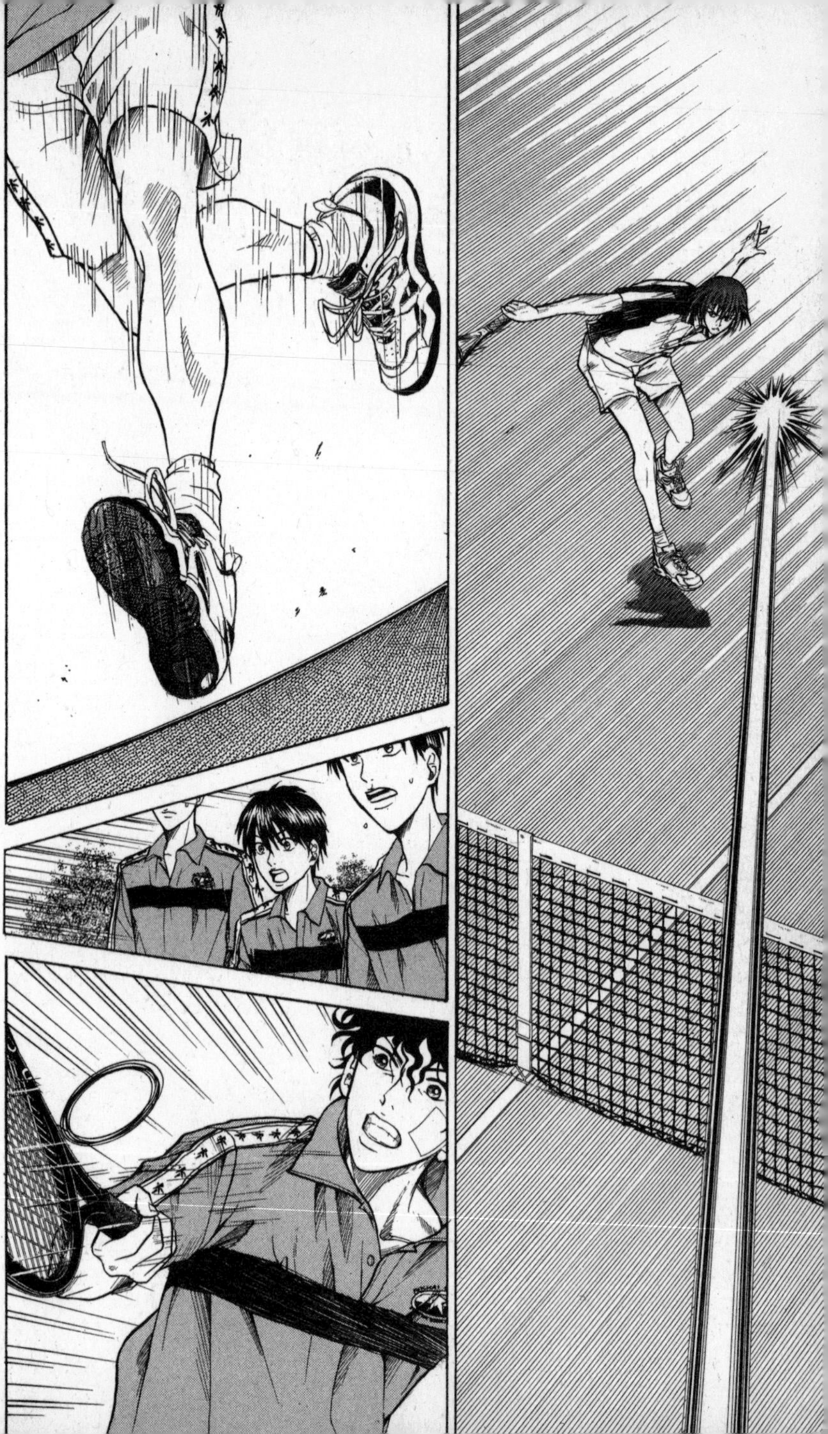

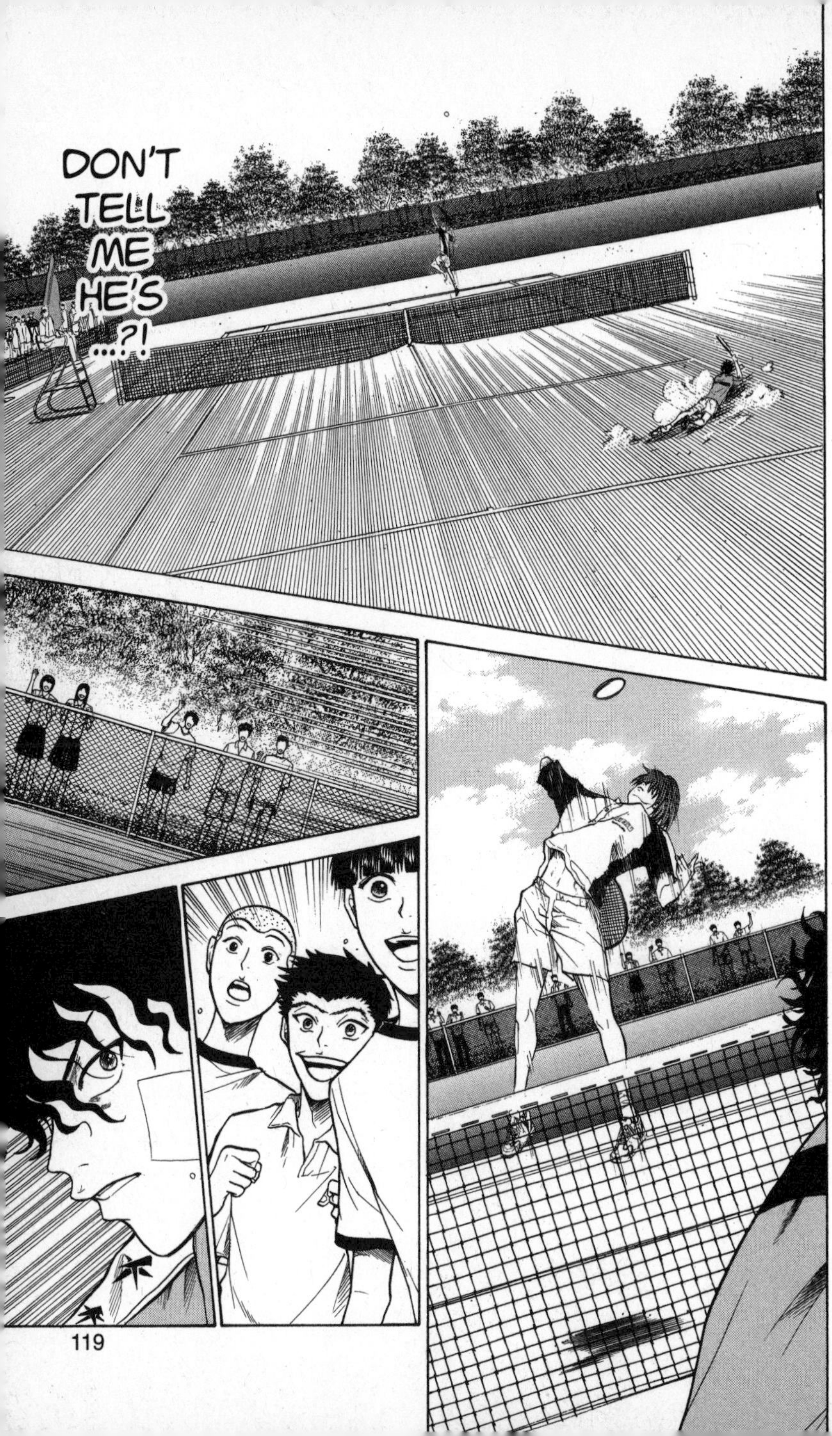
DON'T TELL ME HE'S ...?!

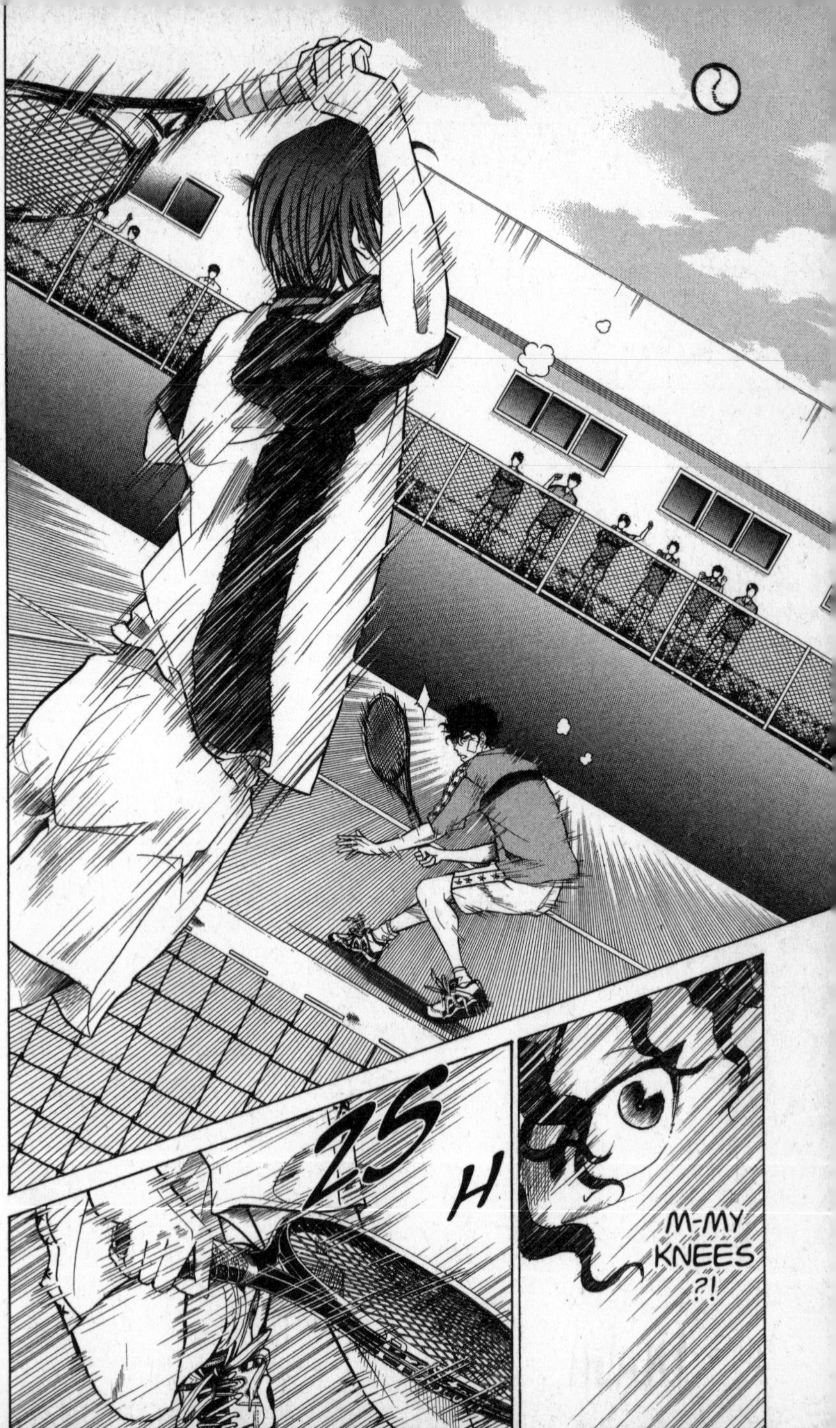
ZSH
M-MY KNEES ?!

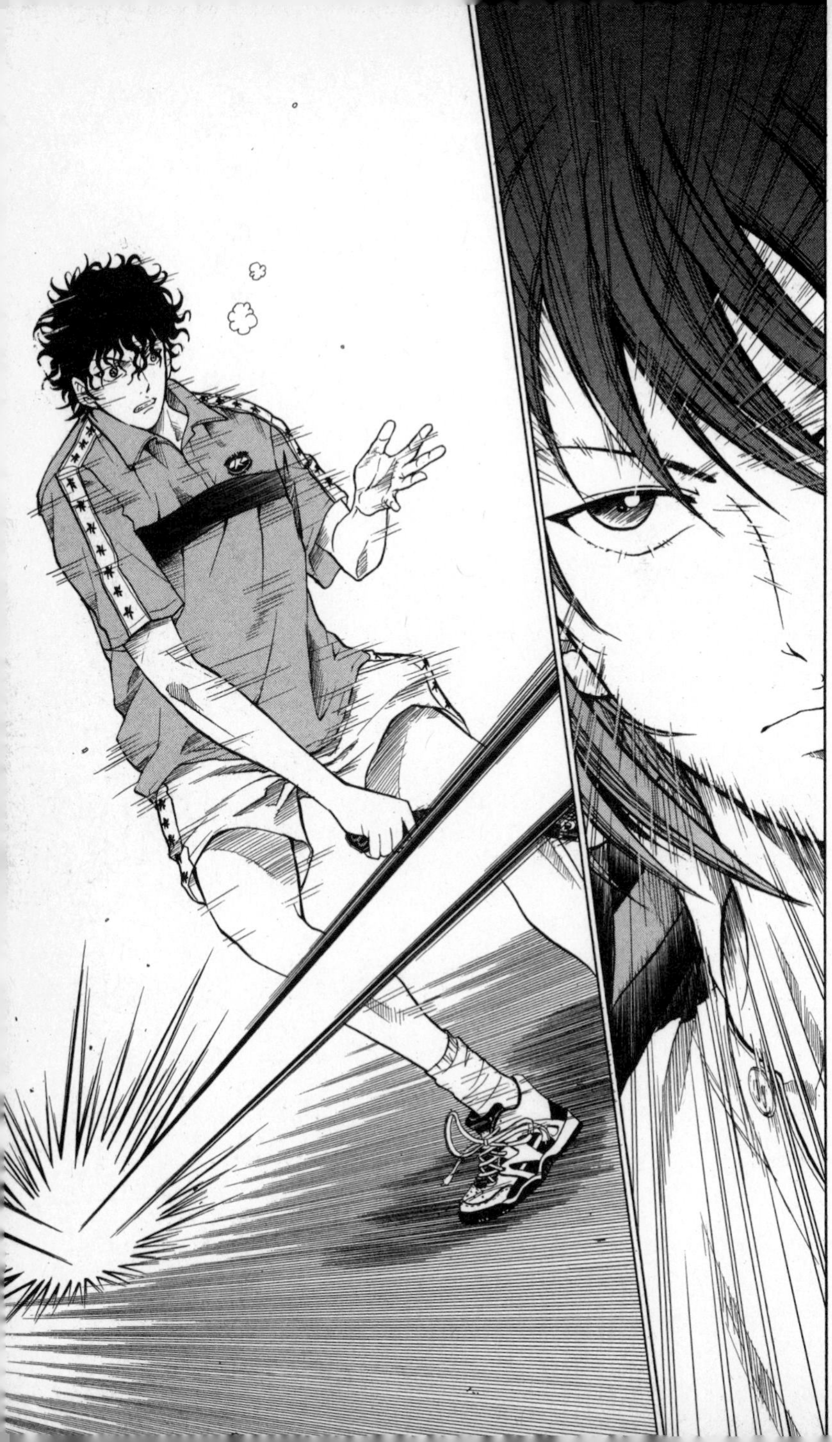

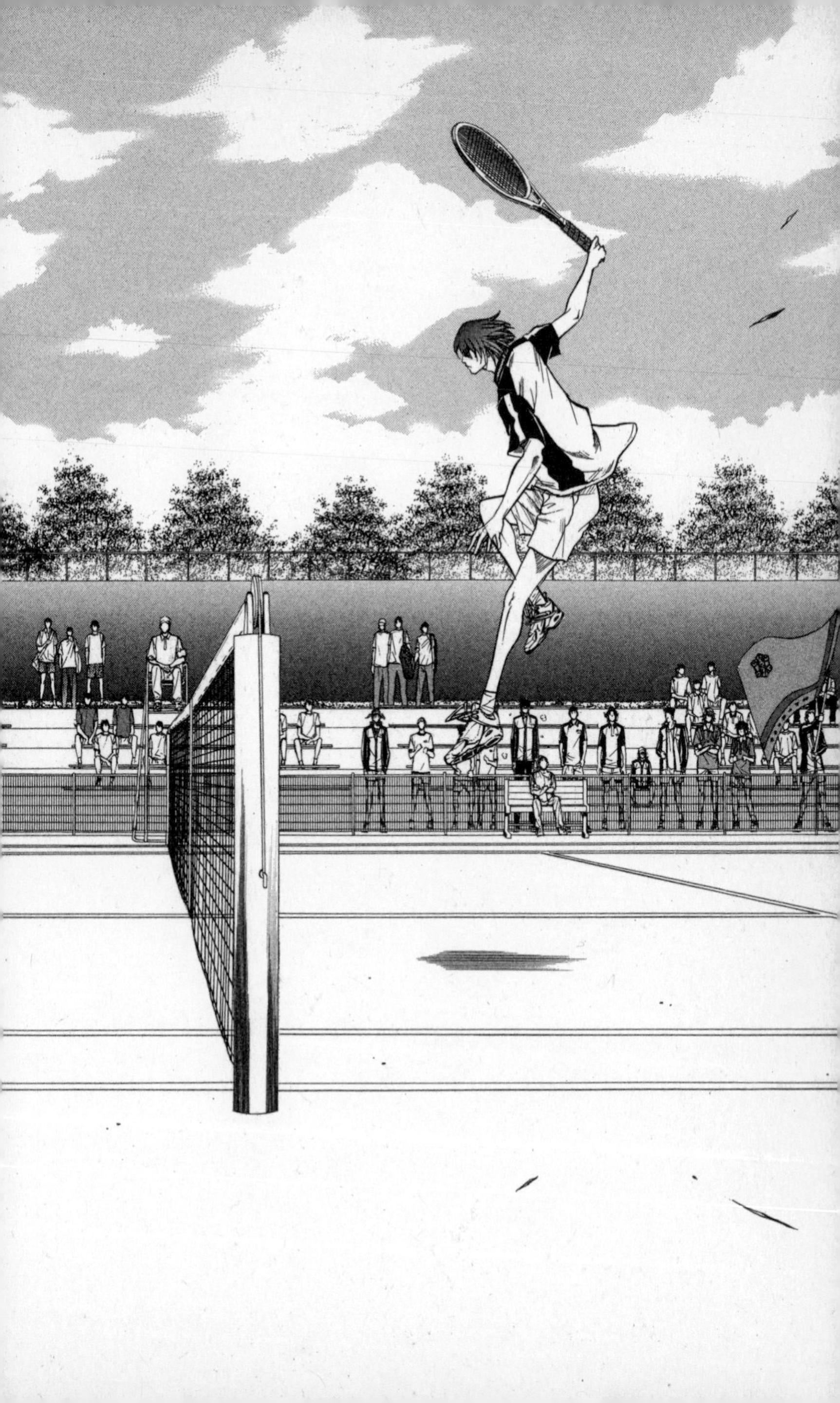

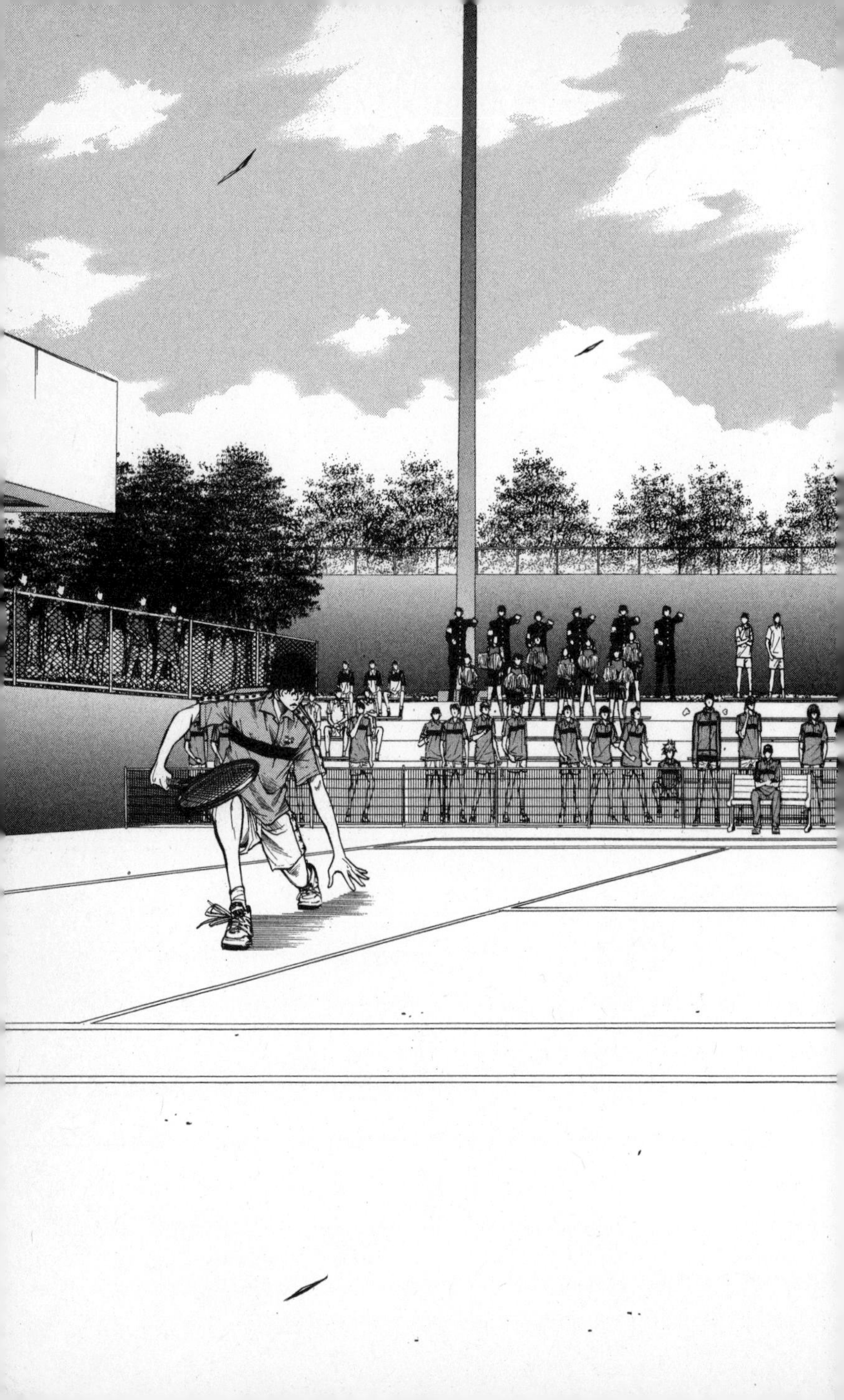

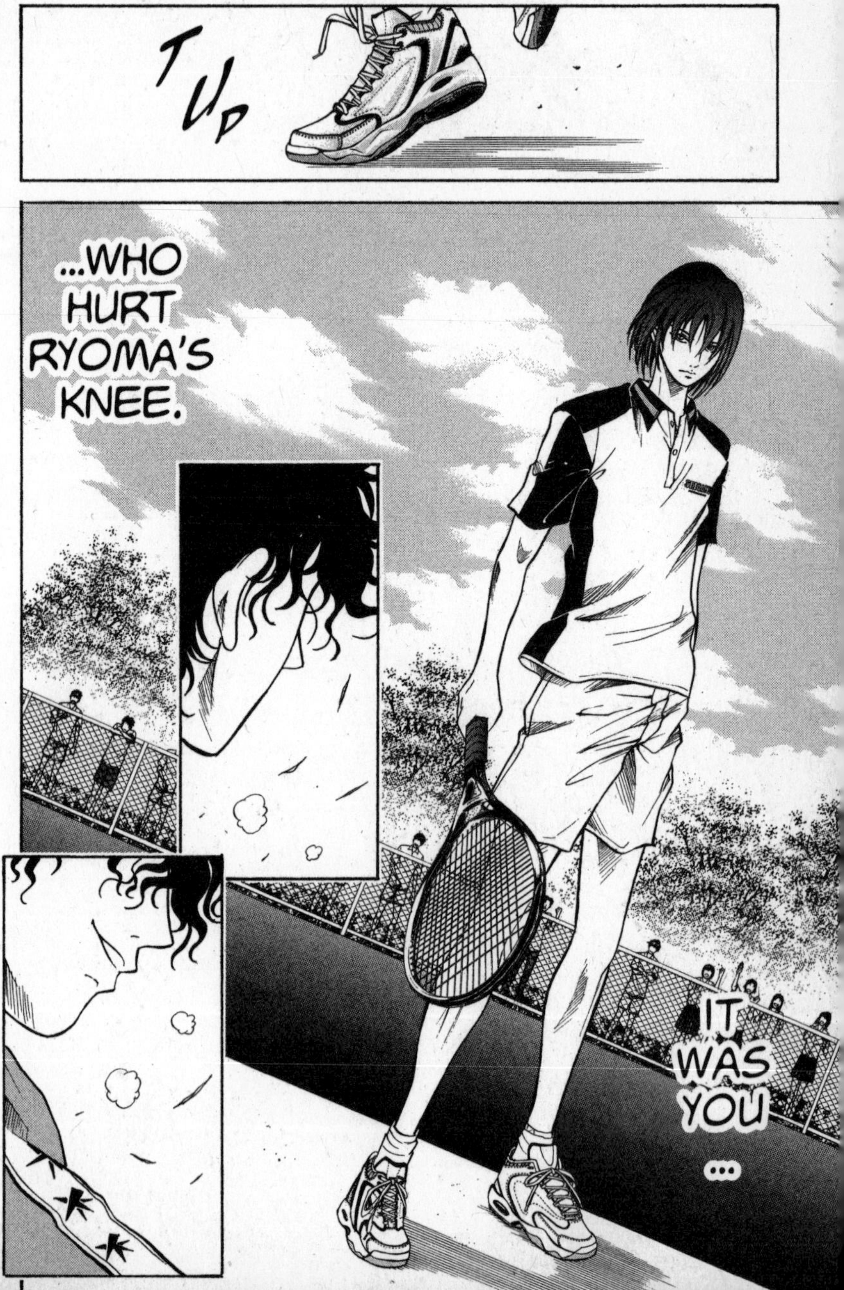
TUP
IT WAS YOU ...
...WHO HURT RYOMA'S KNEE.

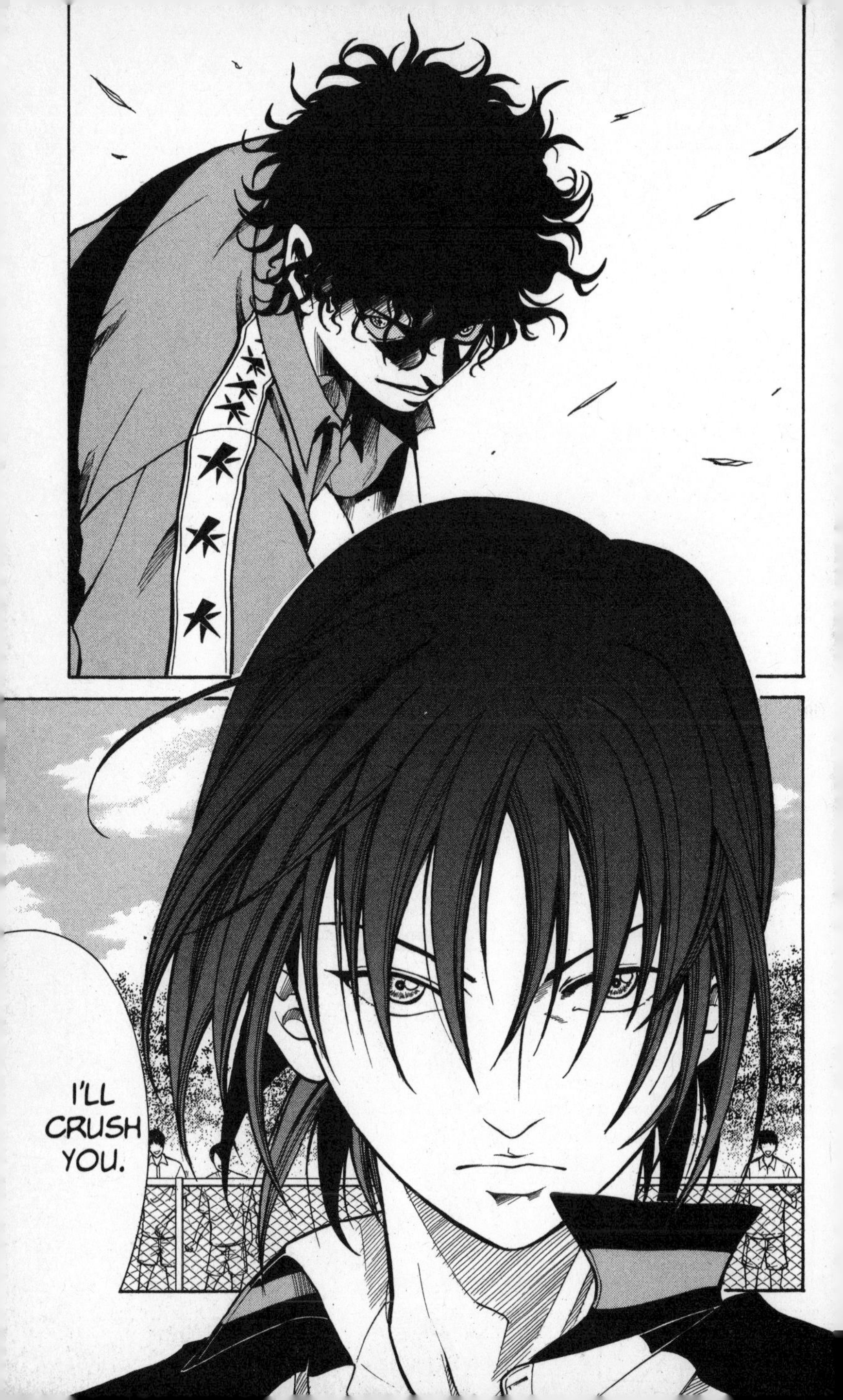
I'LL CRUSH YOU.

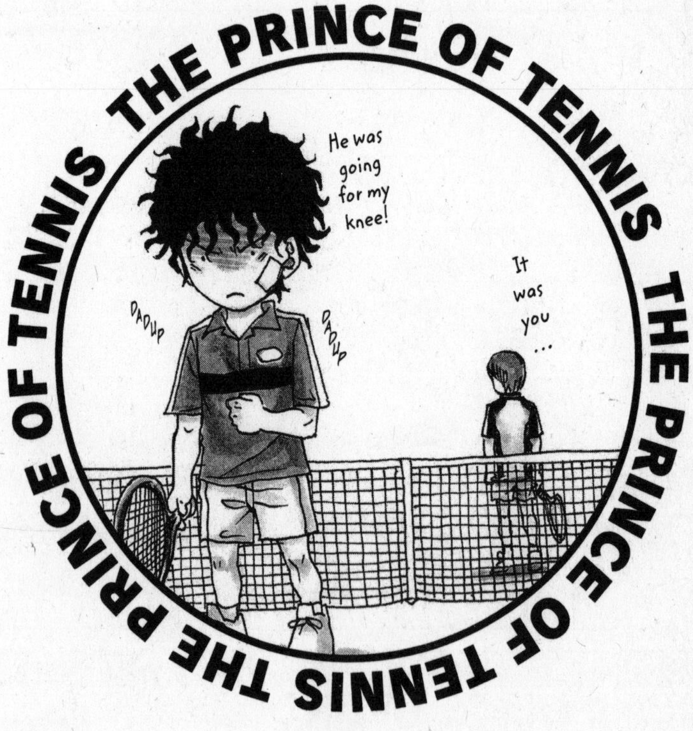
THE PRINCE OF TENNIS THE PRINCE OF TENNIS THE PRINCE OF TENNIS
He was going for my knee!
It was you ...
DADUP
DADUP

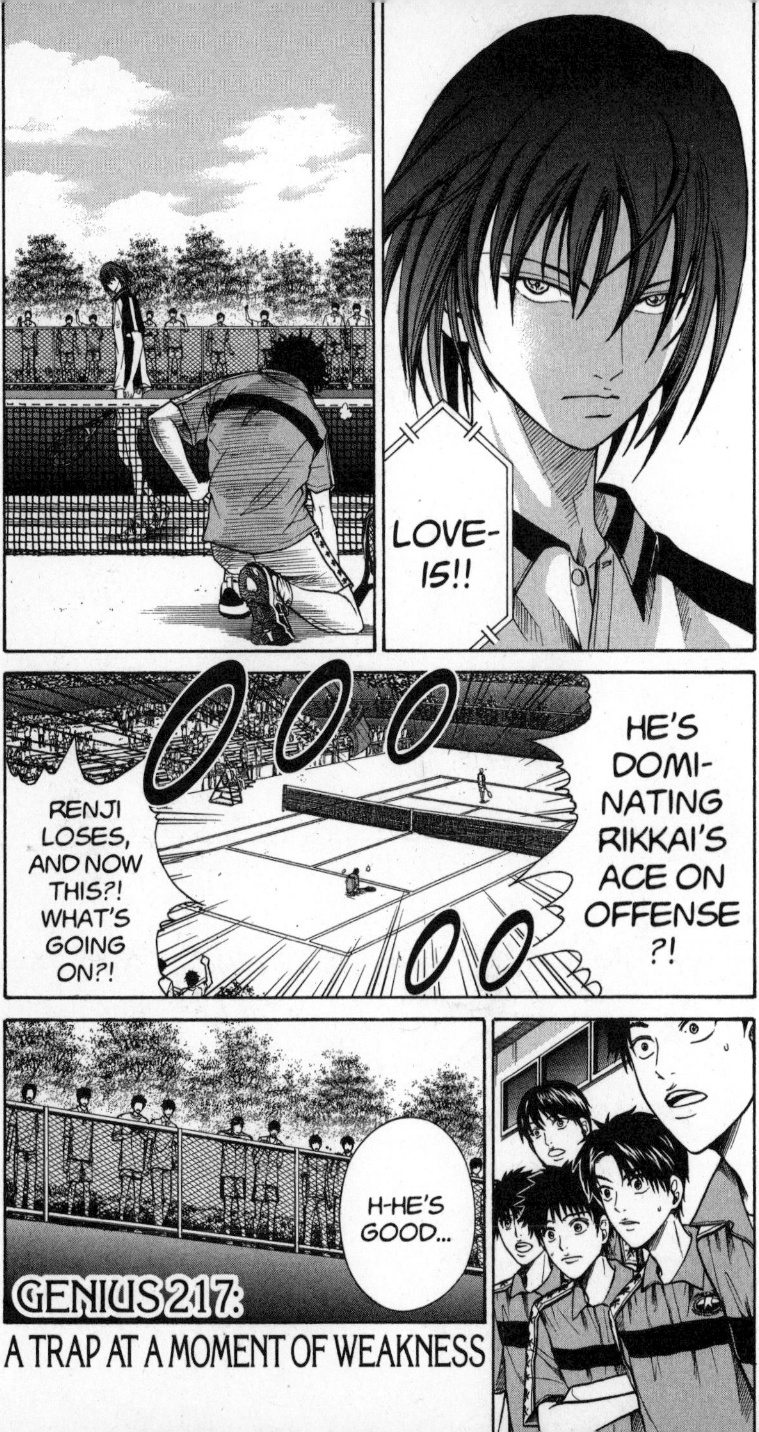
LOVE-15!!
HE'S DOMINATING RIKKAI'S ACE ON OFFENSE?!
RENJI LOSES, AND NOW THIS?! WHAT'S GOING ON?!
H-HE'S GOOD...

GENIUS 217: A TRAP AT A MOMENT OF WEAKNESS

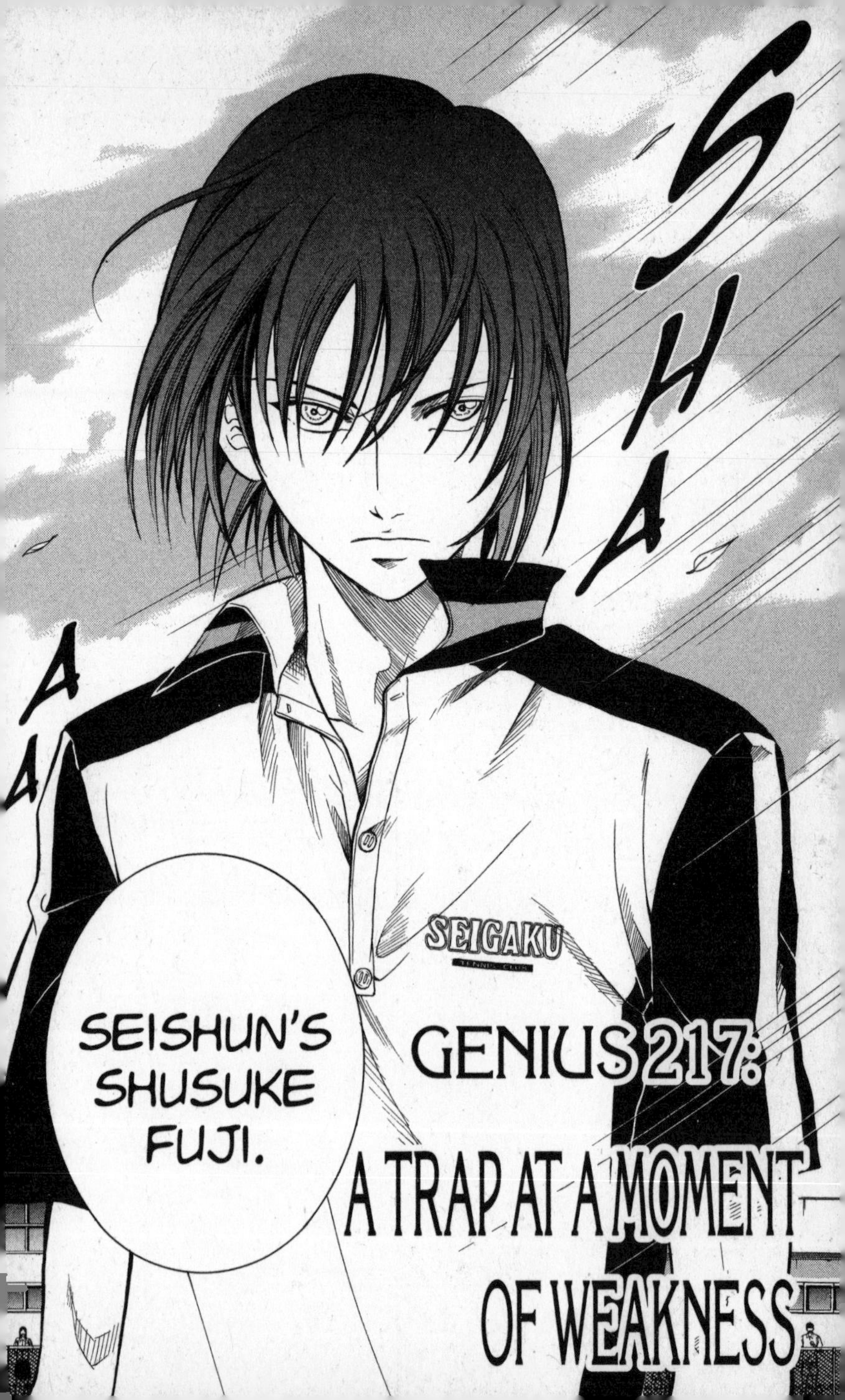
SHAAA
SEIGAKU
SEISHUN'S SHUSUKE FUJI.
GENIUS 217:
A TRAP AT A MOMENT OF WEAKNESS

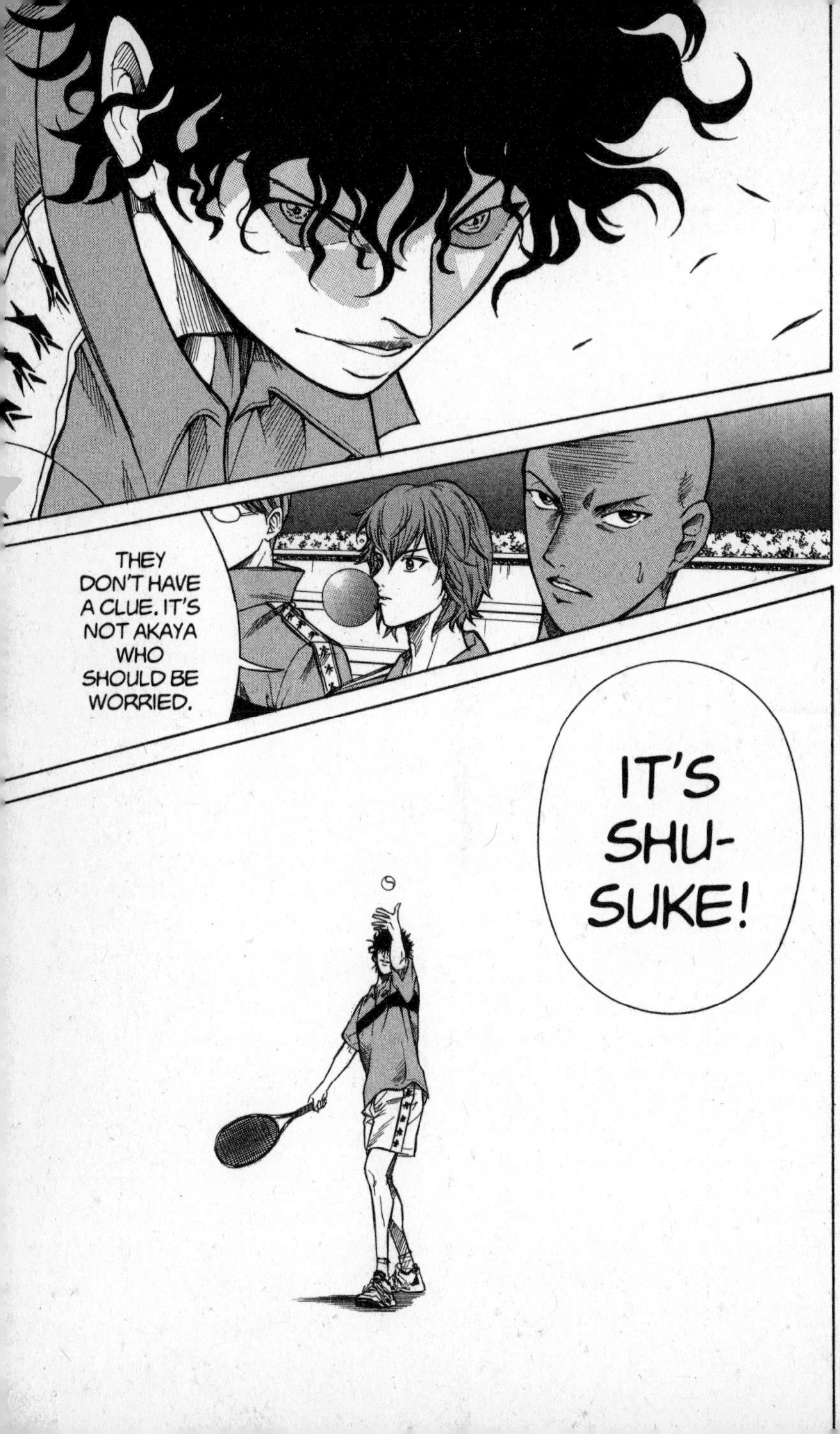
THEY DON'T HAVE A CLUE. IT'S NOT AKAYA WHO SHOULD BE WORRIED.
IT'S SHU-SUKE!

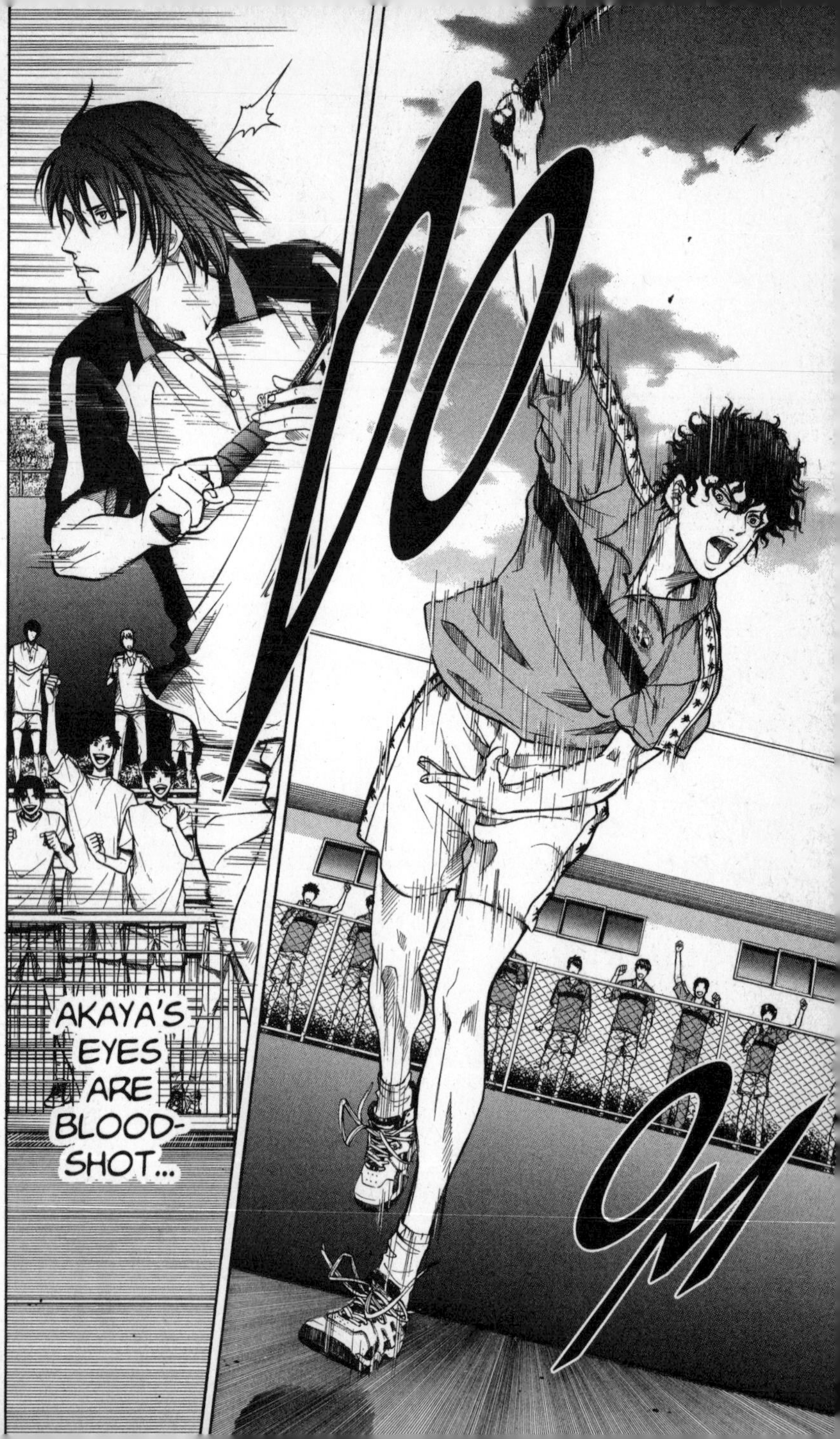
AKAYA'S EYES ARE BLOOD-SHOT...

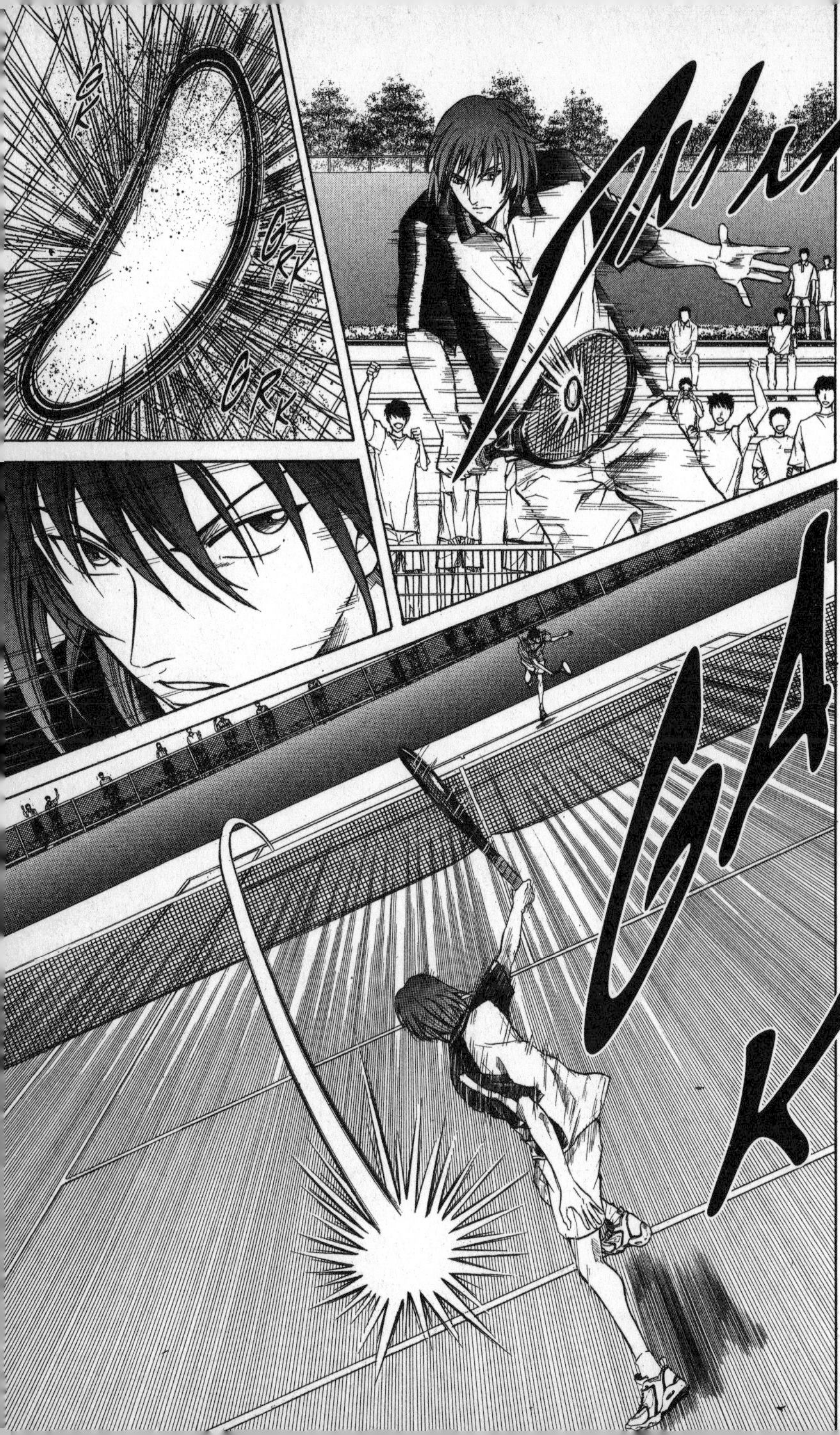
GRK
GRK
GAK

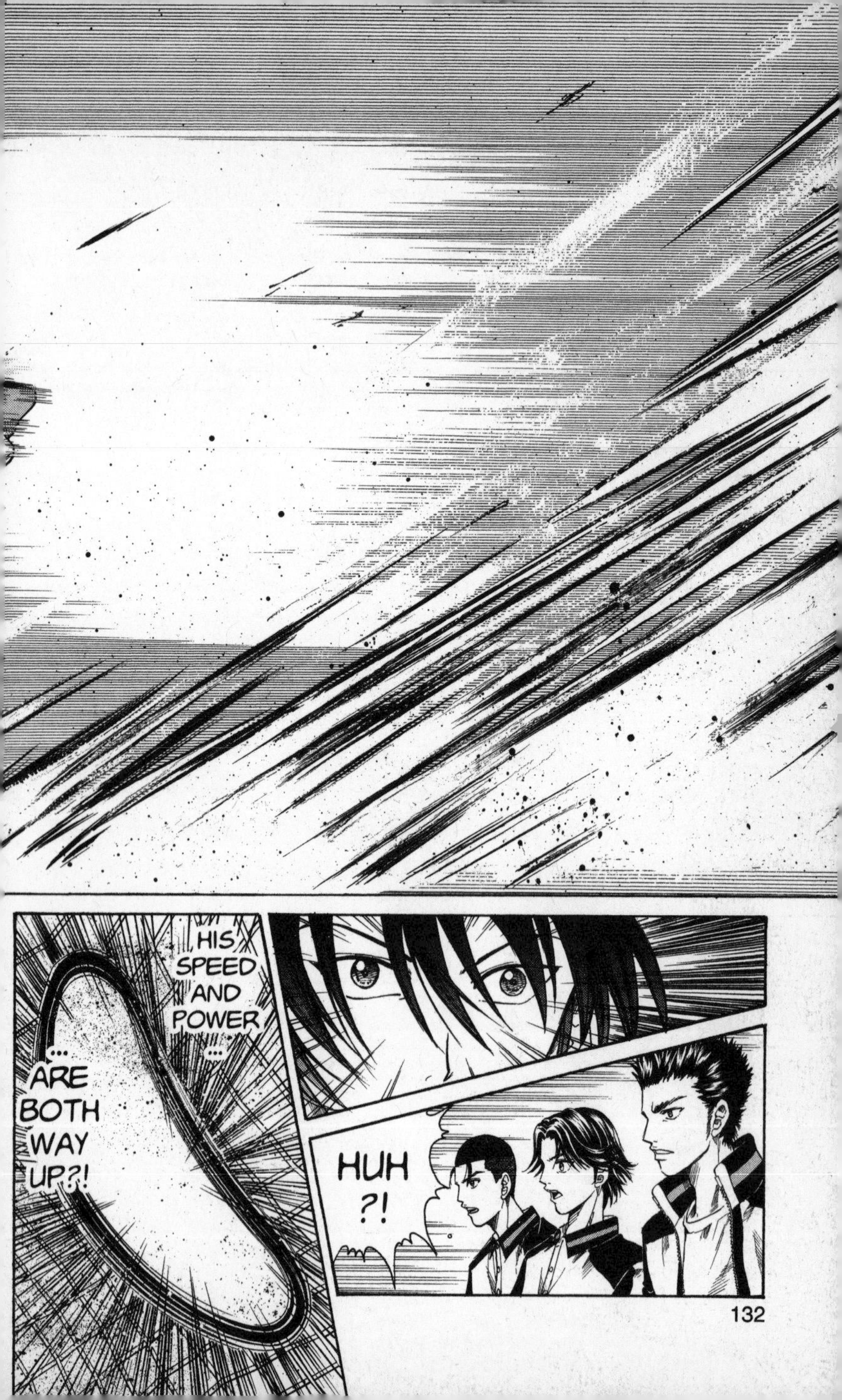
HIS SPEED AND POWER ...
... ARE BOTH WAY UP?!
HUH ?!

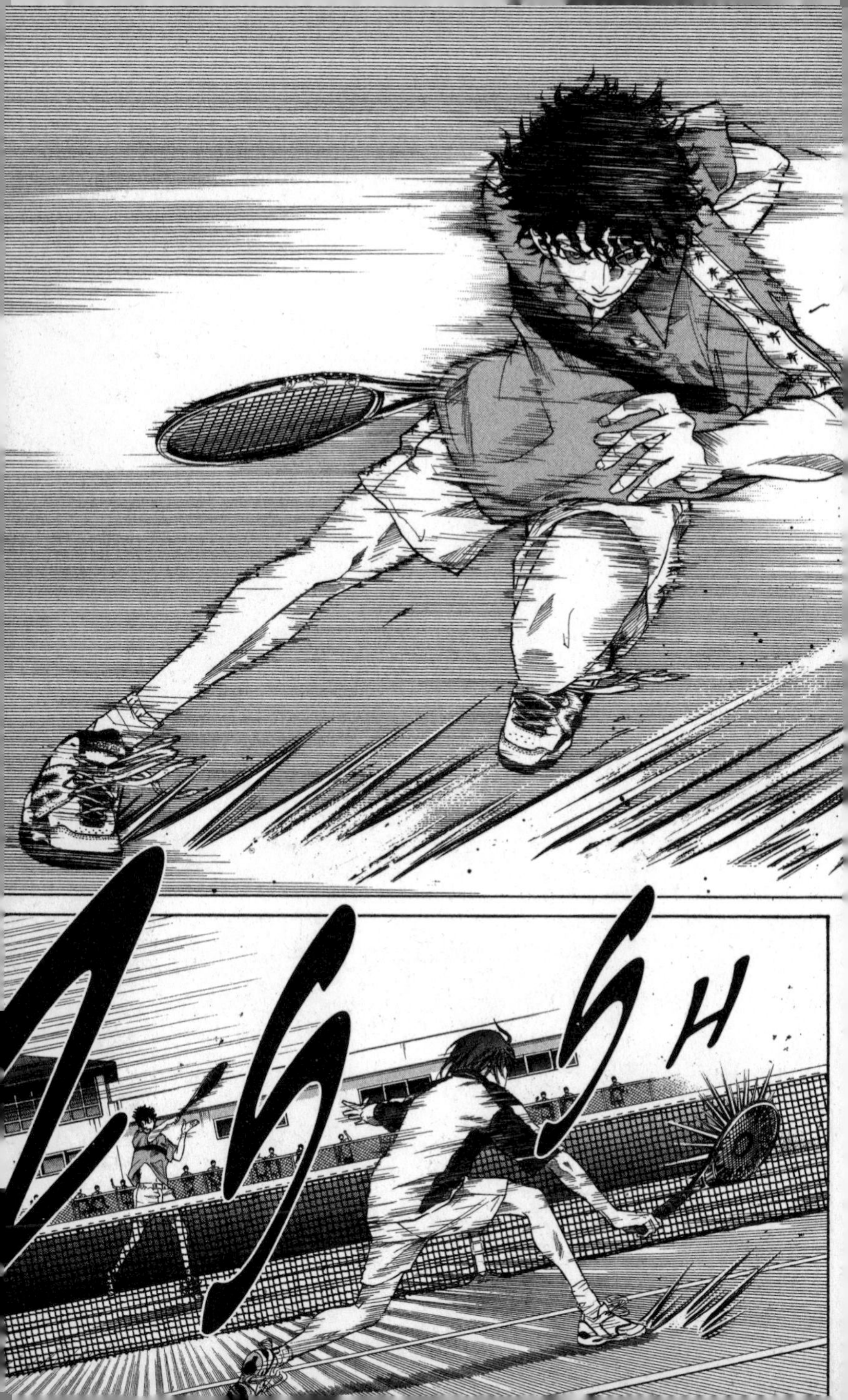
SWISH

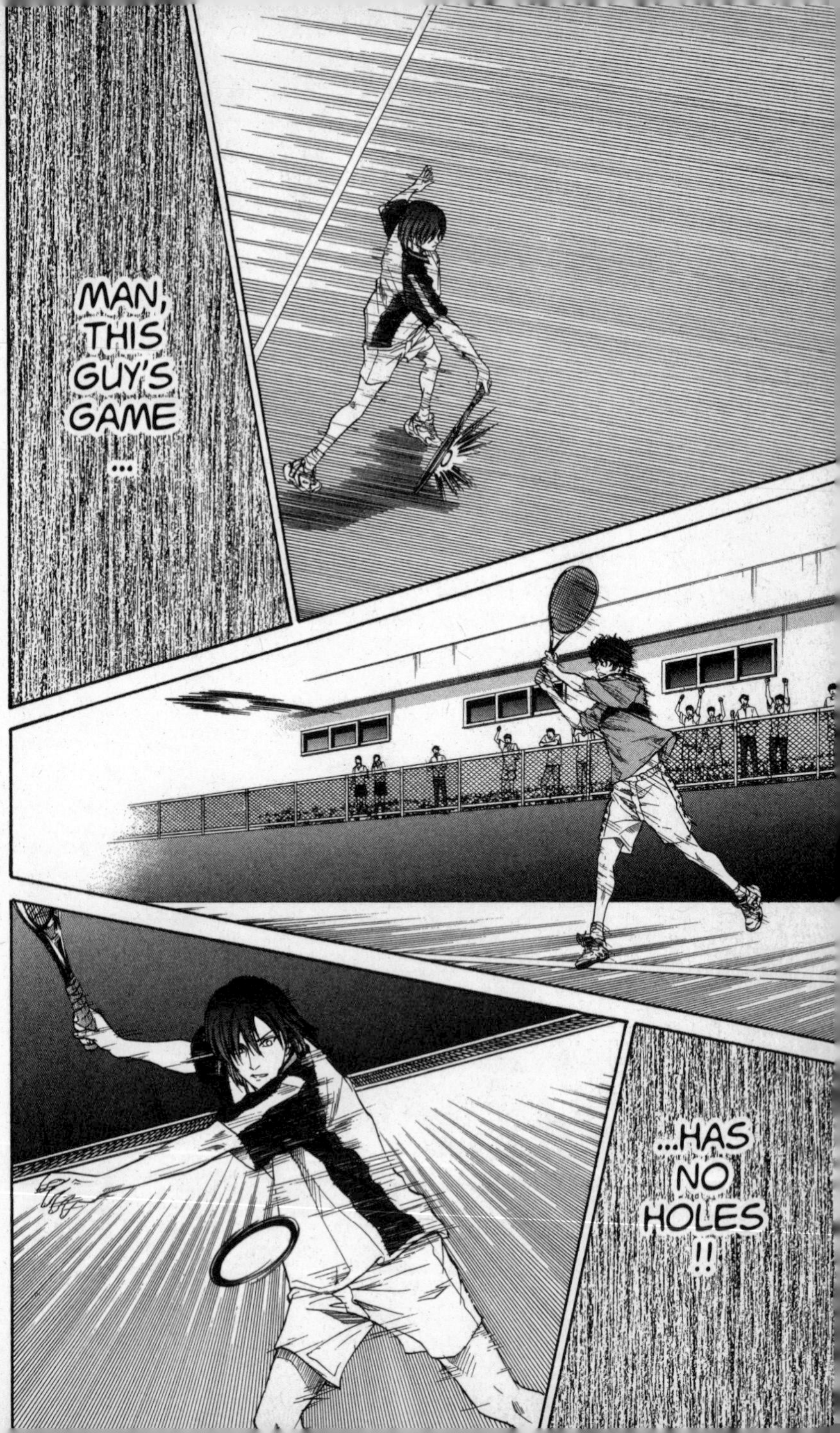
MAN, THIS GUY'S GAME ...
...HAS NO HOLES !!

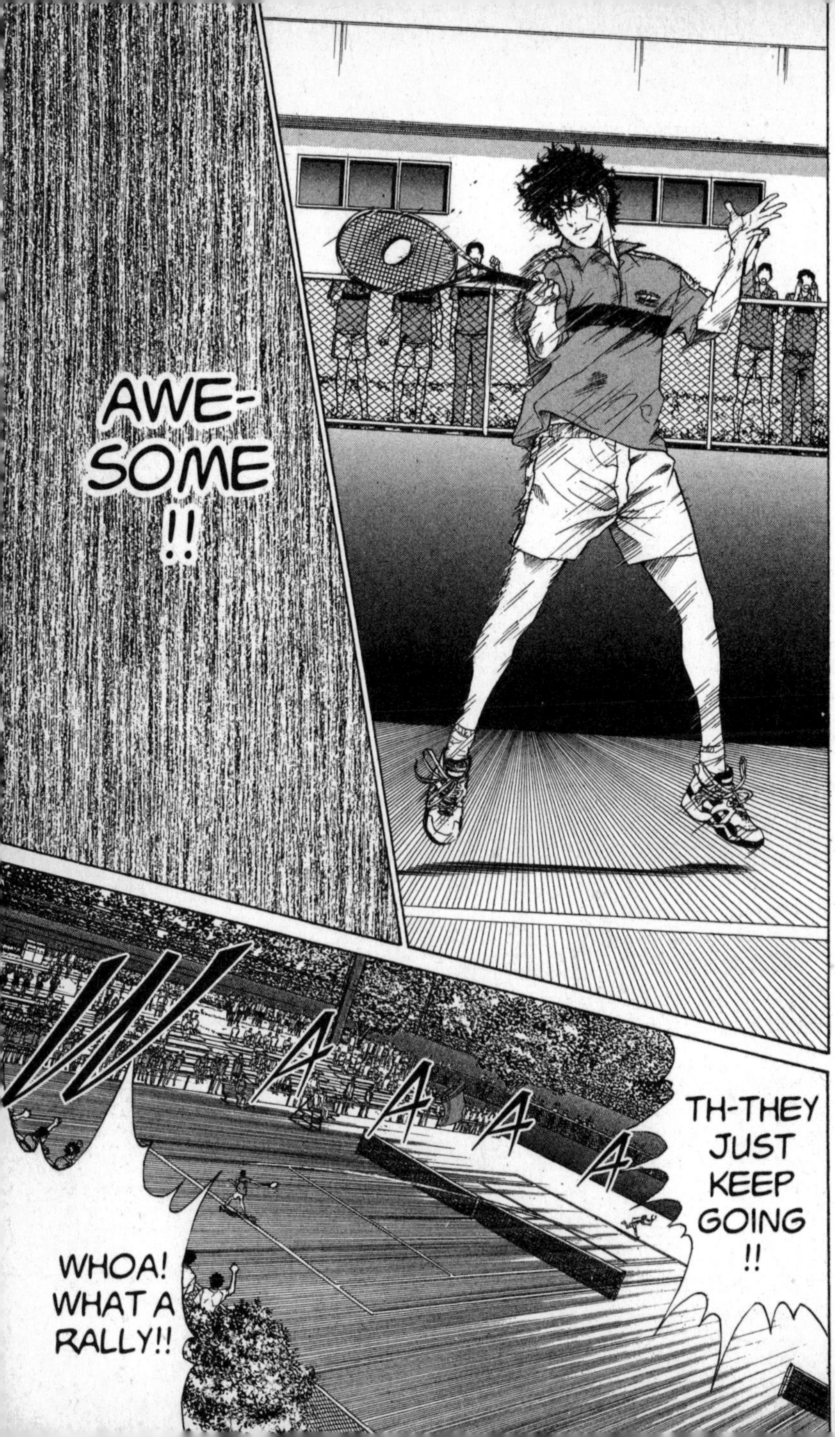
AWE-SOME!!
TH-THEY JUST KEEP GOING!!
WAAAA
WHOA! WHAT A RALLY!!

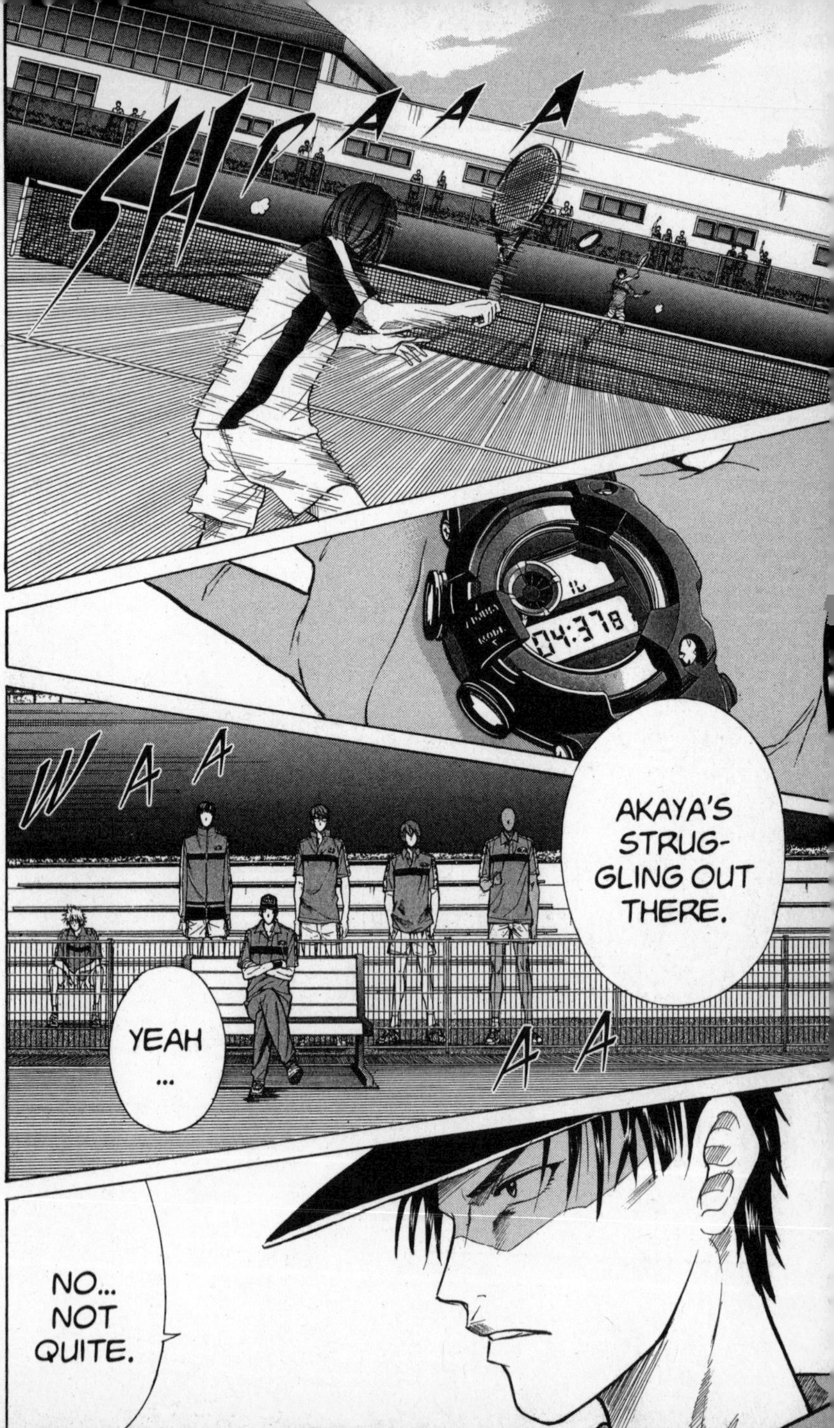
SHPAAAA
WAA
AKAYA'S STRUG-GLING OUT THERE.
YEAH ...
AA
NO... NOT QUITE.

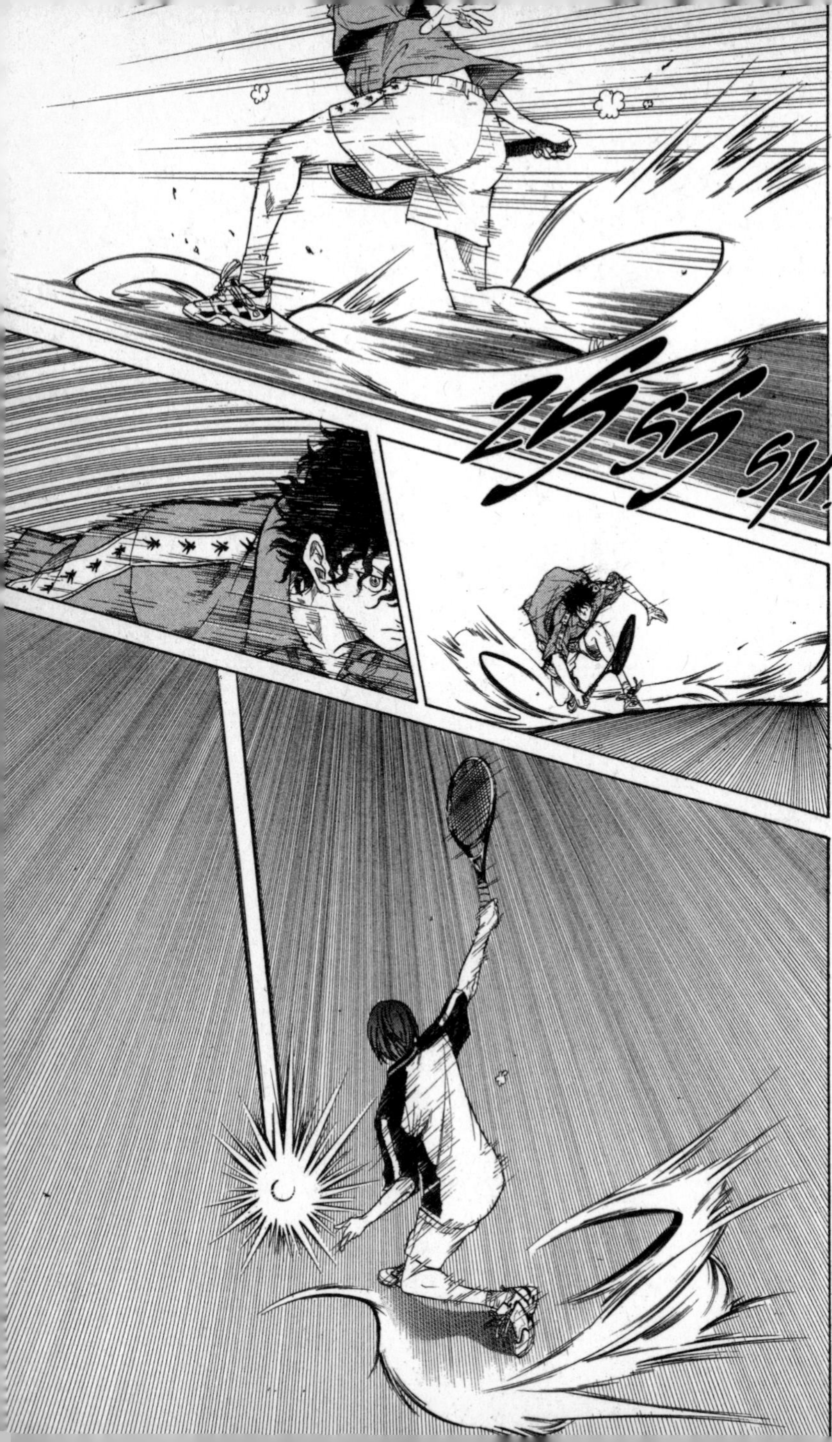
ZSSSSH..

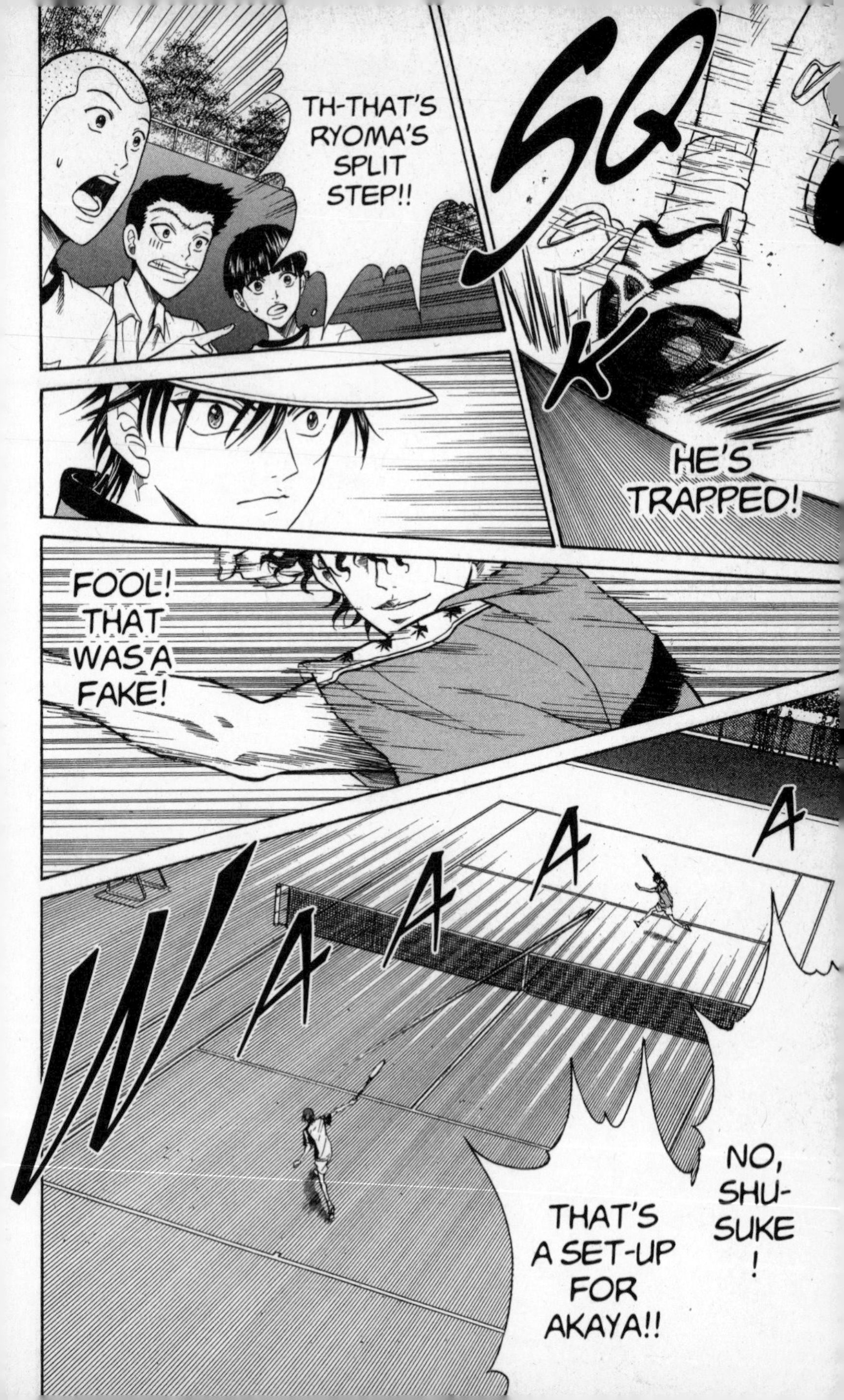
SQK
HE'S TRAPPED!
TH-THAT'S RYOMA'S SPLIT STEP!!
FOOL! THAT WAS A FAKE!
WAAAAA
NO, SHUSUKE!
THAT'S A SET-UP FOR AKAYA!!

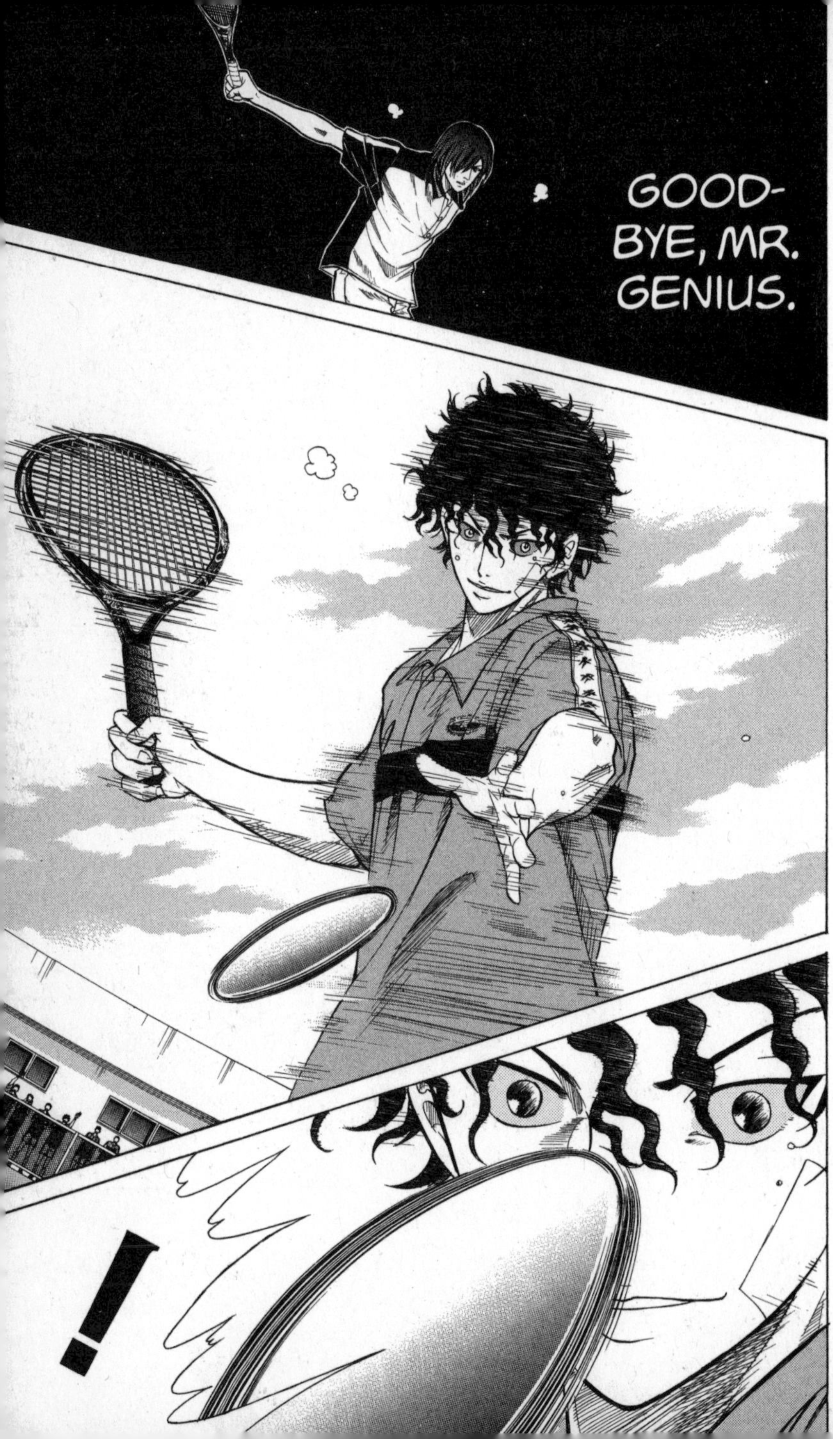
GOOD-
BYE, MR.
GENIUS.
!

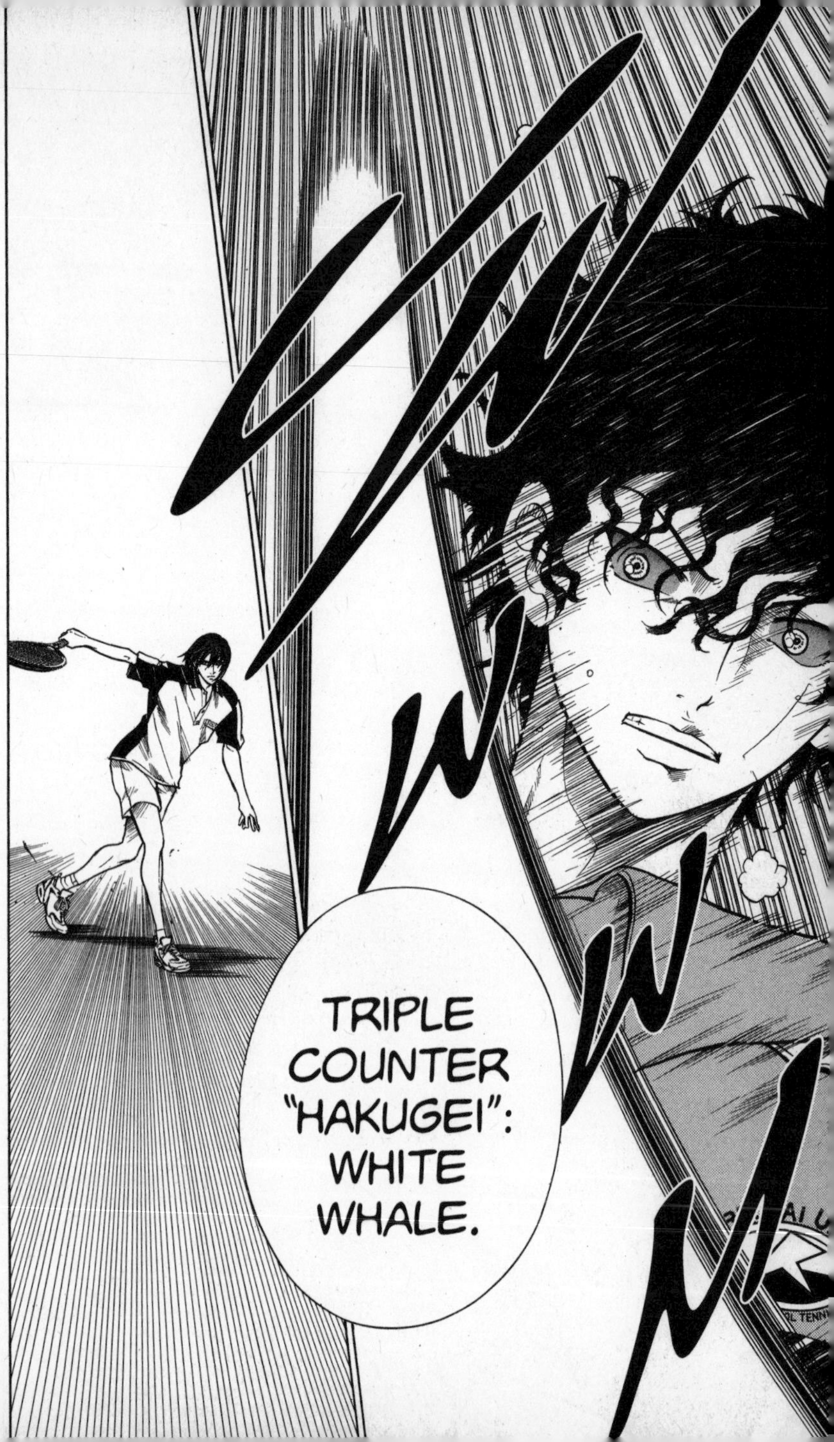
TRIPLE COUNTER "HAKUGEI": WHITE WHALE.

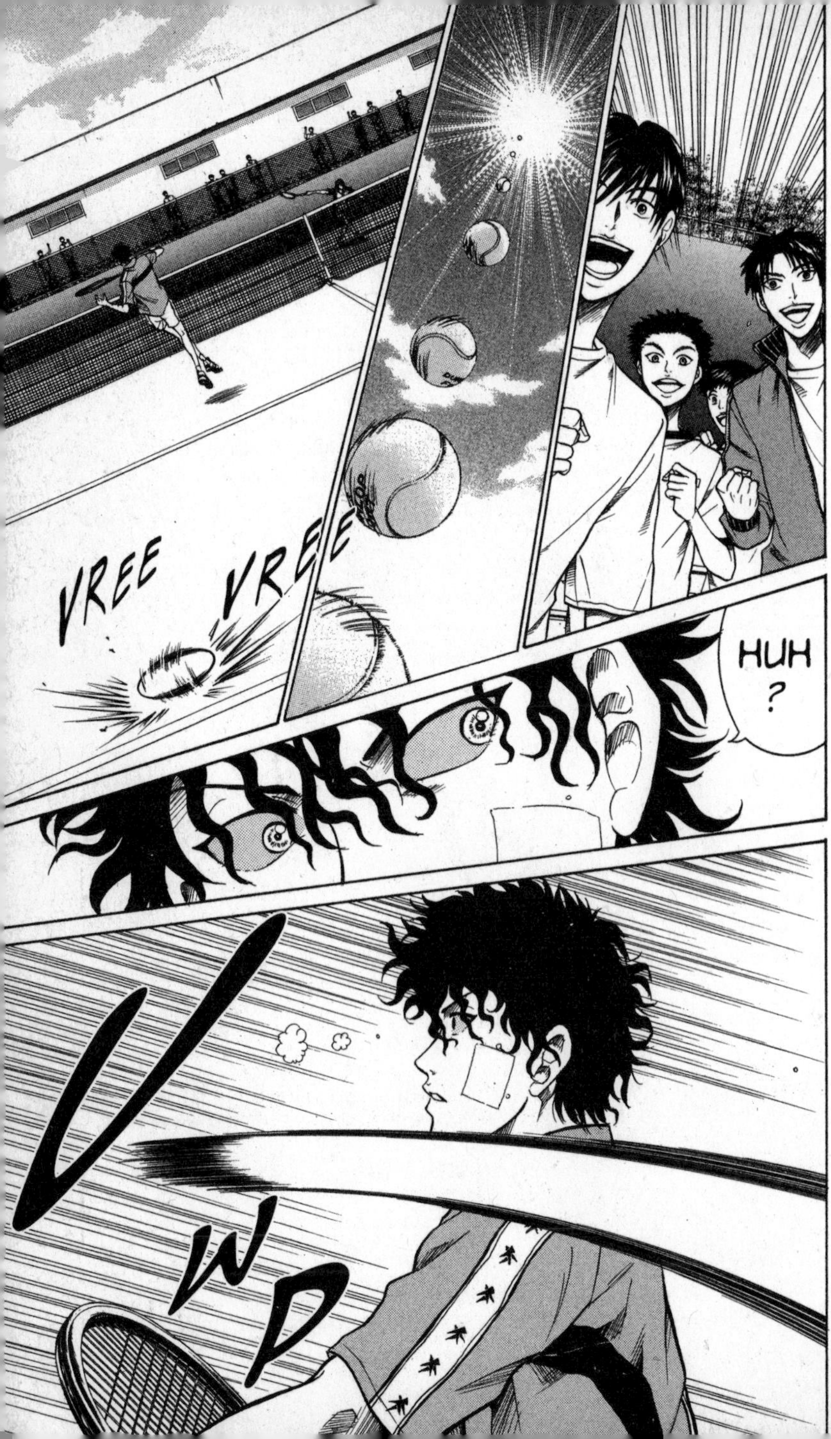
VREE
VREE
HUH?
VWD

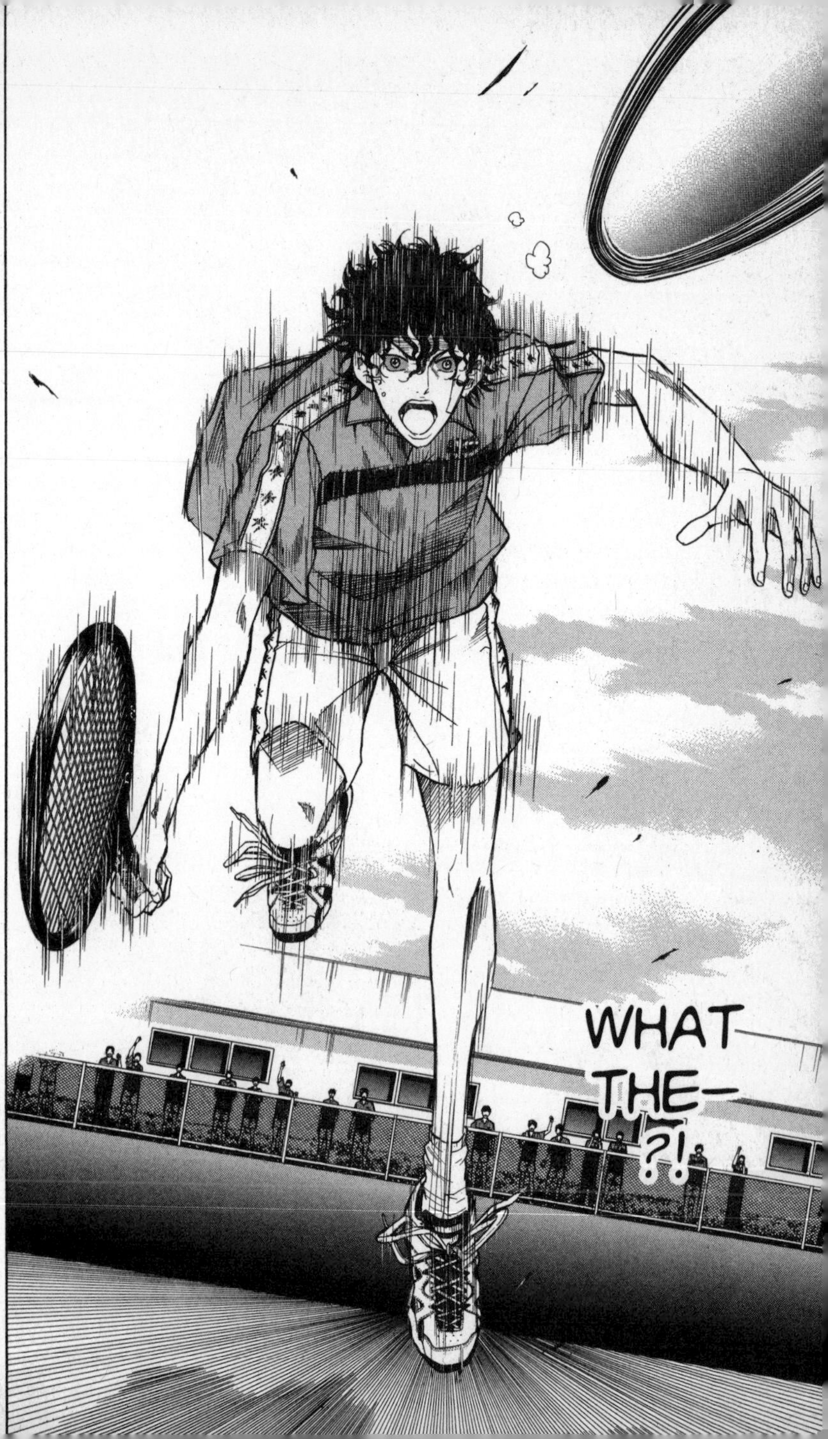
WHAT
THE—
?!

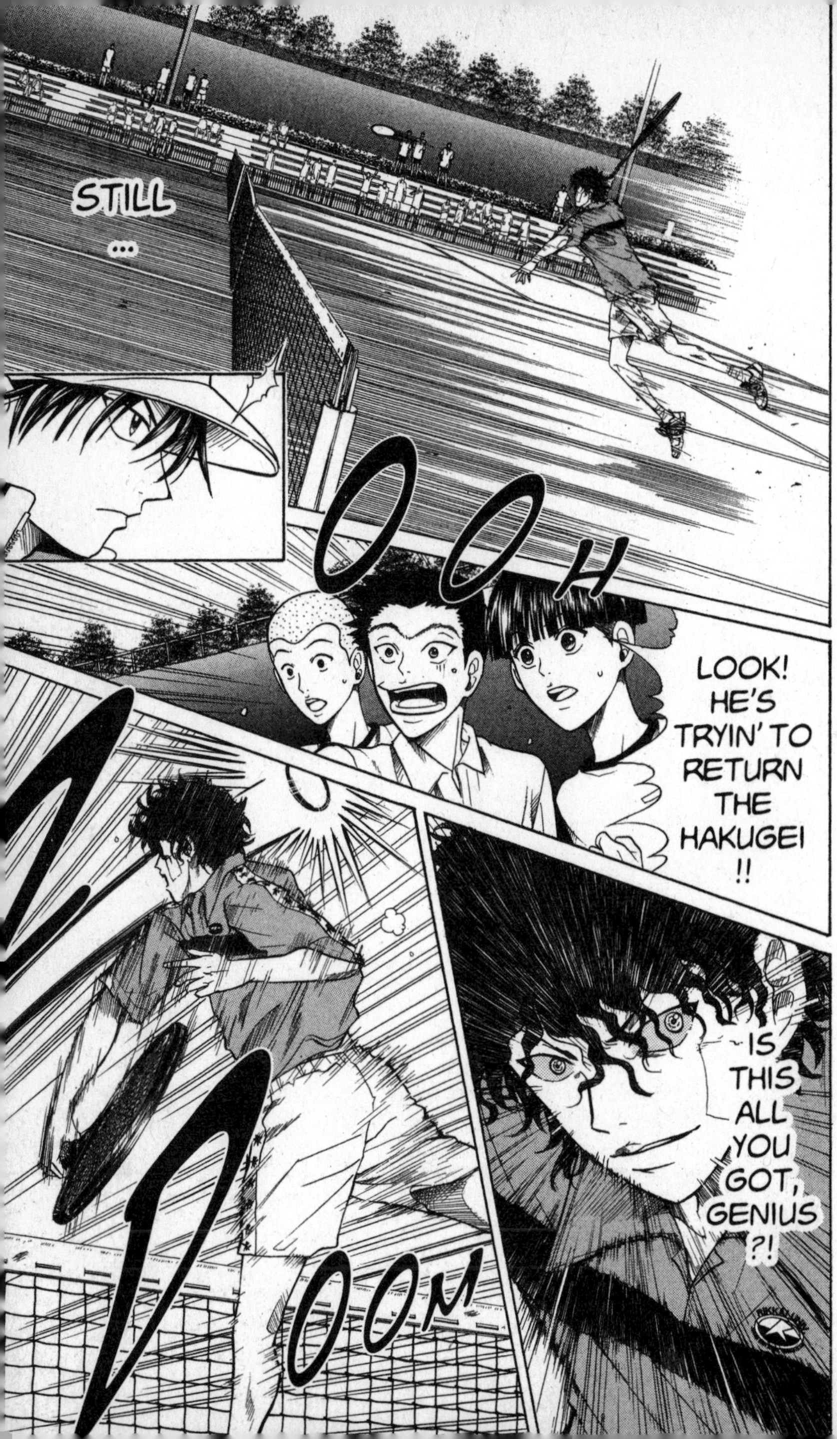
STILL
...
OOH
LOOK! HE'S TRYIN' TO RETURN THE HAKUGEI!!
IS THIS ALL YOU GOT, GENIUS?!

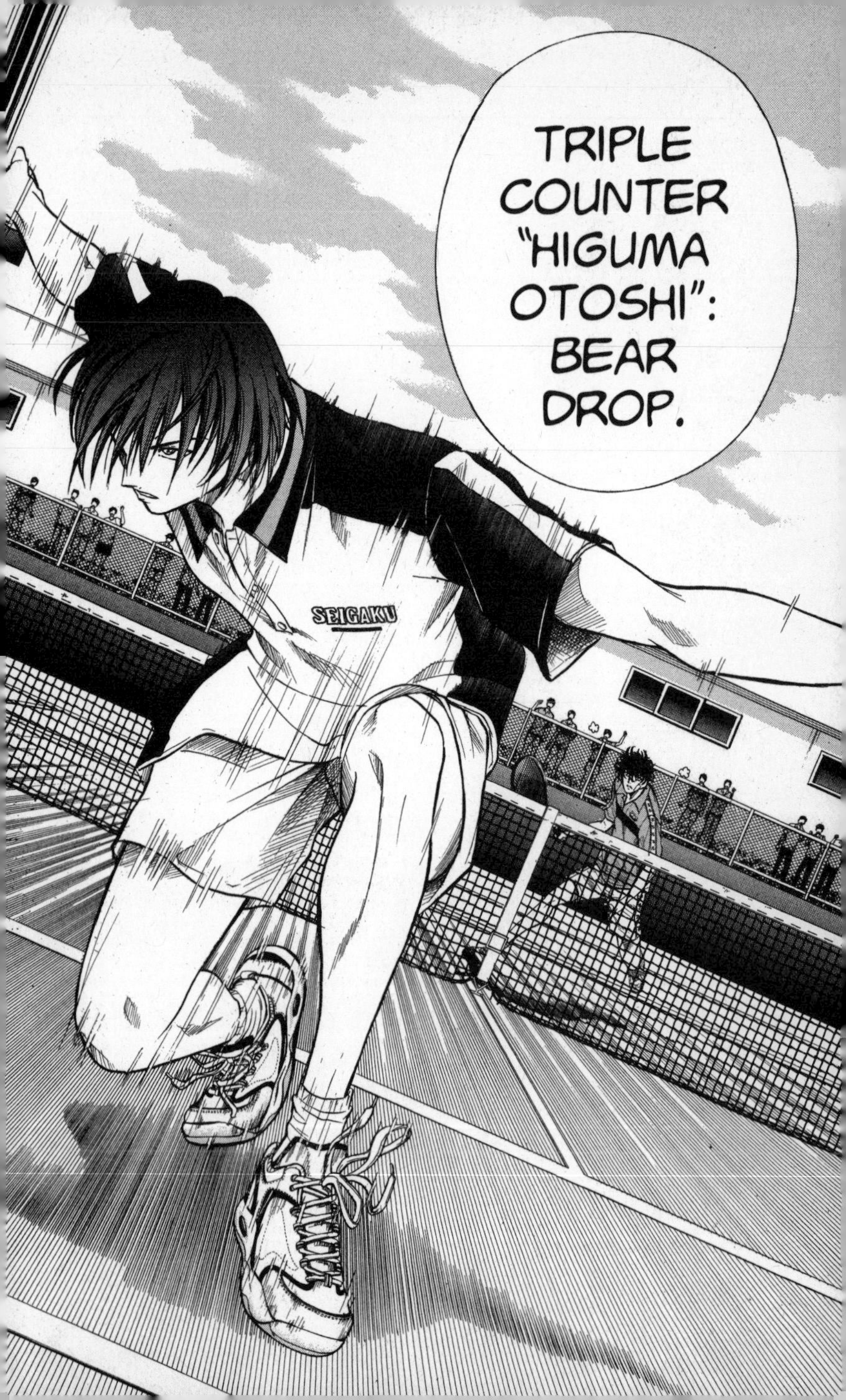
TRIPLE COUNTER "HIGUMA OTOSHI": BEAR DROP.
SEIGAKU

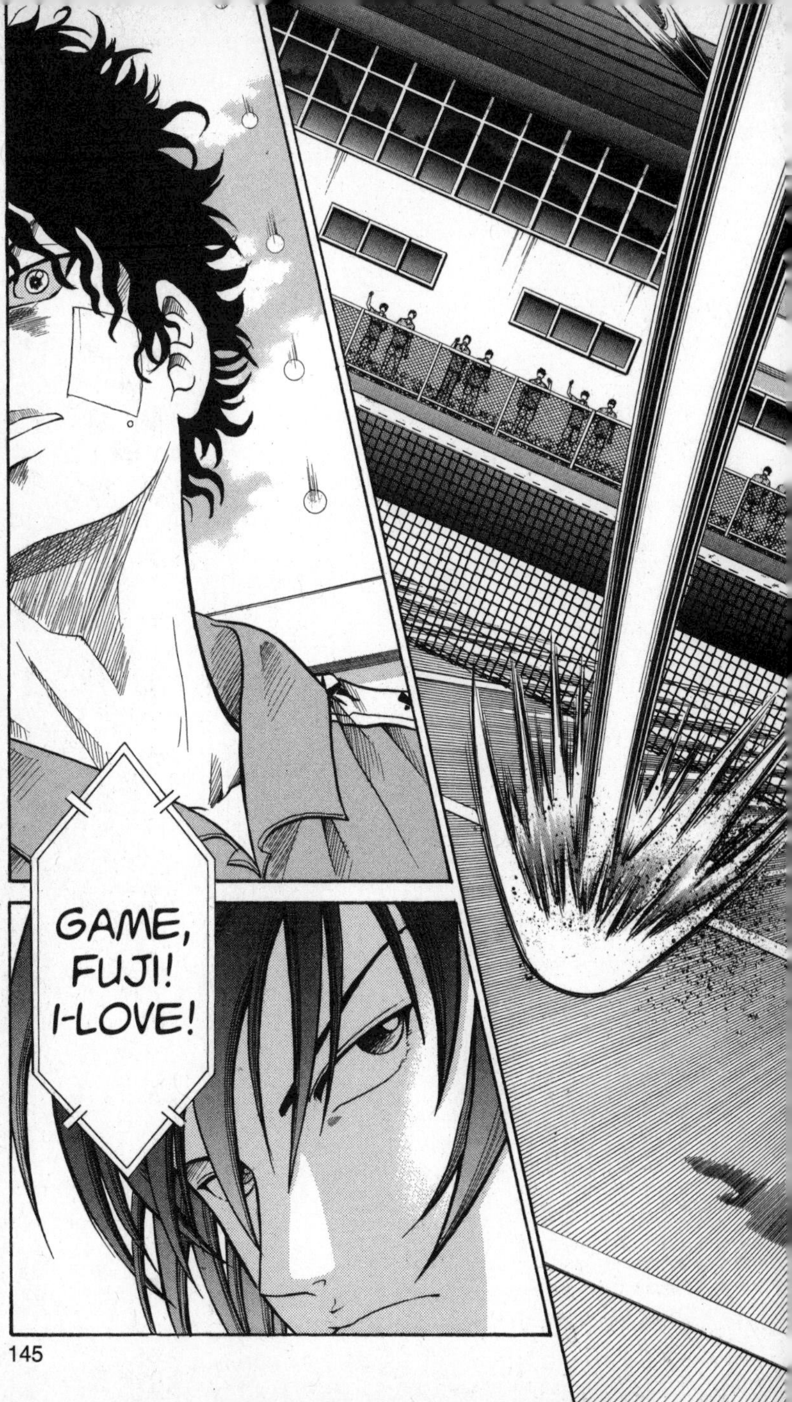
GAME, FUJI! I-LOVE!

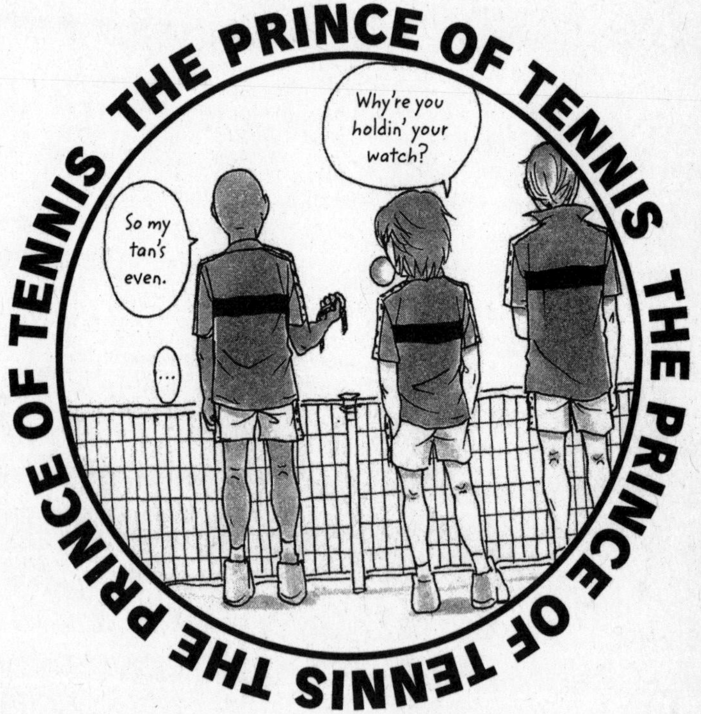
THE PRINCE OF TENNIS THE PRINCE OF TENNIS THE PRINCE OF TENNIS
Why're you holdin' your watch?
So my tan's even.
...

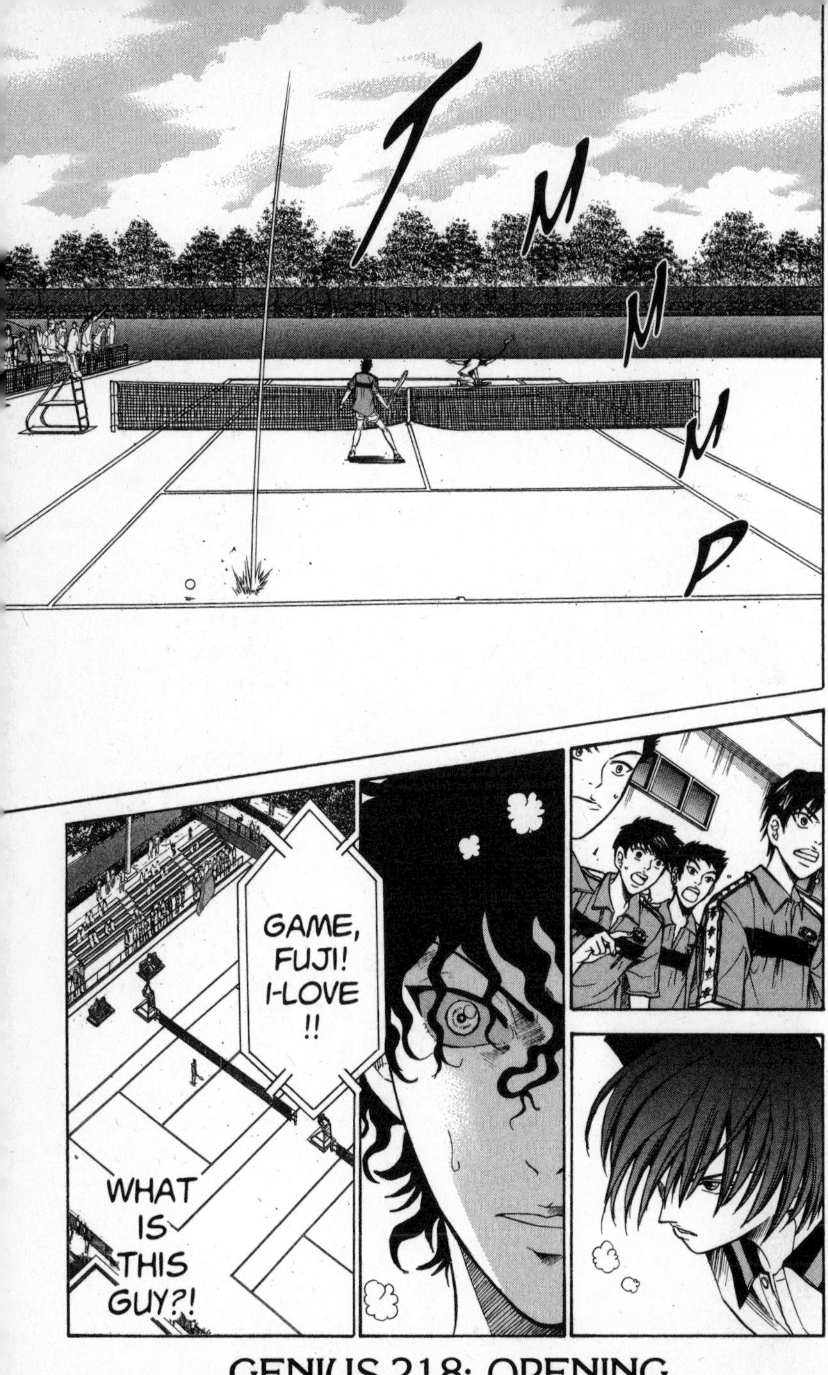
TMMMP
GAME, FUJI! I-LOVE !!
WHAT IS THIS GUY?!

GENIUS 218: OPENING

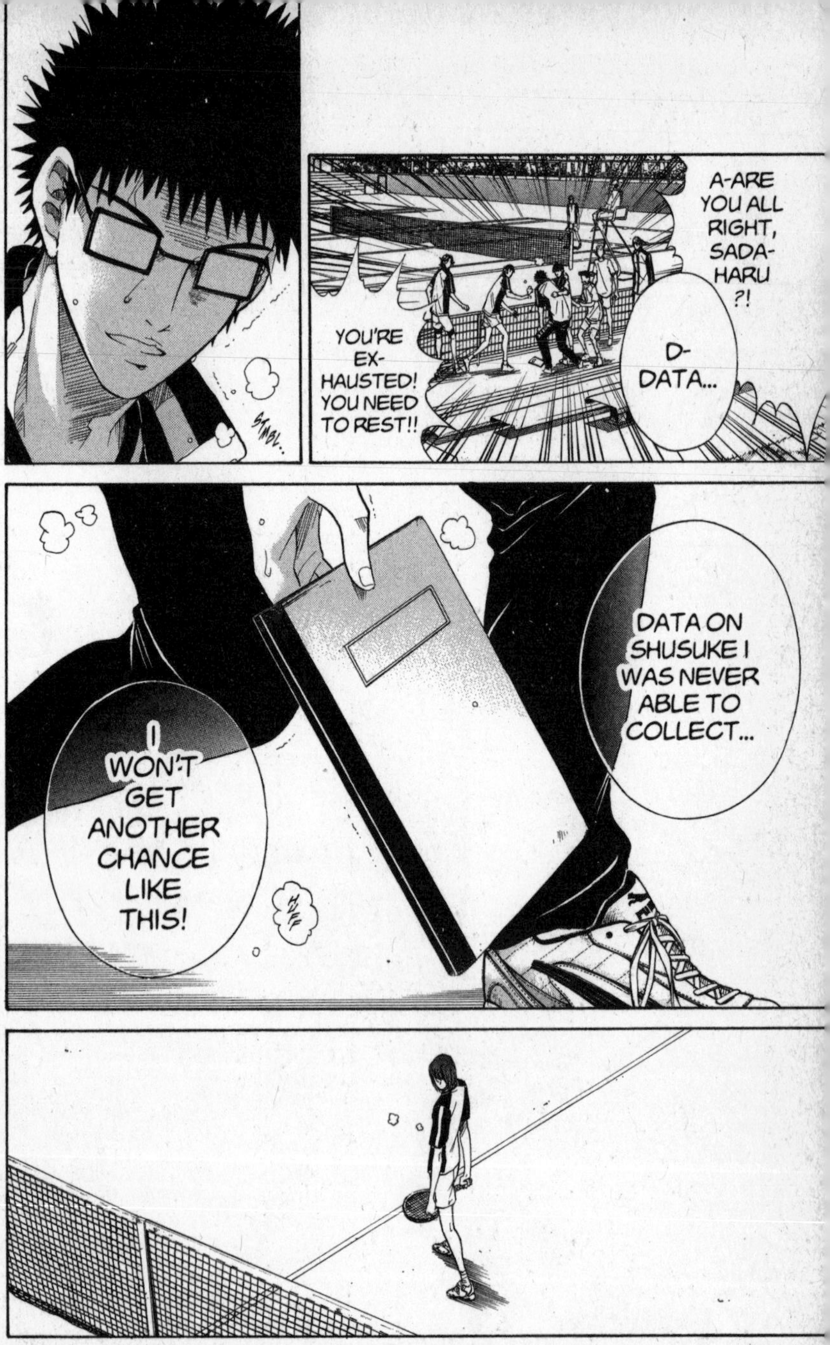
A-ARE YOU ALL RIGHT, SADAHARU?!
D-DATA...
YOU'RE EXHAUSTED! YOU NEED TO REST!!
STMBL...
DATA ON SHUSUKE I WAS NEVER ABLE TO COLLECT...
I WON'T GET ANOTHER CHANCE LIKE THIS!
HUFF

READ THIS WAY

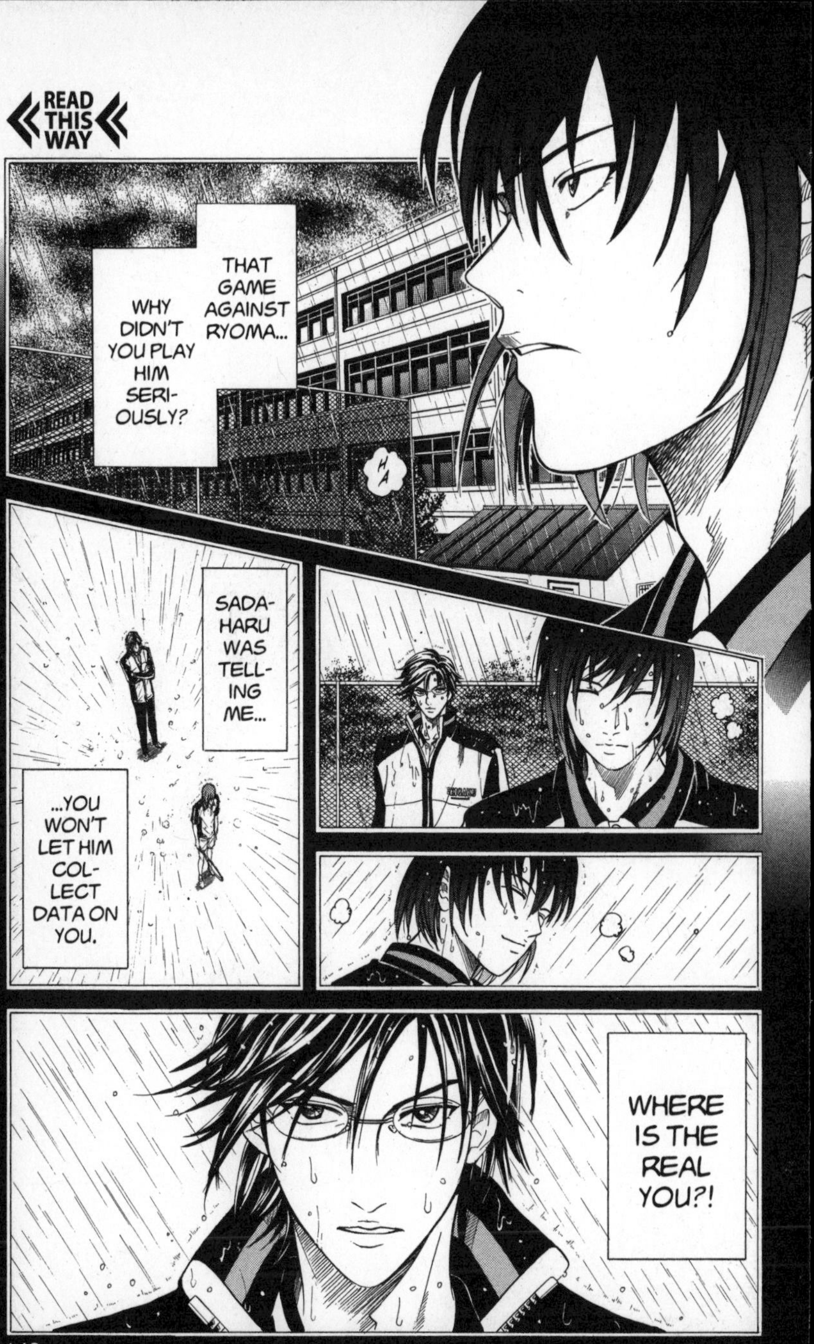
THAT GAME AGAINST RYOMA...
WHY DIDN'T YOU PLAY HIM SERI-OUSLY?
HA
SADA-HARU WAS TELL-ING ME...
...YOU WON'T LET HIM COL-LECT DATA ON YOU.
WHERE IS THE REAL YOU?!

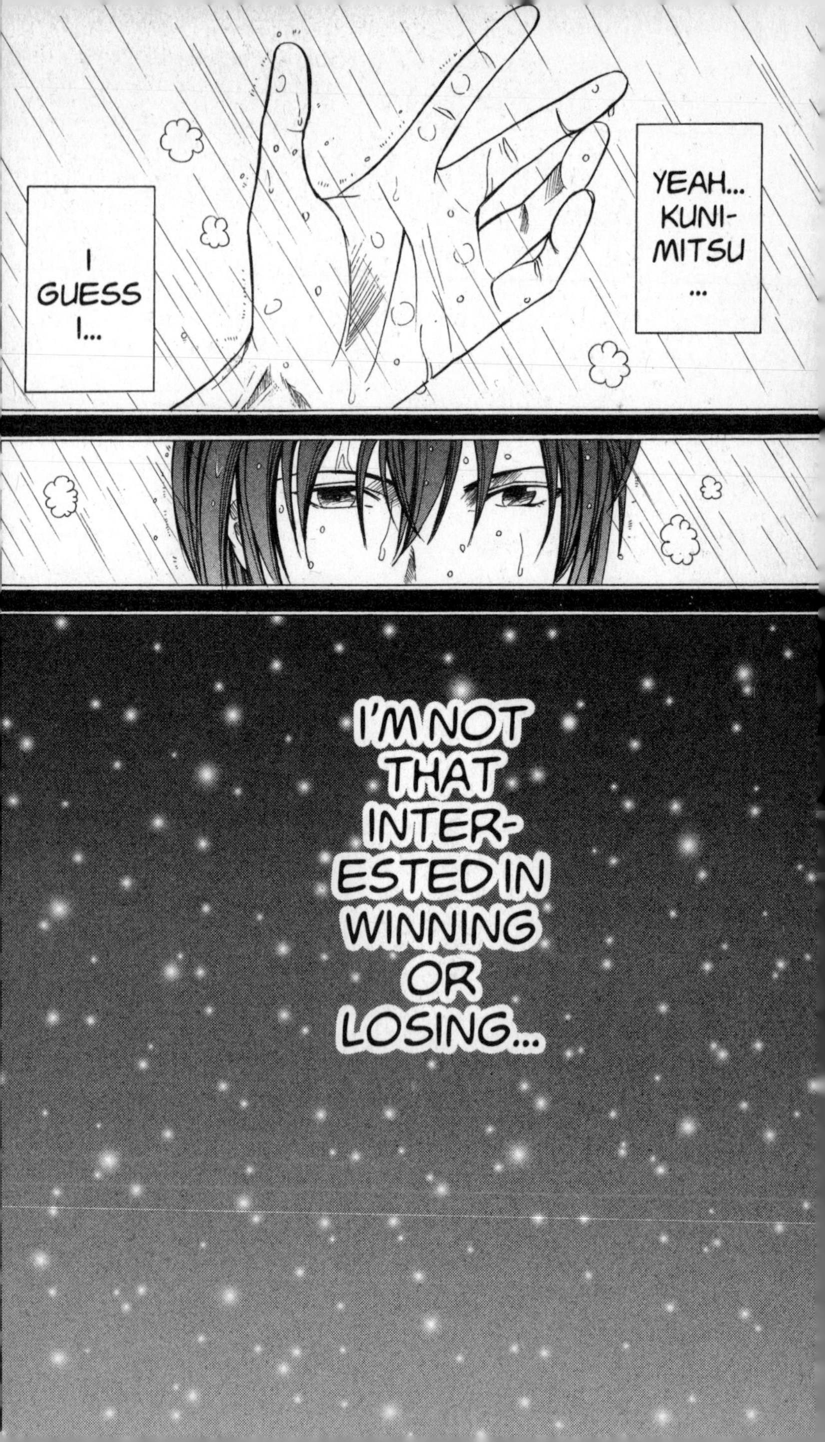
YEAH... KUNI-MITSU...
I GUESS I...
I'M NOT THAT INTER-ESTED IN WINNING OR LOSING...

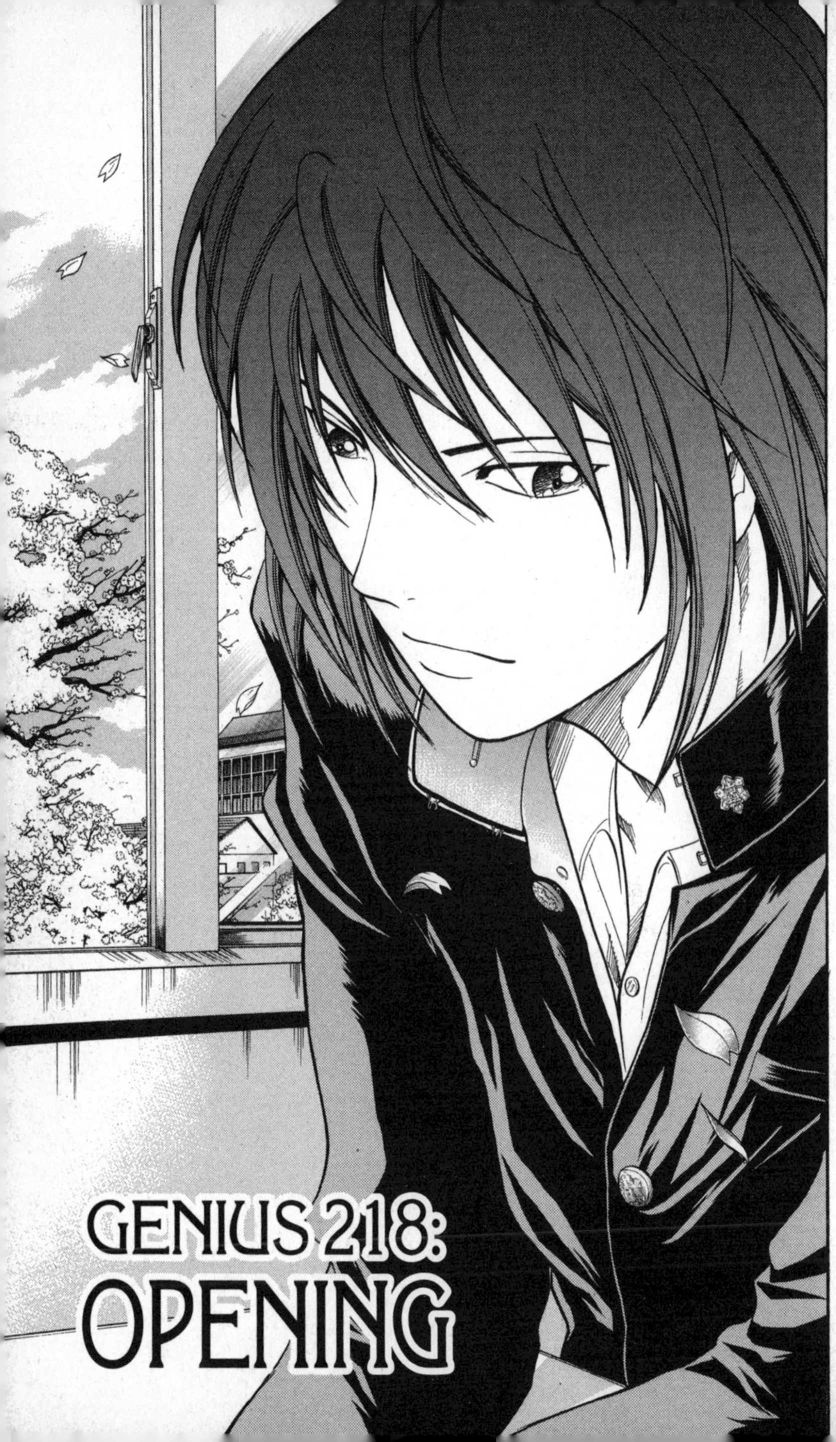
GENIUS 218:
OPENING

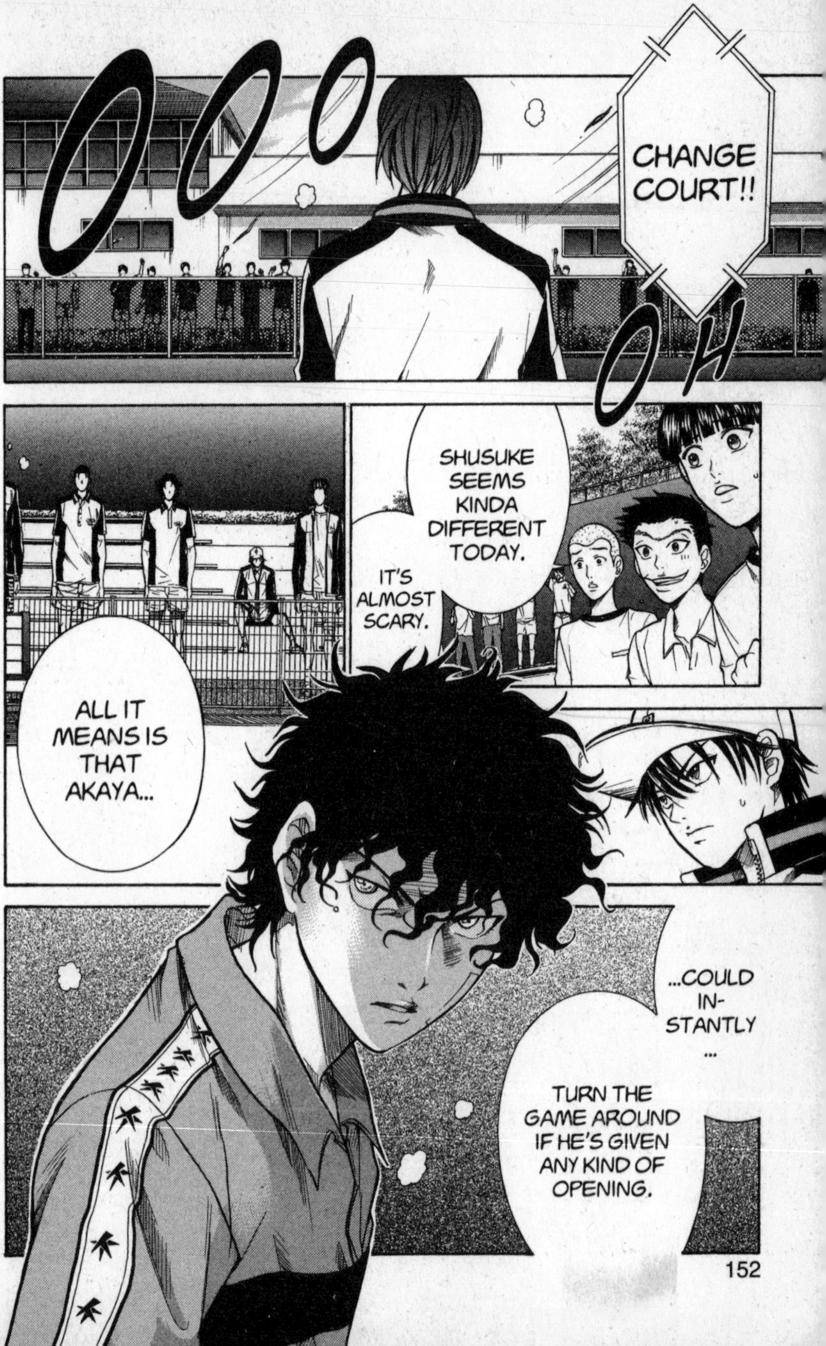
OOOOH
CHANGE COURT!!
SHUSUKE SEEMS KINDA DIFFERENT TODAY.
IT'S ALMOST SCARY.
ALL IT MEANS IS THAT AKAYA...
...COULD IN-STANTLY...
TURN THE GAME AROUND IF HE'S GIVEN ANY KIND OF OPENING.

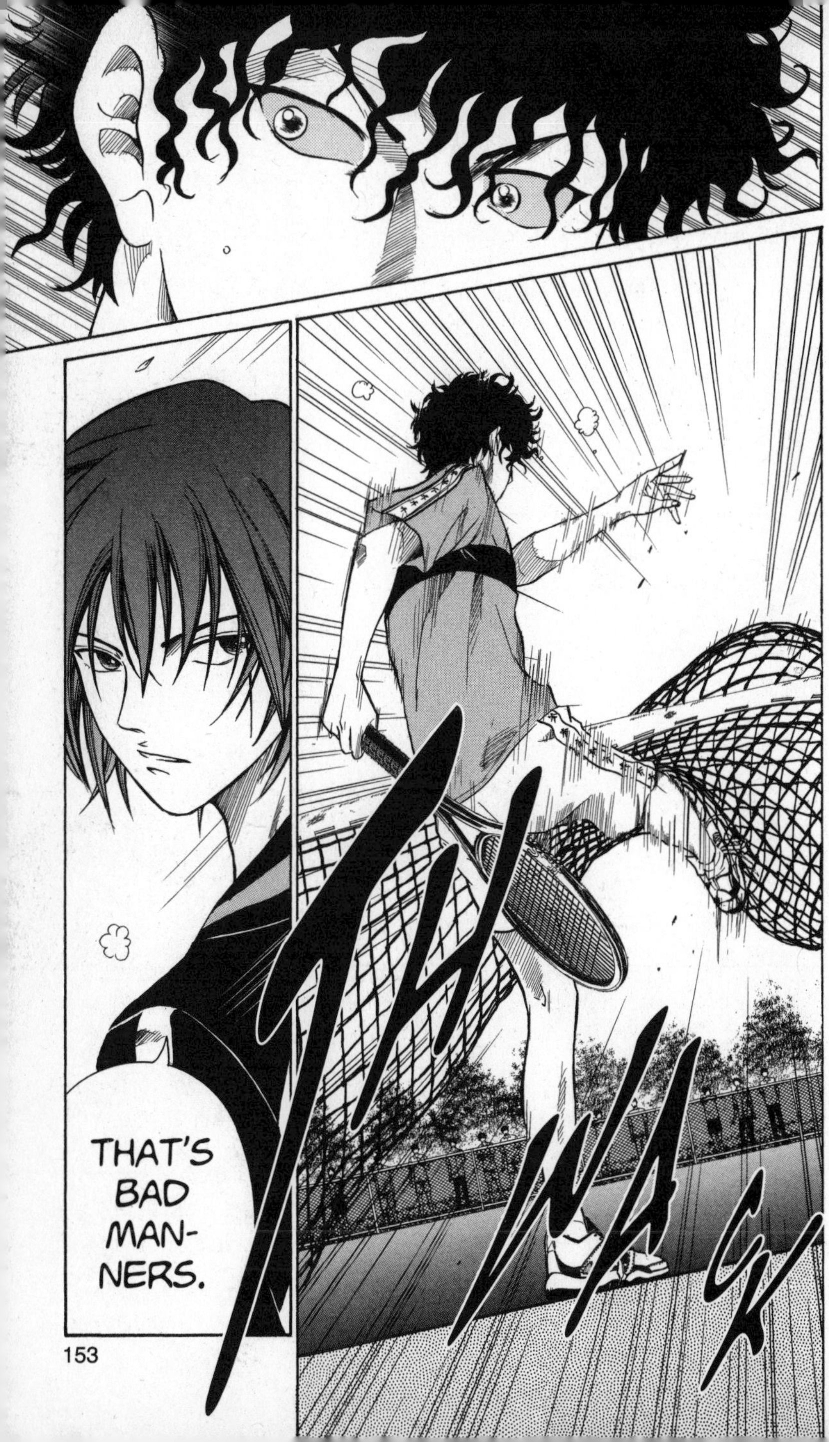
THAT'S BAD MAN-NERS.

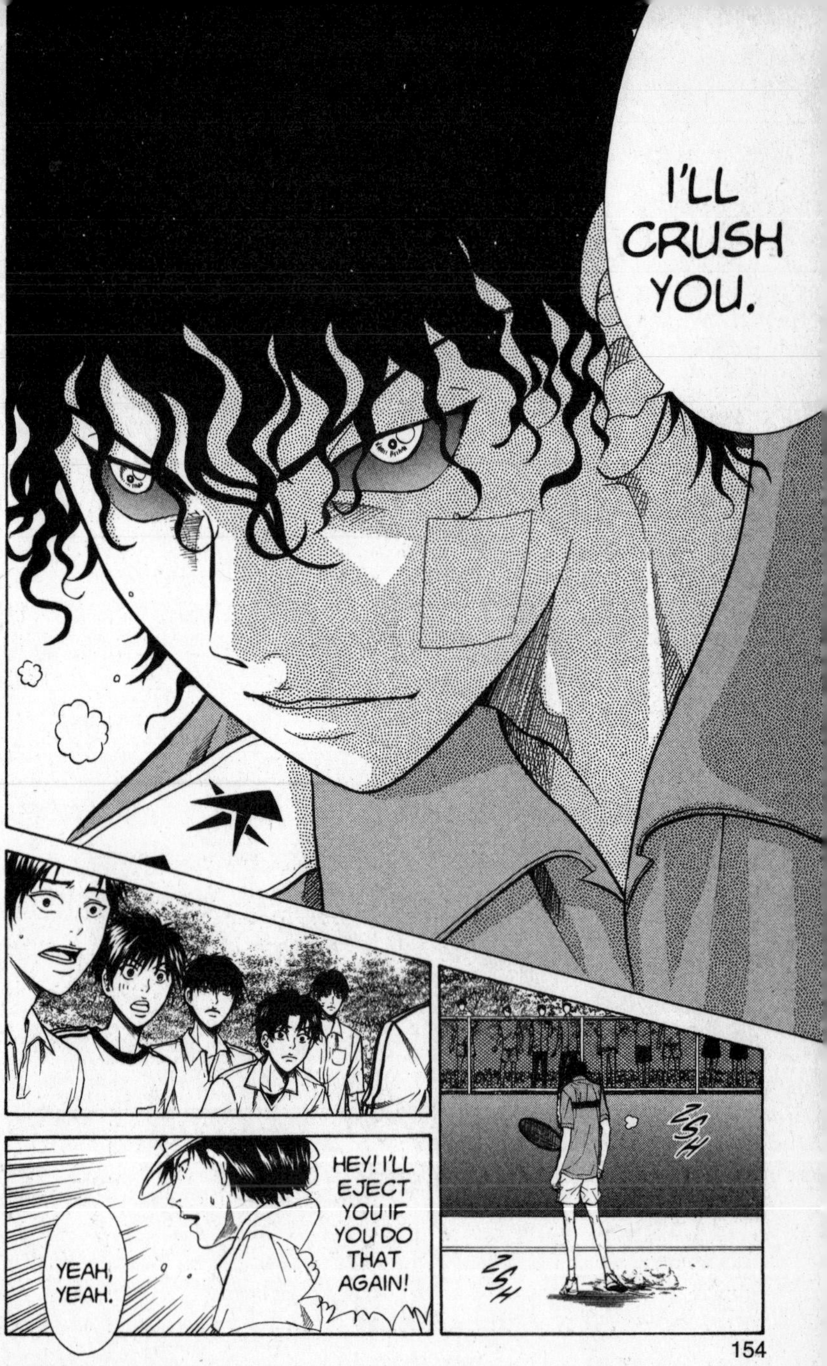
I'LL CRUSH YOU.
ZSH
ZSH
HEY! I'LL EJECT YOU IF YOU DO THAT AGAIN!
YEAH, YEAH.

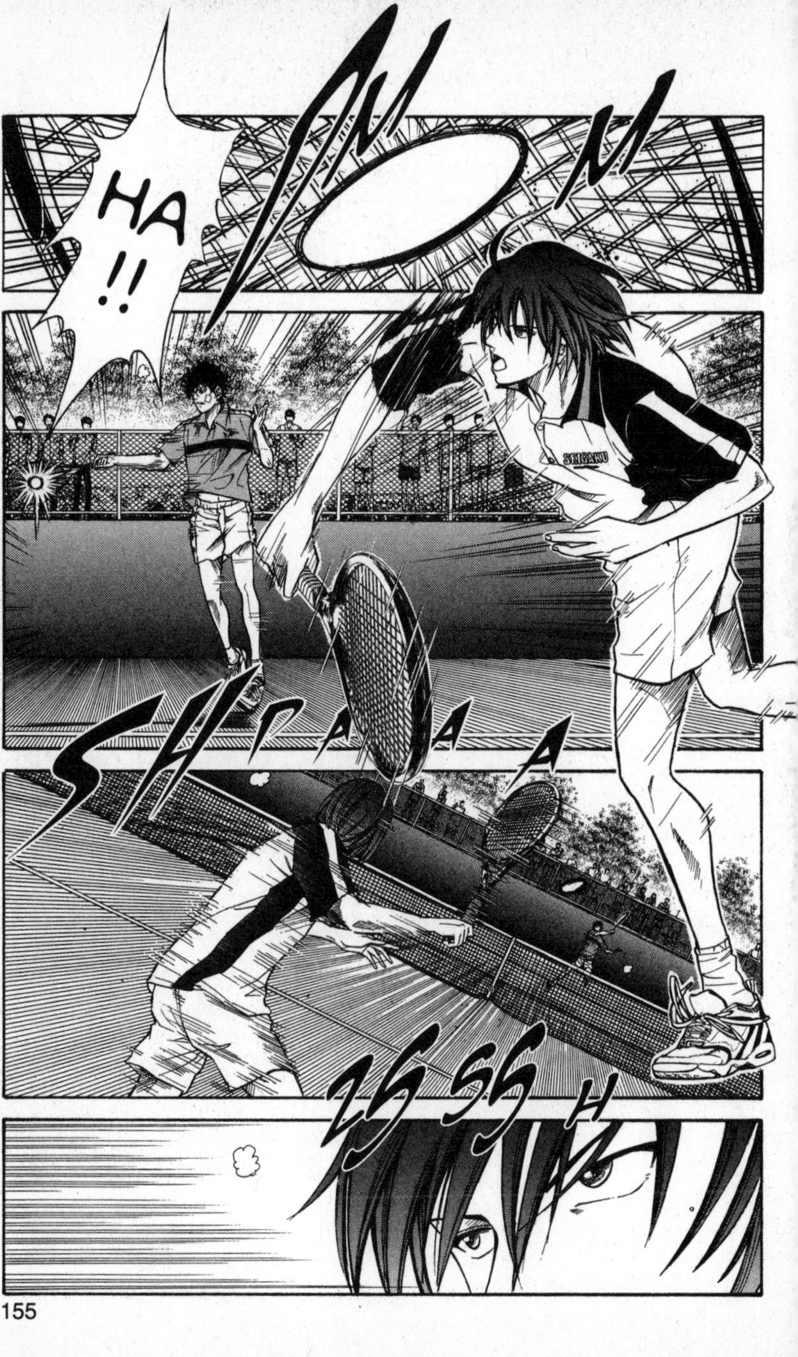
HA!!
WOM
SHPAAA
ZSSSH

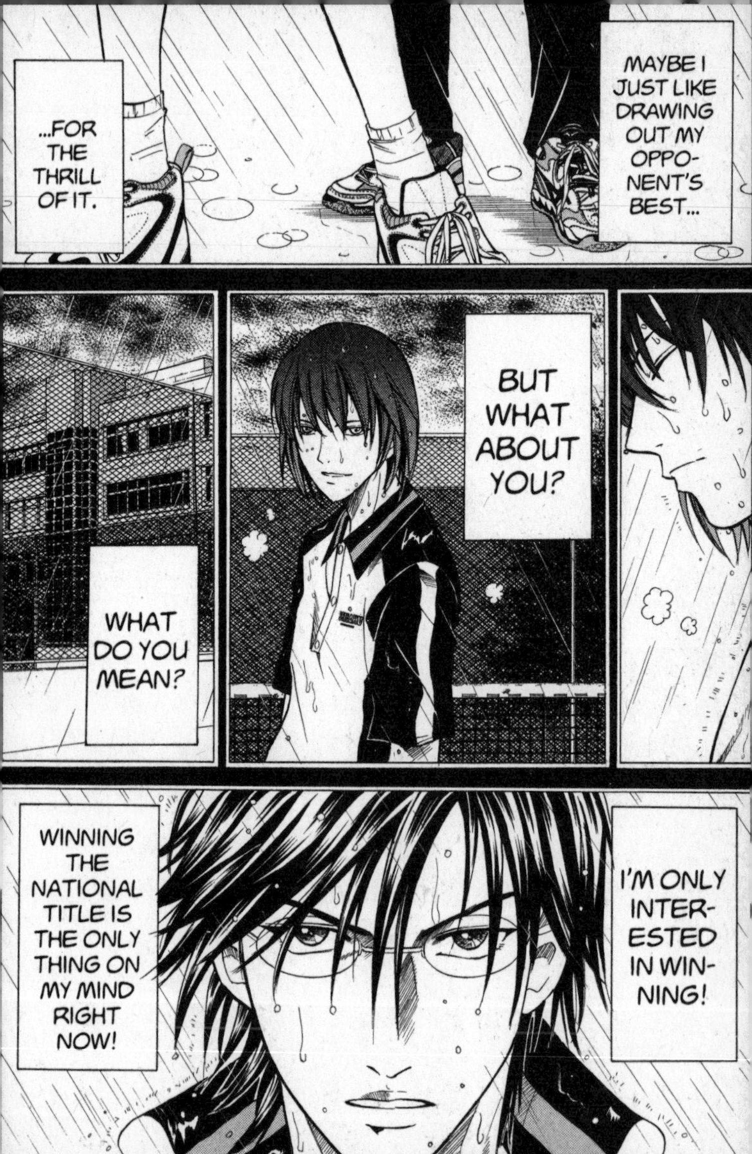
MAYBE I JUST LIKE DRAWING OUT MY OPPONENT'S BEST...
...FOR THE THRILL OF IT.
BUT WHAT ABOUT YOU?
WHAT DO YOU MEAN?
I'M ONLY INTERESTED IN WINNING!
WINNING THE NATIONAL TITLE IS THE ONLY THING ON MY MIND RIGHT NOW!

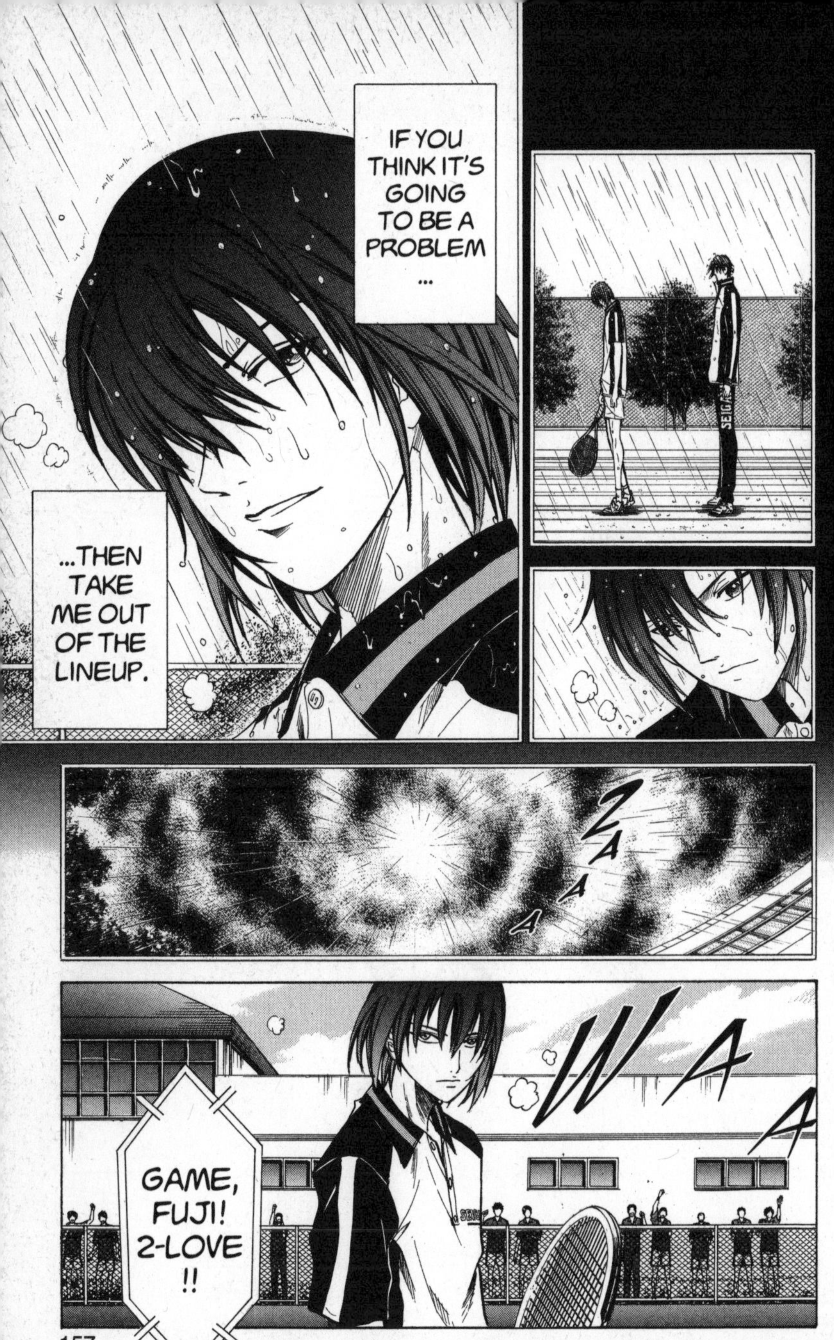
IF YOU THINK IT'S GOING TO BE A PROBLEM ...
...THEN TAKE ME OUT OF THE LINEUP.
ZAAAA
WAA
GAME, FUJI! 2-LOVE !!

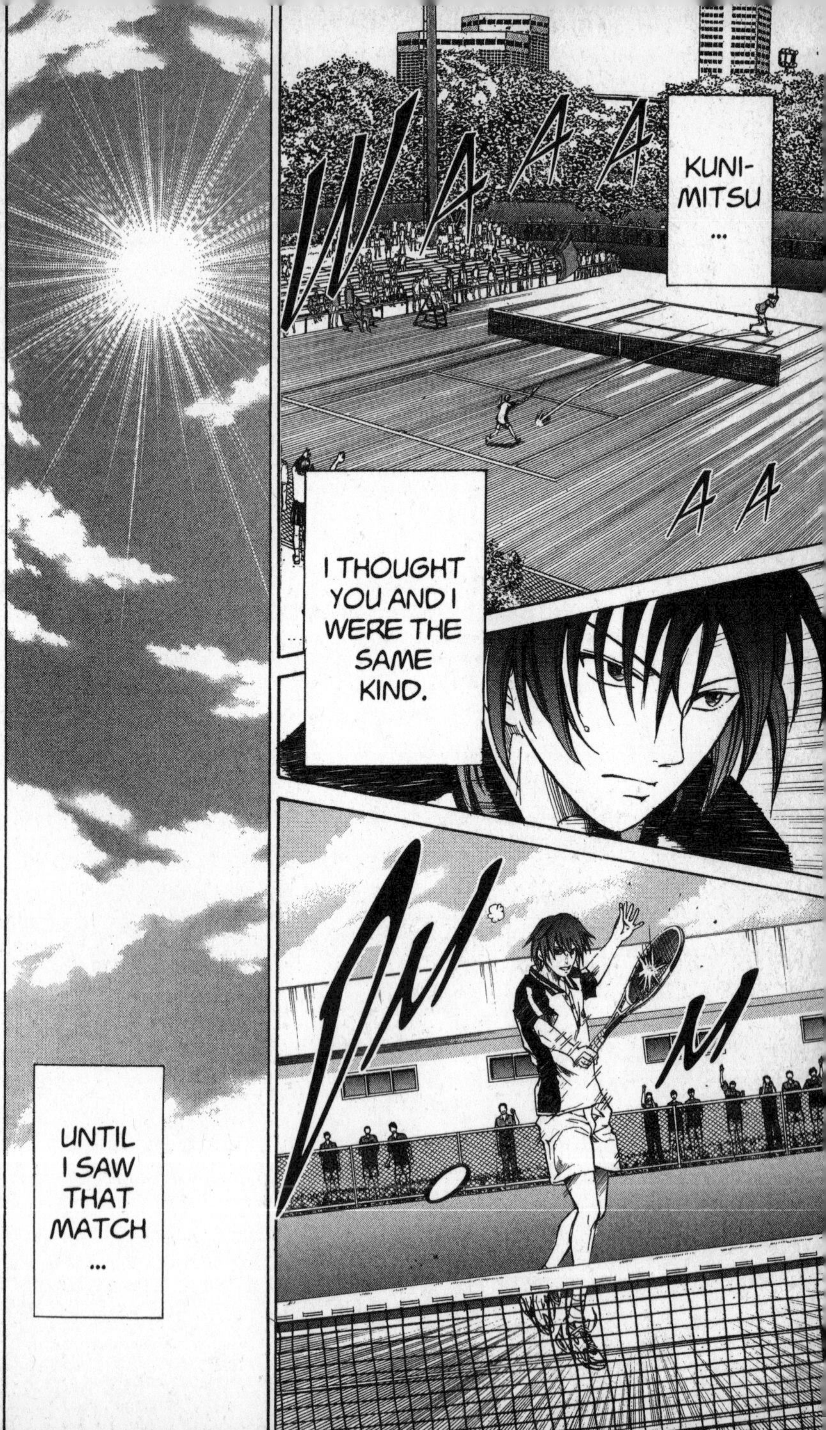
WAAAA
KUNIMITSU...
AA
I THOUGHT YOU AND I WERE THE SAME KIND.
UNTIL I SAW THAT MATCH...

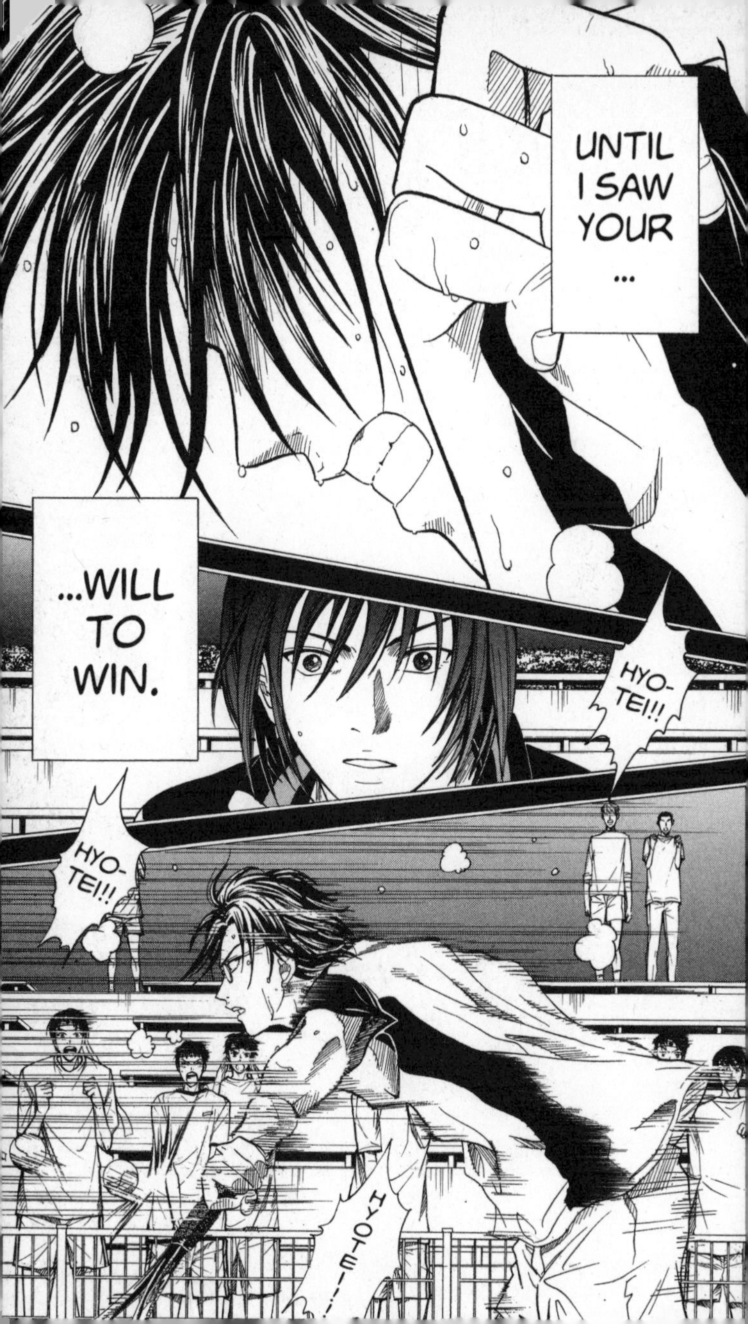
UNTIL I SAW YOUR ...
...WILL TO WIN.
HYO-TEI!!!
HYO-TEI!!!
HYOTEI!!!

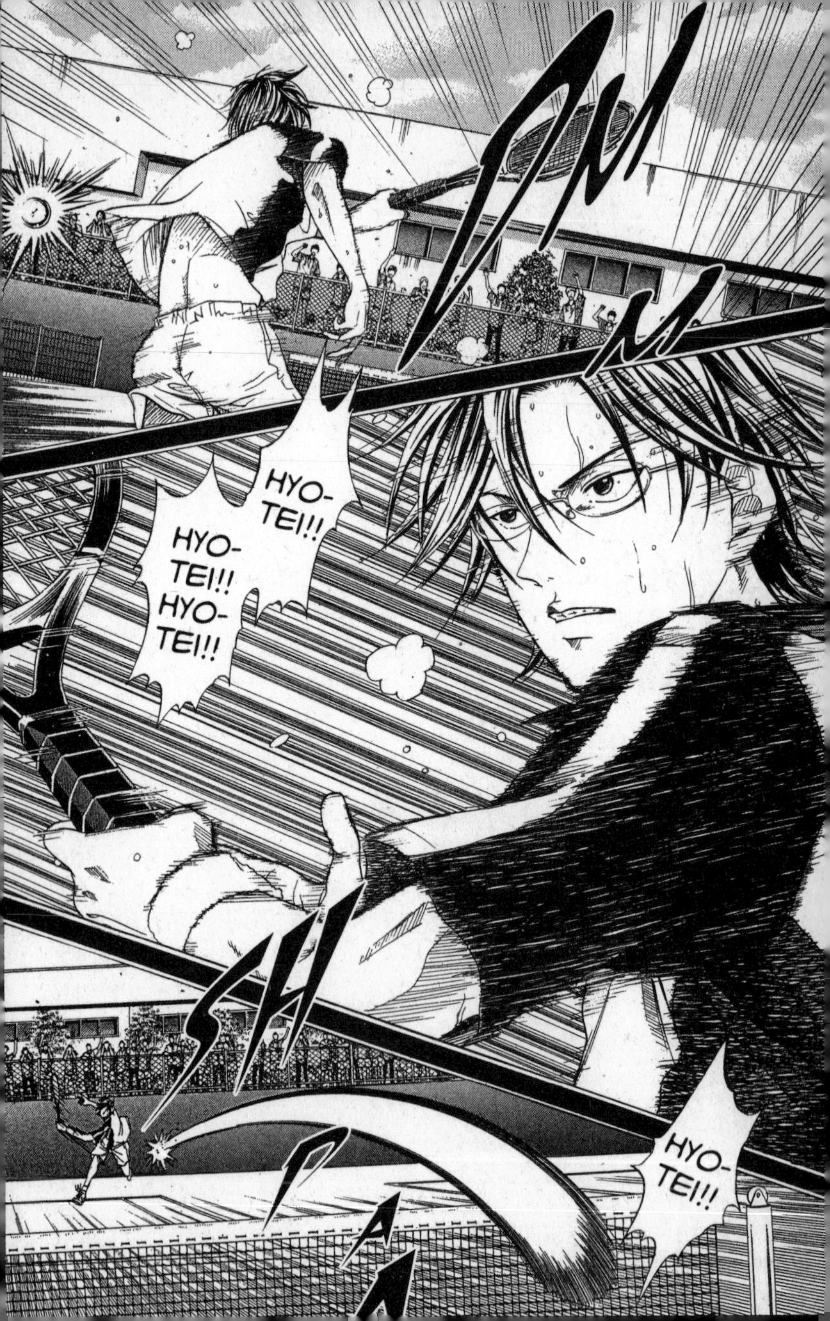
HYO-TEI!!
HYO-TEI!! HYO-TEI!!
HYO-TEI!!

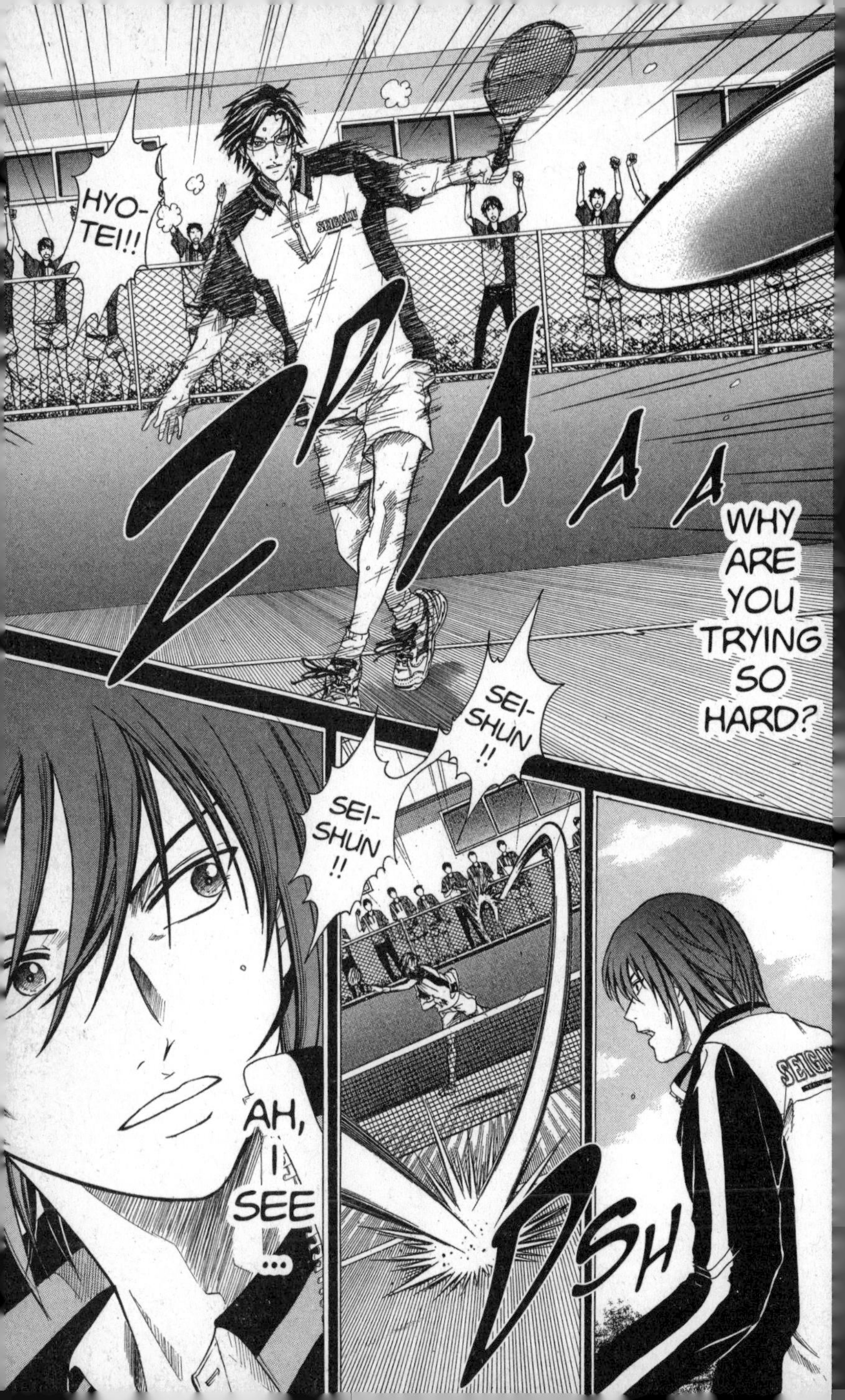
HYO-TEI!!
ZBAAA
WHY ARE YOU TRYING SO HARD?
SEI-SHUN!!
SEI-SHUN!!
DSH
AH, I SEE...

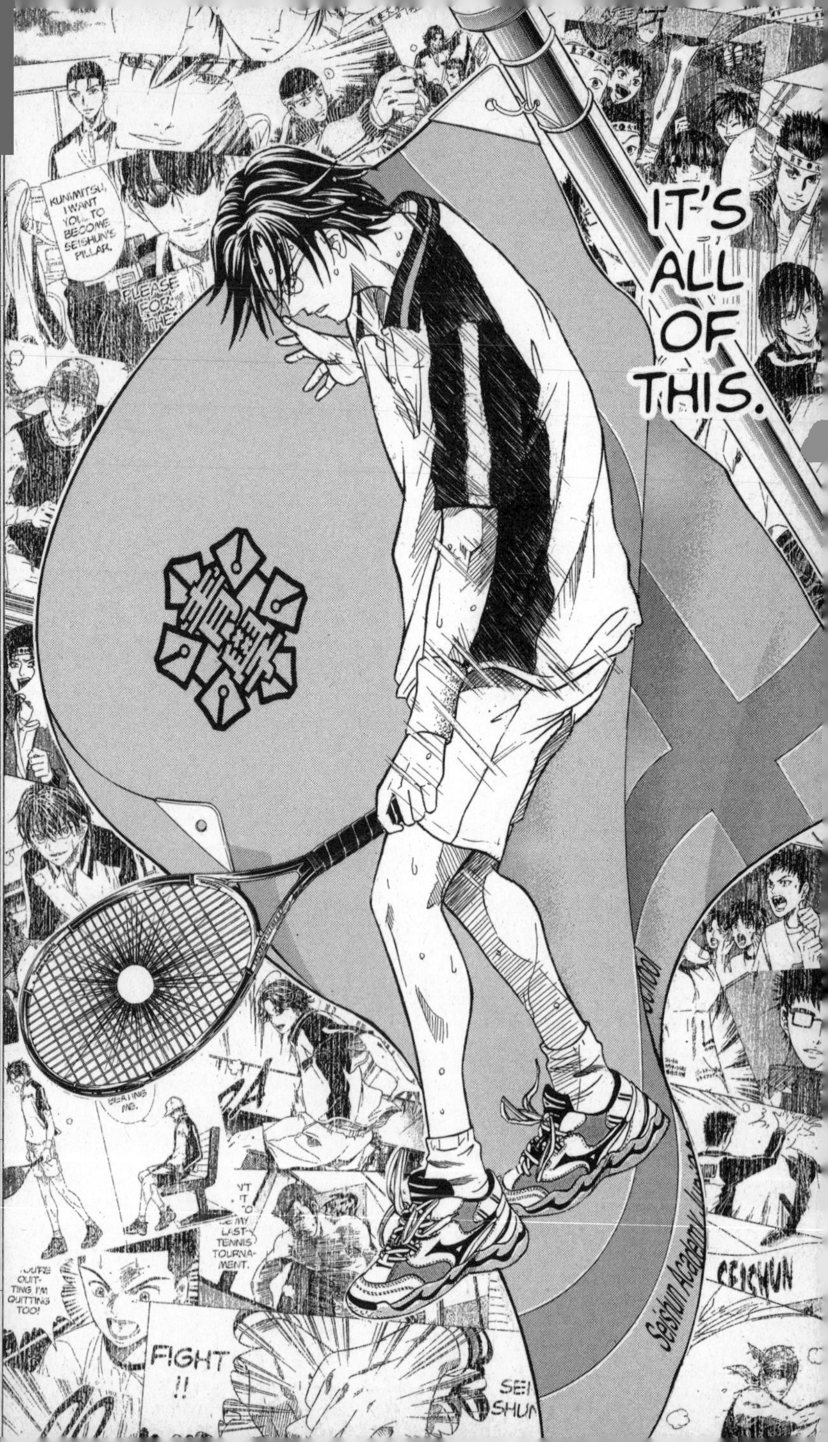
IT'S ALL OF THIS.
KUNIMITSU, I WANT YOU... TO BECOME SEISHUN'S PILLAR.
PLEASE FOR THE
SEISHUN
Seishun Academy
BEATING ME.
MY LAST TENNIS TOURNAMENT.
QUITTING I'M QUITTING TOO!
FIGHT !!
SEI SHUN

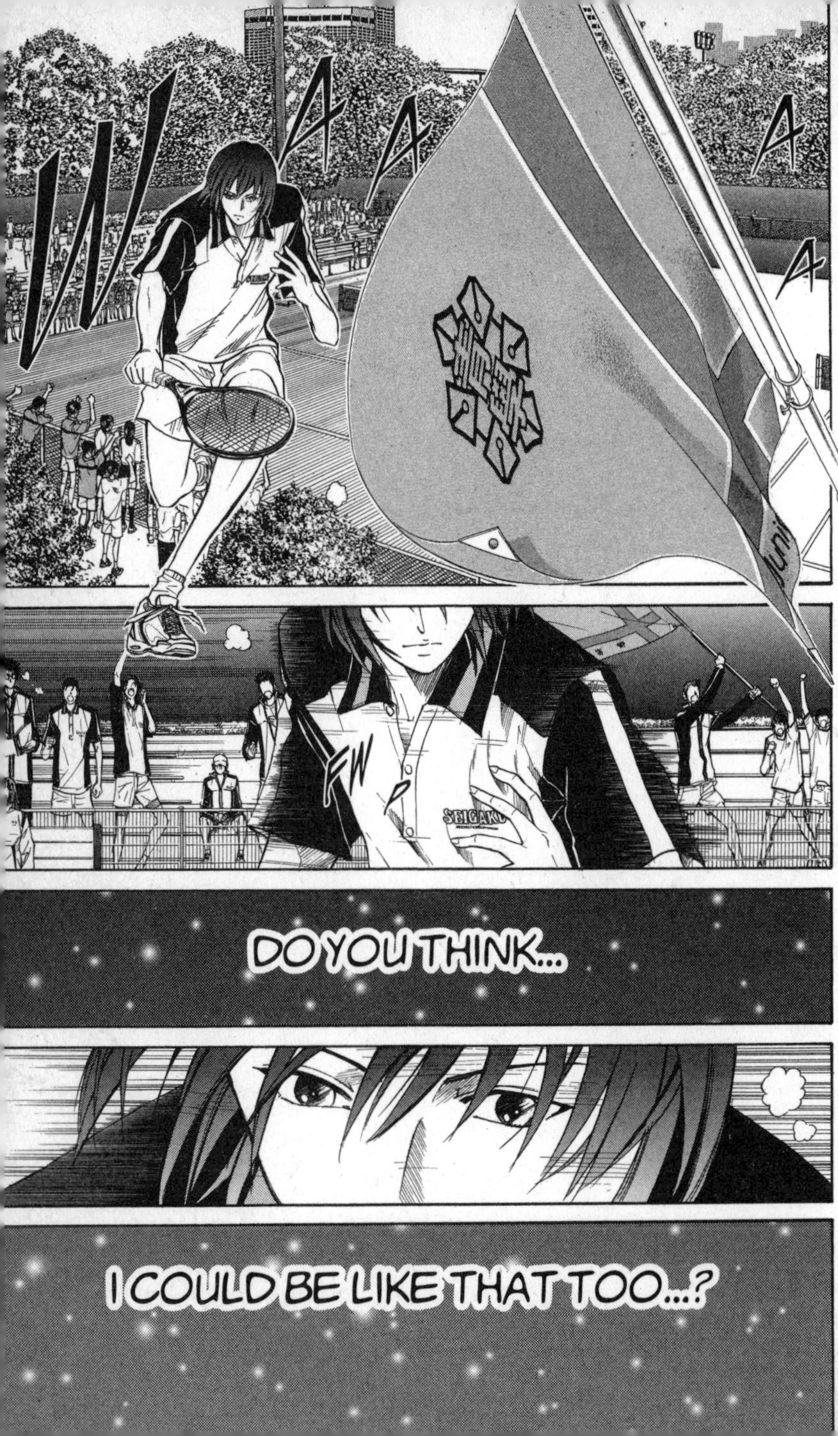
WAAAA
FWP
SEIGAKU
DO YOU THINK...
I COULD BE LIKE THAT TOO...?

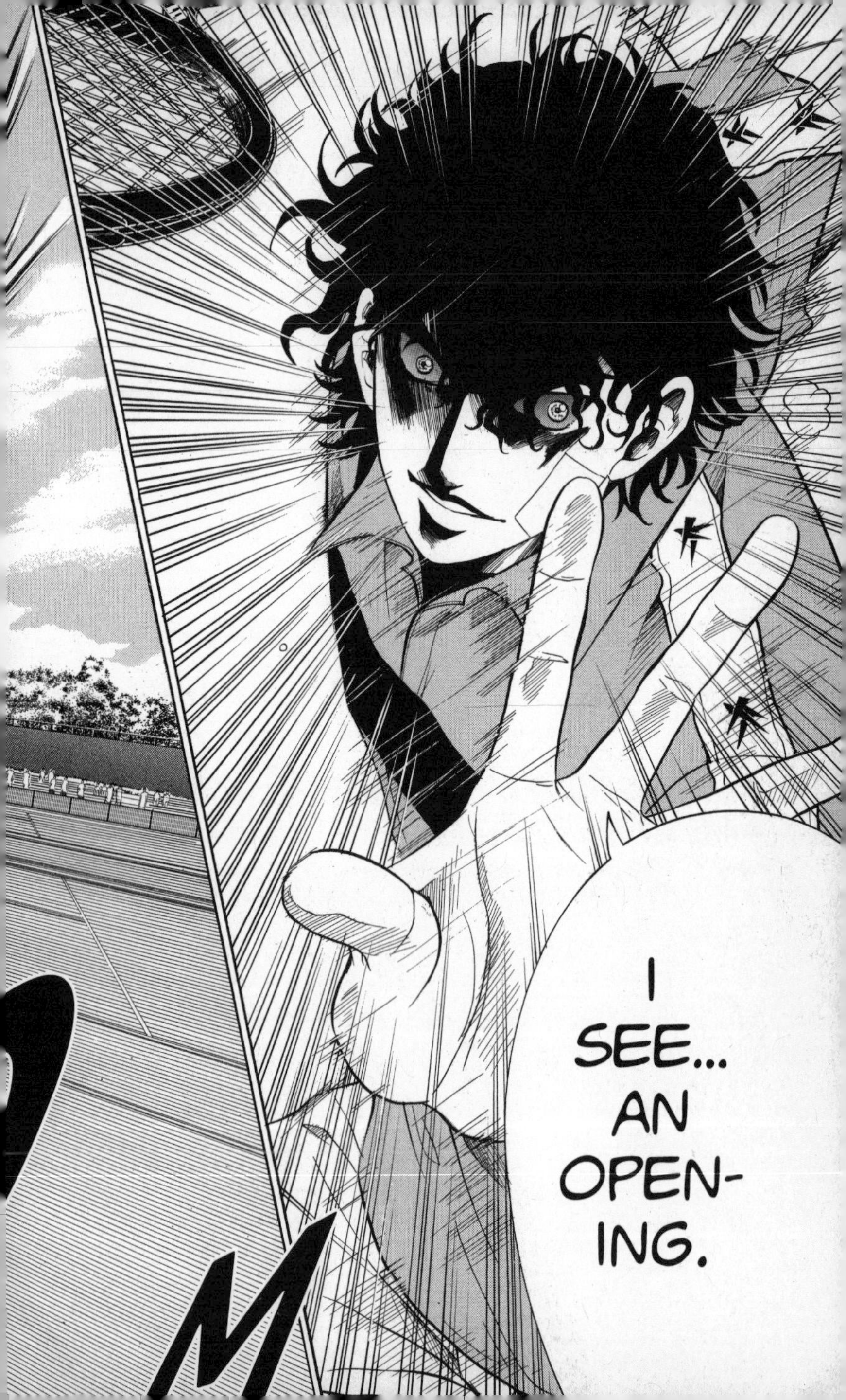
I SEE... AN OPEN-ING.

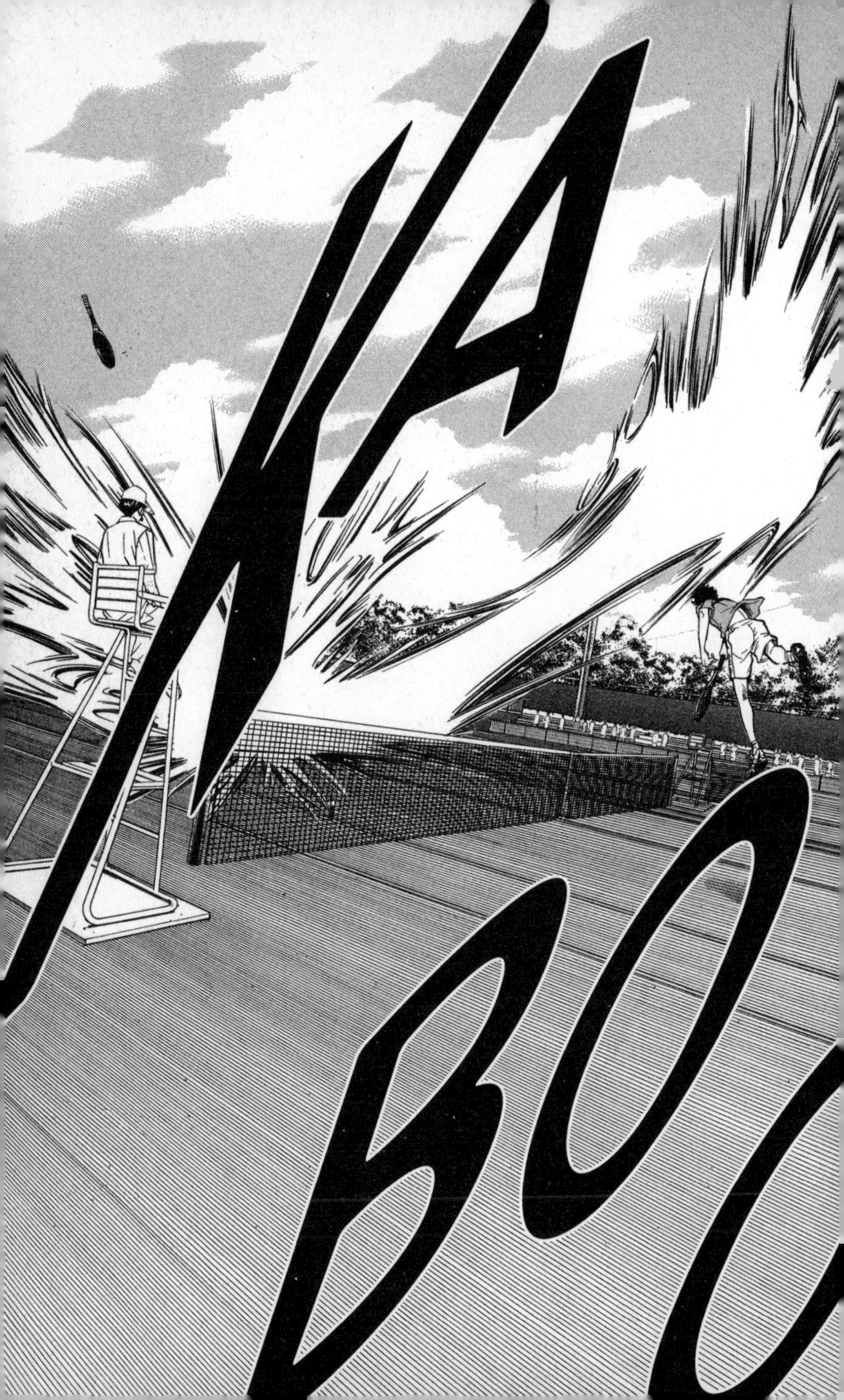
KA
BO

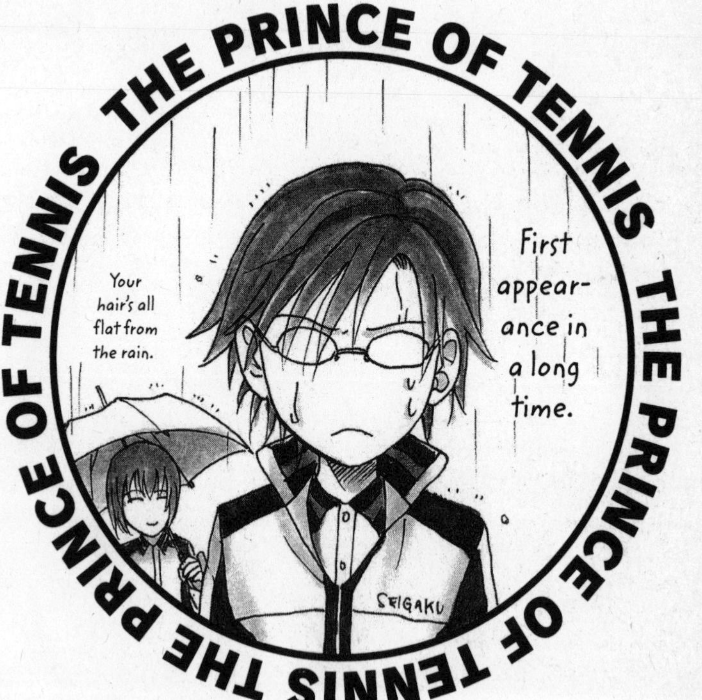
THE PRINCE OF TENNIS THE PRINCE OF TENNIS THE PRINCE OF TENNIS THE PRINCE OF TENNIS
First appearance in a long time.
Your hair's all flat from the rain.
SEIGAKU

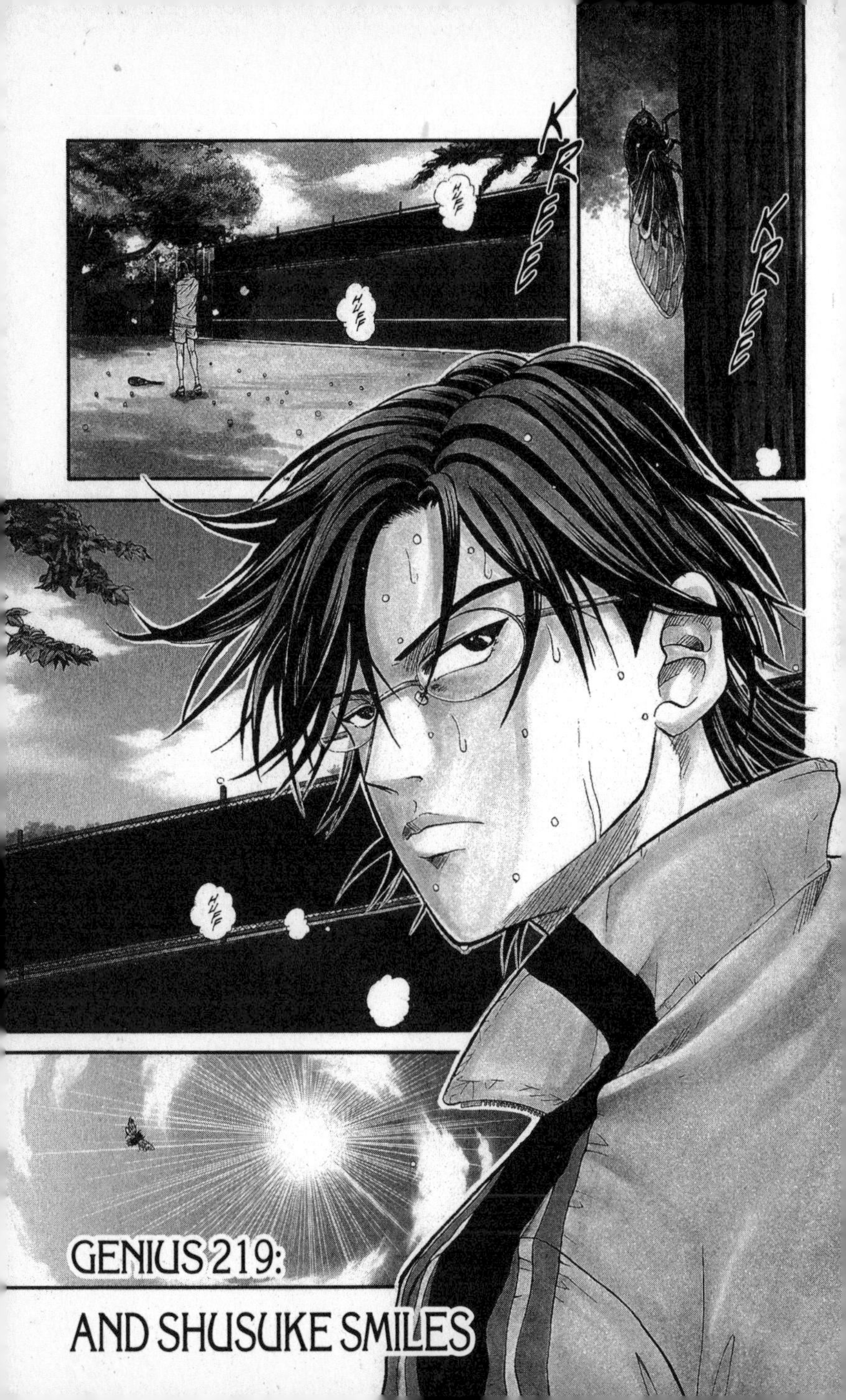
KREE
KREE
HUFF
HUFF
HUFF

GENIUS 219:

AND SHUSUKE SMILES

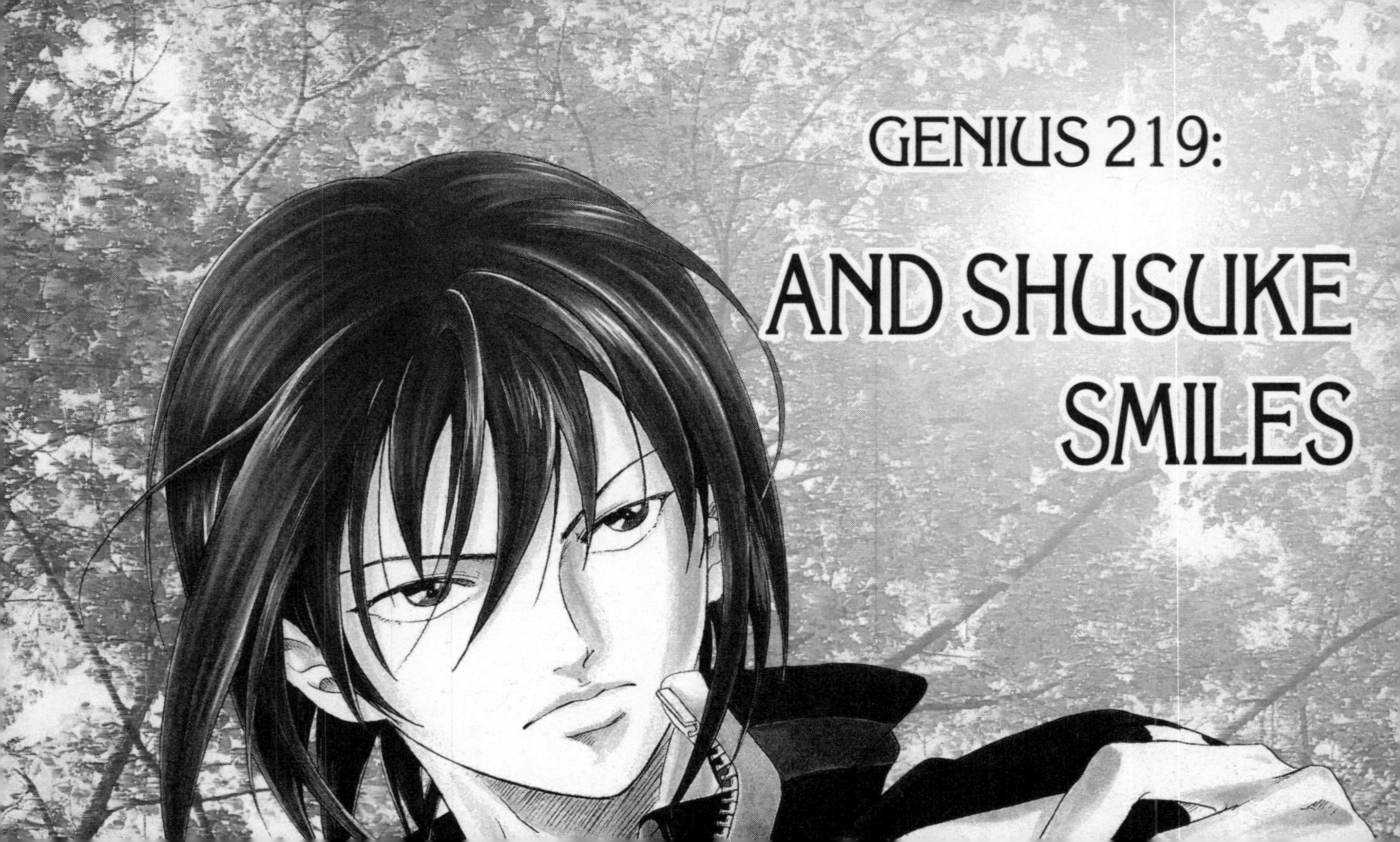
GENIUS 219:
AND SHUSUKE SMILES

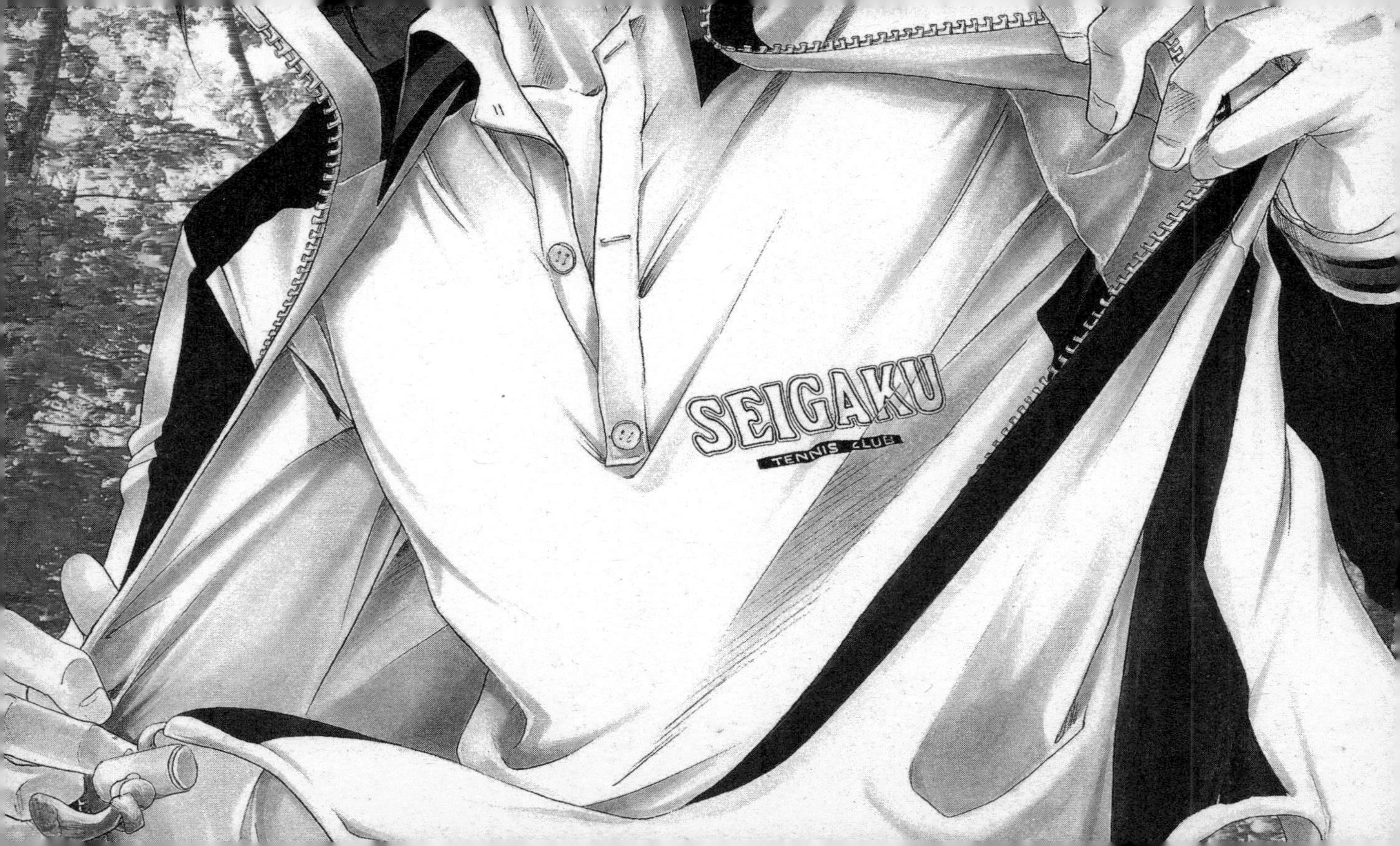
SEIGAKU
TENNIS CLUB

テニスの王子様
THE PRINCE OF TENNIS

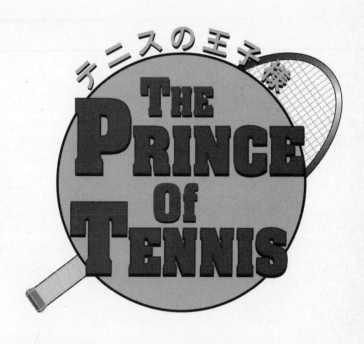

KLUNK...

SHU-
SUKE
!!

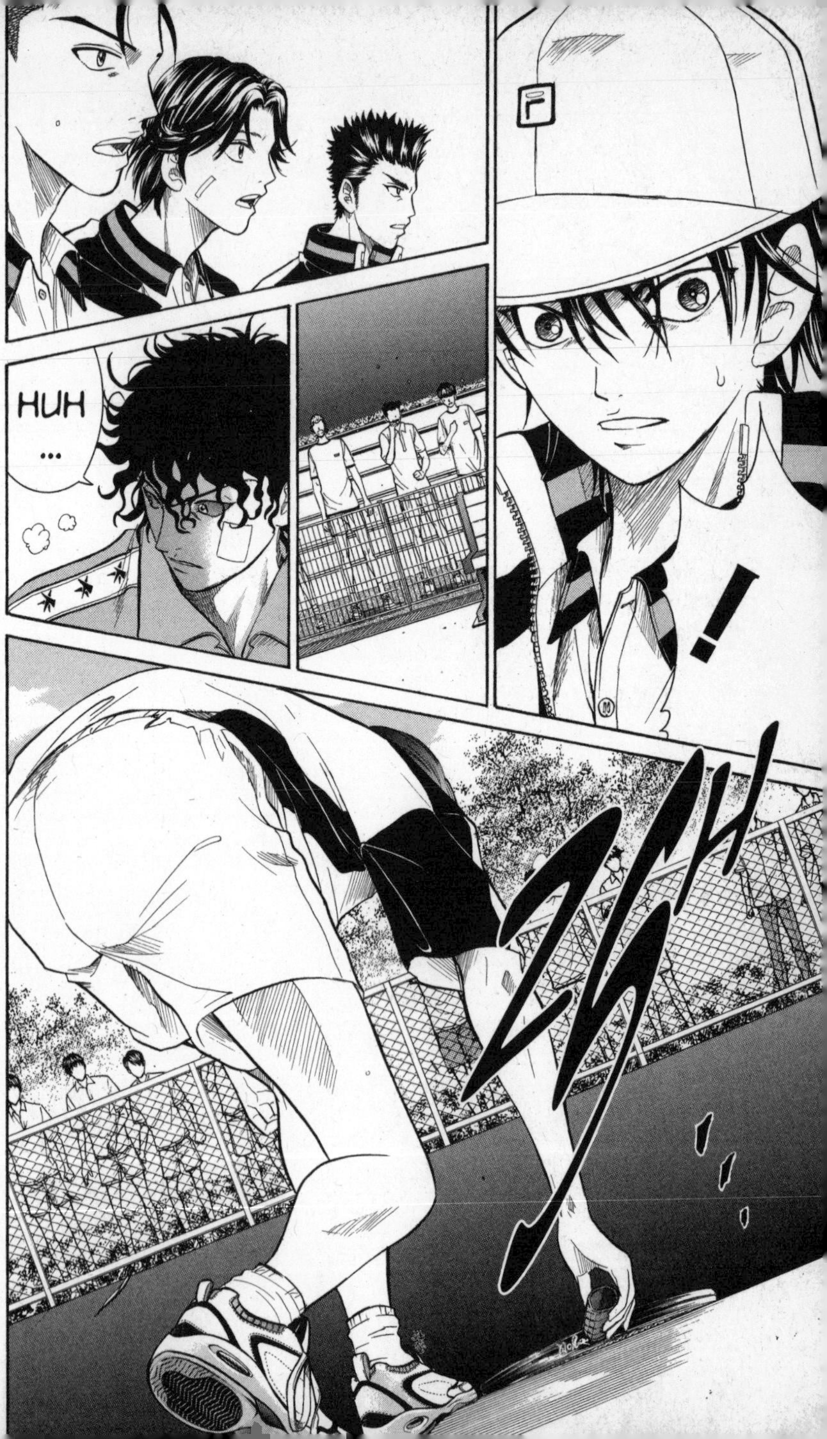
HUH
...

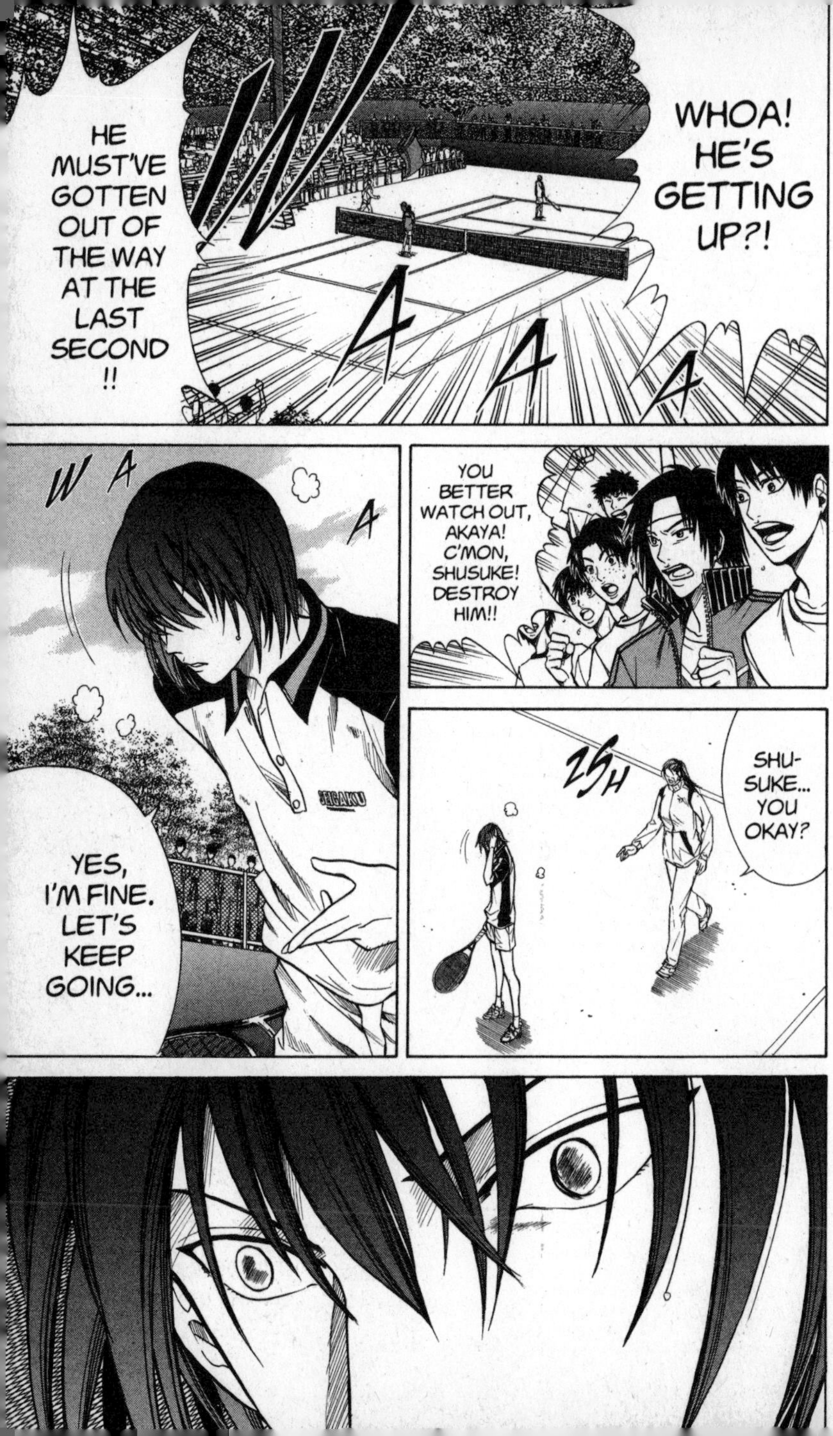
WHOA! HE'S GETTING UP?!
HE MUST'VE GOTTEN OUT OF THE WAY AT THE LAST SECOND!!
WAAAA
YOU BETTER WATCH OUT, AKAYA! C'MON, SHUSUKE! DESTROY HIM!!
ZSH
SHU-SUKE... YOU OKAY?
WAA
YES, I'M FINE. LET'S KEEP GOING...

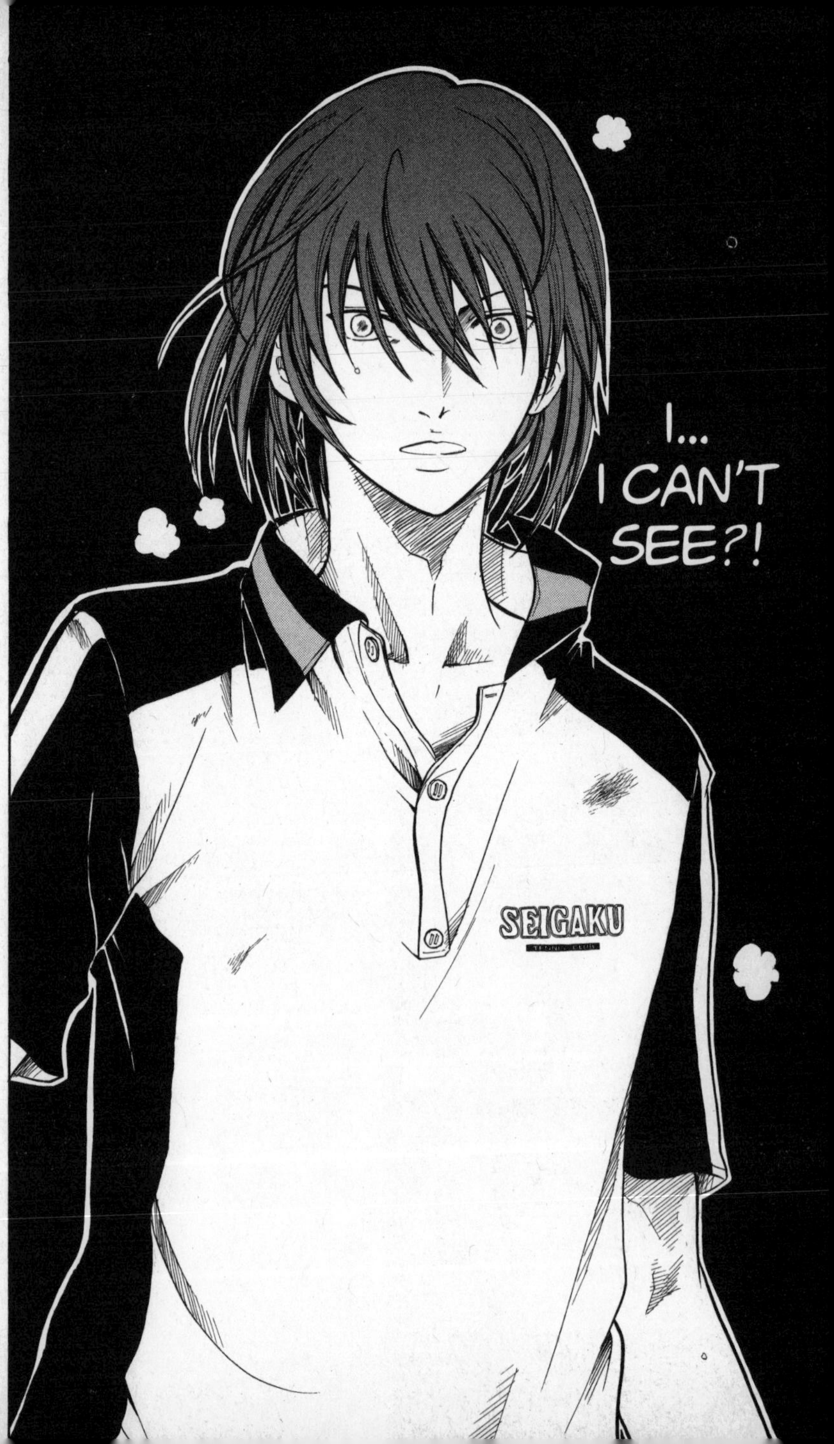
I...
I CAN'T
SEE?!
SEIGAKU

READ THIS WAY

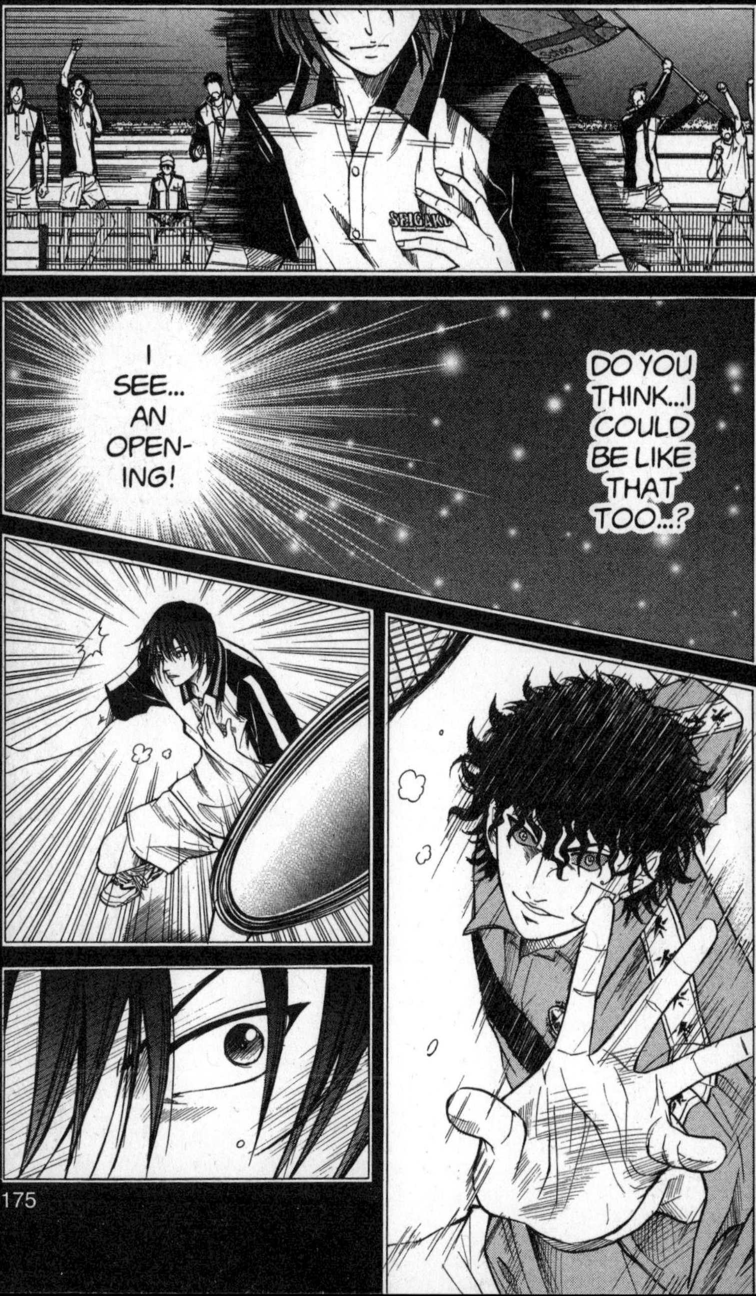
DO YOU THINK...I COULD BE LIKE THAT TOO...?
I SEE... AN OPENING!

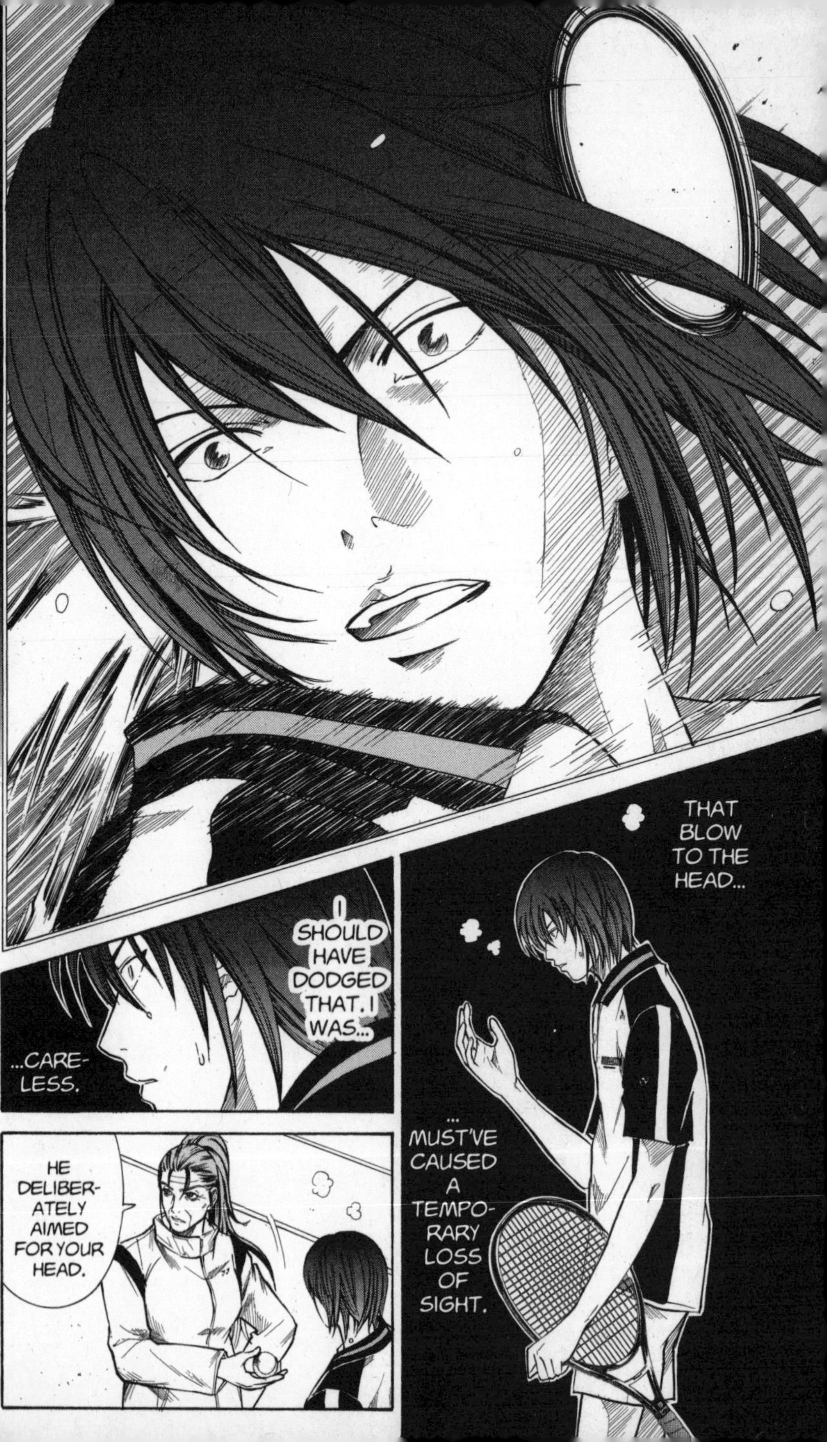
THAT BLOW TO THE HEAD...
...MUST'VE CAUSED A TEMPORARY LOSS OF SIGHT.
I SHOULD HAVE DODGED THAT. I WAS...
...CARELESS.
HE DELIBER-ATELY AIMED FOR YOUR HEAD.

READ THIS WAY

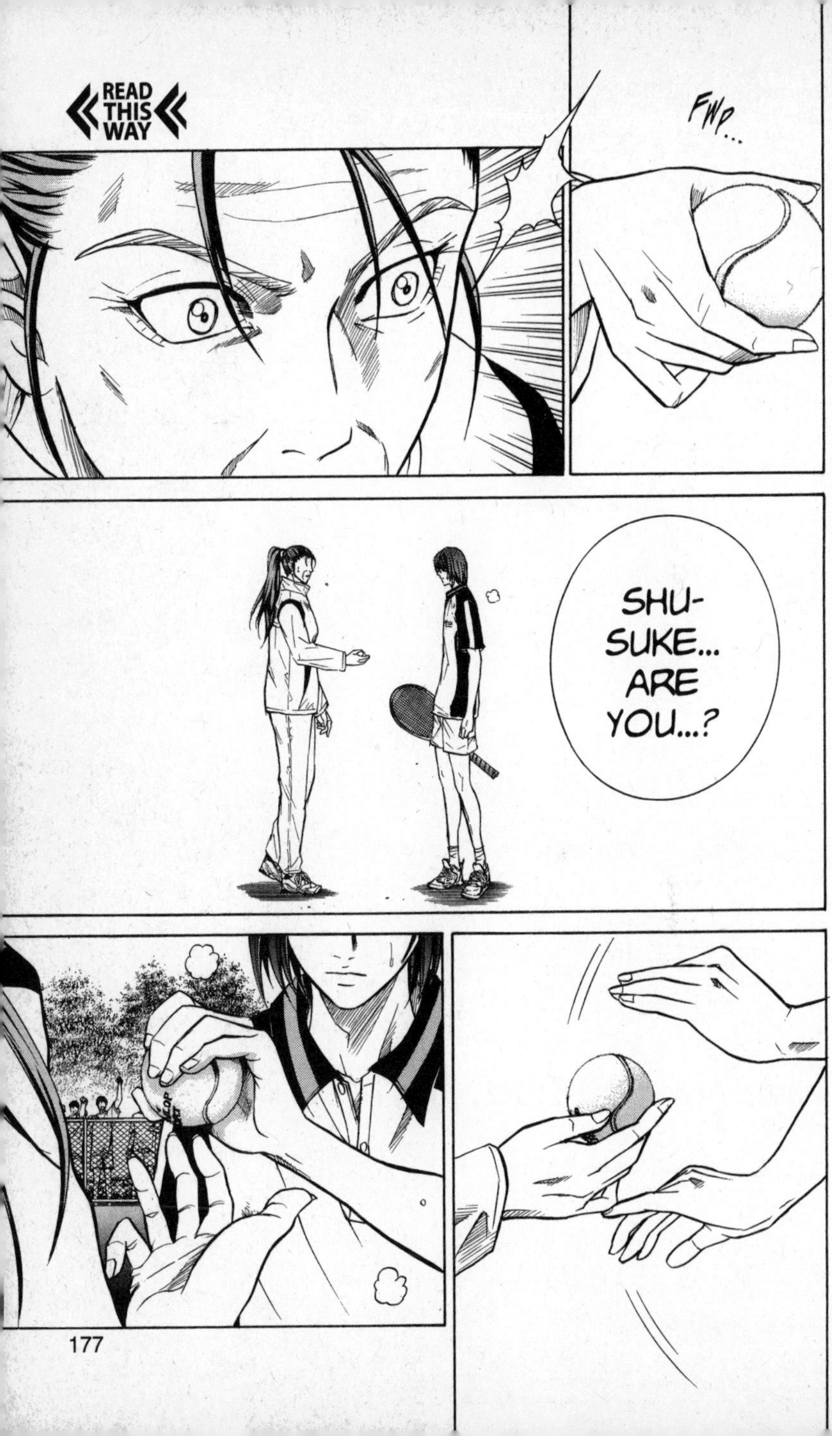
FWP...
SHU-SUKE... ARE YOU...?

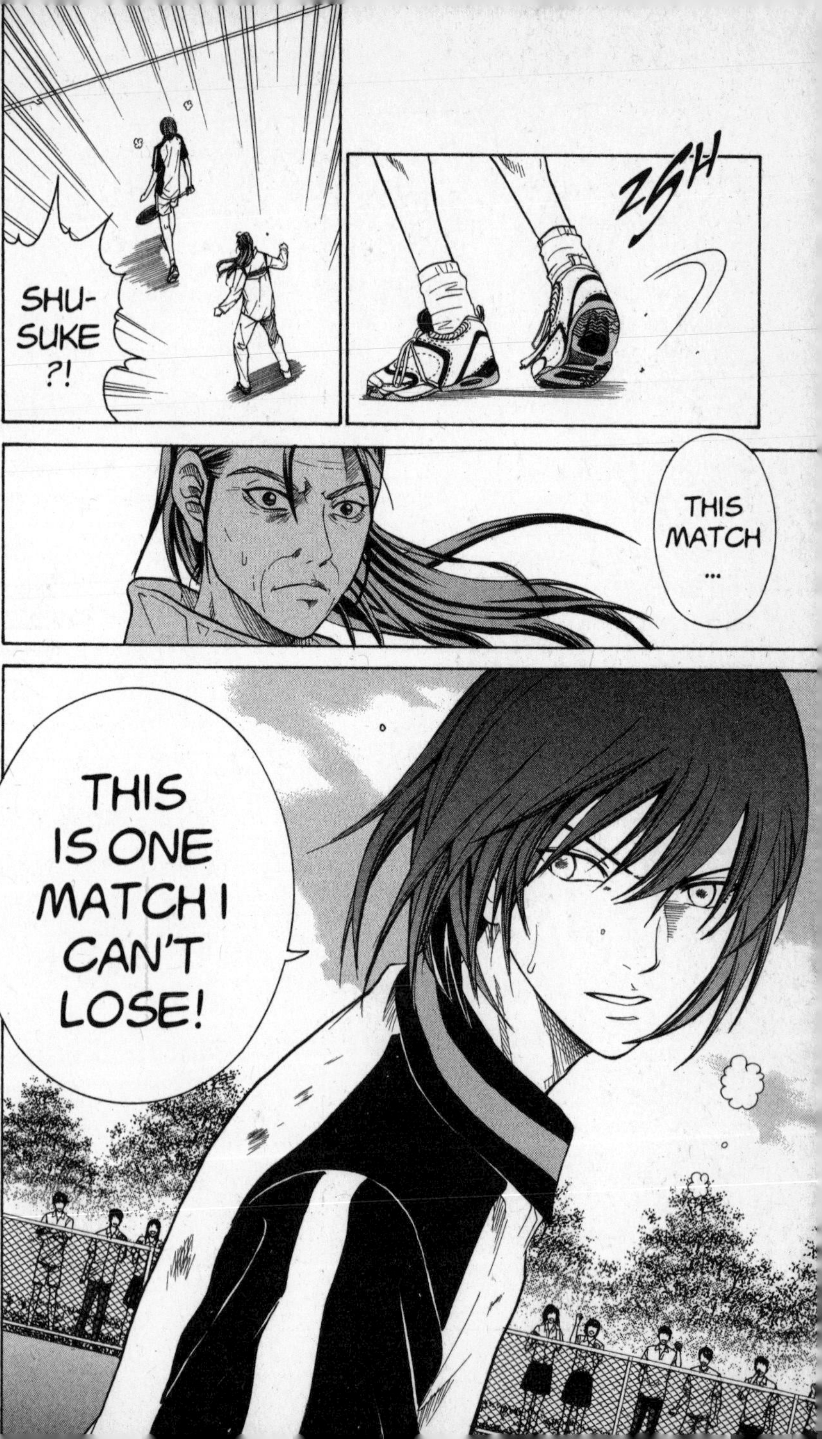
ZSH
SHU-SUKE ?!
THIS MATCH ...
THIS IS ONE MATCH I CAN'T LOSE!

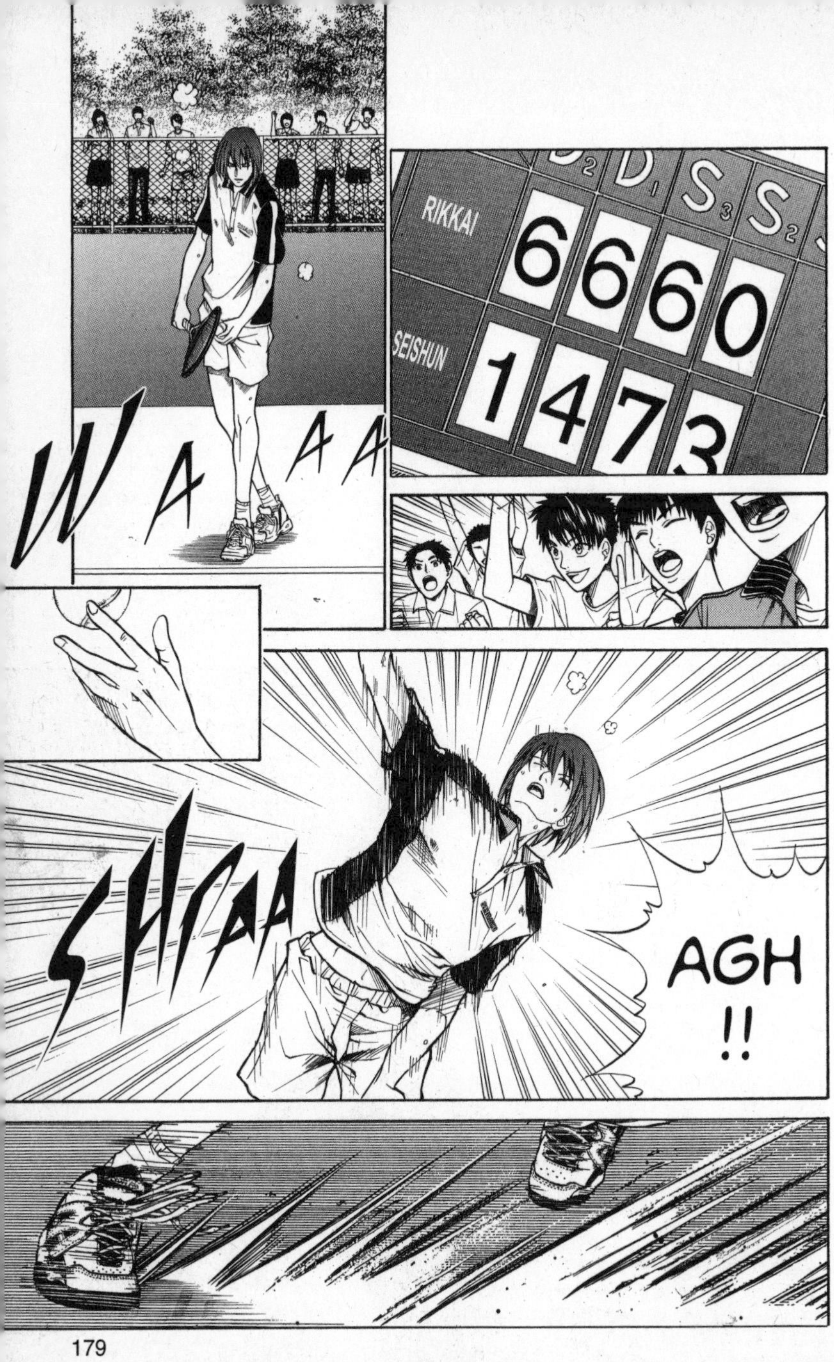
D2 D1 S3 S2
RIKKAI 6 6 6 0
SEISHUN 1 4 7 3
WA A A
AGH !!
SHRAA

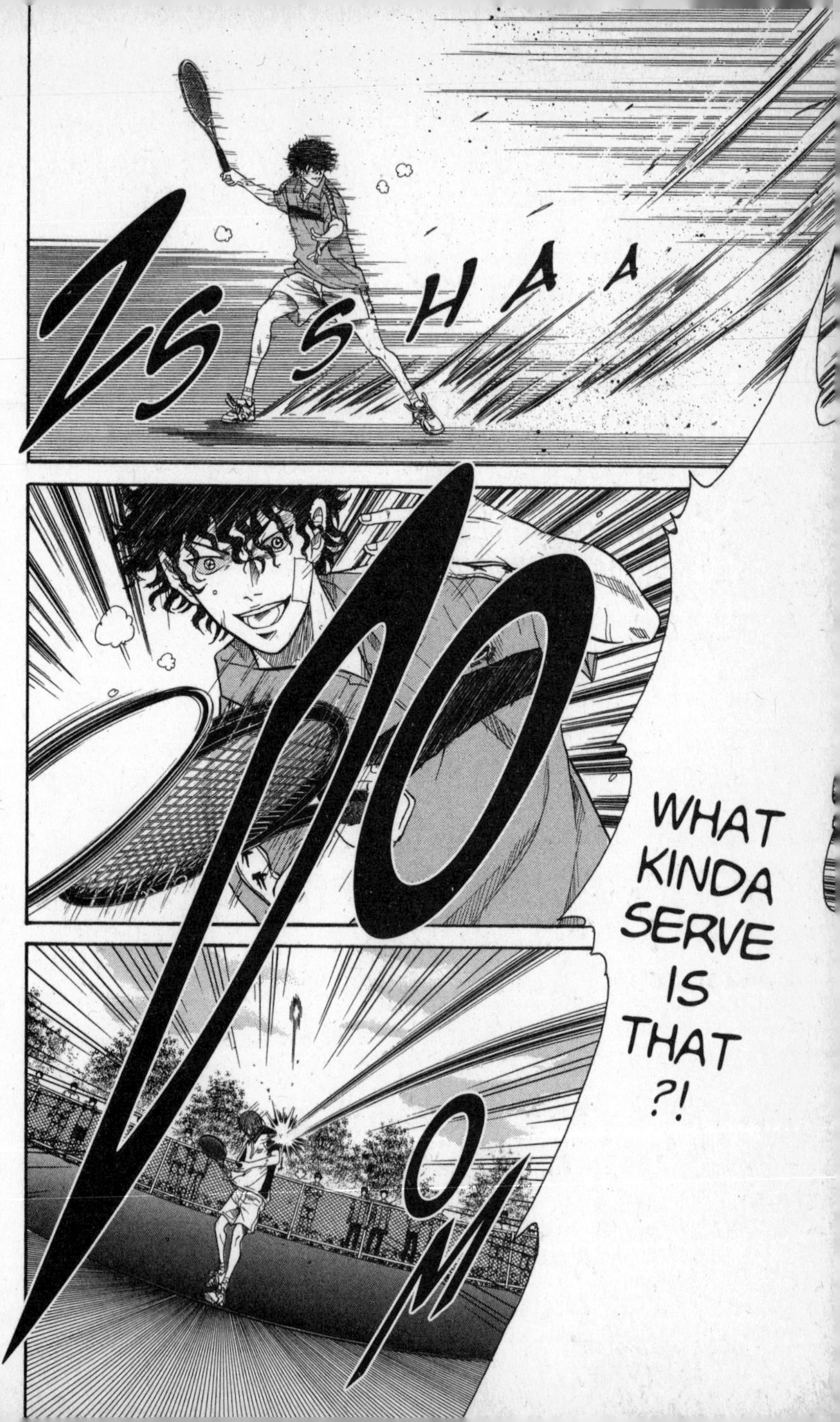
ZSSHAA
ZOOM
WHAT KINDA SERVE IS THAT ?!

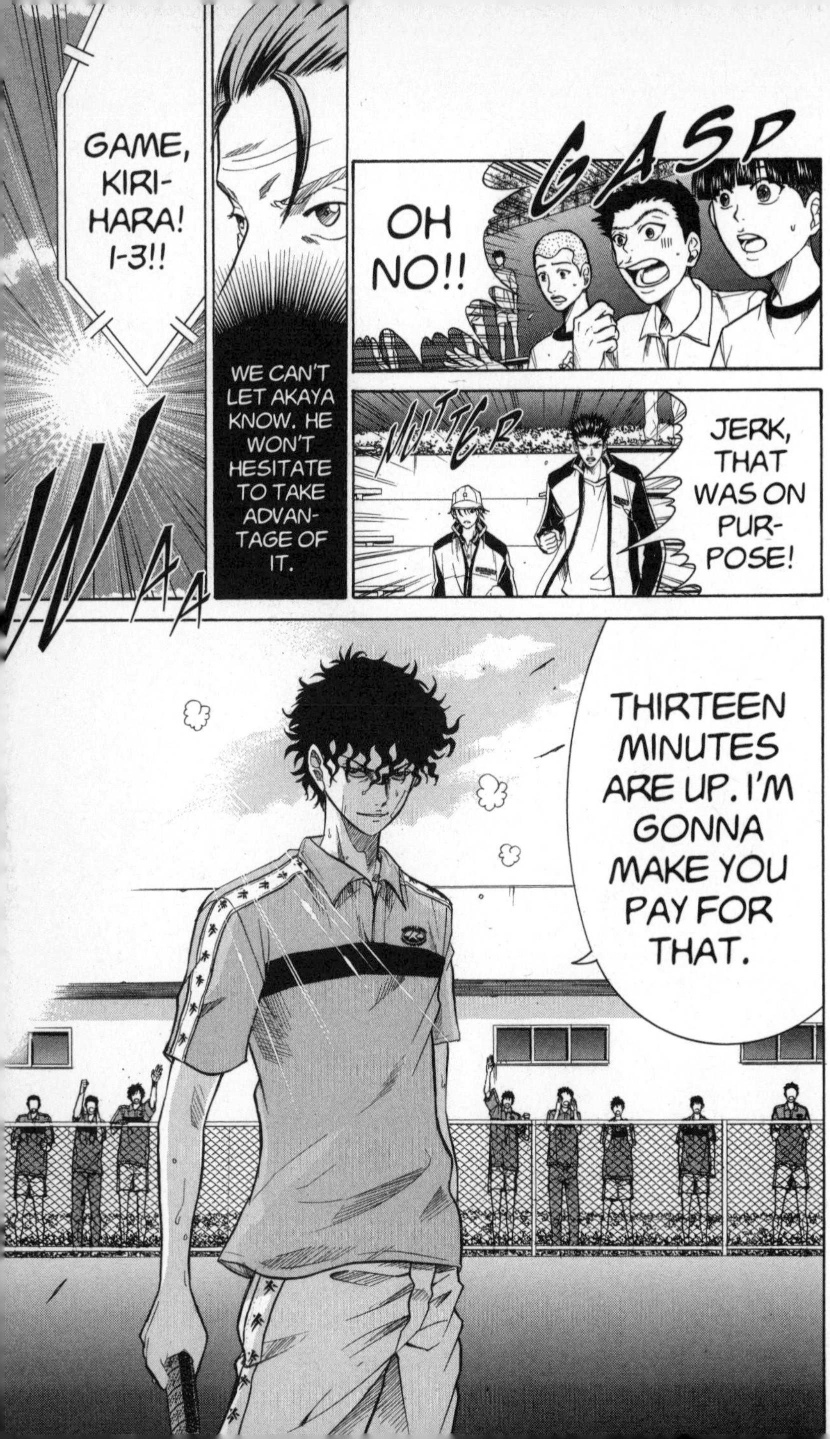
GASP
OH NO!!
JERK, THAT WAS ON PUR-POSE!
MUTTER
WE CAN'T LET AKAYA KNOW. HE WON'T HESITATE TO TAKE ADVAN-TAGE OF IT.
GAME, KIRI-HARA! 1-3!!
WAA
THIRTEEN MINUTES ARE UP. I'M GONNA MAKE YOU PAY FOR THAT.

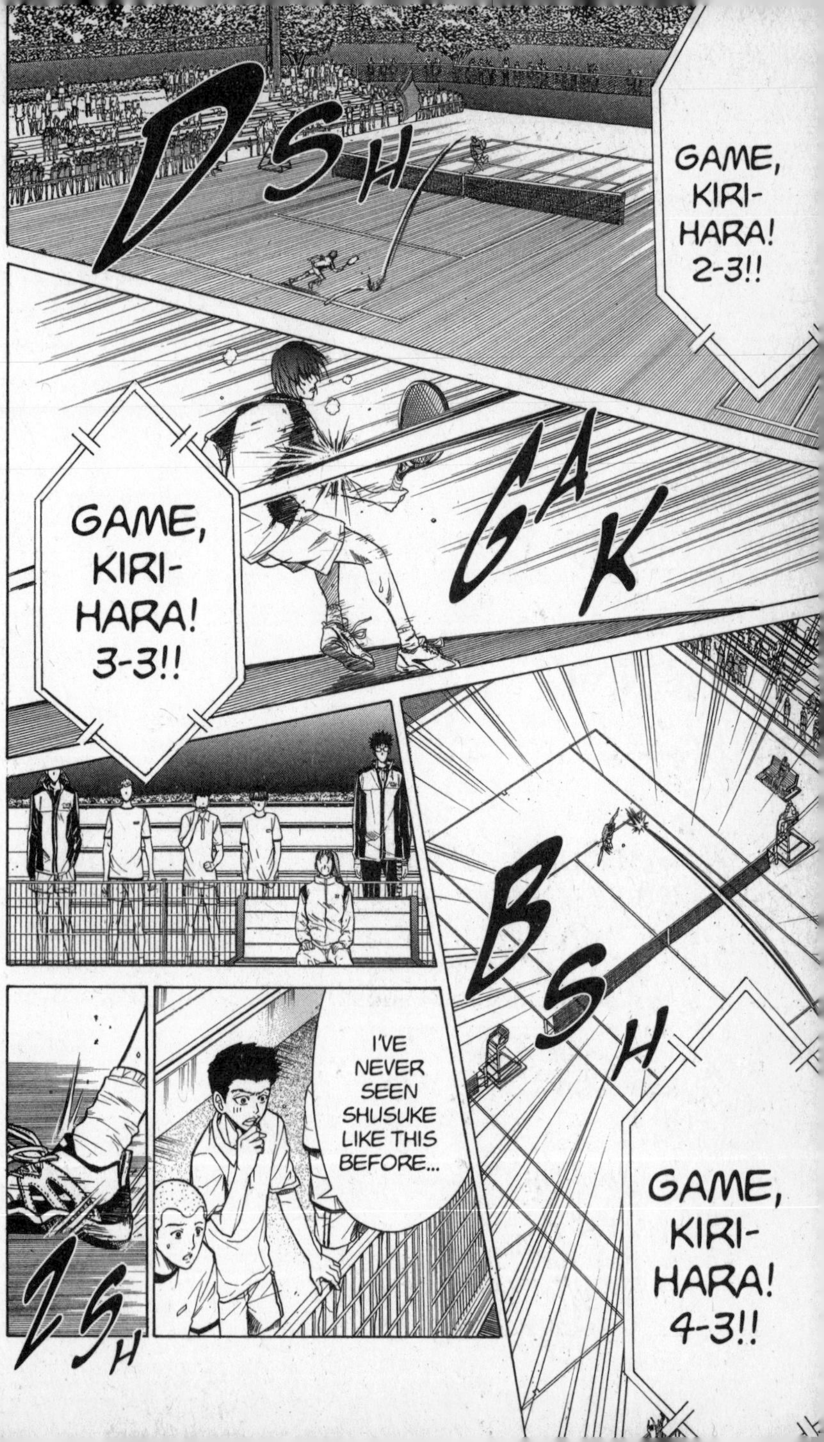
DSH
GAME, KIRI-HARA! 2-3!!
GAK
GAME, KIRI-HARA! 3-3!!
BSH
GAME, KIRI-HARA! 4-3!!
I'VE NEVER SEEN SHUSUKE LIKE THIS BEFORE...
ZSH

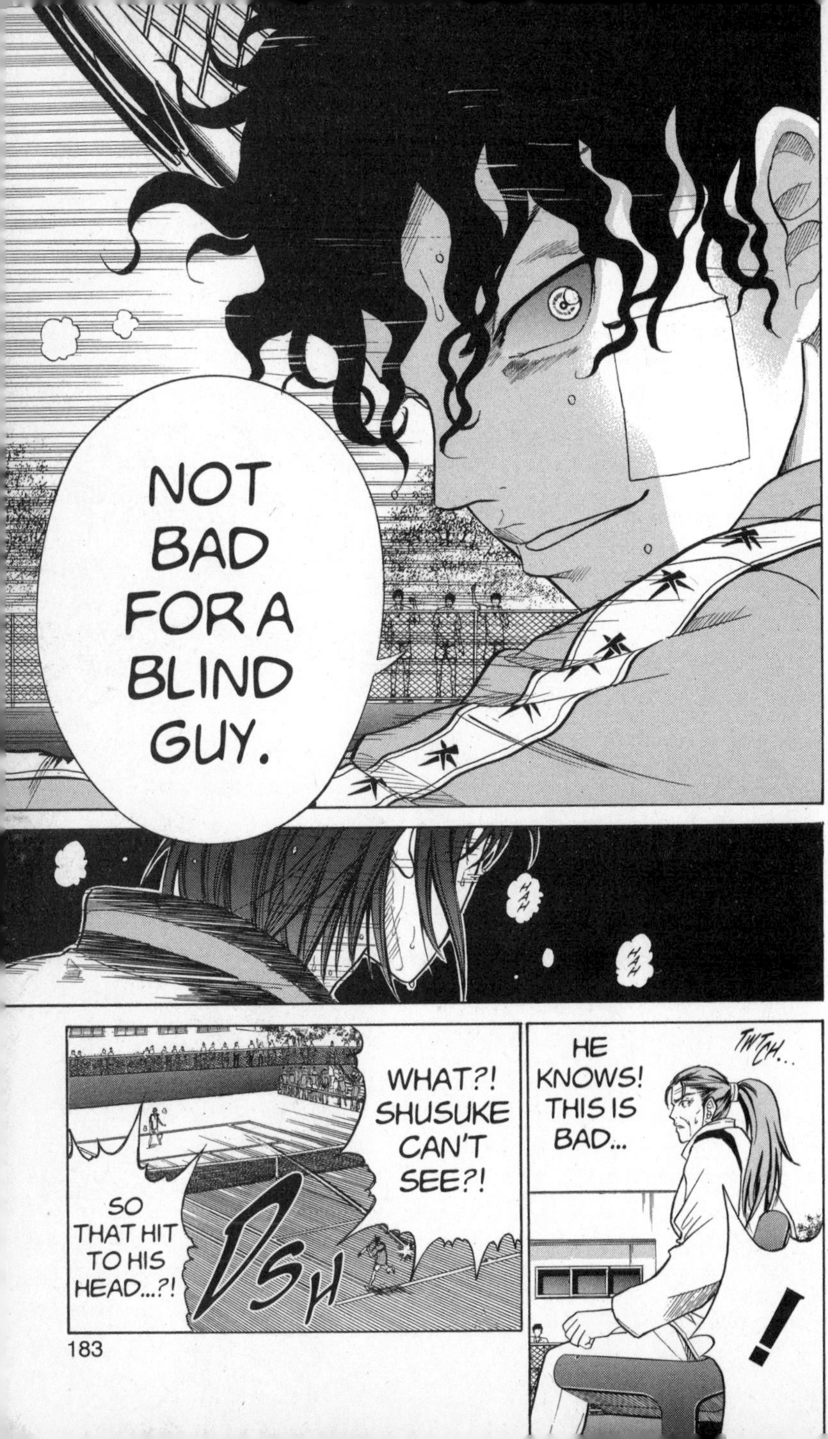
NOT BAD FOR A BLIND GUY.
HAH
HAH
TWITCH...
HE KNOWS! THIS IS BAD...
!
WHAT?! SHUSUKE CAN'T SEE?!
SO THAT HIT TO HIS HEAD...?!
DSH

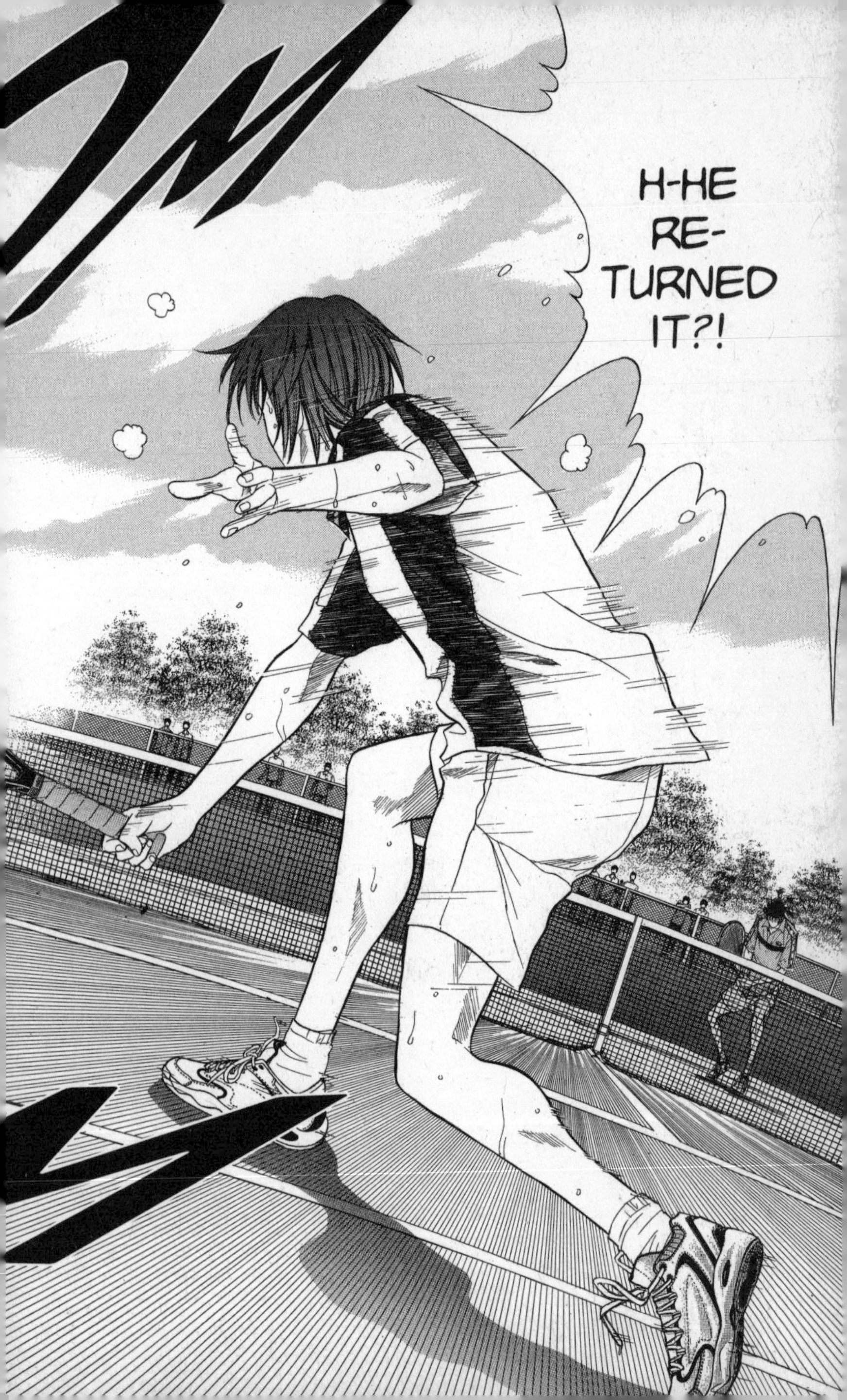
H-HE RE-TURNED IT?!

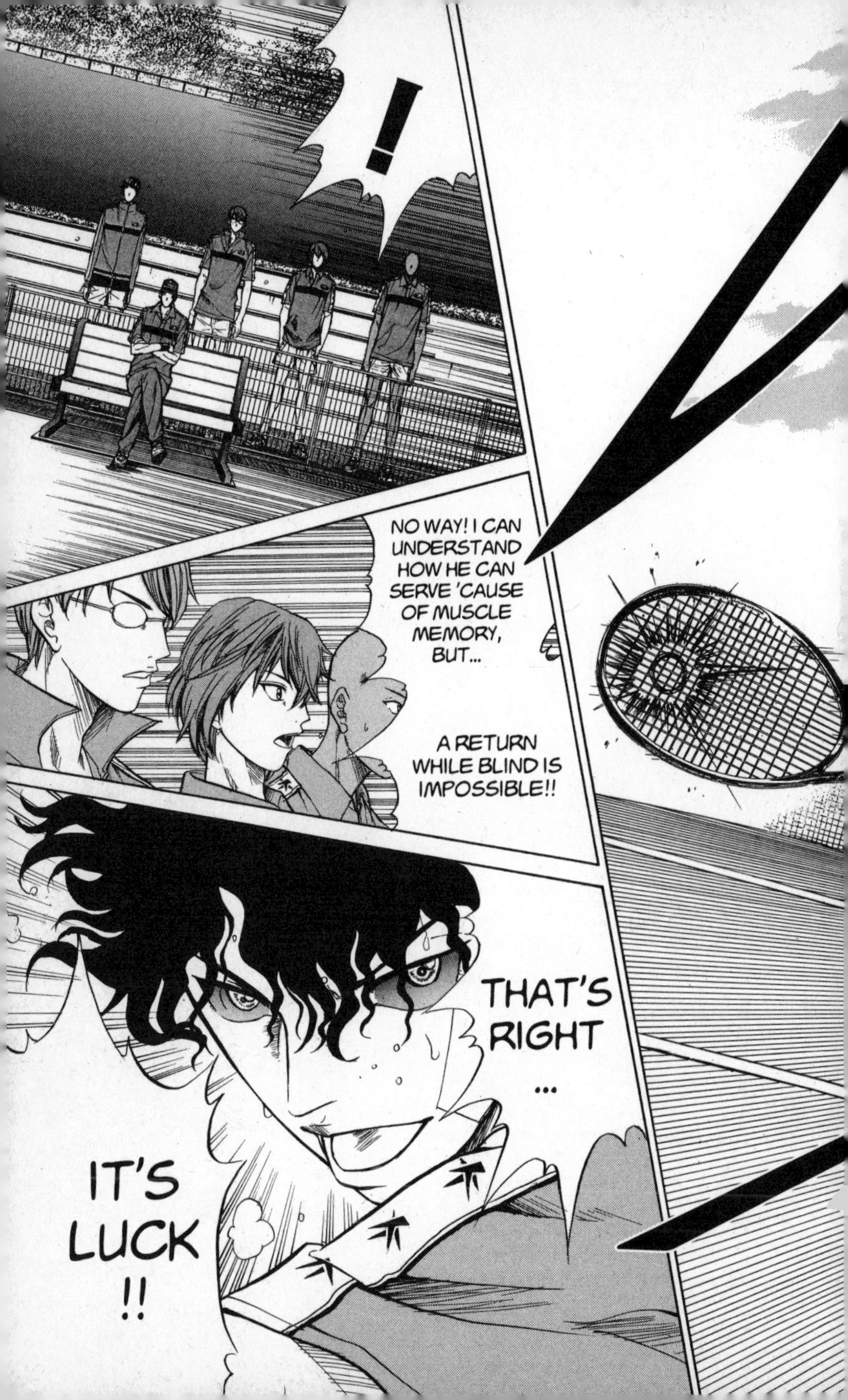
!
NO WAY! I CAN UNDERSTAND HOW HE CAN SERVE 'CAUSE OF MUSCLE MEMORY, BUT...
A RETURN WHILE BLIND IS IMPOSSIBLE!!
THAT'S RIGHT ...
IT'S LUCK !!

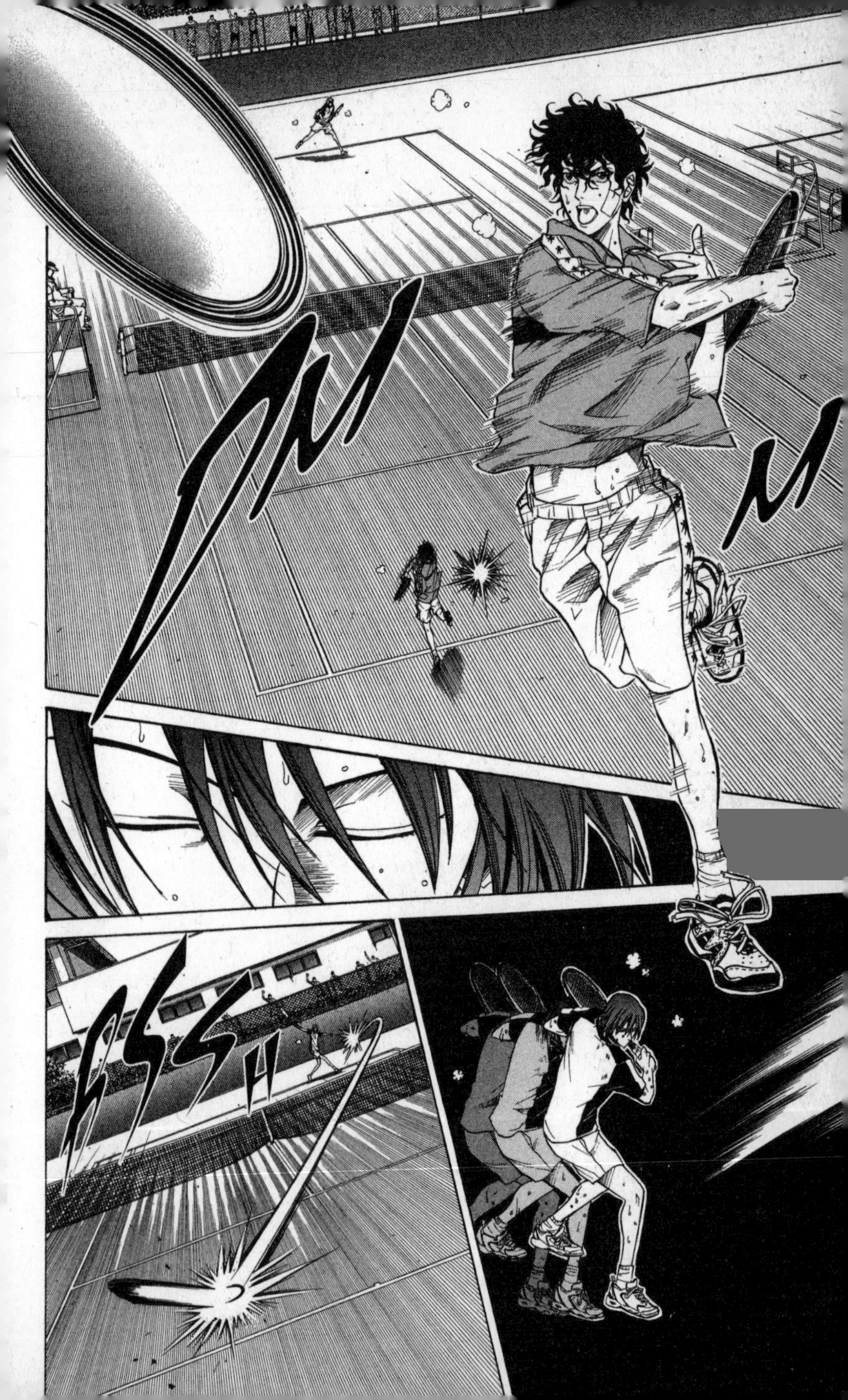
SSSH

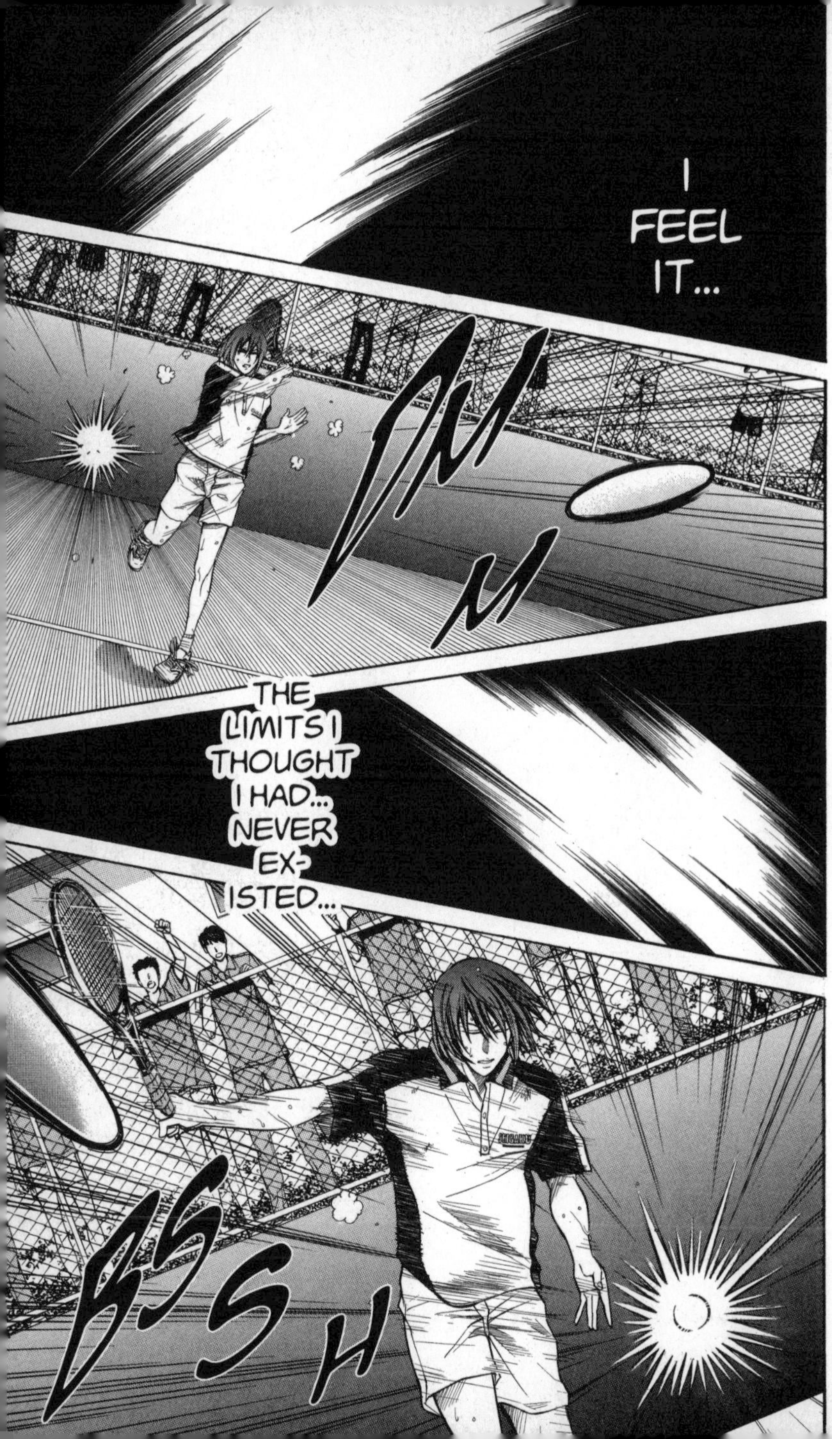
I FEEL IT...
VMM
THE LIMITS I THOUGHT I HAD... NEVER EX-ISTED...
BSSH

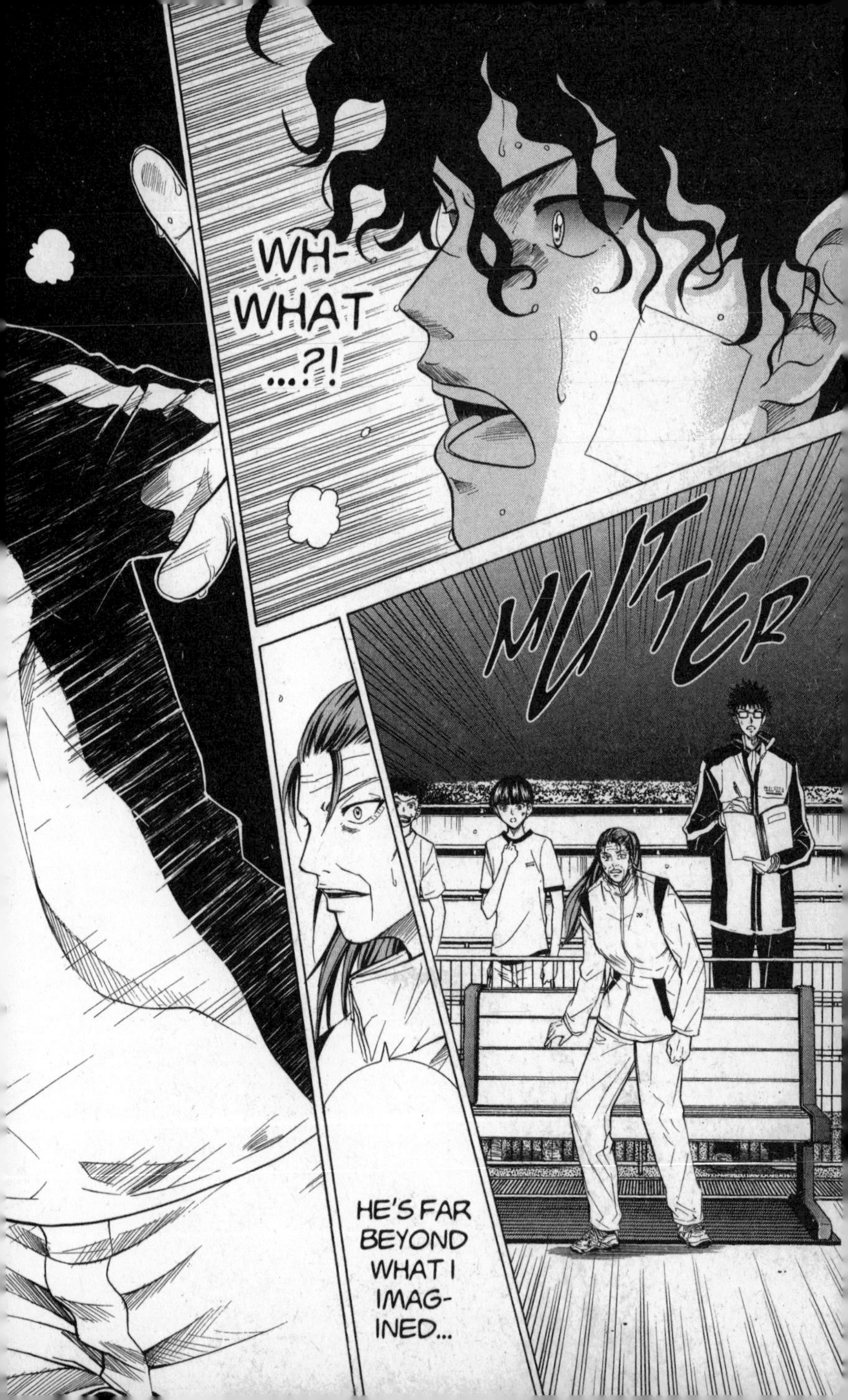
WH-WHAT...?!
MUTTER
HE'S FAR BEYOND WHAT I IMAGINED...

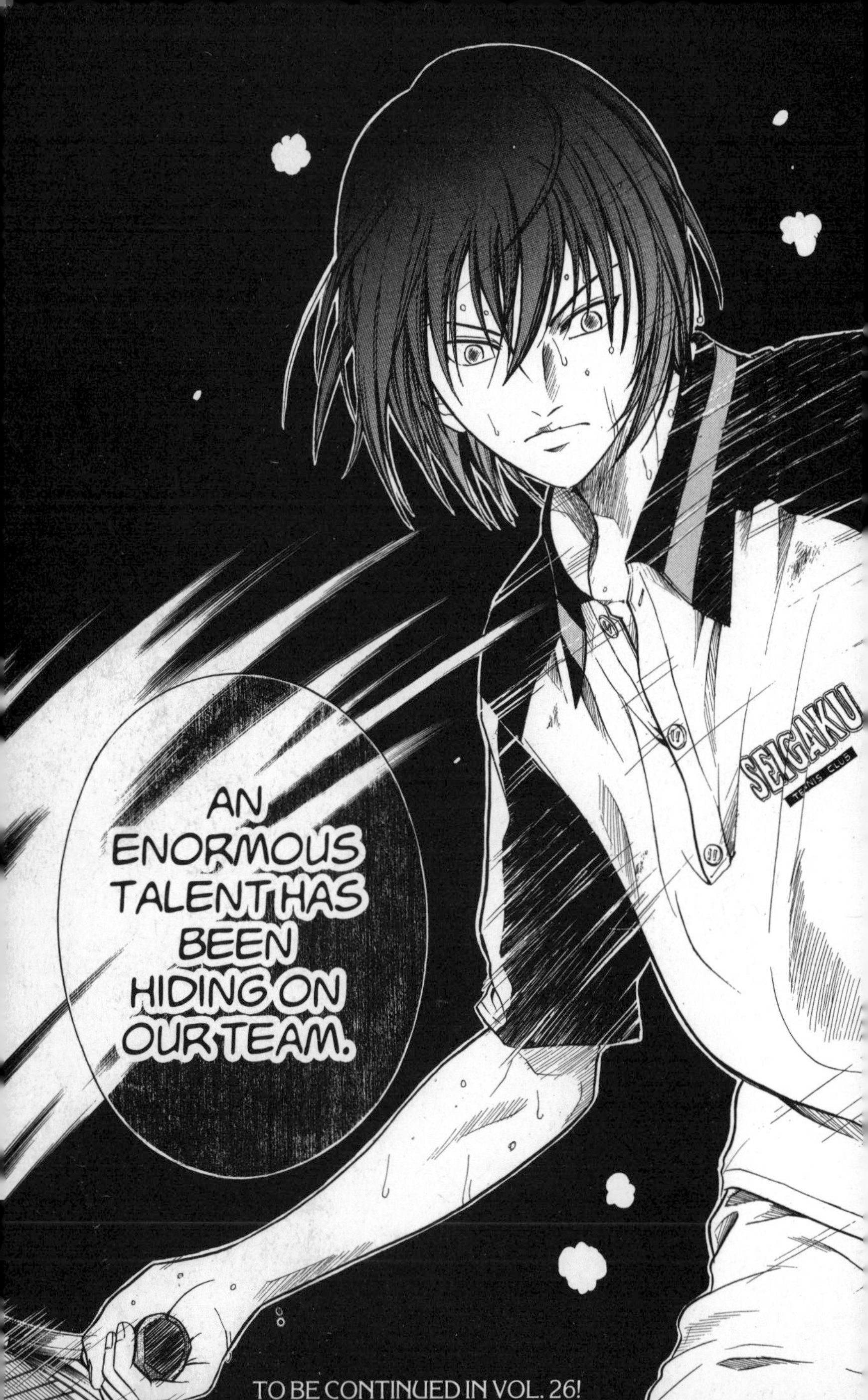
AN ENORMOUS TALENT HAS BEEN HIDING ON OUR TEAM.
SEIGAKU TENNIS CLUB
TO BE CONTINUED IN VOL. 26!

In the Next Volume...

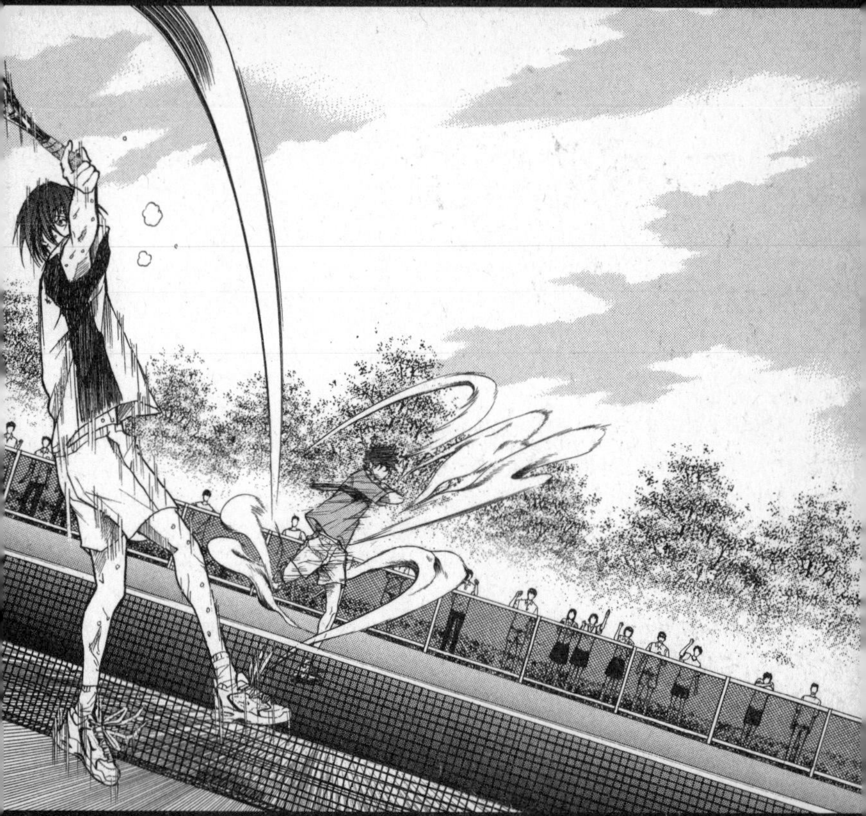

Ryoma Echizen vs. Genichiro Sanada

The Kanto Tournament Finals are down to the last two matches, with the top players for the two best teams—Seishun and Rikkai—engaged in a fierce battle for dominance. As Shusuke and Akaya's match reaches its surprising end, the final showdown begins: Ryoma vs. "Emperor" Genichiro Sanada.

Available July 2008!

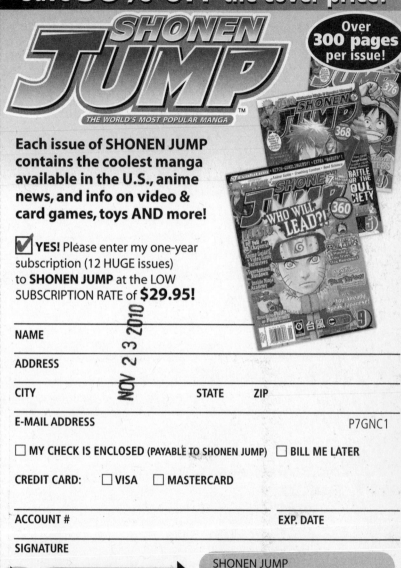